QUANTUM GENESIS

Speculations in Modern Physics and the Truth of Scripture

QUANTUM GENESIS

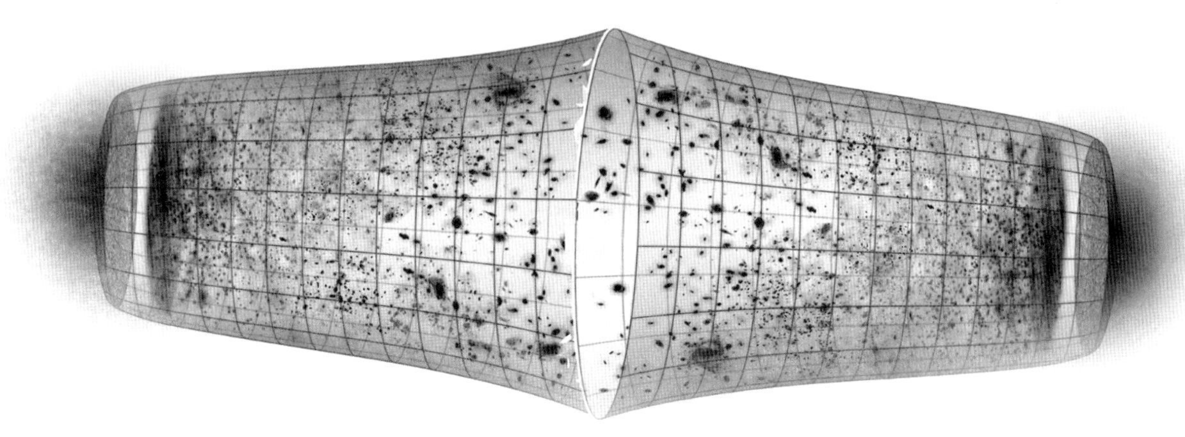

Speculations in Modern Physics and the Truth of Scripture

STUART ALLEN

Published by Deep River Books
Sisters, Oregon
www.deepriverbooks.com

Software used to develop protein images includes:
NGL imager by A.S. Rose, A.R. Bradley, Y. Valasatava, J.M. Duarte, A. Prlić and P.W. Rose. *Web-based molecular graphics for large complexes*. ACM Proceedings of the 21st International Conference on Web3D Technology (Web3D '16): 185-186, 2016. doi:10.1145/2945292.2945324 and AS Rose and PW Hildebrand. *NGL Viewer: a web application for molecular visualization*. Nucl Acids Res (1 July 2015) 43 (W1): W576-W579 first published online April 29, 2015. doi:10.1093/nar/gkv402

Vsualization software, VMD, developed by the Theoretical and Computational Biophysics Group in the Beckman Institute for Advanced Science and Technology at the University of Illinois at Urbana-Champaign

ISBN – 13: 9781632694720
Library of Congress: 2018946985

Printed in China

Cover design by Joe Bailen, Contajus Design

Cover image: "Spacetime,"adapted from *Timeline of the Universe*, by NASA/WMAP Science Team and Ryan Kaldari, 2010, https://en.wikipedia.org/wiki/Big_Bang. Public domain.

Contents

Figures

00

Introduction

"Because of its indispensable role in science, many scientists—especially physicists—invest the ultimate reality of the physical world in mathematics. A colleague of mine once remarked that in his opinion the world was nothing but bits and pieces of mathematics. To the ordinary person, whose picture of reality is tied closely to the perception of physical objects, and whose view of mathematics is that of an esoteric recreation, this must seem astounding. Yet the contention that mathematics is a key that enables the initiate to unlock cosmic secrets is as old as the subject itself."
—Paul Davies, The Mind of God

"It's only cranks who try to solve the big problems at one go."
—Martin Rees, "In the Matrix," The Edge Foundation

This story began with my wife's young student, Luke.

A youth leader at our church responded to a question about Genesis with the "God in the Gaps" naturalist interpretation: the creation story is allegorical, there are millions and billions of years to the earth's history—not six literal days of creation nor the mere thousands of years counted up in Genesis genealogies.

Luke's parents are Young Earth Creationists; they hold that what the Lord said in His ten commandments (and wrote on stone tablets) is true: he made "heaven and earth, the sea, and all that in them is" in six literal days (Exodus 20:11). In their view, a church leader had told their son that Scripture is false. They began looking for a different church.

All concerned—youth leader, student, and parents—are dedicated Christians, obedient to our Lord. But they are being divided by an interpretation of theology and science.

My fellow believers in Christianity, we have a problem. The most common interpretations of the Genesis creation story do not seem to be compatible with the most common perceptions of what science and natural philosophy tell us about this world. The apparent conflict between Scripture and science has encouraged division in our body, discouraged belief in Scripture, and emboldened the opponents of our faith.

Dear readers, there may not actually be a conflict between Scripture and science. If we alter our interpretation of Genesis just a little, if we accept some conjectures of modern physics regarding the nature of our world as possibly valid, then the conflict between Scripture and science can shrink to a minor disagreement.

Given the nature of the science involved, I wish to stress this point: this book tells a story, and only a story. There will be a great deal of modern science involved in telling it, so it may start to seem as if some parts of the story have an air of reality. And perhaps they do. But in the end, no point of this argument can be *proven.* It is really important that you always remember—it's just a story.

This is a book of speculations, which are really just stories: speculations in theology and speculations in science and natural philosophy, especially physics. Speculation in theology is nothing new, of course. There is always lots of speculation in theology. Christian and Jewish theology both depend on Scripture, on the Bible, but there are many, many parts of Scripture where we can only guess at meaning. About the creation story in Genesis 1, pretty much all we have is speculation. Nobody knows how something like the world we see around us could have been made, so all we can really do is tell stories about it. This book just offers one more interpretation, one more creation story.

It may come as a surprise to some readers, though, that the situation is very similar in physics. In many areas of physics, the details of why stuff does what it does are unknown—all we can do for now is guess. That is especially true for the fundamentals of physics: what our universe is made of and how it basically works. We know a lot about what stuff in our universe *does,* but almost nothing about what stuff *is.* A little history may help show the limits of our scientific knowledge.

For many centuries, at least since the time of the ancient Greeks, the study of our world and how it works was called natural philosophy. Part of natural philosophy turned into what we now call physics in the 1600s, when Galileo Galilei, Isaac Newton, and others had tremendous success applying mathematics to explain and predict the physical behavior of the world. Newton, for example, used a newly developed branch of mathematics now called calculus (a mathematics describing changing conditions) and a simple mathematical description of the force of gravity (force = Gm_1m_2/r^2) to exactly predict the motions of the planets, the changing phases of the moon, the times of future lunar and solar eclipses, and the tides in the oceans. The motions of the planets had been studied and debated for thousands of years; the ocean tides were thought to have something to do with the moon, but the details were unknown. Newton's mathematical analysis provided answers, or at least a path to answers, for almost all of these questions.

But there was at least one question Newton could not answer: what causes the gravitational force? We know quite a bit more about gravitation today, but we still have no definite answer to that question. In 1915 Albert Einstein explained gravitational force with a mathematical model that describes space and time bending and curving in the presence of mass-energy. Einstein's model, like Newton's model before it, has been successful at predicting and describing some very odd physical behavior, but it adds more questions: Space can bend? Time can bend? Wouldn't that mean they are made of something bendable? What are they made of? What is mass-energy, and how does it bend space and time? Why are space and time physically connected? Nobody knows.

Natural philosophers, now called physicists and mathematicians, applied the mathematical approach of Galileo and Newton to the observable world for the next two hundred years. They developed a large body of mathematical models, now called classical physics, which accurately described and predicted the physical behavior of the world as they saw it.

The models of classical physics, based on observed behavior, often provide nearly complete insight into the questions of how and why physical objects do what they do. But some observations, some experiments, could not be explained by classical physics. It all started to fall apart around 1890, and by 1930 or so, classical physics had been completely replaced by what we call modern physics. With this new era, all certainty withered away. Einstein led the way with his theories of special and general relativity: mathematical models that describe a curving spacetime. Heisenberg, Schrodinger, and many others developed quantum mechanics: mathematical models that describe the tiny bits and pieces that make up our world as physically existing but forever hidden possibilities. Particle physics began to be developed around 1900. Mathematical models inspired by particle behavior have gradually revealed a world made of flitting ghosts that can only be described by abstract, unreal mathematics.

Classical physics showed us a picture of a sensible, understandable world. Classical physics, however, was wrong; it could not accurately predict some physical behaviors (mostly relating to the interactions between matter and electromagnetic radiation). Modern physics is capable of extremely accurate predictions of behavior and has shown us physical possibilities that could not have been found any other way. But modern physics paints a picture of a world that is not, as far as we know, sensible—and is not, so far, understood.

Of course, many guesses have been made by various physicists and philosophers about how the world works. But so far, none have been convincingly proven by experiment. So just as we can only speculate about the meanings of some parts of Scripture, we can only speculate about how the physical world really works and what it really is.

That is why this book can only be read as speculation—as a story.

In this particular story, some of our more obscure speculations about the physical nature of the world will be used as a setting for some of the more obscure events of Scripture. The goal of the story is to see how physics and Scripture might fit together. In your author's opinion, modern physics and Scripture fit together pretty well. Not perfectly, but well enough to be surprising, well enough that they could both be true. Scripture, at least the creation story in Genesis 1, does not fit particularly well with classical physics—but that might be because classical physics is wrong, not because Scripture is untrue.

The physical setting for Genesis 1 offered here uses some mainstream physics, plus a couple of very unconventional streams. The mainstream physics are the theories of special and general relativity, the Copenhagen interpretation of quantum mechanics, and the standard model of particle physics. The unconventional streams are the Feynman-Stueckelberg interpretation of antimatter and the notion described in the quote at the beginning of this introduction—that our entire reality might actually have a mathematical basis.

The major conflict between Scripture and science has always been the time scale of the Genesis creation story: the six days of creation versus the millions and billions of years of cosmological and geologic time. The Feynman-Stueckelberg interpretation of antimatter supports a very different perspective of time, a perspective that allows both Genesis and science to be literally true. As Saint Augustine said long ago in his *Confessions* (11:40, written in 397–400 AD): God's time and our time are not the same. The six days of creation are in God's time. The millions and billions of years are in ours. Much more on this subject later.

The idea that our reality might have a mathematical basis is not a requirement for the speculations in this book, but it is convenient. It is convenient because it paints a picture of how our world might work that hangs comfortably between truth and understanding: detailed enough to possibly shed light on a process that is really beyond us, but still simple and familiar enough for us all (with a little preparation) to follow the story.

Christians are the intended audience for this book. Scriptural theology and doctrine are woven intimately into the presentation. I have tried to keep the presentation of the science impartial, but I realize that to a nonbeliever, much of this book will probably seem a little "weird." There is an inescapable difference in perspective between nonbelievers and believers as we regard our universe. To nonbelievers, this reality is basically a pile of rocks. It can be an interesting pile of rocks, even quite attractive in parts, but it is still just a pile of rocks: a wholly natural world that just happened. It is the way that it is because that's the way it is.

To believers, this is our Lord's creation, made for his own pleasure. It is, at least partly, a work of art; it is beautiful because part of its purpose is to be beautiful. As with all works of art, it shows us some of the character of the artist (he likes beauty).

Living in this art museum, in this Louvre, believers see sculpture and paintings where nonbelievers see only oddly shaped stones and dried glop on canvas. The best example of this that I can give is bacteria. Microbiologists study them mostly in self-defense because they sometimes cause human diseases. Among the larger community of biologists, the prevailing attitude seems to be that bacteria are primitive organisms worthy only of a cursory glance before passing on to larger, more interesting critters. When I first encountered bacteria in some detail, I saw something quite different: they are a tough, resilient, astoundingly adaptive community of organisms that, together, form the foundation of life on this planet. None of us could survive without them. To a believer they are an absolutely brilliant solution to a very tough (but crucial) biological design problem, that of packing enough DNA to allow adaptability into an organism small enough to live on low natural nutrient concentrations. To use engineering design terminology, bacteria are not primitive; they are elegant. What many do not understand is that simple, compact, effective things are by far the hardest to make.

The intended audience for this book is also specifically Christians who do not have any formal training in physics or science. The first chapters briefly present the basics of modern physics along with some additional science and natural philosophy that will be used in the interpretation of the Genesis creation story. Although the presentation of the science is, I think, as brief as it can reasonably be and only covers the highlights, there is still a lot of material to go through.

A few features have been included in this book to help you follow the presentation. A glossary and subject index are located in the back. The glossary includes definitions of some of the more important terms used in the science. In some cases, the definitions in the glossary are more complete than the descriptions of terms and concepts in the book.

It is customary in technical books written for nontechnical readers to emphasize important points with pages and pages of description. There is some of that in *Quantum Genesis,* but only for a few, really crucial parts of the presentation—namely energy and quantum object localization. Many other points are also important, but to keep the book as short as possible, your author has mentioned them only briefly. To help identify them, points of moderate importance will be emphasized (like this sentence here).

Because there is so much material and because the narrative frequently jumps from topic to topic before it all comes together later in the discussion of Genesis, it can be easy to get lost. I hope the following map of the argument will help to keep all of the bits and pieces in their proper places (next page).

A quick look at the map will reveal that there is more to the book than just the interpretation of Genesis. Apologies, dear readers, but I just could not resist the temptation. So many apologetics doors stand open after a presentation of modern physics that I just had to go through some of them. This book makes several apologetic arguments based on modern physics:

- The Genesis creation story can (and probably should) be interpreted using modern physics.
- The Genesis creation story (interpreted using modern physics) is compatible with the millions and billions of years of geology and cosmology.
- The Genesis creation story (interpreted using modern physics) is compatible with the geology and fossil record we see on Earth.
- Modern physics is probably not in conflict with the prophecies and miracles in Scripture.
- It is possible to postulate a reality that would likely result in the physical existence of a being resembling God.

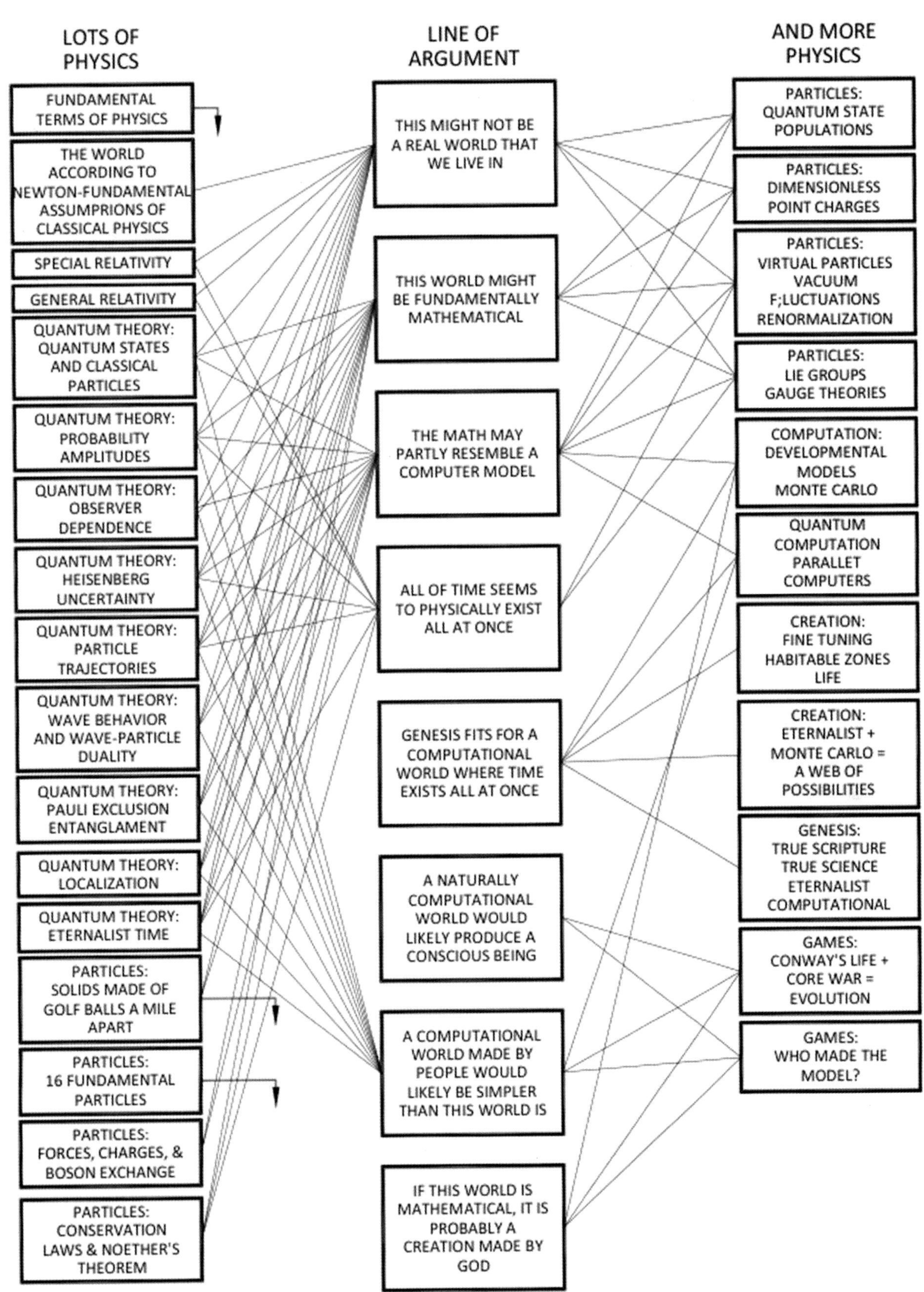
LOTS OF PHYSICS
FUNDAMENTAL TERMS OF PHYSICS
THE WORLD ACCORDING TO NEWTON-FUNDAMENTAL ASSUMPRIONS OF CLASSICAL PHYSICS
SPECIAL RELATIVITY
GENERAL RELATIVITY
QUANTUM THEORY: QUANTUM STATES AND CLASSICAL PARTICLES
QUANTUM THEORY: PROBABILITY AMPLITUDES
QUANTUM THEORY: OBSERVER DEPENDENCE
QUANTUM THEORY: HEISENBERG UNCERTAINTY
QUANTUM THEORY: PARTICLE TRAJECTORIES
QUANTUM THEORY: WAVE BEHAVIOR AND WAVE-PARTICLE DUALITY
QUANTUM THEORY: PAULI EXCLUSION ENTANGLAMENT
QUANTUM THEORY: LOCALIZATION
QUANTUM THEORY: ETERNALIST TIME
PARTICLES: SOLIDS MADE OF GOLF BALLS A MILE APART
PARTICLES: 16 FUNDAMENTAL PARTICLES
PARTICLES: FORCES, CHARGES, & BOSON EXCHANGE
PARTICLES: CONSERVATION LAWS & NOETHER'S THEOREM
LINE OF ARGUMENT
THIS MIGHT NOT BE A REAL WORLD THAT WE LIVE IN
THIS WORLD MIGHT BE FUNDAMENTALLY MATHEMATICAL
THE MATH MAY PARTLY RESEMBLE A COMPUTER MODEL
ALL OF TIME SEEMS TO PHYSICALLY EXIST ALL AT ONCE
GENESIS FITS FOR A COMPUTATIONAL WORLD WHERE TIME EXISTS ALL AT ONCE
A NATURALLY COMPUTATIONAL WORLD WOULD LIKELY PRODUCE A CONSCIOUS BEING
A COMPUTATIONAL WORLD MADE BY PEOPLE WOULD LIKELY BE SIMPLER THAN THIS WORLD IS
IF THIS WORLD IS MATHEMATICAL, IT IS PROBABLY A CREATION MADE BY GOD
AND MORE PHYSICS
PARTICLES: QUANTUM STATE POPULATIONS
PARTICLES: DIMENSIONLESS POINT CHARGES
PARTICLES: VIRTUAL PARTICLES VACUUM F;LUCTUATIONS RENORMALIZATION
PARTICLES: LIE GROUPS GAUGE THEORIES
COMPUTATION: DEVELOPMENTAL MODELS MONTE CARLO
QUANTUM COMPUTATION PARALLET COMPUTERS
CREATION: FINE TUNING HABITABLE ZONES LIFE
CREATION: ETERNALIST + MONTE CARLO = A WEB OF POSSIBILITIES
GENESIS: TRUE SCRIPTURE TRUE SCIENCE ETERNALIST COMPUTATIONAL
GAMES: CONWAY'S LIFE + CORE WAR = EVOLUTION
GAMES: WHO MADE THE MODEL?

- Modern physics and the interpretation of the Genesis creation story offered in this book can provide strong rebuttals for many of the most common arguments made against Scripture by opponents of our faith.
- Modern physics implies that it is logically most likely that we are living in a creation made by God.
- As Scripture says, this creation attests to the existence and the power of God.

First, though, we need to begin with a little science.

An Aside for Terminology: Science and Natural Philosophy

Before the scientific method became really popular, what we now call science was called "natural philosophy." In my opinion, the term still applies to some of the observational information we will be using to interpret Genesis 1. Most definitions of "science" today are quite complex, and different definitions often do not agree in the details. I suspect that some of the difficulty results from trying to lump together areas of study that are based on scientific method (like physics) with areas of study where scientific method is mostly impractical (like geology, paleontology, and archeology). The fundamental difference is that, in science, the theories that win are those verified by experiment. In natural philosophy, the theories that win are the ones that seem the most reasonable to the majority of the practitioners. Plenty of science is used in the various areas of natural philosophy, but it only goes so far; there is often not enough of it available to be conclusive.

For the rest of this book I will try to use the term "science" for concepts that have been entirely derived using scientific method (physics, chemistry, astrophysics, and cosmology) and "natural philosophy" for ideas that haven't (geology, paleontology, and evolutionary biology). Natural philosophy isn't necessarily wrong; it just has not been proved in the same way. There will be quite a lot of natural philosophy used to interpret Genesis 1.

01

A Speculation in Physics

Physics is the study of how the world works—and since about the mid-1600s AD, it has been all about applying mathematics to that study. Physicists take careful measurements of the behavior of some physical system, then develop mathematical models based on those measurements to try to predict the future behavior of the same or similar systems. All of physics boils down to this very simple process, which has been repeated over, and over, and over.

In physics, a "theory" is a detailed mathematical model that predicts some aspect of physical behavior. Theories in physics are verified by experiment: a carefully arranged situation wherein physical behavior can be accurately measured. The results are compared to the predictions of the theory's mathematical models, and if measurements and theoretical prediction agree, the theory is considered to be verified.

Isaac Newton's theory of universal gravitational attraction (proposed in 1687) was accepted as valid because it accurately predicted the motions of the planets and moons in our solar system which had earlier been measured by astronomers Tycho Brahe (1546–1601) and Johannes Kepler (1571–1630). Albert Einstein's theory of general relativity (proposed in 1915) was first accepted as valid because it accurately predicted the angle at which light from a distant star is bent as it passes near the sun. Both theories, both mathematical models, are still accepted as valid today because they continue to make accurate mathematical predictions of physical behavior whenever they are used.

The particular math techniques used in physics may at times seem to be a rather odd choice. Especially when it comes to quantum mechanics and particle physics, I think most physicists would not disagree with that perception! The thing to remember is that the mathematical approaches used in physics are all chosen for exactly the same reason: because they work. If there is ever any question as to why the math is done in this or that particular way, the answer is always the same: because it's what works. Quantum mechanics has been described as not only stranger than anyone imagines, but stranger than anyone *can* imagine. The reason the mathematical theory of quantum mechanics is used is that it works, and no matter how very odd it is, it's the only theory that works.

Any presentation of modern physics has to be about the mathematics because that is what modern physics is. This book is no exception. Especially for subjects like particle physics or quantum mechanics, where the events are far too small and fleeting for us to see them, mathematical descriptions are all that exist for us. They are our only point of interaction with the realities we describe. What follows, therefore, is mostly a description of mathematics, with a few equations added in for illustrative purposes. For the most part, it will not be necessary to understand the equations or know how to use them; they are included because some people (me, for example) like to see them.

Numerous other books provide the same information with much more detailed and complete explanations. The following is a list of some of the books I have found useful for readers who may be interested in explanations that are rather more complete than will be found herein. Please bear in mind that some of the material is challenging; it might not make sense the first time it is read. I have frequently found that, like the Bible, it can be necessary to read physics presentations more than once before they start to make any sense at all.

QED, The Strange Theory of Light and Matter, by Richard Feynman. This book is a great introduction to quantum mechanics. Dr. Feynman was one of the acknowledged stars in quantum physics and had a passion for explaining the subject to anyone who was willing to sit through a lecture. The example calculations focus on Feynman's path integral formulation.

Quantum Reality: Beyond the New Physics by Nick Herbert. This is a good introduction to quantum mechanics using Schrodinger's wave mechanics for the calculation examples. *Quantum Reality* emphasizes the implications of physics on the nature of our existence. It does a pretty good job of presenting some of the major interpretations of quantum mechanics. Just for reference, the view of quantum mechanics that will be presented in this book is a slight twist on Von Neumann's extension of the Copenhagen interpretation (as Nick Herbert describes it, it wasn't actually proposed by Von Neumann, but it was based on his work).

Quantum Reality: Theory and Philosophy by Jonathan Allday. This is a very thorough (and long, but totally worth the time) introduction to the details of quantum mechanics with some introduction to quantum field theory. This book is a more challenging read; it uses Dirac's notation and includes frequent presentations of how the mathematics for quantum mechanics is done. It also has sections that discuss some of the major interpretations of quantum mechanics and their historical development.

The Quantum Challenge: Modern Research on the Foundations of Quantum Mechanics by George Greenstein and Arthur Zajonc. In my opinion, this is the best book out there about quantum physics. The book has a very thorough discussion of the interpretational issues in quantum mechanics and the experiments that have been done to try to resolve them. This book is not an introduction. It is possible to get through it with no preparation, but it will make more sense after reading one or more of the introductory works mentioned above.

Deep Down Things: The Breathtaking Beauty of Particle Physics by Bruce Schumm. This book is a very nice introduction to the standard model of particle physics; it's one of my favorites. Dr. Schumm does a particularly effective job of discussing some of the limitations of the physical theories; it's surprising how many of the experts forget to mention those little tidbits. It may be challenging for readers who have not been trained in introductory physics.

By the way, the title is a quote from Gerard Manley Hopkins' poem "God's Grandeur":

> THE WORLD is charged with the grandeur of God.
> It will flame out, like shining from shook foil;
> It gathers to a greatness, like the ooze of oil
> Crushed. Why do men then now not reck his rod?
> Generations have trod, have trod, have trod;
> And all is seared with trade; bleared, smeared with toil;
> And wears man's smudge and shares man's smell: the soil
> Is bare now, nor can foot feel, being shod.
> And for all this, nature is never spent;
> There lives the dearest freshness deep down things;

And though the last lights off the black West went
Oh, morning, at the brown brink eastward, springs—
Because the Holy Ghost over the bent
World broods with warm breast and with ah! bright wings.

A Universe From Nothing: Why There Is Something Rather Than Nothing by Lawrence Krauss. This is a pretty good presentation of the naturalist side of the cosmology first cause argument. It includes a good presentation of the observational justification for the Big Bang cosmology.

New Proofs for the Existence of God: Contributions of Contemporary Physics and Philosophy by Robert Spitzer. This book presents the creationist side of the cosmology first cause argument. It mentions a few things that Krauss left out (must have slipped his mind). It also has an interesting presentation of metaphysics for those unenlightened persons (like me) who think philosophers are mostly pretty goofy.

A final caution before we start. This book will build like a tower of blocks, beginning with some basic terms used in physics and going on from there. In order for the conclusions at the end to make sense, it is pretty important that you be reasonably familiar with the material at the beginning and all the way through.

At the same time, to get the most from this book you won't need to develop a thorough understanding of the details of the physics or the mathematics. A general impression of how it works is really good enough. When we reach our interpretation of Genesis—the pinnacle of the book—we won't be using any calculations or equations at all.

Finally, let's begin our tour of the science. And welcome. Welcome to our Lord's creation.

Fundamental Terms

Our presentation now begins with a few definitions of basic terms that we will be using later. Physics uses a lot of jargon: words that are only used in physics to describe concepts nobody else really cares about. Physics also uses many terms, such as work and energy, that are in common usage. It is important to remember that, in physics, all terms, especially work and energy, have very specific mathematical definitions.

Cartesian Coordinates

According to tradition, the mathematician and philosopher Rene Descartes (1596–1650) was not a healthy man. The inspiration for the most fundamental tool of physics, the Cartesian coordinate system, came while he was lying in bed watching a fly crawl around on the tiled ceiling. It occurred to him that he could write a mathematical description of the position of the fly by counting tiles up from the wall at his feet and over from the left wall. A description of the movement of the fly could then be written using a clock and recording the various positions of the fly at certain times.

In physics Cartesian coordinates are usually measured in meters instead of tiles, but the principle is the same. Pick any convenient spot to measure from (called the origin) and the orientations of three perpendicular directions to measure in (called the X, Y, and Z axes), and any position in the universe can be described by the three distances along the axes (x, y, and z). Positions in front of the origin are described by positive numbers (greater than 0); positions behind the origin are measured by negative numbers (less than 0).

Negative numbers are very useful here because they allow us to put an origin in any convenient position that makes the math easier to do. Without negative numbers, we would always have to put our origin in the most remote corner of the universe and measure positions in megaparsecs (a distance unit in astronomy, equal to 3.26 million light years).

Incidentally, our universe is described as having three spatial dimensions (3-D) because it always takes three Cartesian numbers to fully describe any position (Figure 1, next page).

The Cartesian coordinate system unified the mathematical disciplines of geometry and algebra by allowing numbers to be used to describe shapes and shapes to be used to display numbers. In the pages that follow, this concept of using shapes to

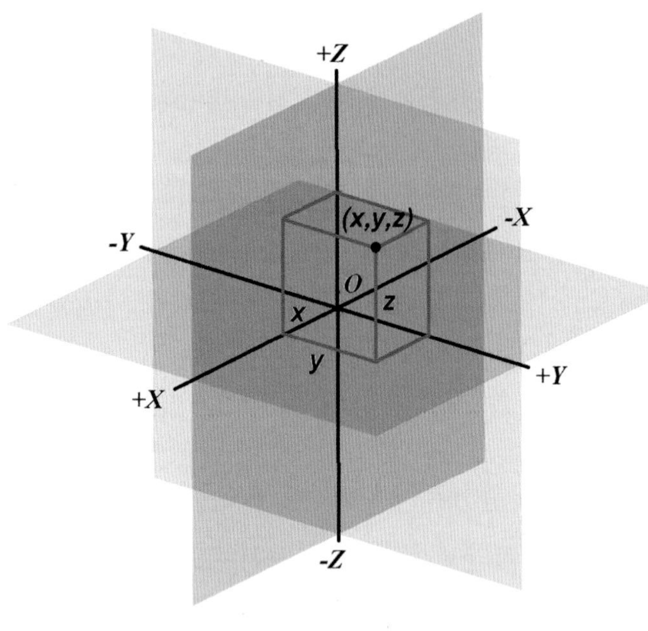

Fig. 1. 3-Dimensional Cartesian Coordinates

display numbers is going to be really useful; it is much easier to see patterns in drawings of shapes than it is in long lists of numbers.

Cartesian coordinates are used everywhere in physics. Any time x, y, or z pop up in equations, it's a safe bet that they mean positions along perpendicular axes.

Figure 2 shows an example of a geometric shape (a circle) and the algebraic formula for a circle. The x and y variables are the distances along the X and Y axes; r is the radius of the circle. By shuffling letters and numbers around, we can write the formula to figure out the value of the Y axis positions of any point on the circle given the value on the X axis.

One thing to notice here is that the square root operation gives two solutions, and therefore, two positions on the Y axis for each value of x—one positive and one nega-

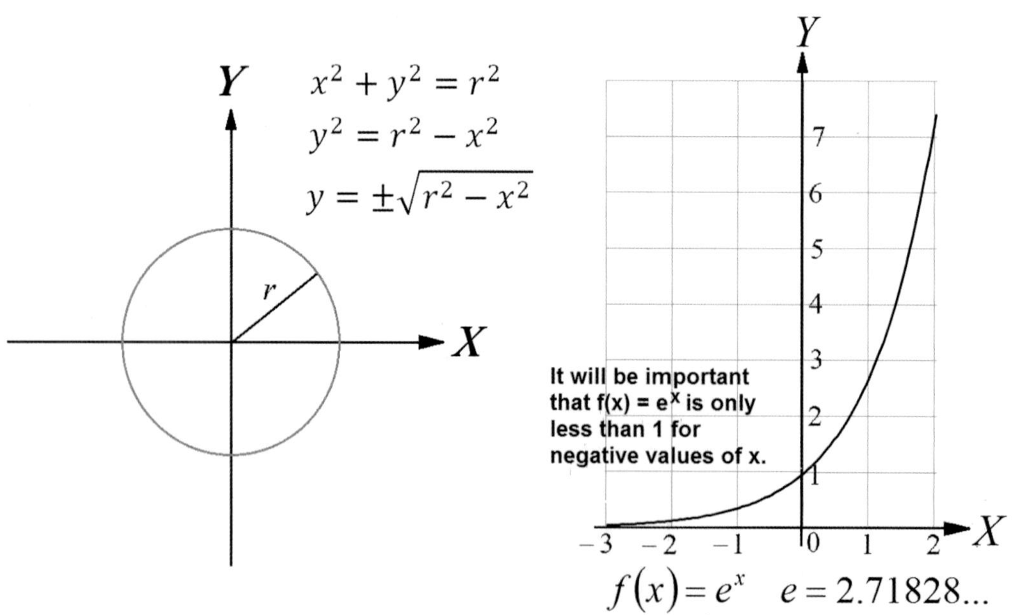

Fig. 2. A Circle and Function in Cartesian Coordinates

tive. This is appropriate to describe a circle, because the circle does have two y positions for each x position (except at the ends). This is going to be really important later on when we get to particle physics, because the mathematic descriptions of antimatter are similar to the negative solutions for a square root. As might be expected, it is a little more complex than that, but it's the same sort of thing.

The f(x) notation in the other example means that the vertical axis positions can be thought of as being a function of the x position. A *function* in algebra is a rule for changing one number (X axis position, in this case) into one other number (vertical axis position, in this case) in some useful way. The notation used in algebra—the constants (only e here), variables (x, y, r), exponents (lots of twos plus one x), and operation symbols (+ and =)—are just a shorthand way of writing the rule. The circle formula technically can't be a function, because a function isn't allowed to have two y values for each x value.

Function notation is used all over the place in physics. In fact, most of the mathematical models that are used to describe physical behavior are written as functions. The only important thing to remember here is that the function notation just means some number that is calculated from other numbers: f(x) means a number calculated from the x axis position; f(x, y, z) means a number that is calculated from all three Cartesian coordinates for a position. We will be using the e^x function later in probability distributions. The important feature of the e^x function here is that it is only less than 1 for negative values of x.

Complex Numbers

Another odd thing that can come from the square root operation is a type of number called a complex number. Complex numbers are written with two terms, one "real" term with a normal number and one "imaginary" term with an i factor (i is the square root of negative 1). Imaginary numbers are square roots of negative numbers. The problem is that a positive number times the same positive number is a positive number, while a negative number (less than 0; behind the origin) times the same negative number is also a positive number. No real number can be multiplied by itself to get a negative number. So mathematicians made up a new kind of number called an imaginary number.

It should not be a surprise that a complex number can be represented as a line or arrow in Cartesian coordinates by designating one of the axes, usually the vertical

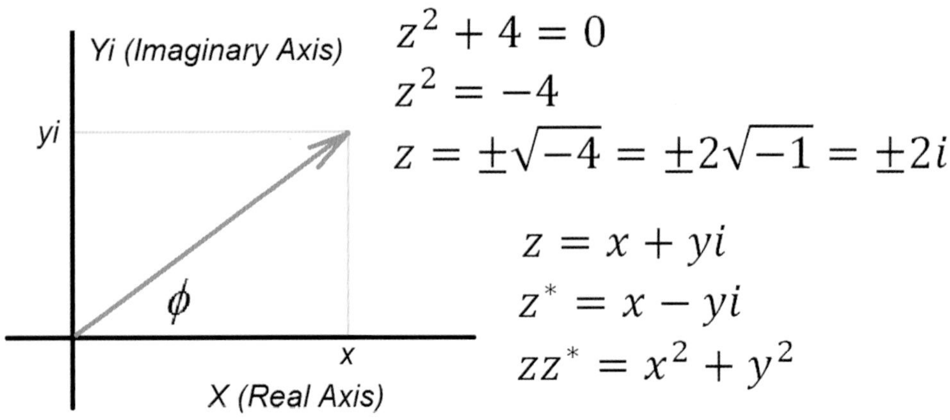

Fig. 3. Complex Number in Cartesian Coordinates

axis, as imaginary. The Greek letter phi (ϕ) in the figure above represents the angle between the x axis and the arrow that represents the complex number value; it is called the phase of the complex number.

The arrow representation for complex numbers will be used most of the time here because it is much easier to see the interactions between complex numbers displayed as arrows than it is by using just the numbers themselves.

Complex numbers are important in modern physics because the equations for quantum mechanics use complex numbers, not just real numbers. Mostly, the results of quantum mechanics calculations are phase relationships (angles) between complex numbers (represented by arrows).

The z^* equation is called the *complex conjugate* of a complex number z; it's just the same complex number with the imaginary part subtracted instead of added. Complex conjugates will be important because multiplying the complex number results of quantum mechanics calculations by their complex conjugate is how we will get the answers from the "imaginary" world back to our real world.

Is this all starting to sound a bit odd yet? Good. It should. Things are going to get much, much worse.

Scalars and Vectors

Physics frequently needs to describe things that have directions. Particles move in directions; forces push in directions. Quantities with directions are called vectors, and they are described using a slight modification of (what a shocker) the Cartesian coordinate system. Quantities in physics that do not have a direction are called scalars.

Vectors will show up a little in some of the term definitions in this book, but other than that we won't use them much. They are included here simply because they are a huge part of physics calculations. The only thing that might be handy to remember later is that vectors have three dimensions and require three numbers, like the (x, y, z) for a position vector in Cartesian coordinates. Scalars are just a single number.

Vectors are treated as little arrows, much like complex numbers; they are drawn as arrows, and vector quantities in equations have little arrows over them. The i, j, and k quantities in the example below are vectors with length equal to 1 in the X, Y, and Z axis directions (called unit vectors).

Vectors have their own special rules for mathematical operations. They are added by lining them up blunt end to pointy end; the sum is a vector from the blunt end of

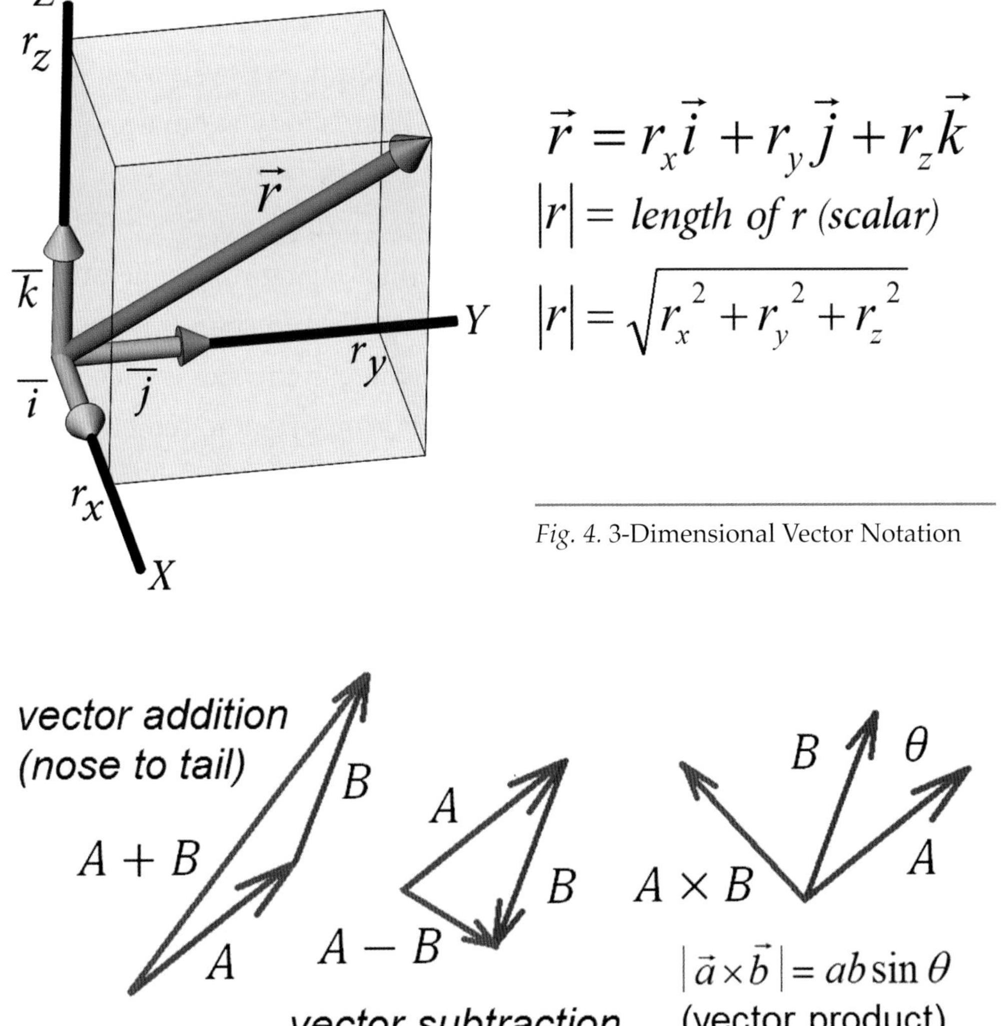

Fig. 4. 3-Dimensional Vector Notation

Fig. 5. Vector Addition and Multiplication

the first to the pointy end of the last (red + blue = purple). In subtraction, a vector with the opposite direction is added (red − blue = purple). There are two kinds of multiplication for vectors: a vector product (which gives a vector result, red × blue = purple) and a scalar product (that gives a scalar result—just a number with no direction). The circle-bar symbol is the Greek letter theta, which is frequently used to represent angles in physics; here it represents the angle between the red and blue vectors.

The Derivative Operator

Functions change numbers into other numbers in useful ways; operators change functions into other functions in useful ways. Operators are going to be used a few times in this book because the mathematics of quantum mechanics is based on operators. This section and the next give descriptions of two operators, the derivative operator and the integration operator, that are used constantly in physics. For anyone interested in the details of the mathematics used, it will be handy to have an idea of how derivatives and integrals work.

First, the derivative operator. It is often really useful in physics to know how fast values are changing. Velocity is how fast a position is changing; acceleration is how fast a velocity is changing. Velocities and accelerations both change in response to forces. The technique used to calculate rates of change in physics is called the derivative (or differential) operator. The only thing that is important to remember here is that the d/dx notation (the derivative operator) just means rate of change.

The derivative operator is based on the rules for calculating changes in the Cartesian coordinate system. The triangle (Greek capital letter delta) in figure 6 is a math symbol that means change—the last value minus the first value ($x + \Delta x - x = \Delta x$). In the Cartesian coordinate system, change is represented by the slant, or slope of a line. Slope can be calculated as the ratio of the differences between two positions on the X axis (x and $x + \Delta x$ in this example) and the corresponding positions on the Y axis. So slope is the change in y divided by the

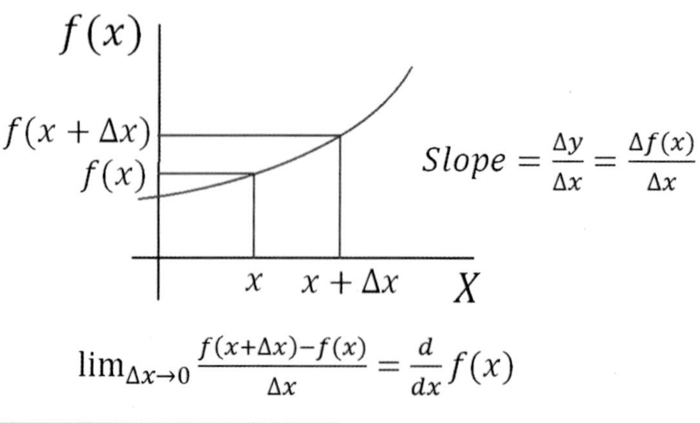

Fig. 6. Derivative Operator

change in x. For a curved line, the slope calculation will get more and more accurate as Δx gets smaller and smaller. The "lim" symbol stands for limit, meaning the value that the function will theoretically get to as Δx gets really, really close to 0. We need to use the limit concept, because it is not actually allowed to divide by 0.

As Δx becomes (theoretically) zero, the slope calculation is finally accurate. The calculation of the slope for a (theoretical) zero value of Δx is what the derivative operator does. It is a set of rules for changing one function into another function that will give the slope of the original function at every point on the original curve. The derivative of a position curve is the velocity (the rate of change of position) at every point in the curve; the derivative of a velocity curve is the acceleration (the rate of change of velocity) at every point in the curve.

The Integration Operator

It is also useful in physics to multiply quantities together. Multiplying constant scalars (numbers that don't change) is not difficult. Multiplying changing functions is more challenging. Physics sometimes uses another operator, the integration operator, to do that kind of thing. Like the derivative operator, the integration operator won't be used very much in this book. Even so, it will be convenient to know what the really tall S symbol means.

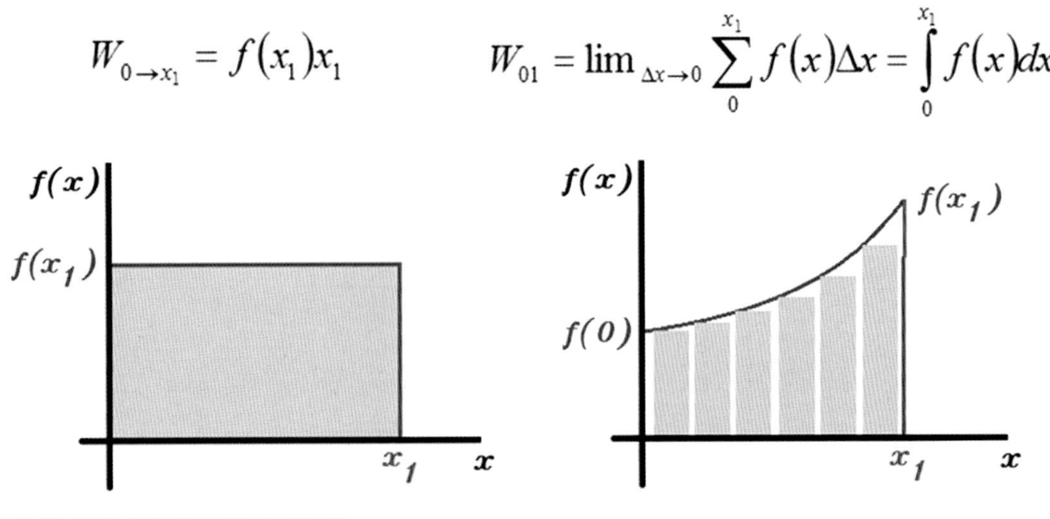

Fig. 7. Integration Operator

We are going to use our old friend the Cartesian coordinate system to represent the operation (that thing is really handy!).

If we put constant scalars on the horizontal and vertical axes, we get a rectangular figure. The product is just the area of the rectangle; length times height in this example. To multiply changing values, we are going to do the same thing—it is just a little more difficult to calculate the area under the curves (Figure 7, previous page).

The area is calculated by breaking it up into little boxes, each with a width of Δx. Like the derivative operator, the calculation is going to become more and more accurate as Δx gets smaller and smaller and creates more and thinner boxes. The integration operator is the calculation of the area for the limit as Δx gets really, really close to 0. Also like the derivative operator, the integration operator is a set of rules for changing a function into another function that will give the area under the curve for every point in the curve.

The angular E symbol is the Greek capital letter sigma; it means summation, in this case the sum of the areas of all of the little rectangular boxes. The subscript (0) and superscript (x_1) mean that the addition of areas is only between the 0 and x_1 values on the X axis. The tall S symbol and dx indicate the integration operator.

Momentum

Next on our list of terms are three words that not only serve as physics jargon but are also used in normal conversation: *momentum, work,* and *energy.* All three terms have precise, mathematical definitions in physics that are similar to but not the same as the English language definitions everyone uses. The physics definition of *momentum* is pretty easy to understand; *work* is a little more difficult; energy is complicated. Unfortunately, the concept of energy is really crucial in science, and we will be using it constantly in this book—so complicated or not, we will need to deal with it.

First, though, we get to define momentum (assigned the lowercase letter "p" in physics):

$$\vec{p} = m\vec{v}$$

$\vec{p}$ = *momentum (vecor)*
m = *mass (scalar)*
$\vec{v}$ = *velocity (vector)*

That's it. Momentum is just the product of mass times velocity. Momentum (p) is a vector (it has the little arrow over it in the equation) because velocity (v) is a vector (things move in directions). Because momentum is a vector, it will always take three numbers (p_x,p_y,p_z) to specify the value and direction of momentum.

It turns out that momentum is a pretty useful quantity, more useful than mass or velocity by themselves. This is because forces change momentum, not mass or velocity alone. Most of the equations in modern physics that involve motion use momentum instead of velocity.

Work

Next is the mathematical definition of work. We will only be using the physics concept of work in this book because it's part of the definition of energy; outside of that context, it won't show up again.

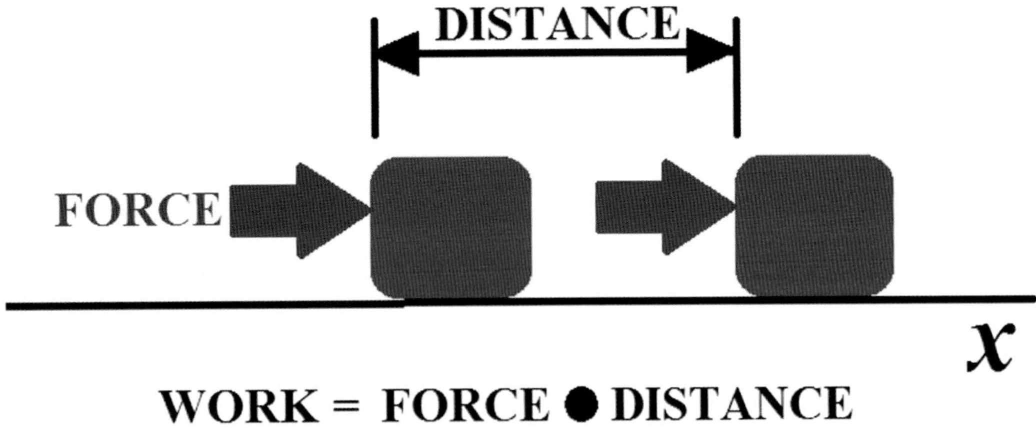

Work is the product of the magnitude of a force that pushes on an object and the distance that the object moves in response to the force. Both the force and the distance are vectors (they push and move in directions), but the quantity of work is a scalar (just a single number, no direction) because the calculation of work uses the scalar version of a vector multiplication product (the dot symbol shown in the illustration). Work can be positive or negative, depending on the directions of the force and motion.

Because the force can, and often does, change, we need to use the integration operator to do the multiplication. In the equation below, the F(r) notation means a variable force that changes with position (r). Unfortunately, it looks a lot like the f(x) notation for a function, which we saw used earlier. I apologize for the confusion. Mathematicians and physicists have very inconsiderately chosen to use the same letter, f, to mean two different things: function and force. One way around the problem is used here: a lower case, italicized *f* usually means function; uppercase F usually means force.

For a constant force:

$$W = \vec{F} \bullet \vec{r}$$

$W = work\ (scalar)$
$\vec{F} = force\ (vector)$
$\vec{r} = position\ (vector)$
$\bullet = scalar\ product$

For a changing force:

$$W = \int_{r_1}^{r_2} f(r)dr$$

The calculation for work can be a little tricky to do, because there must be both force and movement in order for the result to count as work. Push on a wall with all of your strength; if the wall does not move, then no work is done. An example from baseball: a bat does work on a ball to send it out into the field, but mathematically, only the tiny amount of time when the bat is actually in contact with the ball counts as work. The flight of the ball has movement, but there is no force on the ball, so there is no work done during the flight (in this example, we're ignoring gravity).

When a fielder catches the ball and stops it, that will also count as work. It has the same value as the work done by the bat, but if the work done by the bat is considered positive, the work done by the fielder's glove on the ball would be considered negative. They cancel out to leave the ball at rest, just like adding positive and negative numbers.

The positive or negative sign for work is determined by the directions of the force and movement vectors in the Cartesian coordinate system: force and/or movement in positive X, Y, or Z directions (directions that increase positive numbers) give positive work; negative work has force and/or movement in negative directions (directions that increase negative numbers).

Energy

Energy is the key concept in physics. The wind blows because of energy. Rain falls and water flows because of energy. The sun and stars shine because of energy. Our hearts pump and our blood flows because of energy. Our entire universe is what it is and behaves as it does because of energy.

The purpose of physics is to describe and understand the behavior of the world we live in. Almost all of that behavior—certainly all of the parts that change or move—can be mathematically described as changes in the form of energy. One of the most surprising revelations of modern physics has been that everything in our world is made entirely of energy and nothing but energy ($E = mc^2$).

Energy comes in many forms:

chemical energy, which causes chemical reactions to happen or not happen;
mechanical energy stored in springs or compressed gases, which pushes on objects;
electric energy, which powers lights, sound systems, and computers;
magnetic energy, which turns motors;
radiant energy, which heats and lights the earth;
nuclear energy, which generates heat and light from the sun;
thermal or heat energy, which warms things up;
sound energy, which lets us hear;
gravitational energy, which pulls stuff down;
and many more.

The tricky thing about energy is that while it cannot be created or destroyed, it can and does change form. As an example, a story of energy: Nuclear energy in the sun generates heat energy, which flows to the surface and is radiated to the earth as light and heat (a kind of light). The light and heat are captured by algae on the earth's surface and used to drive the chemical reactions that cause the algae to grow, storing chemical energy. Some of these algae are buried in sediment, and as the sediment piles up over a long time, gravitational energy compresses and heats the dead algae and turns them into oil and natural gas. Mechanical energy pushes oil and gas out of the ground and then pushes it again to refineries, where it is heated by thermal energy and separated into useful fuels. The fuel is burned, turning stored chemical energy into thermal energy to heat water and vaporize it into steam, which then provides mechanical energy to drive turbines. The turbines turn generators, which use magnetic energy to make electrical energy. This flows out over wires to houses, where it is used to light lights and power computers to write and to read this book. All of those events are actions driven by energy changing form over time.

Now that we're all properly impressed, here is the definition of energy as the term is used in physics: the energy of an object is the aggregate quantity of work that has been done to the object. Because energy cannot be created or destroyed, the energy of an object is also the numerical capacity of that object to do work on other objects.

In the figure on the next page, the triangle symbol is the Greek capital letter delta, which means change in physics, so

Δ = later value − earlier value:

$\Delta x = x_{later} - x_{earlier}$,

$\Delta E = Energy_{later} - Energy_{earlier}$.

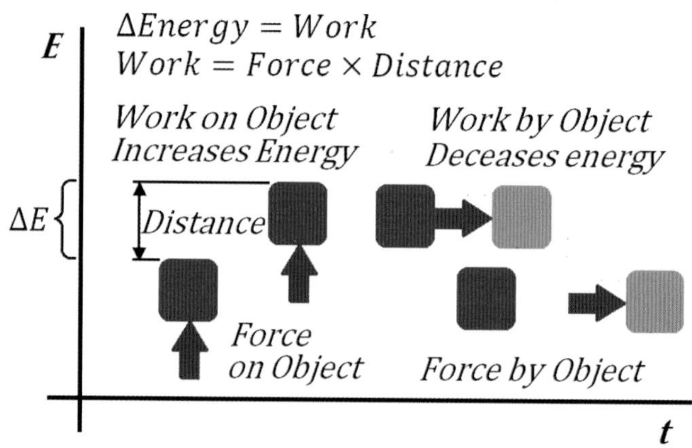

Remember that work is force and motion. Down in the tiny world of the particles that make up all of the material we think of as the universe, objects will always move in response to forces. It is not far wrong to think of the energy of a particle as the net sum of all the forces that have ever pushed on the particle, which is exactly equal to the total capacity of the particle to push on other particles. From that perspective, it is not unreasonable to think of energy as a kind of stored force.

Also down in the tiny world of particles, there are only two forms of energy we need to worry about for now: kinetic energy and potential energy. Since, as far as we know, everything in the universe is made of particles, all of the forms of energy we've discussed are variations on the themes of kinetic and potential energy. Detailed analyses of the physical processes involved above also reduce down to kinetic and potential energy and (almost) nothing else.

In quantum mechanics, we use certain mathematical techniques to do detailed analyses like these. One of the ways of doing the calculations, called Schrodinger's wave mechanics, is based on the transitions between kinetic and potential energy.

There is a third kind of energy, rest or intrinsic energy, that we will get to later as we discuss relativity. Rest energy is the quantity of energy that a particle must have in order to be a particle ($E = mc^2$ again). The total energy of a particle is the sum of its kinetic energy, potential energy, and rest energy. The various energies still change forms: rest energy can (and does) change into kinetic and potential energy; kinetic and potential energy can (and do) change into rest energy.

Kinetic Energy

Kinetic energy is the simplest of these three, so we'll define it first:

$$E_K = \frac{1}{2} m\vec{v}^2$$

E_K = *Kinetic Energy (scalar)*
m = *mass (scalar)*
$\vec{v}$ = *velocity (vector)*

The mathematical description of kinetic energy is one half the product of the mass of a particle and the square of its velocity. Remember that energy is all about force. The harder a particle is pushed, the faster it goes. The faster a particle goes, the harder it must be pushed in order to be stopped.

Potential Energy

Potential energy is the energy a particle can acquire by being pushed into a force field. Thanks to Hollywood, the image that pops up when we hear that statement is of some hapless little particle being shoved into an invisible wall that acts like a bug zapper (bzzzt!). That's not quite what it means.

In both mathematics and physics, a field is a volume of space that can have some number assigned to every point in it. A force field is a volume of space that can have a value and a direction for a force assigned for every point in the volume (remember, force is a vector). All that really means is that a force field is a part of space where we can calculate what the forces are.

I'll use a gravitational force field as an example to help explain potential energy. Since we all live in one, we are pretty familiar with how it works!

A particle acquires potential energy if work is done on it—if it is pushed over a distance, against the forces of a force field. Potential energy decreases if the particle moves in response to the field forces. In order to have potential energy, the particle must be in a force field of some kind.

The earth has a gravitational force field all around it. Gravitational force directions are always toward the center of the earth. The value of the force can be calculated using Newton's law of gravitation (force = Gm_1m_2/r^2). Near the earth's surface, Newton's law is usually simplified to force = mg.

Pick a ball up off the floor. Work has been done to the ball. The value of the work is the force (the weight of the ball, F_g = mg, in this case) times the distance (h for height) it was picked up. The ball now has potential energy equal to the work that was done to it (E_p = mgh).

Let the ball go. The gravitational force field will push the ball down toward the center of the earth. The ball will speed up as it falls, meaning that the kinetic energy of the ball increases as the potential energy (proportional to the height) decreases. When the ball hits the floor, it will have exactly as much kinetic energy (= $mv^2/2$) as it had potential energy (= mgh) when it was dropped.

F_g = gravitational force
G = Newton's gravitational constant $\left(1.069 \times 10^{-9} \frac{ft^3}{lbm-s^2}\right)$
m = mass of objects
M_E = mass of the Earth
g = gravitational acceleration at the surface of the Earth $\left(32.174 \frac{ft}{s^2}\right)$
E_P = gravitational potential energy
h = height of object above Earth's surface

$$F_g = \frac{Gm_1m_2}{r^2} = \frac{GM_Em}{r^2} = m\left(\frac{GM_E}{r^2}\right) = mg$$

$$E_P = Work = \vec{F} \bullet \vec{r} = Fr\cos\theta = mgh$$

Fig. 8. Earth's Gravitational Field

Toss a ball straight up into the air. Your hand does work on the ball to speed it up, which gives it kinetic energy. Once it leaves your hand it starts to slow down as it gets higher in the gravitational force field; kinetic energy is changing form into potential energy. The top of its travel will be at a height where the potential energy matches the kinetic energy it had when it left your hand. Falling back to your hand, the ball's potential energy will be turned back into the same amount of kinetic energy it had when it left your hand.

When a particle moves into the force field of another particle, the physics is exactly the same. Kinetic energy changes form to potential energy and then back to kinetic energy. The change in the form of energy from kinetic to potential and back to kinetic as particles "bounce" off each other is exactly how collisions are analyzed in particle physics experiments. Welcome to particle physics.

Electrostatic (Coulomb) Force

There are several force fields that are important among particles (gravity generally is not one of them). Throughout this book, we will mostly be discussing the forces generated by electrostatic attraction and repulsion. Electrostatic forces are called Coulomb forces in honor of Charles de Coulomb, the physicist who developed the equations for calculating them in 1785.

Science tells us that there are four forces that hold our existence together. Two of them, the strong and weak nuclear forces, only act to hold atomic nuclei together;

they don't really show up much outside of the centers of atoms. The other two, gravitational and electromagnetic forces, form and manipulate everything else. All of the light and colors that we see are electromagnetic force interactions. Atoms are bound into molecules by arrangements of electrical charges and engage in chemical reactions that are controlled by them.

$+p$ $+p$ (repel); $-e$ $-e$ (repel); $-e$ $+p$ (attract)

$-e$ *is the symbol for an electron*
$+p$ *is the symbol for a positron, an antimatter electron*
F_e *= electrostatic force*
π *= ratio of the circumference of a circle to its diameter*
e_0 *= electrical permittivity of vacuum*
q *= electric charge*
r *= distance between charges*
E_p *= potential energy due to the electrostatic force*

$$F_e = \frac{1}{4\pi e_0}\frac{q_1 q_2}{r^2}$$

$$E_p = Work = \int F_e dr = \int_{r=0}^{r} \frac{1}{4\pi e_0}\frac{q_1 q_2}{r^2} dr = \frac{1}{4\pi e_0}\frac{q_1 q_2}{r}$$

Some objects and particles have electric charges that make them subject to electrostatic (or Coulomb) forces. Objects and particles that do not have an electric charge are not affected by electrostatic forces. Electric charges come in two kinds, called positive (+) and negative (–). If the charges on two particles are the same kind (+ and + or – and –) the force is a repulsion; it pushes the particles apart. If two particles have an opposite charge (+ and –), the force is an attraction and pulls the particles toward each other.

The term *electrostatic* is used when the charges are not moving. When electric charges move, they generate magnetic forces so that particles are affected by the combination of electrical and magnetic forces. Calculations for particles subject to combined electromagnetic forces are a bit more difficult (see intimidating equation, above).

Maxwell's Equations for electromagnetic interactions

Differential Form:	**Integral Form:**
$\nabla \cdot E = \frac{\rho}{\varepsilon_0}$	$\oiint_{\partial V} E \cdot dA = \frac{Q(V)}{\varepsilon_0}$
$\nabla \cdot B = 0$	$\oiint_{\partial V} B \cdot dA = 0$
$\nabla \times E = \frac{\partial B}{\partial t}$	$\oint_{\partial S} E \cdot dl = -\frac{\partial \Phi_{B,S}}{\partial t}$
$\nabla \times B = \mu_0 J + \mu_0 \varepsilon_0 \frac{\partial E}{\partial t}$	$\oint_{\partial S} B \cdot dl = \mu_0 I_S + \mu_0 \varepsilon_0 \frac{\partial \Phi_{E,S}}{\partial t}$

The upside-down triangle represents a three-dimensional derivative operator (rate of change). The backward 6 is also a particular kind of multidimensional derivative operator. The dot and the x represent vector multiplication: the dot is scalar multiplication of the vectors (just a single number); the x is vector multiplication that gives a vector result. The circles on the integral signs mean that the integral is done over a closed circle or surface.

Probability Distribution

This is our last term definition. It is also the most important (or maybe energy is; it's hard to be sure). Probability distributions are crucially important in modern physics because the results of quantum mechanics calculations are always probability distributions: quantum mechanics does not make any definite predictions of behavior.

Physical systems in quantum mechanics can be represented by a thing called (in English) a probability amplitude, or $\Psi(x, y, z, t)$. The trident symbol is the Greek capital letter psi. $\Psi(x, y, z, t)$ means that the probability amplitude is a function dependent on the values of the three coordinates of spatial position and time. It is a kind of complex (meaning $x + yi$, not meaning complicated) square root of a probability distribution. The French term for $\Psi(x, y, z, t)$ translates as "probability essence," which, I think, offers an interesting perspective on the whole concept.

The purpose of this book is to propose a worldview derived from modern physics that is compatible with the Bible. One of the key parts of that worldview (Feynman-Stueckelberg) will be based on a restriction of the values that $\Psi(x, y, z, t)$ can have because it is related to a probability distribution.

In physics, probability distributions are used to describe the results of events that can have many different outcomes. The chance that any particular result may occur is the probability for that outcome. The list of all possible outcomes, with their associated chances (probabilities), is a probability distribution. If the outcomes can be assigned a number, then the probability distribution can be represented by a function and be displayed in the Cartesian coordinate system (what a surprise).

To understand probability distributions, let's start out with something familiar: the rolling of two six-sided dice and adding up the sum. We'll then see how the same concepts are used in physical analysis. In quantum mechanics, probability distributions will predict the chances that a particle will be here or there, will have one or another value of momentum (= mv), will have more or less energy, or will arrive at a later or sooner time. In particle physics, probability distributions will describe how particles are changed or deflected when they interact with other particles.

						6, 1	6, 2	6, 3	6, 4	6, 5	6, 6	Total
					5, 1	5, 2	5, 3	5, 4	5, 5	5, 6		
				4, 1	4, 2	4, 3	4, 4	4, 5	4, 6			
			3, 1	3, 1	3, 3	3, 4	3, 5	3, 6				
		2, 1	2, 2	2, 3	2, 4	2, 5	2, 6					
	1, 1	1, 2	1, 3	1, 4	1, 5	1, 6						
Sum of Dice Rolls	2	3	4	5	6	7	8	9	10	11	12	
Number of Combinations	1	2	3	4	5	6	5	4	3	2	1	36
Fractional Probability	1/36	2/36	3/36	4/36	5/36	6/36	5/36	4/36	3/36	2/36	1/36	36/36
Decimal Probability	0.0278	0.0556	0.0833	0.1111	0.1389	0.1667	0.1389	0.1111	0.0833	0.0556	0.0278	1.0000

Fig. 9. Probability Distribution of Sums for two Six-Sided Dice

Figure 9 is a table of all of the possible results of rolling two six-sided dice and adding the two top sides together. There are 36 (= 6 × 6) possible results for the dice roll event. The sum can have any integer value between 2 and 12. The chance, or probability, for each sum is the number of ways that the same value can occur divided by the total number of possible rolls. The table shows both fractional and decimal values for the probability; they are the same values. The total of the probabilities for a probability distribution will always be equal to 1. Since a probability distribution will always list all of the possible results of an event, it is guaranteed (probability = 1) that something on the list will happen.

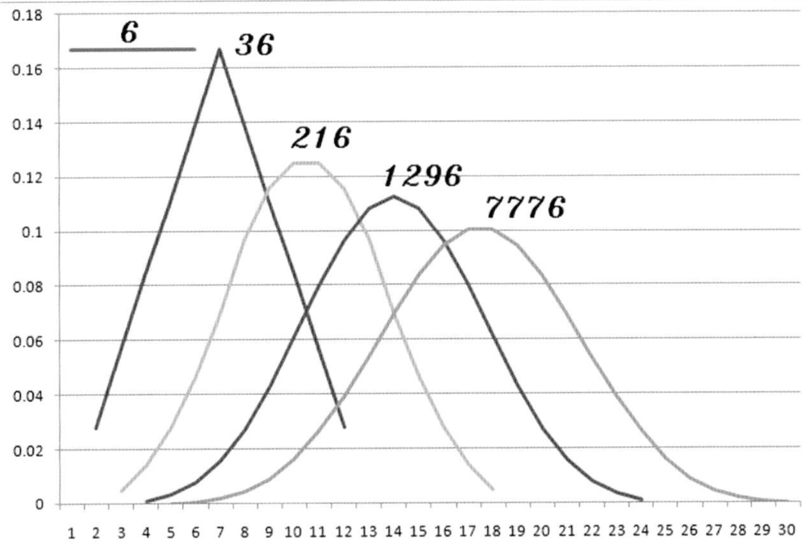

Fig. 10. Probability Distributions for Sums of 1, 2, 3, 4, & 5 Six-Sided Dice

Figure 10 (previous page) shows the probability distributions for the sums of different numbers of the six-sided dice (1D6 through 5D6). The numbers at the tops of the curves are the total number of possible results for the dice rolling events ($6 \times 6 \times 6 \times 6 \times 6 = 7{,}776$). They all share the basic requirements for a probability distribution: all probability values in the distribution have to be less than or equal to 1, and the sum of all the probabilities for all of the possible outcomes must be equal to 1.

Like the limit concept we used for the derivative and integration operators, the curve for a probability distribution gets smoother and smoother as the number of possible outcomes increases toward infinity.

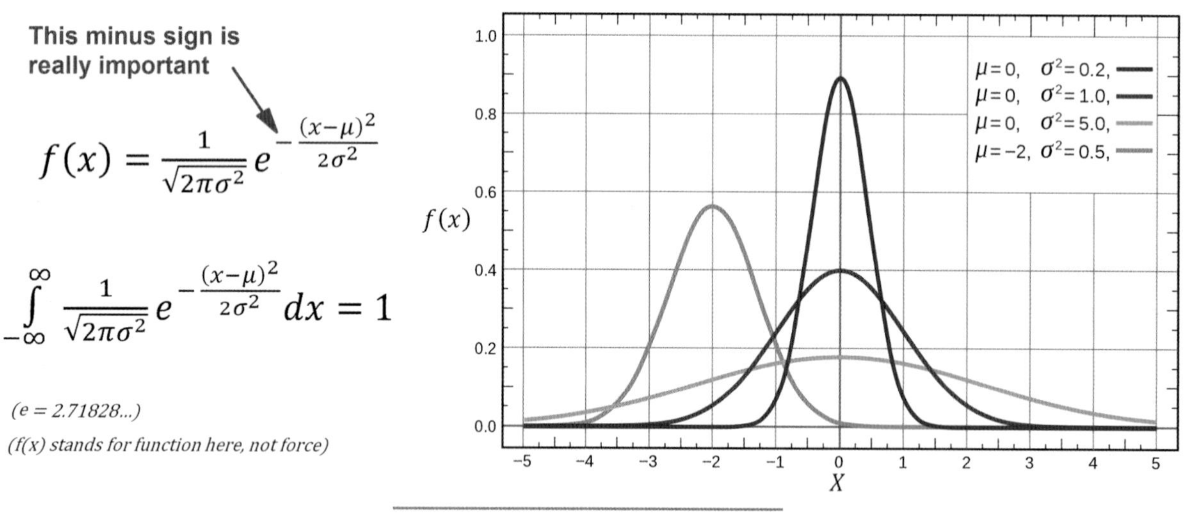

Fig. 11. Normal Distribution

Figure 11 shows equations and a Cartesian representation for a probability distribution called a normal distribution. While there are many probability distributions in mathematics with different "shapes" in Cartesian coordinates, the normal distribution is common. The normal distribution is frequently used in statistical analysis as an approximation for situations that may involve the sums of large numbers of variables (like the sum of a million six-sided dice); these actually crop up surprisingly often in physics. The Greek letter mu (μ) represents the average value of the distribution; the Greek letter sigma (σ) represents a measure of the shape of the curve called the standard deviation.

We won't be using the normal distribution at all in this book's ideas, but the form of it is very similar to a probability amplitude (Ψ), which will be important. Both formulas use a factor times e raised to an exponent with the function variable in the exponent (x, in this case). e is an important number for the derivative and integration operators and shows up frequently in solutions for calculations that use them (like Maxwell's equations in the Coulomb force section).

The important thing here is that e is greater than 1. That means that the exponent for e must be negative ($e^{-x} = 1/e^{x}$) in order for the values of the function to all be less than 1. All values for a probability distribution or a probability amplitude must be less than or equal to 1. The sum of all the probabilities for all the possible results must be equal to 1. Because the normal distribution is continuously changing, we use the integration operator to calculate values for the normal distribution. The integration is done from minus infinity to plus infinity because the normal distribution function is theoretically infinite.

The World According to Newton

"There is nothing new to be discovered in physics now. All that remains is more and more precise measurement."—Lord Kelvin, 1894

"Physics is essentially complete. There are just two dark clouds on the horizon."—Lord Kelvin, 1900

In 1687, Isaac Newton published *Mathematical Principles of Natural Philosophy* (in Latin, the *Philosophiae Naturalis Principia Mathematica*; in physics jargon generally, the *Principia*) in 1687. In the book, he described the development of calculus, including the derivative and integration operators mentioned earlier, the analysis of the motions of bodies in response to forces using calculus, and the law of universal gravitation.

To capture the mood of this momentous publication, we should probably loose a fanfare of trumpets and a roll of drums, but those are really hard to do in print. At the time, Newton's achievement opened the doors to the secrets of the natural world. Natural phenomena that had been a mystery, like the movements of the planets and moons and the ocean tides, could now be analyzed and calculated with precision. The application of the derivative and integration operators and Newton's three laws of motion (shown next page) to the behavior of objects provided the intellectual foundation for the industrial revolution that followed soon after.

For the next two hundred years, physicists expanded and improved on Newton's analytical techniques, developing what is now called classical physics with such an

An object in motion will tend to remain in motion; an object at rest will tend to remain at rest.

$$F = 0 \Rightarrow \frac{dp}{dt} = 0$$

A force applied to an object will cause it to accelerate at a rate inversely proportional to its mass.

$$F = \frac{dp}{dt} = \frac{d(mv)}{dt} = m\frac{dv}{dt} = ma$$

For every action, there is an equal and opposite reaction.

$$F_{12} = F_{21}$$

$F = Force$
$p = momentum\ (= mv)$
$m = mass$
$v = velocity\left(\frac{\Delta position}{\Delta time}\right)$
$t = time$
$a = acceleration\left(\frac{\Delta velocity}{\Delta time}\right)$

Fig. 12. Newton Laws of Motion

unfailing success that Lord Kelvin could express with conviction the idea contained in the quotations above: physicists understood it all, and there were no mysteries left.

This book is about worldviews; that is, about ideas of how the world works. While the details of classical physics will not be much discussed, we will take a look at the assumptions and attitudes regarding the operation of our existence that were the basis for classical physics and that still hold sway among many people today. As you might expect from the discussion so far, the basic assumptions of classical physics will mostly serve as examples of assumptions that turned out to be wrong.

Along with Newton's laws and calculus, classical physics was based on some very common-sense interpretations of how our existence works. Among these are some perspectives that are worth discussing here:

The world is deterministic: All of the objects that make up our existence, from planets to particles, have repeatable, predictable behavior. They all move in response to forces—and *only* in response to forces. Once forces and initial movements are known, all future motions can be calculated and predicted with accurate certainty.

The world is real: Objects have their own existence. They have their own properties: shape, size, and, if they are particles, charges—like electric charges—for each of the four forces. All objects have attributes like position, momentum, and energy, which can change over time. Most importantly, objects have properties and attributes that always exist, that are completely unaffected by what we might think of them or whether we are paying any attention to them.

The world is material: Objects are made of stuff. The official term for "stuff" in classical physics was *matter*, and matter was defined as having mass and taking up space. As we will see, the concept of stuff in modern physics is a little more nuanced.

In classical physics, everything is made of stuff; stuff and forces are all that is.

The world is separable: Objects interact with the rest of the world only through the physically real forces that act on them. Excepting forces, objects can be accurately considered as separated from the rest of the universe. This sounds like one of those deep philosophical questions where the only real question is whether it has any relevance to anybody or anything. But separability is a really big deal in physics because a lot of the derivations for the mathematical models that make up the body of classical physics depend on it.

The world is reducible: The behavior of any complex system can be accurately explained by reducing it to simpler component objects and their interactions. The whole is always the sum of the parts and nothing but the sum of the parts.

Finally, in classical physics, time is absolute. Time progresses at the same rate and the same direction for all objects everywhere.

Down the Rabbit Hole

"[T]he 'paradox' is only a conflict between reality and your feeling of what reality ought to be."
—Richard Feynman, The Feynman Lectures on Physics, vol. III

In modern physics, the world is a different sort of place. The observable differences from the world of classical physics are subtle; they only

Fig. 13. Four Forms of Matter: Solid, Liquid, Gas, Plasma.
Quartz © 2014 by Didier Descouens; Drop Closeup © 2009 by Jos Van Zetten; Purple Smoke by Wikipedia Commons user Macluskie; Plasma Lamp © 2004 Luc Viatour/https://Lucnix.be.

show up when we peek into dark corners and look behind curtains, but they are there. Even in "doing physics" they can often be ignored, as they were in classical physics, and most calculations will still produce results that are close enough for all practical purposes (FAPP).

But our quest here is not for the answer to a homework problem; our quest is for the truth. The worldview we are trying to develop here is one of understanding how God sees this existence. What we are trying to understand (as much as anyone can) is God's perception of this world, so that we can come closer to understanding what he is saying when he talks about it in his Scripture.

Modern physics shows us a reality that is very different from the sensible world of classical physics:

In truth, the world is not deterministic; it is fundamentally uncertain. The detailed behavior of particles can only be predicted with probability distributions—with possibilities of what they might do—not because the specific details are unknown or can't be measured, but because they literally do not exist.

In truth, the world is probably not real. The implication of the science is that objects do not have definite values for their properties and that the behavior of objects depends on our participation: on our perceptions and our choices.

In truth, the world is not material. It is not made of stuff; it is completely insubstantial, made only of light and shadow. The only reason it seems solid to us is that we are in it.

In truth, the objects and behaviors of this world are not separable. They must always be analyzed as linked systems, where both beginning and end are inextricably bound together to form a behavior.

In truth, the world is not reducible, just as it is not separable.

In truth, time is not absolute. Time certainly progresses at different rates for different objects, and it arguably progresses in different directions.

In our search for a divine worldview, we are going to be looking at particles because everything in this creation is made of particles. We are going to be using physics because, so far, physicists are the only ones who have brought candles to illuminate corners and peek behind curtains. In the rest of this chapter, we are going to look at what modern physics has to say about this world that is different from the account given by classical physics. (Hint: it's all different.)

So first, here is a brief description of our true existence, courtesy of relativity, quantum mechanics, and particle physics.

Special Relativity

Special relativity, the simplified version of relativity that applies only to the special case of objects moving at constant speed with no forces on them, is obsessed with light. Classical physics assumed that light traveled at a constant speed in some stationary, universal Cartesian coordinate system called the luminiferous aether. Measurement of the speed of light should, it was thought, produce different results depending on how fast and in what direction the measuring apparatus was moving. Careful measurement by Michelson and Morley in 1887 revealed, however, that light always travels at the same speed (called "c") regardless of the movement of the observer.

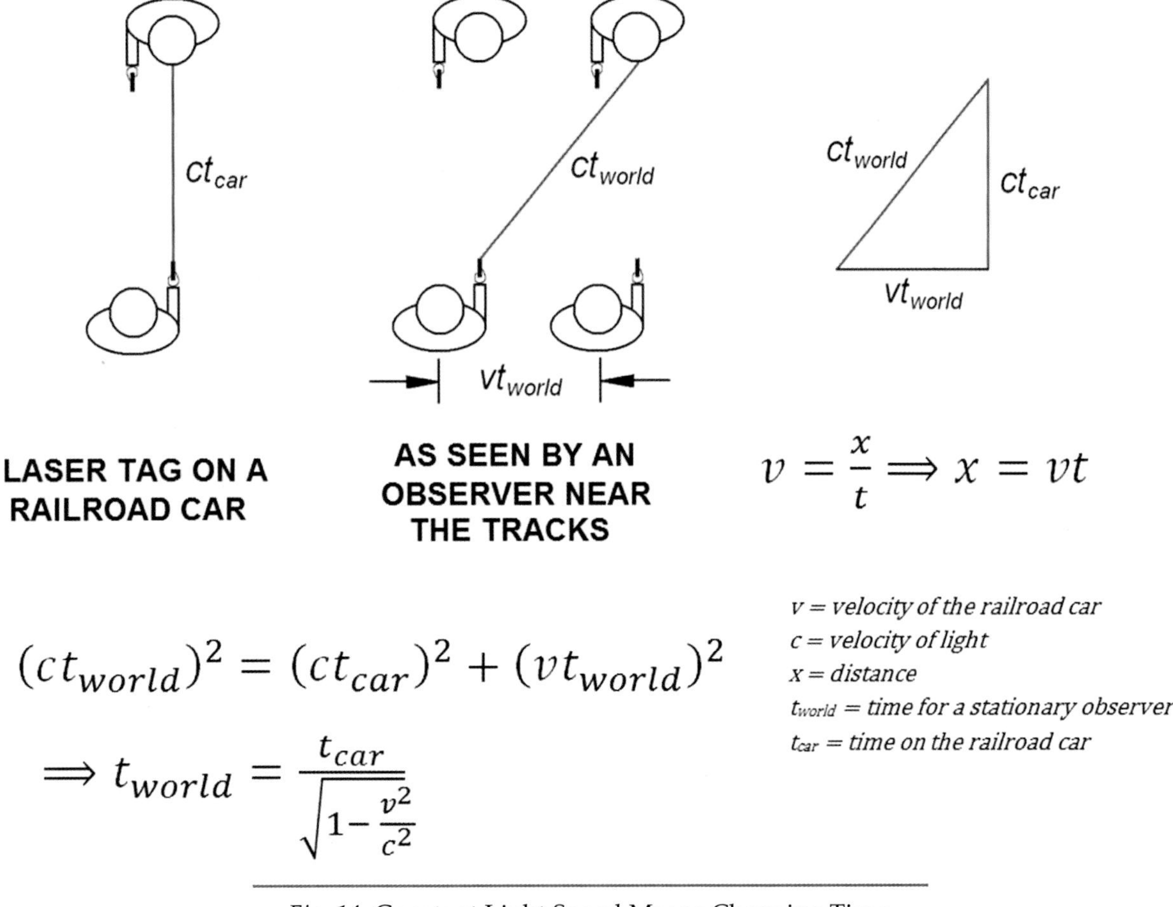

Fig. 14. Constant Light Speed Means Changing Time.

In 1905, Albert Einstein proposed the simple analysis shown in Figure 14. Two guys on a railroad car perpendicular to the direction of travel see light pass straight between them at speed c. Someone standing beside the tracks sees the light traveling a longer distance because the car travels some distance (x = vt) while the light travels across the car. But to the observer beside the tracks, the light travels at the same speed (c). The light as seen from the ground travels a longer distance than the light as seen on the car, but they both travel at the same speed (c). Because the light moves at the same speed (c) for both observers but travels different distances, it must be that the time it takes for the light to travel from one guy on the train to the other guy on the train is different for the guys on the train than it is for the observer standing beside the tracks. Time on the car must be slower than time on the ground (t_{car} is less because the light goes a shorter distance). As it turns out, the guys on the train will also see the observer on the ground as advancing more slowly in time.

Nothing material, no particle, can move faster than c, the speed of light. From the equation for the relative "speed" of time (called a Lorentz contraction):

$$\Rightarrow t_{World} = \frac{t_{Car}}{\sqrt{1 - \frac{v^2}{c^2}}}$$

As v increases, time measured in the world will be more than time measured on the car; time passes more slowly on the car. If v = c, then the square root in the denominator is 0, and t_{World} is infinitely more than t_{car}; time stops for an object traveling at the speed of light.

Photons, the particles that we think of as light, have no rest energy (mass) and always travel (to us) at the speed of light. They do not experience time. For them, emission and absorption, birth, and death happen in the same instant, no matter how far apart (to us) those events occur.

To calculate time difference, the light beam is seen as moving perpendicular to the direction of travel. The same kind of analysis can be applied to light beams in the same direction as the relative motion to derive the results shown in figure 15 (next page).

Guys on the car see the light travel from A1 to A2 and back to A1 at speed c. Once again, because the car moves while the light travels, the distance is not the same for an observer on the ground. This time, the result is that an observer on the ground sees the distance along the line of motion shrink; a moving railroad car (or anything else) literally gets shorter while it is moving. (Its width, on the other hand, does not change.)

Again, when two objects pass each other, each will see the other as shorter (figure 16).

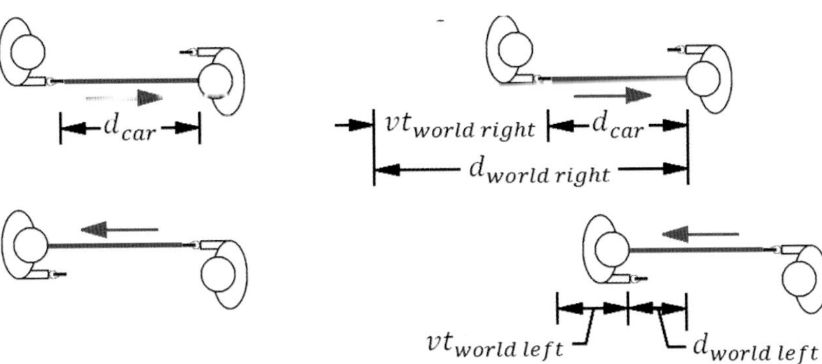

Laser Tag on a railroad car

As seen by an observer near the tracks

Distance is less on the car

$$d_{world} = \frac{d_{car}}{\sqrt{1 - \frac{v^2}{c^2}}}$$

Simultaneous events on the car happen at different times for a stationary observer

$$\Delta t_{world} = \frac{d_{car} v}{c^2}$$

t_{car} = time on the railroad car
t_{world} = time for a stationary observer
v = velocity of the railroad car
c = velocity of light
d_{car} = distance between laser tag players on the railroad car
d_{world} = distance between laser tag players for a stationary observer

Fig. 15. Distance Contraction and Simultaneity

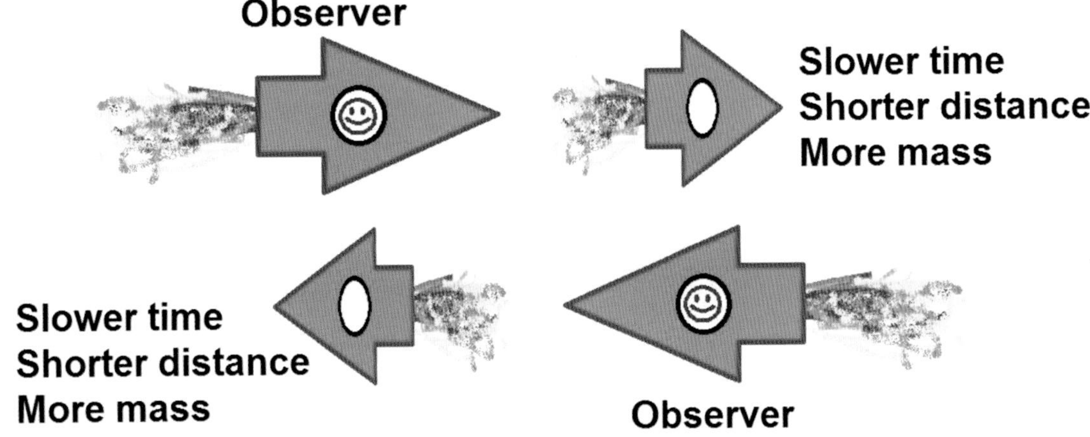

Fig. 16. Observations From Moving Objects

The same kind of calculation can be done to show that events separated along the direction of travel that happen simultaneously for an observer traveling at one speed happen at different times for another observer moving at a different speed.

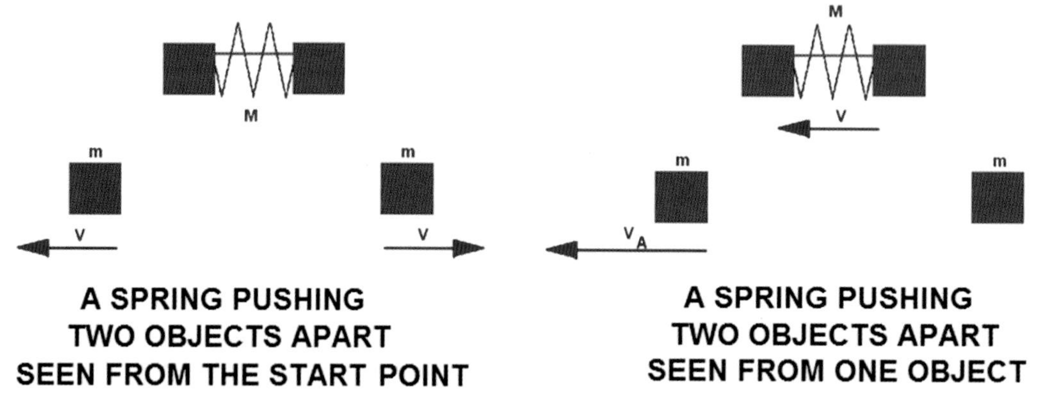

Fig. 17. Momentum and Kinetic Energy in Special Relativity

Also in 1905, Albert Einstein published another calculation for the situation shown in Figure 17 using the results of his light calculations above to show what happens to momentum and kinetic energy. The result (Helliwell, *Introduction to Special Relativity*, 1972) was surprising at the time:

$$M = \frac{2m}{\sqrt{1-\frac{v^2}{c^2}}} \qquad E = E_K + E_M = \frac{mc^2}{\sqrt{1-\frac{v^2}{c^2}}}$$

$$E_K = mc^2\left(\frac{1}{\sqrt{1-\frac{v^2}{c^2}}} - 1\right) \Rightarrow E_M = mc^2$$

M = total mass (m + m)
m = mass of one object
v = velocity
c = velocity of light
E = total energy
E_K = kinetic energy
E_M = rest energy (minimum energy of mass)

Maybe it is still surprising.

Mass changes along with distance and time as velocity increases. As was mentioned earlier, mass is energy: rest energy plus kinetic energy plus potential energy. Rest energy is the minimum mass of an object, the mass when it has no kinetic or potential energy. As an object acquires potential energy or kinetic energy, its mass will change as energy increases.

Remembering the definition of energy, what energy truly is, this means that all objects, from particles to planets, are composed of "something" that we describe as the numerical capacity to apply force to other objects—and nothing else.

All of the predictions that special relativity makes about the behavior of the physical world have been proven by experiment. The change in the flow of time has been measured. The compression of distance has been measured. Change in mass has been measured. Real particles with real mass have been observed to change into energy; energy has been seen to change into real particles.

In spite of the way that everything changes between two objects (A and B) moving at different speeds, physicists have managed to find calculated quantities that do not change. One of these deals with space and time and is called the space-time interval:

$$x_B{}^2 + y_B{}^2 + z_B{}^2 - c^2 t_B{}^2 = x_A{}^2 + y_A{}^2 + z_A{}^2 - c^2 t_A{}^2$$

Another similar calculation deals with momentum and energy:

$$p_{xB}{}^2 + p_{yB}{}^2 + p_{zB}{}^2 - \frac{E_B{}^2}{c^2} = p_{xA}{}^2 + p_{yA}{}^2 + p_{zA}{}^2 - \frac{E_A{}^2}{c^2}$$

The space-time interval mathematically unifies space and time. The mathematics for calculating changes in the values of physical quantities between frames of reference traveling at different, constant speeds (called inertial frames) is also much easier using something called a four-vector (x, y, z, ict) instead of trying to keep space (x, y, z) and time (t) separate. i is the square root of −1 and is often used in the four-vector because of the time sign in the space-time interval. c is, as always, the speed of light. The equivalent quantity for momentum and energy is called the four momentum (p_x, p_y, p_z, iE/c).

Because of calculations in special relativity, physicists (and philosophers) have started to think of our reality as being four dimensional instead of three dimensional, an idea they call spacetime, where time is another coordinate just like the x, y, and z of the Cartesian coordinate system. More about that later.

General Relativity

"General relativity fulfills Einstein's conviction that 'space is not a thing': the ever changing relation of matter and energy is reflected by an ever changing geometry. Spacetime does not have an independent existence; it is nothing but an expression of the rela-

tions among physical processes in the world." —Ta-Pei Cheng, *Relativity, Gravitation, and Cosmology: A Basic Introduction*

General relativity is the version of relativity that applies to the general case of objects that spin and accelerate in response to forces. General relativity derives not from the motion of light, but from the motion of objects in gravitational fields. The strange thing about the effect of gravity on movement is that it does not depend on the mass of the object; all objects move the same regardless of their size or weight. In the equations for gravitational force and Newton's second law of motion, the mass cancels out.

$$F_G = \frac{GMm}{r^2} = m\left(\frac{GM}{r^2}\right)$$

$$F = \frac{dp}{dt} = \frac{d(mv)}{dt} = m\frac{dv}{dt} = ma$$

$$\Rightarrow ma = m\left(\frac{GM}{r^2}\right)$$

$$\Rightarrow a = \frac{GM}{r^2}$$

F_G = gravitational force
G = Newton's gravitational constant
M = mass of stationary object
m = mass of moving object
r = distance between objects
p = momentum (= $m \times v$)
v = velocity
a = acceleration (= $\frac{\Delta velocity}{\Delta time}$)

Albert Einstein (again, this time in 1915) deduced that the reason objects move in curved paths in gravitational fields is not that there is a force acting on them; rather, objects travel in curved paths in gravitational fields because space and time are curved there. He derived a field equation describing the curvature:

$$R_{\mu\nu} - \frac{1}{2}Rg_{\mu\nu} + \Lambda g_{\mu\nu} = \frac{8\pi G}{c^4}T_{\mu\nu}$$

$R_{\mu\nu}$ = Ricci tenser, a 4 × 4 matrix that describes the volumetric deviation of a curved spacetime from that of a straight Cartesian spacetime
R = Ricci scalar, a constant that describes the average curvature of spacetime
$g_{\mu\nu}$ = metric tenser, a 4 × 4 matrix that describes the angular deviation of a curved spacetime from a straight Cartesian spacetime
Λ = cosmological constant that represents the energy density of vacuum
G = Newton's gravitational constant
c = velocity of light
$T_{\mu\nu}$ = stress tenser, a 4 × 4 matrix that describes the local changes in momentum and energy density

General relativity holds that the fabric of space and time can bend and stretch—that distances, directions, and the flow of time all warp and twist in the presence of mass (which is really energy, which is a sort of stored force). Time slows as any object is accelerated to higher speeds. Time passes faster closer to a massive (energetic, forceful) object and slows further away from such an object. In the presence of enough mass, space and time kink into knots called black holes; astronomers find them now and then.

Special and general relativity are accepted, settled physics. Everything mentioned above has been verified by experiments many, many times. The implications for physical reality are widely accepted. With FAPP (For All Practical Purposes) calculations, the distortions in time and space can mostly be ignored, because in relation to the objects we experience in our daily existence, they are really tiny. But if we are searching for truth and not just for practical application, we need to realize that because all particles are in constant motion, all objects (composed of particles) pass through time at their own, different rates.

Incidentally, we can occasionally apply special and general relativity in everyday life. Figure 18 shows the change in the rate of time for satellites orbiting the earth. Things done with and by satellite often have to use relativity calculations in order to get accurate results. GPS locations, for example, have to be corrected for the different rates of time passage and for the curvature of space between the satellite and the receiver. Without corrections for special and general relativity, GPS locations would be accurate to only about six miles.

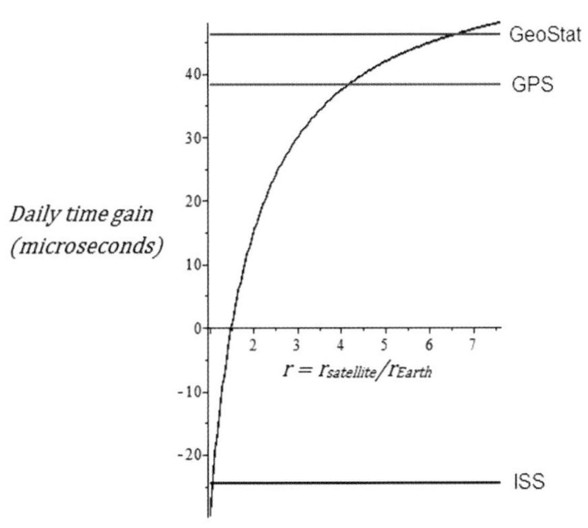

Fig. 18. Daily Time Gain for Satellites in Orbit

In special relativity, it is convenient to include time in the spacetime four-vector (x, y, z, ict) for calculations that deal with the transformations of coordinates between objects moving at different speeds—the math is easier if you do.

Calculations in general relativity must use the space-time four-vector or the results do not match our measurements of the world. Time and space bend together in the presence of mass. As we will see again in quantum mechanics, physics tells us that we live in a spacetime, not a space with time.

Quantum Mechanics

"By nature I am peacefully inclined and reject all doubtful adventures. But a theoretical interpretation had to be found at all costs, no matter how high . . . I was ready to sacrifice every one of my previous convictions about natural laws."—Max Planck, who made the breakthrough discovery that led to quantum theory

"The world is not what it seems. Behind the apparent solidity of everyday objects lies a seething shadow world of potentiality. This world defies easy description, as its form is so different from our everyday experience. Yet our common or garden world of solid tables, cricket balls, stars, and galaxies somehow arises from what transpires underneath. We do not know how this comes about.

"There is a theory of how the underlying world works: quantum theory. It is probably the most successful scientific theory that has yet been created, and it has profoundly changed our view of the world. Yet for all its success, quantum theory remains utterly baffling."—Jonathan Allday, *Quantum Reality, Theory and Philosophy*

Quantum mechanics, up next on our tour, has an unusual relationship to physical truth. Quantum theory, the mathematical models used to predict the behavior of particles, is the most completely verified theory in physics. Calculations using these models produce predictions that are accurate to the limits of our ability to check them, and they have done so without error for thousands of experiments. But the mathematical models of quantum theory were derived to match experimental data. The relationship between these mathematics and whatever deep-down events actually occur in our existence is unknown.

Physicists have proposed lots of guesses—these are called "interpretations" of quantum mechanics—but none have yet been verified by experiments with enough assurance to be considered conclusive. The guess that is nominally considered the most likely version is called the Copenhagen interpretation. Copenhagen is philosophically simple: it holds that what the mathematics says is happening is what is actually happening. In that sense, a description of the Copenhagen interpretation is also a description of the mathematics.

We will begin the discussion of quantum mechanics with a discussion of particles. Physically and mathematically, particles are described by a combination of properties and attributes. Properties are characteristics that make a particle a particular kind of particle. In the standard model of particle physics, *properties* are a particle's charges, which determine, among other things, how it will respond to the four known forces: the strong nuclear force, the weak nuclear force, electromagnetic forces, and gravity. *Attributes* are characteristics of a particle that describe where it is and what it is doing, like position, momentum, energy, and time.

Particles can exist in one of two states: a classical state, where they properly behave like particles; or a quantum state, where their behavior is more like that of waves (often called *quantum objects* because, in quantum state, particles are not really particles). The physical term for this one-state-or-the-other existence is wave-particle duality. Particles in the classical state have definite values for both properties and attributes; their behavior can be accurately described using classical physics. In the quantum state, however, even properties constantly shift. Quarks morph into electrons, which dissolve into energy as objects flicker in and out of existence. Quantum state particles don't have specific attributes at all; position, momentum, energy, and time share a blended, complex ($x + yi$) kind of probability distribution called a probability amplitude (the Ψ function mentioned earlier). Only the mathematical models (theories) called quantum mechanics can accurately describe the behavior of particles in the quantum state; classical theories are useless.

It might be reassuring if it were true that particles, and the objects of our experience that particles compose, existed mostly in the classical state—if quantum state particles were rare, shy creatures, difficult to find and challenging to capture. But, dear readers, the opposite is true.

Everything that can be touched, heard, smelled, or tasted is and must be in the quantum state. Solids exclude solids to give us the sensation of touch. Gases push on gases to transmit the sounds we hear. Chemicals react to stimulate taste and smell. All of these are the interactions of the probability amplitudes of quantum state particles. Particles in the classical state don't do those things.

Everything we touch, hear, smell, and taste is in the quantum state. Only what we see involves classical particles. Every beam of light that strikes our eyes originates in the interactions of quantum state particles, causing changes in the shape and size of probability amplitudes. But for our perception of light, where one or a few photons trigger single light receptor cells in our eyes, the photons must be in classical state in order to produce sharp, clear images.

Quantum state particles are everywhere—and they are nowhere. No physicist has ever measured, photographed, or detected a particle in the quantum state. The particles that we see are always, always, always classical, but *where* they show up can only be explained by quantum state behavior.

An aside about terminology: because the probability amplitude for attributes resolves into specific values when particles make the transition from quantum state to classical state, particles in the classical state are most often referred to as being localized. The transition from quantum state to classical state is most often called localization.

Another aside for accuracy: the descriptions of quantum mechanics and particle physics presented here are based on "classical" quantum mechanics. Like classical physics, classical quantum mechanics is no longer regarded as an accurate model of physical behavior. The much more accurate models of quantum field theory provide most of the proofs for quantum theory. However, classical quantum mechanics is still a useful framework and is much easier to understand, hence its usage here. In my opinion, the implications for theology evident in classical quantum mechanics are the same in quantum field theory—the same but stronger.

Probability Amplitudes

> *"Erwin with his psi can do*
> *Calculations quite a few.*
> *But one thing has not been seen:*
> *Just what does psi really mean?"*
> —Erich Hückel, translated by Felix Bloch (referring to Erwin Schrodinger)

To make predictions, quantum mechanics always uses probability distributions derived from Ψ, the probability amplitude (sometimes called a possibility wave). In quantum theory, no particle ever has localized attributes; particles exist only as patterns of possibility waves that spread out from their points of origination to reflect and combine like ripples in a puddle of

Fig. 19. Wave Interference.
Photograph by Oliver Walker. Used with permission.

water. Like waves in water, crests of probability amplitude meet other crests and build to produce higher crests. Troughs combine with troughs to produce deeper troughs. Crests and troughs cancel each other to produce regions of zero probability. The addition of probability amplitudes is called superposition (the same term used for other types of waves). The patterns of probability that result from the superposition of probability amplitudes are called interference (the term used for for water or light waves).

Observer Dependence

Exactly when, where, and how particles show up in experiments depends on how we look for them. If a physicist constructs an experiment to measure the positions of particles, they will show up as predicted by a position probability distribution that is derived from the probability amplitude (Ψ). If the experiment is set up to measure the momentum (speeds) of particles, then the results will have the distribution for momentum that is also derived from the probability amplitude (still the same Ψ).

The derivations of the position distribution and the momentum distribution are different. The shapes of the distributions and the ways the particles will show up are different. Remember that any particle that is measured in an experiment will always be in a localized, classical state, not a quantum state. This means that the particle will always be localized in the course of an experiment that measures anything about the particle. The results of the experiment, then—the when, where, and how that a particle is localized—will always depend on the relationship between the state of the particle (described by Ψ) and the particular kind of measurement that is made. Neither the resulting particle nor the kind of measurement can ever be independent of the other.

Heisenberg Uncertainty

> *"A highway patrol officer pulls over an electron. Walking up to the electron's window, the officer says, 'Sir, did you know that you were going 85 miles an hour?' The electron replies, 'Oh, great! Now I'm lost.'"*—Physics joke, original source unknown

Some attributes of particles break down into complementary pairs:

Position is complementary to linear momentum.
Orientation is complementary to angular momentum.
Time is complementary to energy.

(Angular momentum is similar to linear momentum (= mv) but is calculated for the rotation of an object rather than motion in a direction. The calculation is pretty involved, not nearly as simple as p = mv, and is not really relevant to the speculations of this book, so it will not be described here.)

When a momentum measurement of quantum state particles causes them to localize, they will each have definite values for all of their attributes. The distribution of all the attribute values for the group of particles will be as predicted using the probability amplitude Ψ. The shape of the position distribution, which is complementary to momentum, changes depending on how accurately the momentum measurement is made. The more accurate the momentum measurement is, the larger the area where localized particles will appear. A sloppy momentum measurement will produce localized particles with a smaller range of positions. Theoretically, if the momentum could be measured exactly (like our highway patrolman with his radar in the joke above), the localized particles would appear randomly throughout the entire universe.

The same thing happens with measurements of other complementary attributes: a more accurate measurement of time results in a broader range of particle energies; a more inaccurate measurement of energy produces a narrower range of times.

Werner Heisenberg derived mathematical expressions called "uncertainty relationships" to describe the behavior of complementary attributes. Here are the ones for position/momentum and energy/time:

$$\Delta x \Delta p \geq \frac{h}{4\pi}$$

$$\Delta E \Delta t \geq \frac{h}{4\pi}$$

x = position
p = momentum (= m × v)
h = Planck's constant
π = ratio of the circumference of a circle to its diameter
E = energy
t = time

The star relationship is that of position/momentum; it is most often used to illustrate Heisenberg uncertainty. However, we won't use it again as it doesn't have much relevance for our discussion in this book. The energy/time relation, on the other hand, has a huge impact in the most common narrative for particle physics; literally, our universe could not hang together without it. We will spend more time with this one.

Heisenberg uncertainty is often taught as a sort of consequence of the physical act of measurement: if a particle position is measured by bouncing a photon off it, the collision changes the momentum of the particle in unknowable ways. While that does occur, it is not what Heisenberg uncertainty is. Heisenberg uncertainty is an inherent characteristic of the probability amplitude Ψ. For quantum state particles, more definite values for attributes simply do not exist; uncertainty is a fundamental and necessary part of their being.

Trajectories

Classical state particles have trajectories: they move from here to there, occupying a contiguous chain of specific points in between at successive times. Quantum state particles don't do anything remotely like that. They do not have trajectories at all. Rather, quantum particles originate at some location. The probability amplitude for the particle ripples outward from the point of origination in all directions that are available to it, much like the small waves when a water puddle is disturbed. The ripples superpose and interfere to produce a probability distribution that depends on the physical environment, just like the pattern of waves in a puddle will depend on the shape and size of the puddle. Any measurement will see classical particles as its result, but the positions in which the classical particles appear will be in the pattern set by the superposition and interference of the probability amplitude.

For example: physicists use particle accelerators to break material apart so they can try to figure out how it was originally put together. Particle accelerators use detectors around the point of collision where particles strike a target. A particle detector measures the passage of particles produced by the collisions.

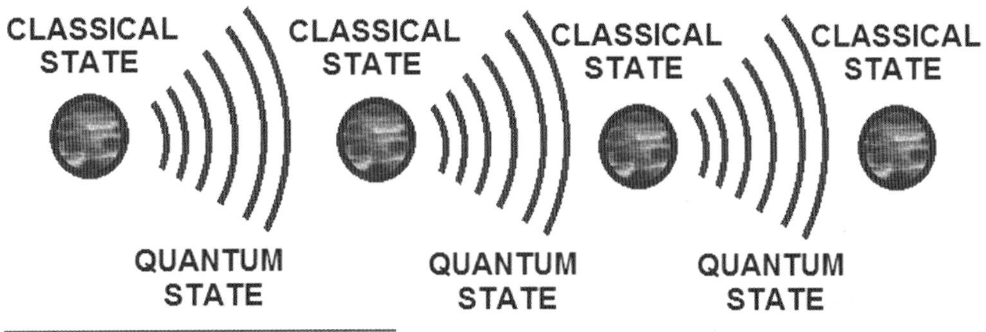

Fig. 20. Particle Track Detection

Particle detectors "see" particle tracks as strings of points—dotted lines—not as continuous lines. Even when detectors are sensitive enough that they should be able to see between the points, they still see separate points of detection. The reason fast-moving particles show up as strings of points instead of lines is because they are oscillating between quantum state (when we can't see them) and classical state (when we can). Each point of detection serves as an origin point for a new probability amplitude wave that spreads out to form the basis for a probability distribution of the next point of detection.

Understanding Quantum Mechanics

This could all be starting to sound a little weird, so I think it might be a good idea to take a short break here to provide a little reassurance (to wit: you are not wrong; it really is weird). I want to share some quotations from two physicists who played major parts in the development of quantum mechanics: Niels Bohr and Richard Feynman.

> *". . . for those who are not shocked when they first come across quantum theory cannot possibly have understood it."*—Niels Bohr

> *"I think I can safely say that nobody understands quantum mechanics."*—Richard Feynman, in *The Character of Physical Law*

Fig. 21. "Dr. Niels Bohr, 1885–1962," Wikipedia by AB Lagrelius & Westphal

Fig. 22. "Dr. Richard Feynman, 1918–1988," Wikipedia by the Nobel Foundation

As Dr. Feynman was fond of saying: if quantum mechanics seems really strange and impossible to understand, don't worry about it—that's a completely normal reaction. Nobody understands quantum mechanics.

So back we go to the rabbit hole. We've only just begun to fall; it goes much, much deeper.

Standing Waves = Quantization

Probability amplitude waves have some of the same characteristics as physical waves like sound waves or water waves: namely, they have wavelength and amplitude. The upside-down y in Figure 23 is the lowercase Greek letter lambda, which is the standard symbol in physics for wavelength.

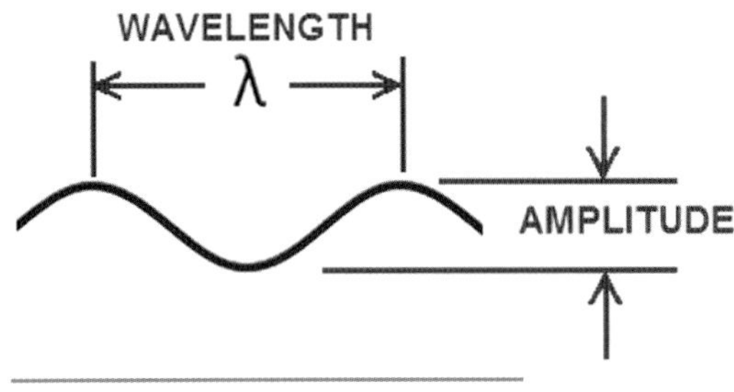

Fig. 23. Wave Measurements

Particle probability amplitudes have a wavelength that depends on the momentum of the particle. This was proposed by Prince Louis de Broglie, pronounced "de Broy," in 1924.

$$\lambda = \frac{h}{mv} = \frac{h}{p}$$

λ = wavelength
h = Planck's constant
m = mass
v = velocity
p = momentum $(= m \times v)$

Photons, the particles that we think of as light, have very little mass and therefore very little momentum. Consequently, their probability amplitudes have relatively large wavelengths. Up until the twentieth century, photons were the only particles with wavelengths big enough to cause anyone to notice their wave behavior.

The other particles that compose our existence, electrons and quarks and such, have much larger masses and momentums, so their wavelengths are really tiny. It takes very special equipment to see wavelengths for them. Currently, physicists *are* able to build equipment to see waves that small, and they have seen wave behavior (the same as light) for particles as large as C_{60} molecules (buckminsterfullerene, or bucky-balls to their friends).

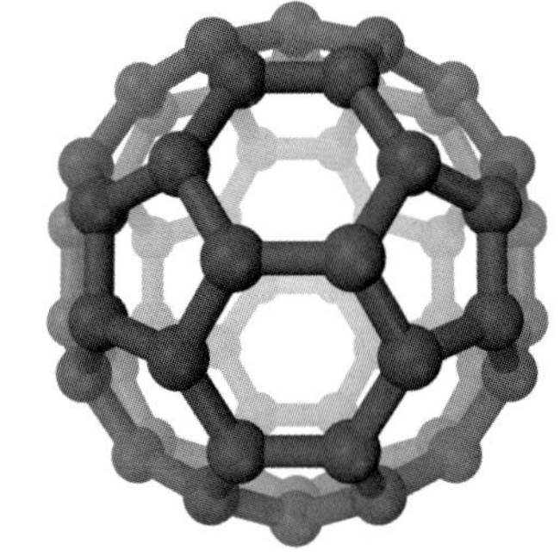
Fig. 24. Buckminsterfullerene.

One part of wave behavior that physical waves (like water waves) and probability amplitudes share is that of standing waves. Textbooks most often show standing waves in figures like the left part of Figure 25. The idea is that a wave trapped between two walls will bounce back and forth. If the distance between the walls is an exact number of half wavelengths, the wave oscillation will superpose to form a standing wave where the high points and zero points don't move. If you have ever been in a car with one window open and felt the air pulsing like a drum, that was a standing wave formed inside the car by the passing air.

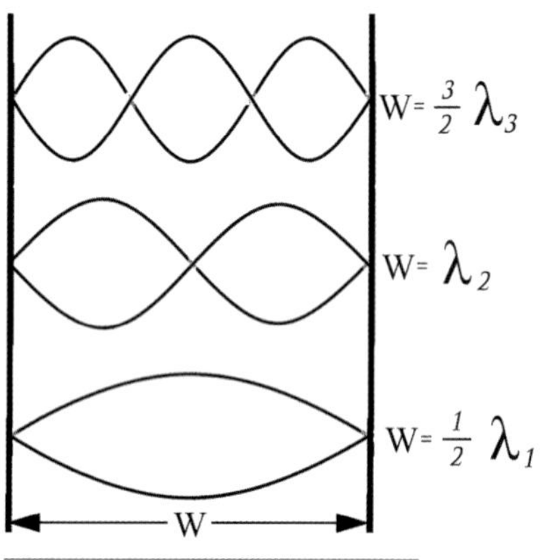

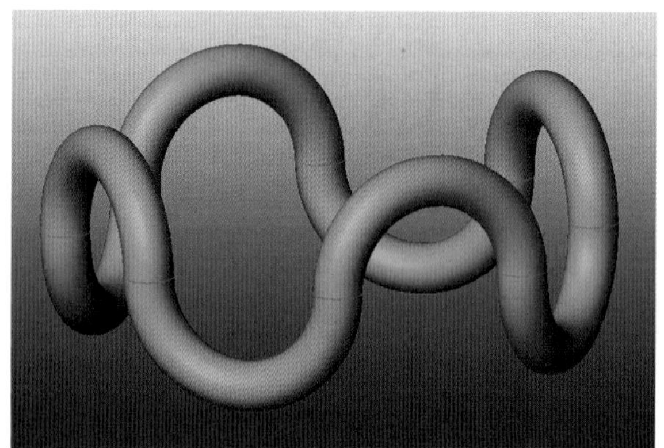

Fig. 25. Standing Waves

Probability amplitudes are not trapped inside cars or between walls, so it is useful to think of the standing waves they form as being more like the circular standing wave shown in the right side of Figure 25. Real standing waves for probability amplitudes are actually three-dimensional, so even the circular wave is a simplified picture of what they really do.

The shapes of the standing waves that probability amplitudes actually form depend on their local environment, in particular upon the arrangement of charges that affect potential energy. A relatively simple example is the probability amplitudes for the electron in a hydrogen atom. A hydrogen atom is one electron with one proton in the nucleus. For a single point charge like the proton, the electric field is spherical, just like the earth's gravitational field. The standing waves formed by the electron probability amplitude are mathematically based on the oscillations of the surface of a sphere; the technical term is spherical harmonics. (For further information, Wikipedia has a pretty nice article on spherical harmonics with graphics and videos that show the oscillations.)

The pictures of spherical harmonics should be familiar to present or former chemistry students. They are the shapes of electron orbitals for the hydrogen atom, the 1s, 2s, 2p, 3s, 3p, 3d, etc. Hydrogen electron orbitals are actually standing waves in the probability amplitude for an electron in the spherical electric field generated by the proton.

Fig. 26. Spherical Harmonics.

The essence of an electron in a hydrogen atom must always reside in one or another of the standing wave patterns. An electron bound in an atom cannot take any form that is not one of the standing waves. Interactions with the outside world (exchanges that increase or decrease the energy of the electron) can cause it to shift from one standing wave to another standing wave, but the energy has to be just right for it to do so. Any potential interaction with the wrong energy, where the electron would not end up in a standing wave, the electron will just ignore.

Because they only inhabit standing waves, electrons in atoms can only accept or emit energy (photons) in certain very exact amounts. In physics, an object that can only have certain exact values (and no other values) is described as being quantized. The various possible values are called quanta. A single one of these values is called a quantum. Quantum theory got its name because the pickiness of electrons when they emit or absorb photons is the first aspect of quantum behavior that physicists noticed.

Photons do not have mass (rest energy) but they do have energy. The wavelength of a photon (and hence the color of the light that we see when we perceive one) depends on the energy in a relation first proposed by Max Planck in 1900 (next page):

$$E = \frac{hc}{\lambda} = h\nu$$

E = energy
h = Planck's constant
c = velocity of light
λ = wavelength
ν = frequency

Because electrons in atoms can only make transitions between standing waves in probability amplitude, they can only interact with photons that have certain values of energy. What physicists originally saw was that electrons in atoms only emit or absorb certain colors of light (and not others). Every kind of atom has a different, distinctive pattern of light colors that it emits and absorbs, which is called a light spectrum.

There's just one more little step in our discussion of quantum standing waves. Electrons in atoms are not the only objects that inhabit standing waves in probability amplitudes. All of the objects that we experience and think of as matter, that is, all particles that are bound into the structures we think of as matter, are mathematically described as standing waves in probability amplitudes. In our Copenhagen interpretation (where things are what the math says they are), particles in matter actually are standing waves of possibility.

While they all form standing waves, the shapes of the waves for different particles are very different. Probability amplitude shapes are partly determined by potential energy, by the strength and direction of the forces that act on the particles. Charges and forces for different particles vary, so potential energy contributions also change. Quarks have color charge and respond to the nuclear strong force. Electrons have electric charge and mostly respond to electrostatic forces. The shapes, sizes, and behavior of the probability amplitude standing waves of an electron and a quark are not the same. But both particles form standing waves with quantized interactions in the structures of matter.

Earlier, I mentioned that particles in quantum state can and do shift from one type of particle to another. They do this constantly. For example: the protons and neutrons in atomic nuclei are made of smaller particles called quarks. Nominally, there are one up quark and two down quarks for a neutron and two up quarks and one down quark for a proton (*up* and *down* here don't refer to directions, they are just names; we will discuss this in more detail later, when we get to particles). From here, the variations are dizzying: The up quark particle spends part of its time as a charm quark or a top quark. The down quark spends part of its time as a strange quark or a bottom quark. The properties of the objects we perceive as neutrons or protons are actually time-based averages of the properties of all of those various quarks. The correct physics description for the averaging of properties is that quantum particles form *statistical ensembles*. The term for the constant shifting of particle types is *fluctuations*.

The variability of quantum state particles can be hard to accept if one thinks of them as being real, solid objects made of the kinds of material that we experience: steel or plastic or wood. But quantum state particles are not made of solid material; there (probably) isn't any solid material in them. Instead, they are standing waves of probability amplitude (whatever that is physically; nobody really knows). When they shift from one type of particle to another, all they are actually doing is shifting from vibrating one way to vibrating a different way.

Pauli Exclusion

Quantum state particles are not made of solid material, but they can be very territorial; they do not share attributes. They share properties, the characteristics (charges in this case) that distinguish different types of particles. But they do not share attributes—the characteristics like position and energy that specify where they are and what they are doing. Quantum state particles must be in different places doing different things. The separation of quantum state particles is called Pauli exclusion. Wolfgang Pauli developed the rule for quantum state particle exclusion in 1925:

No two identical fermions may occupy the same quantum state.

Fermions are a family of particle types; we will discuss them in much more detail in the description of particles coming up. They make up what we think of as matter. Electrons are fermions. The quarks that compose protons and neutrons are also fermions. "Quantum state" here basically means the particular values (for properties) and the probability amplitude (for attributes) that each individual particle has.

For example, a maximum of two electrons can occupy a spherical harmonic. The probability amplitude (Ψ) is a blend of distributions for the attributes of electrons: position, momentum, orientation, angular momentum, energy, and time. In order to form a valid spherical harmonic, several of the distributions that make up the probability amplitude have to form standing waves with an integer number of wavelengths.

Electron orbitals (spherical harmonics) in atoms are described by three numbers of wavelengths (called quantum numbers): n, l, and m. Quantum number n describes the number of energy wavelengths; l describes the number of angular momentum wavelengths; and m describes the number of orientation wavelengths.

Only two electrons at a time can have a particular set of quantum number values. Pairs of electrons are allowed in atomic orbitals because a fourth quantity for each orbital, called spin, is associated with the particle property. Spin can be in one of two states, called spin up and spin down. (Again, the *up* and *down* don't actually refer to specific directions; they are just names.) We'll look at spin in more detail later in the section on particles.

Pauli exclusion is what keeps atoms apart so that they form the solids, liquids, and gases we think of as matter. Electrons cluster around atomic nuclei, drawn by the electrostatic force attraction of protons. Electrons that arrive early occupy orbitals close to the nucleus; later electrons are forced into larger orbitals because the smaller ones are already occupied. Atoms are kept separated because the outer electrons can't share the same probability amplitude standing waves (also known as orbitals).

Physicists originally thought that atoms were kept apart by the electrostatic force of electrons repelling each other. In 1967, Dyson and Lenard showed by calculation that electrostatic repulsion is not strong enough to do this; without Pauli exclusion, matter would collapse into much smaller volumes than those we see.

Pauli exclusion is one example of a quantum exchange interaction. Quantum exchange interactions are behaviors that quantum state particles do because they are quantum state particles; classical state particles don't do them. Pauli exclusion, for example, only applies to quantum state particles; classical state particles don't exclude each other.

Therefore, in order for solids, liquids, and gases to form, the atoms involved must all be in quantum state. This means a very simple experiment can be done to see whether the particles of an everyday solid object are in quantum state or in classical state. Poke the object with a finger. If the finger is excluded—if it does not pass through the object—the object is in quantum state. If the finger sinks into the object (that might actually be painful, but it doesn't happen often), then it is in classical state. By the way, this also implies that the finger is in quantum state. (For *Ghostbusters* fans, Egon poked the hotel guest to make sure he was in quantum state.)

Entanglement

Quantum state particles also have a behavior that is called entanglement. Once two quantum particles have met, they may remember each other (it is almost impossible to avoid anthropomorphizing particles). A measurement (localization) of one particle will restrict the probability amplitude, and therefore the results of measurements, of the other particle.

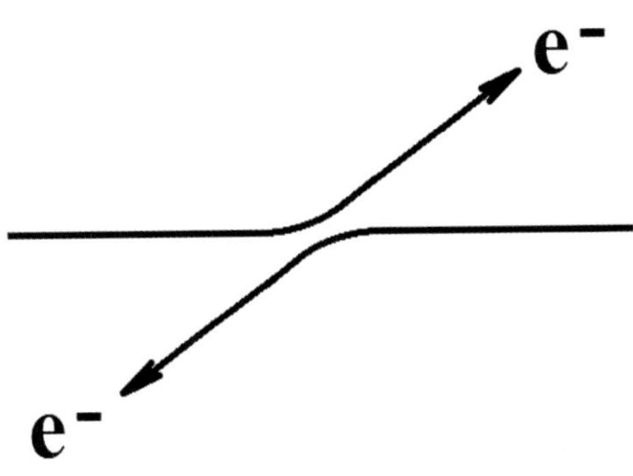

The figure to the right shows a pair of electrons that approach each other and are deflected by the electrostatic force (electric charges that are alike, negative and negative in this example, repel each other). Quantum mechanics tells us that both electrons actually exist as probability amplitudes (Ψ) with a distribution of positions and momentums (speeds and directions). The deflection angles will always depend on the momentums of the two electrons and how closely they approach each other, which means the deflection angles will also have distributions as the probability amplitudes (Ψ) change over time.

The relationship between the angles of the two electrons will always be bound by conservation laws; total momentum and energy will not change. Once the angle and speed of one electron is measured, the angle and speed of the other electron can be predicted with accuracy using classical (Newton's) laws of motion. The probability amplitudes (Ψ) for each electron partly depend on the other electron; the two electrons are entangled. Because they are entangled, the two electrons form a single quantum system: measurement of either of the two electrons will affect both of them.

The details of the physical activity that underlie quantum theory are unknown, but physicists have been able to use experiments with quantum entanglement to provide some clues. Two of the issues that are relevant to the underlying physics are called reality and locality. Reality has already been mentioned; it is the notion that objects have properties and attributes with specific values that do not depend on any observer. Locality comes from special relativity; it implies that the effects of any physical event can only travel from some original position to some other position at the speed of light.

In 1964, John Bell theoretically derived an experimental test to determine whether our world is real and local (both, and at the same time). John Clauser in 1972 and

Alain Aspect in 1982 performed these experiments and demonstrated that our world is not real and local at the same time; meaning that the world is either not real or not local, or neither local nor real. Henry Stapp derived the same theoretical prediction as Bell using only locality in 1985, meaning that the Clauser and Aspect experiments imply that our world is not local. Anthony Legget derived a similar experimental prediction in 2003 for certain kinds of reality. Grolblacher demonstrated experimentally in 2007 that our world is not real, at least for the kinds of reality in Legget's prediction (they relate to the physics of polarized photons but have broader implications).

These experiments all involved the measurement of the polarization of entangled photons. It is actually possible to tell by comparing results which of the two entangled particles was measured first and which second. By careful arrangement of an experiment, it is also possible to measure when the second particle "learns" that the first particle was measured, and knowing the distance between the two events, to calculate the velocity that the news travels from one to the other.

Entanglement information passes from particle to particle at speeds ranging from much, much faster than light to infinite speed (instantaneous transmission of information). Einstein's term for this was "spooky action at a distance." Remember that special relativity told us that no particle can travel faster than light. Whatever it is that travels between entangled particles, it is nothing made of matter (which is really energy). Nobody knows what the information medium is or how entangled particles do it, but it has been verified many times that they do. Entanglement information transmission speeds have been measured at distances of up to eleven miles.

Entanglement information can also "move" backward in time. In a kind of experimental setup called a delayed choice quantum eraser (Wikipedia has a nice description of these), different kinds of measurements on one entangled particle shift the detection results for the other particle. The experiment randomly "chooses" which type of measurement to make, and the detection pattern for the other particle changes to correspond. The detection pattern will always correspond to the type of measurement made, even when the choice of measurement type and the measurement itself happens after the detection (that's the "delayed choice" part of the experiment description).

A note for accuracy: localization, entanglement, and faster-than-light transmission of entanglement information are predictions of the Copenhagen interpretation for quantum mechanics. Other interpretations of quantum mechanics—that is, other explanations of the underlying physical reality—do not include localization or faster-than-light entanglement information. The debate in the physics community over interpretations and the meaning of experimental results is sometimes passionate. It has been going on for many years and does not show any sign of being resolved anytime soon.

Localization

> *"Verily I say unto you, if ye have faith, and doubt not, ye shall not only do this which is done to the fig tree, but also if ye shall say unto this mountain, Be thou removed, and be thou cast into the sea; it shall be done."*—Matthew 21:21

> *"The doctrine that the world is made up of objects whose existence is independent of human consciousness turns out to be in conflict with quantum mechanics and with facts established by experiment."*—Bernard d'Espangnat, recounted by Jonathan Allday, *Quantum Reality, Theory and Philosophy*

Quantum state localization will be a key point in making the connection between physics and theology later on (despite appearances, this book is really about theology, not physics), so, as in the discussion of energy, I am going to go into more detail than usual here.

Localization, the transition between quantum state and classical state, is a hotly debated topic in physics. Within the Copenhagen interpretation of quantum mechanics, there isn't any theory, any mathematical model, of what happens during localization or why it happens—or even if it does happen. The strict Copenhagen interpretation, originally developed by Niels Bohr and Werner Heisenberg, describes localization as caused by measurement. Essentially: quantum state probability amplitudes are localized to classical particles by the physical interaction with the detector used in an experiment. The

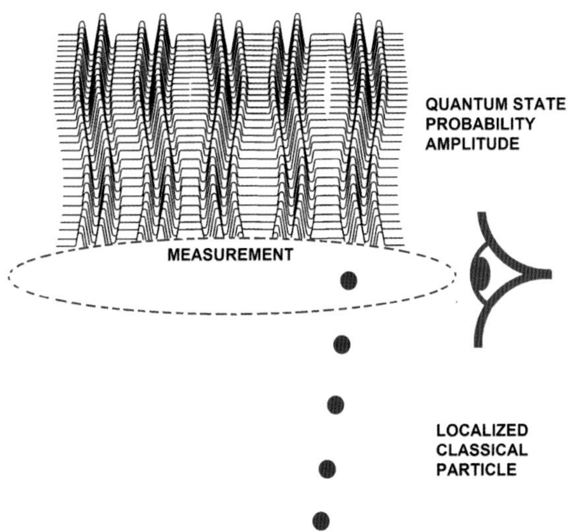

kind of detector and the physical way the detector works are pretty much irrelevant.

Fritz London and Edmond Bauer suggested a modification of the Copenhagen interpretation, a different mechanism for localization based on the work of mathematician John Von Neumann, the same Von Neumann who developed the logical organization of some modern computers. Von Neumann did a mathematical analysis that called the Copenhagen view of localization into question. He pointed out that the sequence of events that compose a measurement (called a Von Neumann chain) are all quantum interactions—except for one.

For example, an experimental photon interacts with an electron in a molecule in a piece of film and causes a chemical change. More chemistry (still quantum state; chemistry is always quantum state) develops the film, and the molecule affected by the photon shows up as a different color. More photons from a light reflect off the colored film into the eye of a physicist (a quantum state interaction). Chemical reactions in the eye trigger an electrical signal through nerves to the brain, where the physicist perceives the distribution of dots with a conscious mind.

What Von Neumann noticed was that the only event in the chain that is not a quantum state interaction is *the perception by a conscious mind.* London and Bauer therefore proposed that localization is caused by perception; that the world that we see is there because we are looking at it. This also implies the contrary inference: that when we are not looking at the world, when nobody has seen it, it isn't really there. At least it is not localized.

With this active role for conscious minds already on the table in physics, another possible cause for localization may seem reasonable. A tiny minority of physicists, widely regarded to be eccentric cranks, have pointed out that measurements are not random events. While all other events in quantum mechanics are completely random, measurements are the result of choices by whoever builds an experiment, choices that necessarily decrease the randomness (uncertainty) that is so fundamental to quantum mechanics and that can provide information about quantum state particles. The implication here is that localization may be caused by a conscious choice or action, which decreases the possibilities available to probability amplitudes in a way that can provide information to an observer, to a conscious mind—in other words, to one of us.

Albert Einstein, the physicist who developed special and (with some help) general relativity, argued passionately against both the Copenhagen interpretation proposed by his friend Niels Bohr and the proposal that conscious perception plays a role in physical events. Bohr once asked him, "You revolutionized physics yourself. Why are you having a problem with this?"

Einstein replied, "You only tell a good joke once."

The controversy continues. Disagreement exists about whether localization is an actual event at all; many physicists hold that particles are always in quantum state and that particles only look localized because we can't see them the way they really are. Another viewpoint, called decoherence theory, holds that localization is caused by the chaotic interference of the gazillions of probability amplitudes that are always present in the real world.

To understand decoherence theory, remember that the key experimental behavior used to identify quantum state is the superposition and interference between different possibilities (terms) in the probability amplitude (Ψ). Analyses of interactions with observers or with the chaotic real world cause the possibilities described by the probability amplitude to separate into terms (called eigenstates) that no longer affect each other. Superposition and interference disappear to yield classical behavior with localized values for particle attributes. The separation of probability amplitude terms into eigenstates that no longer interfere with each other is called decoherence.

The problem with decoherence theory is that, while particles now have a more classical behavior with no interference, there are still multiple possibilities in the probability amplitude. According to quantum mechanics, the interaction of a particle probability amplitude with an observer or with the real world does not produce a single classical particle (which is what we see in experiments); rather, it produces the possibilities of many classical particles. One of the more passionate debates in the physics community relates to this discrepancy between what quantum mechanics predicts (many classical particle possibilities) and what we actually see in experiments (single classical particles).

We have come to an issue where (in my opinion) support for one interpretation of quantum mechanics or another can be strongly influenced by religious attitudes. For a believer, the notion that physical events could be influenced by the thoughts of our conscious minds is not unreasonable. Our Lord told us that we have the capability to change the physical world with our thoughts (see the quote from Matthew at the beginning of this section). I support the Copenhagen interpretation because it fits so very well with Scripture. As we speculate together on the events of Genesis later in this book, I will include some reasons why a modified Copenhagen/Von Neumann view of reality (possibilities changed to actual events by the choices of conscious minds) might be exactly what we could expect to see in a creation made by God.

On the other hand, for a nonbeliever living in a wholly natural world, it is not possible that our conscious thoughts and choices could affect reality. They are just electrochemical signals in our brains. Physicists have proposed several other interpretations of quantum mechanics that do not include a link between conscious minds and localization. The logical obstacle that alternate interpretations must deal with, however, is the discrepancy between the many particle possibilities predicted by quantum mechanics calculations and the single particles that we see in experiments.

As an example of other theories put forth, here are just a couple of the major alternate interpretations:

Many Worlds: All of the decoherent possibilities predicted by quantum mechanics have a real, physical existence. Our universe exists as an essentially infinite number of parallel universes spawned by the multiplication of quantum possibilities. We only perceive a single actual event (and a single universe) because our individual consciousness is limited to a single one of the possible universes. Like the universe itself, our minds and bodies are copied into multiple physical realities, but we can only see the one that we happen to be in.

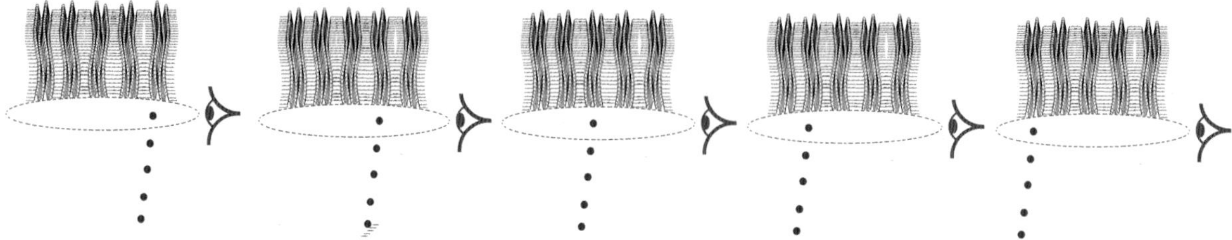

The many worlds interpretation of quantum mechanics has a lot of supporters in the physics community, probably more than the Copenhagen interpretation does. Many worlds has the same philosophical simplicity as Copenhagen (what the mathematics says is happening is what is actually happening), but while the Copenhagen interpretation has quantum behavior stop at a measurement, many worlds sticks with the mathematics to the bitter end: quantum behavior never stops; there is no localization.

Consistent Histories: The consistent histories interpretation is an attempt to derive mathematical models for quantum mechanics that produce classical behavior without some unknown, magical process of localization. Consistent histories theories have

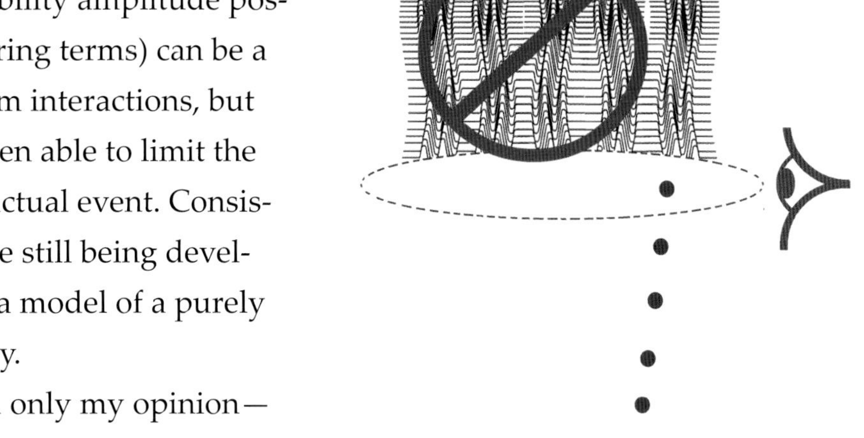

been successful at showing that decoherence (the separation of probability amplitude possibilities into noninterfering terms) can be a natural result of quantum interactions, but they have not (so far) been able to limit the possibilities to a single actual event. Consistent histories theories are still being developed and may produce a model of a purely quantum world someday.

In my opinion, and only my opinion—most physicists would probably disagree—the experimental evidence currently favors the Copenhagen/Von Neumann viewpoint that localization is a real event and is caused by the choices of conscious minds. The evidence is not conclusive, but I think it leans in that direction.

The major disagreement regarding localization is whether it is caused by decoherence (the intrusion of the chaotic real world into carefully controlled experimental environments) or by the influence of conscious minds, either by perception or by choice. Both sides have technical merit, but I think experimental evidence favors the influence of conscious minds. To begin with, decoherence is a real effect. Exposure to the chaos of the real world will always cover up quantum state behavior; that is one of the reasons why we do not see quantum state behavior in our ordinary lives. Experimenters have to be extremely careful while designing and building experimental environments to keep decoherence at bay, or quantum behavior may not show up at all.

Thus, experiments that hope to shed light on the cause of localization try to make tiny, nearly inconsequential changes to the environment that will trigger localization but will not introduce decoherence. There is pretty much always an argument over whether or not decoherence was successfully eliminated. If it is, of course, a role for conscious minds would be favored over decoherence theory.

Localization without decoherence implies that localization is caused by one of two events: a reduction in the scope of possibilities available to the probability amplitude alone, or a reduction in possibility that involves a conscious mind—that either actually provides information to a conscious mind or is the result of a choice or action by a conscious mind that can provide information.

As a general rule, all quantum mechanics experiments restrict the possibilities available to probability amplitudes in one way or another. The restrictions do not always cause localization. The distinctive feature that seems to be associated with localization is that possibilities are restricted in a way that either does or can provide information, any information, to one of us human beings.

Physicists S. Durr, G. Nonn, and T. Rempe performed an experiment in 1998 that was arguably successful at triggering localization without introducing decoherence. In the experiment, falling atoms were separated by light into two groups in two different ways.

In the first way, the atoms were in a single energy state and were separated by light alone. The separation was random; any atom might go into either group with equal probability.

This group demonstrated quantum state behavior: the distribution of particles showed the variation between high and low values caused by superposition (called an interference pattern); see the left panel in figure 27.

In the second way, the atoms were held in two energy states with an electric field that influenced the division, such that atoms in the two groups had different energy states. It was therefore possible to detect which kind of atom had gone into which group. The second group did not show quantum state behavior. The distribution of particles did not have the highs and lows of an interference pattern, and there was no superposition behavior. In other words, atoms separated according to their energy states had been localized to classical state.

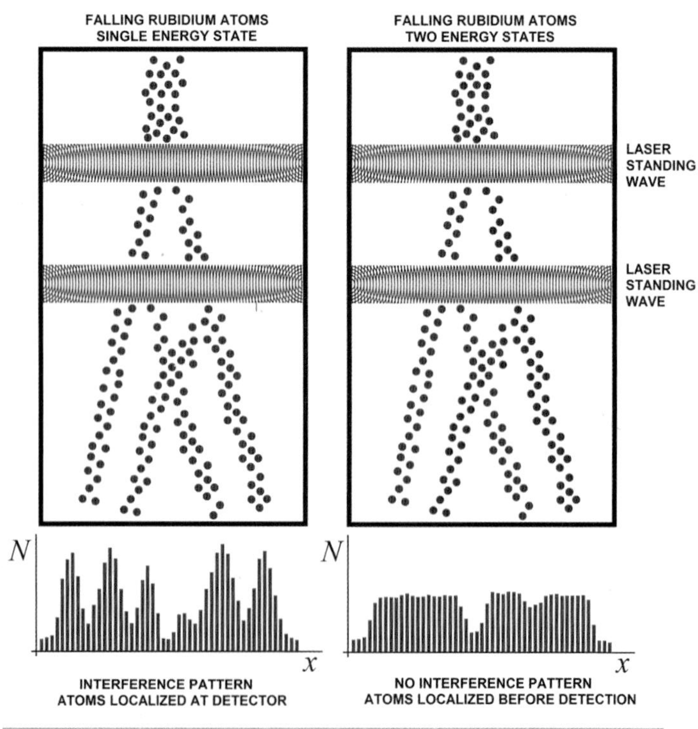

Fig. 27. Durr, Nonn, & Rempe Localization Experiment

Durr, Nonn, and Rempe argued that they had successfully eliminated decoherence because both groups of atoms landed in the same locations; there was no shift in the average positions that would have been the result of any forces that could induce decoherence. Furthermore, while it would have been possible to use a detector to measure the energy states on the falling atoms and so identify them, no such detector was ever installed; no measurements of energy states on the atoms were ever made. There was never any perception by an experimenter or anybody else involved; therefore, localization was apparently caused by a choice that made the information potentially available.

Relativity + Quantum Mechanics = Feynman-Stueckelberg

> *"The past, present and future are only illusions, even if stubborn ones."*
> —Albert Einstein, personal letter

> *"How's the weather on the other side of the bend?"*
> —My genuinely concerned wife, Cynthia

I hope you're enjoying the trip so far. We're about halfway down the rabbit hole at this point—just getting to the really odd bits. This section is an introduction to the Feynman-Stueckelberg interpretation of antimatter. As I mentioned earlier, Feynman-Stueckelberg is the key theory that, in my opinion, brings modern physics and Scripture into the same philosophical room.

The presentation I'll be using for Feynman-Stueckelberg is a shortened version of the one given by Bruce Schumm in *Deep Down Things*. For anyone interested in more detail, I strongly recommend his excellent book.

In 1925 and 1926, several physicists independently developed descriptions of quantum object behavior using different mathematical approaches (called formulations). Werner Heisenberg, Max Born, and Pascual Jordan developed matrix mechanics in 1925. Erwin Schrodinger developed wave mechanics in 1926. In 1930 and 1932, Paul Dirac and John Von Neumann developed the mathematics into the forms most commonly used today. Since then, many more formulations of quantum mechanics have been developed.

All of the formulations, however, give the same answers. Physicists use whichever formulation will be the easiest to solve for the particular kind of problem they are working on.

Schrodinger developed an equation that predicts the time-dependent change of a probability amplitude in response to a physical environment. The probability amplitude (Ψ) can be a list of complex (x + yi) terms, each of which describes the possible state of a system of objects and the associated possibility for each state (possibility, x + yi × complex conjugate of possibility, x − yi = probability, $x^2 + y^2$). For example: if the system is a six-sided die being rolled, the probability amplitude will have six terms, one for each side of the die, with an associated possibility of the square root of 1/6. For a system of one particle moving through space, the probability amplitude will have one term for each possible position the particle could be in (in this case, an infinite number of terms). For a system with two particles moving through space, the probability amplitude would have an infinite number of terms for the *second* particle for each of the infinite possible positions of the *first* particle—sort of infinity squared.

Short Version of Schrodinger's equation:

$$E\Psi = T\Psi + V\Psi$$

Long Version of Schrodinger's equation:

E = total energy operator
Ψ = probability amplitude (or wave function)
T = kinetic energy operator
V = potential energy function
$i = \sqrt{-1}$
h = Planck's constant
π = ratio of a circle's circumference to its diameter
$\frac{\partial}{\partial t}$ = multiple variable version of the derivative operator
m = mass

$$\frac{ih}{2\pi}\frac{\partial}{\partial t}\Psi(x,y,z,t) = \frac{h^2}{8\pi m}\nabla^2\Psi(x,y,z,t) + V(x,y,z)\Psi(x,y,z,t)$$

Schrodinger's equation is basically an energy balance: as the probability amplitude changes over time, the total energy will remain equal to the sum of the kinetic energy and the potential energy. The short version of this equation is also called its operator form. Applying the energy operator to the probability amplitude produces the predicted energy probability distribution (EΨ = energy). Applying the kinetic energy operator to the probability amplitude produces the kinetic energy probability distribution (TΨ = kinetic energy).

In the above versions of the Schrodinger equation, the backward 6 symbol and the upside-down triangle are multidimensional versions of the derivative operator. The 2 exponent on the del operator (the triangle) means that the operator is applied to the function twice.

By the way, the nomenclature for Ψ(x, y, z, t) is not strictly correct in this description. The different formulations for quantum mechanics use different ways of writing the function that describes the possibilities for a system. The descriptive term used so far—probability amplitude—usually applies to the version used with the formulations of Heisenberg, Dirac, and Von Neumann. The symbol Ψ is usually applied to Schrodinger's version of the function and is called a wave function. They are two different ways of describing the same thing.

Because the number of terms in Ψ increases so quickly, solving the mathematics of quantum theory gets really hard for systems with multiple particles. At this time, physicists only have exact solutions for a few, relatively simple systems with one or two particles. Calculations for more complex real-world systems are done using approximations that make the calculations easier, but they are still quite difficult. For example, a calculation of the mass of a neutron based on the quantum interactions of the three quarks that compose it took many physicists using big, fast computers thirty years of effort to get within four percent of the measured value.

The Heisenberg and Schrodinger formulations of quantum theory were known to be wrong—or at least incomplete—when they were first proposed. Although they provided accurate predictions of experimental results, none of them included special or general relativity. Oscar Klein and Walter Gordon (and Vladimir Fock) proposed a version of quantum theory corrected for relativity in 1927:

$$\frac{1}{c^2}\frac{\partial^2}{\partial t^2}\Psi - \nabla^2\Psi + \frac{4\pi^2 m^2 c^2}{h^2}\Psi = 0$$

c = velocity of light
$\frac{\partial}{\partial t}$ = multiple variable version of the derivative operator
Ψ = probability amplitude (or wave function)
∇ = a multiple variable version of the derivative operator
π = ratio of a circle's circumference to its diameter
m = mass
h = Planck's constant

The Klein-Gordon theory was only applicable to a certain type of particles (spin 0; we'll get to them a little later). Paul Dirac proposed a relativistic version of quantum theory for spin 1/2 particles in 1928. The electrons, neutrons, and protons that compose material are all spin 1/2 particles, so the Dirac equation that follows is going to be

$$\left(\begin{bmatrix} \beta_{1,1} & \beta_{1,2} & \beta_{1,3} & \beta_{1,4} \\ \beta_{2,1} & \beta_{2,2} & \beta_{2,3} & \beta_{2,4} \\ \beta_{3,1} & \beta_{3,2} & \beta_{3,3} & \beta_{3,4} \\ \beta_{4,1} & \beta_{4,2} & \beta_{4,3} & \beta_{4,4} \end{bmatrix} mc^2 - \sum_{k=x}^{z} \frac{ihc}{2\pi} \begin{bmatrix} \alpha_{k1,1} & \alpha_{k1,2} & \alpha_{k1,3} & \alpha_{k1,4} \\ \alpha_{k2,1} & \alpha_{k2,2} & \alpha_{k2,3} & \alpha_{k2,4} \\ \alpha_{k3,1} & \alpha_{k3,2} & \alpha_{k3,3} & \alpha_{k3,4} \\ \alpha_{k4,1} & \alpha_{k4,2} & \alpha_{k4,3} & \alpha_{k4,4} \end{bmatrix} \frac{\partial}{\partial k}\right) \Psi(x,y,z,t) = \frac{ih}{2\pi}\frac{\partial}{\partial t}\Psi(x,y,z,t)$$

m = mass
c = velocity of light
Σ = summation, in this case it represents three terms: one for x, one for y, and one for z
$i = \sqrt{-1}$
h = Planck's constant
π = ratio of a circle's circumference to its diameter
$\frac{\partial}{\partial t}$ *= multiple variable version of the derivative operator*
Ψ = probability amplitude (or wave function)

of more interest, since it applies for most of the stuff we encounter in our daily lives:

Both the Klein-Gordon equation and the Dirac equation included some odd mathematical behavior that turned out to relate to antimatter. The probability amplitude (Ψ) that solves the nonrelativistic Schrodinger equation can be factored into two terms, one describing a variation in space and one describing a variation in time. The factor Ψ(t) describing the time variance is:

$$\Psi(t) = e^{-i\alpha Et}$$

Ψ = probability amplitude (or wave function)
e = a constant, (= 2.718282...)
$i = \sqrt{-1}$
α = a constant
E = energy
t = time

Back in the discussion of probability distributions, I mentioned that the sign of the exponent for e in the Ψ function was going to be really important. Here is why. The Ψ function is a kind of square root for a probability distribution. Like a probability distribution function, Ψ must always be less than 1, and the sum of all of the possible values for Ψ must add up to 1. The mathematics do not make any physical sense if those are not true.

Both the Klein-Gordon equation and the Dirac equation include multiple solutions for the factor describing the time variance of Ψ. For the Dirac equation, they are:

$$\Psi(t) = e^{-i\alpha Et} \qquad \Psi(t) = e^{i\alpha Et}$$

The first solution is okay, but the second solution is impossible for a probability distribution or for Ψ. The exponent for e must be negative. Dirac reorganized the second solution a little to get it to work mathematically:

$$\Psi(t) = e^{-i\alpha(-E)t}$$

He called this second solution a negative energy solution and proposed that it must relate to a different kind of matter. Based on the solutions to his relativistic equation, Dirac predicted that a new type of matter particles would have the same properties as the particles we are familiar with, except their electric charges would be opposite. His prediction was confirmed when a positron, an antimatter electron with the same mass but opposite electric charge, was observed in cosmic rays by Carl Anderson in 1932.

Negative energy is still an odd concept, but it is not as odd as a probability distribution with values greater than 1. Remember that energy is the aggregate amount of work done on an object. It is thus a little challenging to picture how energy could be negative; it would imply a particle doing more work than it actually had available. Therefore, Dirac justified the negative energy solutions by proposing that some basic level of energy fills every bit of our universe; kind of like the rest energy associated with mass ($E=mc^2$) but associated with a vacuum instead. Physicists call this the zero-point energy. The idea is that negative energies are just energies below the zero point value, like negative coordinates in the Cartesian system are just positions behind the origin.

The Klein-Gordon equation also produced negative energy solutions, but it had the additional, unfortunate consequence that the negative energy solutions also predicted negative probabilities. That doesn't make any physical sense at all.

Ernst Stueckelberg in 1941 and Richard Feynman in 1949 proposed a slight change to these "negative energy" solutions:

$$\Psi(t) = e^{-i\alpha E(-t)}$$

Their proposal is that the solutions for antimatter don't represent negative energy; they represent negative time. This implies that antimatter particles are the same as matter particles except that they just happen to be traveling backward in time instead of forward like the rest of us. The distinctive feature of antimatter, the opposite electric charge, is only an appearance, not a reality. An antimatter particle with the same charge as a matter particle would actually be repelled by electrostatic forces instead of attracted. But because we are effectively watching the movie running backward, it looks like it is moving the opposite way, as if it were attracted.

The negative time interpretation cures all of the problems with both the Klein-Gordon and the Dirac equations; energies and probabilities all become properly positive. The standard model of particle physics is now based on calculations that include the mathematical assumption that antimatter particles move backward in time. The many experiments that validate the predictions of the standard model also, by implication, validate the mathematical truth that antimatter particles go backward in time.

But no one (except for me and a few other intellectual deviants) thinks that the math represents a physical reality. The community of physicists generally regards the backward time representation of antimatter in particle calculations to be a mathematical convention; it's necessary to preserve particle charge continuity but has no real physical meaning. This might seem like a stubborn refusal by a bunch of reactionary curmudgeons to accept a radical new idea, but it really is not. As we will see when we get deeper into particles, there are lots of odd quantities that have to be accounted for in particle mathematics that don't have any known physical meaning. Backward time is just one more oddity in a garden full of oddities, and it is not at all unreasonable to wait for a little proof before buying into something as revolutionary as negative time particles.

That said, the philosophical implications for negative time particles are quite profound. As Dr. Feynman explains:

> *"This view is quite different from that of the Hamiltonian method which considers the future as developing continuously out of the past. Here we imagine the entire space-time history laid out, and that we just become aware of increasing portions of it successively."*
> —Richard Feynman, "The Theory of Positrons," 1949

When we look at the world, what we see is a now. In a particle sense, we see the photons that happen to be arriving at our eyes at the present moment. These photons originated at different times and in different places, but they all arrive at the same instant to produce our experience of the moment. The objects that we see are mostly what they are and where they are because of events that happened in our past. Physically, the particles that compose those objects have values for position, momentum, and energy that are determined by events and interactions in our past.

If antimatter particles actually do travel backward in time, then the same logic must apply in reverse. The antimatter particles that an experimental physicist sees now are where they are and are doing what they are doing because of events and interactions that "happened" in our future. They have values of position, momentum, and energy that "were" determined by events and interactions that must be quite real, but which, to us, have not happened yet.

For interactions and events to happen in the future that affect our perception of now, there must be a future for them to happen in. This means that the future is just as physically real as the present is and the past was. As Dr. Feynman said, the correct viewpoint is that our experience, our conscious perception, moves along a path, a string of nows, through a past, present, and future that all simultaneously exist. As we saw in general relativity, time is just a coordinate, a position in an expanse of time that we can't sense but that is just as real (and just as big) as the expanse of space that we can see and measure. Just as we saw in relativity, we live in a spacetime, not a space with time.

The Hamiltonian viewpoint that Dr. Feynman referred to in the quote above is an alternate mechanics, an alternate mathematical description of the movements of objects in response to forces. Newton's three laws of motion form the basis for Newtonian mechanics. There are two other formulations for mechanics (different ways of doing the math that get the same answers): Hamilton mechanics and Lagrange mechanics. I won't be going into them here, but for the interested reader, Wikipedia has entries for both.

In 1908, philosopher E. McTaggart proposed the same view of time based on the calculations in special relativity, which showed that events that are simultaneous to one observer happen at different times for an observer traveling at a different velocity. Amongst philosophers, the viewpoint that all of spacetime is physically, simultaneously real is referred to as eternalism, the block universe, or the b-theory of time. (Again, Wikipedia has entries for anyone interested.)

The implications of Feynman-Stueckelberg have never been conclusively tested. No physicist has ever mathematically predicted a distinctive behavior of matter or antimatter that could be measured in an experiment; there is no evidence for or against the notion that particles can and do travel backward and forward in time. There is only mathematics. But the mathematics is truly intriguing.

Theology from Antimatter

While the physical validity of the theory is questionable, Feynman-Stueckelberg does fit rather neatly into Scripture:

> *"Remember the former things of old, for I am God, and there is none else; I am God and there is none like me. Declaring the end from the beginning, and from ancient times the things that are not yet done, saying My counsel shall stand, and I will do all My pleasure."*—Isaiah 46:9–10

Feynman-Stueckelberg has at least two fundamental implications for theology. The first is that spacetime is all laid out, from beginning to end, for God to see. He knows the end from the beginning and things not yet done simply because they are all right there in front of him. From his perspective, Adam and Eve wander in the garden of Eden right now. David rules over Israel now. God knows our grandparents now, and our grandchildren now, as familiarly as he knows us now. Judgment Day and the end of the earth are happening right now.

The second theological implication is a corollary of the first. If God can see all of spacetime laid out from beginning to end (as Scripture tells us he can), he cannot possibly be stuck in it like we are. His time and our time are not the same. It is likely, then, that the description of creation in Genesis is not so much about the formation of the earth alone, but a description of the making of spacetime with the earth as a part of it. Much more on this subject in later chapters.

If Genesis describes a spacetime that God carved into existence all at once, then the duration of spacetime, the interval between beginning and end, has no relationship at all to how long it took to make spacetime and fill it up with interesting things. Nor does the duration of events inside spacetime have anything to do with how "long" it has "been" since spacetime "was" made. There is no measurement that can be taken inside spacetime that will tell us "when" it came into existence. From the standpoint of Feynman-Stueckelberg and from our perceptual perspective (since we are limited to spacetime), the question doesn't even make any sense.

The Genesis creation story is told from God's perspective. It is not unreasonable that he would speak of time in the story of creation also from his perspective. The six days of creation are his days. The mere thousands of years since the creation (as described in the Genesis genealogies) are, possibly, his years.

On this view, the much longer scales of time implied by the observations of science inside spacetime probably have no relationship to the times mentioned in Genesis. They measure something completely different. There is no conflict between the millions and billions of years of science and the six days of creation.

Particles (Hadrons and Leptons and Bosons, Oh My!)

> *". . . physicists are forced to acknowledge the fact that they refer to particles as if they were point-like objects. They speak of their 'trajectories,' of the 'collisions' they suffer with other particles even though they know that this language is entirely allegorical, that 'in reality' the 'particles' have neither positions nor trajectories, and that, indeed, they are not truly distinct beings."*—Bernard d'Espagnat, *On Physics and Philosophy*

Particle physics can be a little overwhelming at first glance. It's a play with a cast of hundreds milling about the stage. Scenes shift and scenery moves while the actors change their names at random intervals. In the end, the whole thing will look like a movie shown on fog.

However, particles are the bricks and mortar of spacetime, as far as we know all material in our universe is made of particles. Particle physics forms the foundation stones (although they are not the cornerstone) of our search for the truth of how this world works. So, welcome to a tour of the strangeness of particle physics. There won't be a test, and it won't be necessary to know the details of particle names or interactions as we continue on from here, but it will be really handy later on to have a feel for what particle physics tells us about spacetime.

So, paraphrasing Michael Behe in *Darwin's Black Box*, don't worry about the details. Just sit back, relax, and savor the power of God.

Empty Space

Before we get into the details of particle physics, I'd like to start with an example to put the particle world into a little perspective. That example is diamond. Diamond is a solid made of the element carbon. It has the honor of being the hardest material that we know of, because carbon atoms can form very strong chemical bonds with each other. (Interestingly, carbon also forms bonds that are not as strong: graphite [pencil lead] is another form of carbon with a different bond structure and is not nearly as hard as diamond.)

One of the characteristics of strong chemical bonds is that they pull the nuclei of the bound atoms closer together than weaker bonds. Diamond, therefore, has a relatively short bond length; its atomic nuclei are closer together than in the average chemical compound.

A couple of measured distances for carbon and diamond:

Carbon nuclear charge radius = 2.472×10^{-15}m
Diamond bond radius = 1.5442×10^{-10}m

For the sake of ease, let's scale those tiny little distances up to something a little more familiar. If we increased the size of the carbon nucleus up to the size of a golf ball (about 1.5 inches diameter), the equivalent bond radius would be 3904 feet, a little less than 3/4 of a mile. In what we would think of as a densely packed solid material (diamond), the atomic nuclei are spaced at a distance roughly equivalent to golf balls a mile apart. For carbon in a classical state, there would also be twelve tiny point charges (six electrons for each of the two carbon atoms in the bond) wandering around and between the golf balls.

For liquids, the distances increase a little, up to golf balls 1.1 miles apart or so. For gases at the pressure and temperature of our atmosphere, the spacing is golf balls 16.5 miles apart.

The point here is that the stuff we think of as solid material should more accurately be thought of as mostly empty space with a few rare and tiny objects waving around in it.

Fundamental Particles

Figure 28 (opposite page) shows the known fundamental particles. As far as we know, everything in the universe is made of these sixteen little guys. Technically, the number is actually twenty-four, because there are eight different types of gluon and two different type of W boson, but the diagram looks much better, more symmetrical, with sixteen—so we'll roll with that.

The three purple and green columns on the left are the fermions, the particles that compose "solid" material. Purple blocks represent particles called quarks. Quarks respond to the nuclear strong force and form the structures of atomic nuclei. Particles represented by green blocks are leptons. Leptons are not subject to the strong force and are able to wander more freely outside of the nuclei of atoms. The reddish column on the right lists the bosons, the particles that fermions (quarks and leptons) exchange to apply forces to each other.

Murray Gell-Mann, one of the physicists who developed the theory that identified quarks in 1964, has a quirky sense of humor (he originally called his theory "the eightfold way"). Quark is a kind of homemade cheese that is popular in Europe. The different types of quarks in Figure 28 he called flavors. The mathematical descriptions of the fluctuations of quarks (up→down, down→strange) are still called "flavor space."

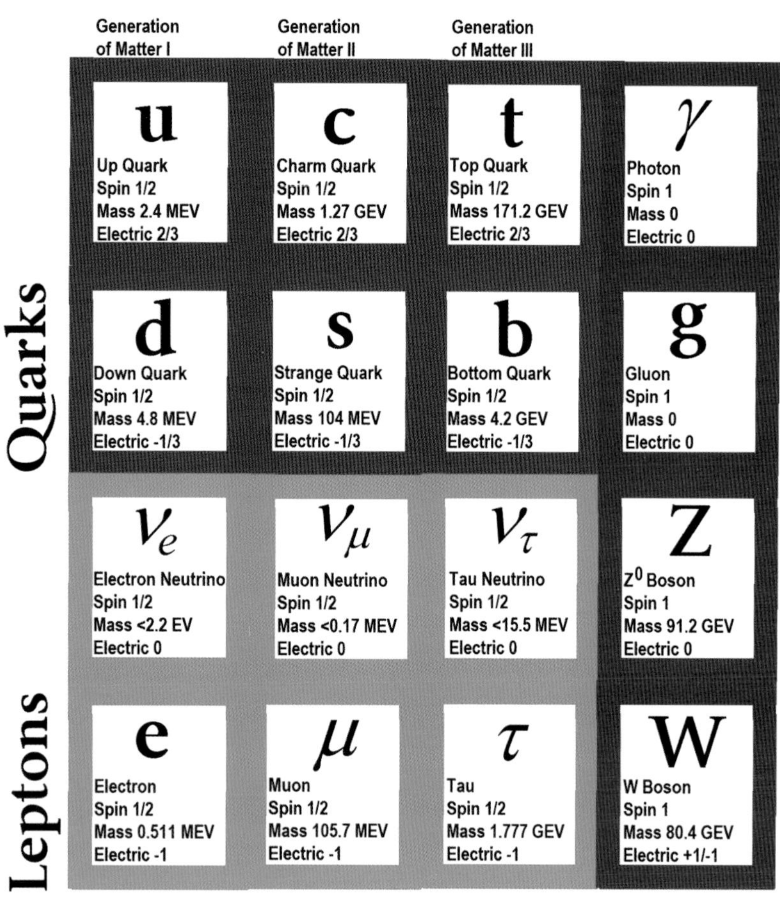

Fig. 28. Fundamental particles of the Standard Model

We'll go into more detail on the particles, but first it will be useful to explain forces. The behavior of particles is all about forces.

Four Forces

There are four known forces that particles can use to push and pull on other particles. They are listed with their relative strengths in the figure below. The table was written by a physicist, so it uses the technically correct term for forces: interactions.

Interaction	Current Theory	Mediators	Relative Strength	Long Distance Behavior	Range
Strong Force	Quantum Chromodynamics (QCD)	gluons	10^{38}	1	10^{-15} m
Electromagnetic Force	Quantum Electrodynamics (QED)	photons	10^{36}	$\frac{1}{r^2}$	∞

Weak Force	Electroweak Theory (ET)	W and Z bosons	10^{25}	$\frac{1}{r}e^{-m_{W,Z}r}$	10^{-18} m
Gravitational Force	General Relativity (GR)	gravitons (hypothetical)	1	$\frac{1}{r^2}$	∞

Fig. 29. Four Known Forces. Based on table by Wikipedia user Chetvorno.

Remembering Newton's laws of motion from the terms section, we get the physical manifestation of what a force is:

$$F = \frac{dp}{dt}$$

F = force
p = momentum (= m × v)
$\frac{d}{dt}$ *= derivative operator*
with respect to time (t)
(rate of change per unit time)

A force is something that changes the momentum of an object. In physics observations, forces have never actually been seen. What *are* seen are changes in momentum; changes in the speed or direction of motion of objects. The existence of forces is inferred based on the assumption that something must be causing the change in momentum.

Classical physics describes forces as fields, like electric fields, magnetic fields, or gravitational fields. A field is some region of space where it is possible to predict what the force on an object will be. More accurately, a field is some region of space where physicists can use mathematical models to predict how the momentums of particles will change.

One other thing to remember from Newton's laws is that forces act in both directions:

$$F_{1\to2} = F_{2\to1}$$

If two particles apply a force to each other (for example, if two electrons repel each other by electrostatic Coulomb force), the forces will act on both with equal strength and in opposite directions. The changes in momentum are always equal and opposite; some amount of momentum is subtracted from one particle and added to the other. This is a classical description of forces.

In the quantum mechanics description of forces, particle momentums are altered because the particles exchange other particles that carry small amounts of momentum between them. In terms of the fundamental particles mentioned above, fermions (quarks and leptons) apply forces to each other by exchanging bosons. In other words, they exchange bosons to pass momentum back and forth.

Each of the four forces uses a different type of boson as a momentum carrier. Boson exchanges between quarks and leptons (the structural particles) are controlled by the charges of each particle. Each type of force has its own type of charge, and each type of exchange boson will only interact with particles that have a charge for the force the boson carries momentum for:

> The strong nuclear force acts by gluon exchanges; gluons only interact with particles that have color charge.
>
> Electromagnetic forces act by photon exchanges; photons only interact with particles that have electric charge.
>
> The weak nuclear force acts by Z, W+, or W- boson exchanges; Z, W+, and W- bosons only interact with particles that have weak isospin charge (or for the charged W bosons, electric charge).
>
> Gravity (hypothetically) acts by (hypothetical) graviton exchanges; gravitons only interact with particles that have mass-energy charge.

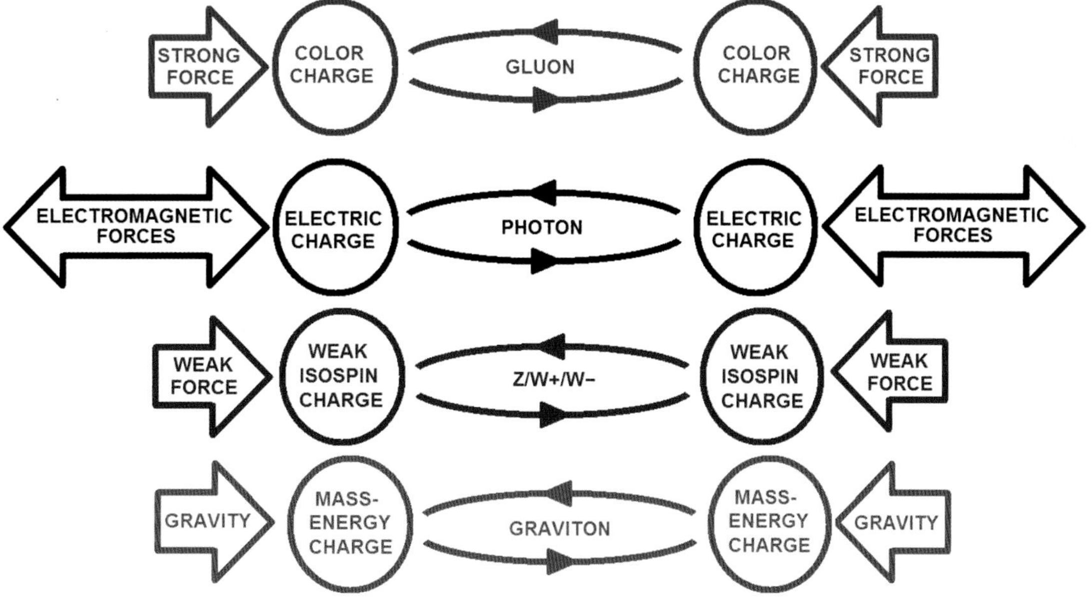

Fig. 30. Forces, Charges, and Bosons

Neutrino particles have very little mass-energy charge and no color charge or electric charge at all. They do have weak isospin charge, but the weak force is very short-ranged and pretty much operates only inside atomic nuclei or very close to them. Because of the very sparse occurrence of atomic nuclei (remember, they are golf balls a mile apart) neutrinos rarely interact at all with other particles. The earth is exposed to a very dense rain of neutrinos from nuclear reactions in the sun, called the solar neutrino flux, but most of them pass through the earth without interacting at all. Neutrino detectors in physics experiments are extremely large and expensive and see neutrino interactions only rarely.

Each boson carries a specific amount of momentum when it is exchanged. Forces are stronger or weaker depending on how often bosons are exchanged. Physically, the charge that each particle has for each force indicates how often the particle emits or accepts the bosons for that force. Particles with higher charges emit bosons more often than particles with lower charges.

An up quark with an electric charge of 2/3 emits photons twice as often as a down quark with an electric charge of −1/3. A neutron is a quark group with one up quark and two down quarks (2/3 + −1/3 + −1/3 = 0). Neutrons are electrically neutral; they do not exchange momentum with other electrically charged particles, because the photons they emit are exactly balanced between positive electromagnetic force photons and negative electromagnetic force photons. Neutrons continuously subtract momentum by photon exchanges and continuously add exactly the same value of momentum by other photon exchanges so that the net change in momentum is zero.

Gravity is described as hypothetical above, because the details of how gravity works are still being developed. The strong nuclear force, electromagnetic forces, and the weak nuclear force all have mathematical models that accurately predict behavior for all known cases

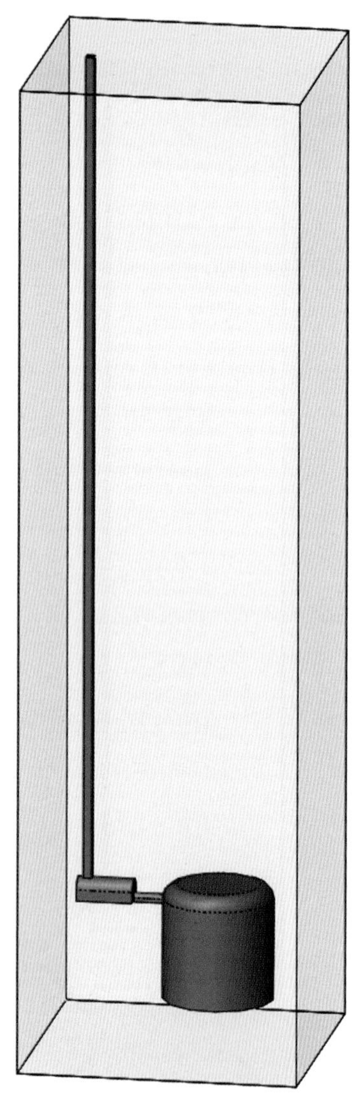

Fig. 31. Super Kamiokande Neutrino Detector. The detector is a stainless steel tank of ultrapure water located 3300 feet underground. The tank is 129 feet in diameter and 136 feet high holding 50,000 tons of water. It is surrounded by 13,031 sensitive light detectors to capture the tiny flashes of light when neutrinos interact with the atoms in water molecules. The Super Kamiokande is near Hida, Japan and is operated by the Institute for Cosmic Ray Research at the University of Tokyo.

where those forces act on particles (called quantum chromodynamics, quantum electrodynamics, and electroweak theory respectively). No one has yet been able to develop a similar model for gravity.

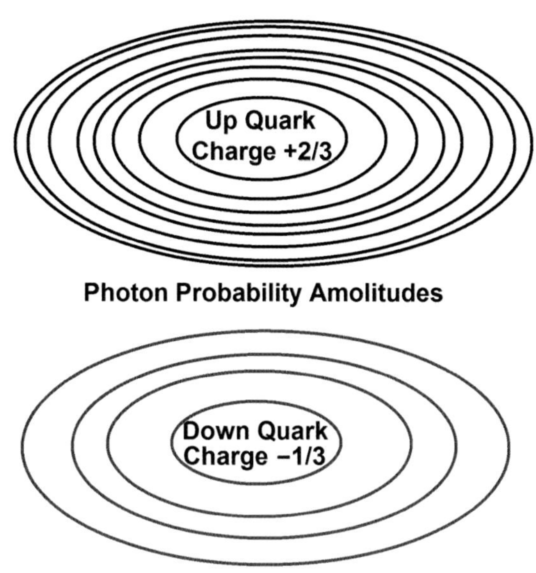

Fig. 32. Photon Emissions by Electrically Charged Quarks

General relativity theory has been tested and works well at distances that are large for particles (>5 × 10^{-6} m is, so far, the minimum distance that has been experimentally verified), but there is currently a conflict between general relativity and quantum mechanics: general relativity predicts black holes at the minimum distances of quantum theory (called the Planck length, 1.6 × 10^{-35}m). We don't see black holes forming outside of large stars, so physicists are pretty sure that something happens to general relativity at distances larger than the Planck length. Nobody knows exactly what.

There have also been attempts to develop mathematical models for gravity based partly on quantum field theory (that's where the notion of gravitons come from) that have some observational support. Some testable predictions have been confirmed in experiments (like gravity waves; see the entry for LIGO in Wikipedia). Other theories that attempt to unite quantum mechanics and gravity have not yet been able to completely match behavior that we have already measured. String theories and M theory, both really popular at the moment in physics, are in that category.

Four Charges

Here is a list of the fundamental particles and their charges:

Bosons:

Particle	Function	Mass-Energy Charge MEV/C²	Electric Charge	Color Charge	Weak Isospin Charge, T³	Intrinsic Angular Momentum (Spin)	Comment
Graviton Boson	Gravity exchange particle	0	0	0		2	Hypothetical, not observed Strength 10^{-30}

Photon Boson	Electro-magnetic exchange particle	0	0	0		1	Observed Strength 10^{-2}
Gluon Boson	Strong force exchange particle	0	0	1	0	1	Indirect observation Strength 1
W+ Boson	Weak force exchange particle	80,000	1	0		1	Strength 1 Observed
W- Boson	Weak force exchange particle	80,000	-1	0	1	1	Strength 10^{-13} Observed
Z0 Boson	Weak force exchange particle	91,000	0	0	-1	1	Strength 10^{-13} Observed
Higgs Boson	Weak force exchange particle	>78,000	0	0	0	0	Strength 10^{-13} Hypothetical, not observed

Fig. 33. List of Bosons and Charges

Lepton Fermions:

Particle	**Function**	**Mass-Energy Charge MEV/C^2**	**Electric Charge**	**Color Charge**	**Weak Isospin Charge, T^3**	**Intrinsic Angular Momentum (Spin)**	**Comment**
Electron	Part of atoms	0.51	-1	0	-1/2	1/2	Observed
Electron Neutrino	Radioactive decay product	0	0	0	1/2	1/2	Observed
Muon		106	-1	0	-1/2	1/2	Observed
Muon Neutrino		0	0	0	1/2	1/2	Observed
Tau		1,784	-1	0	-1/2	1/2	Observed
Tau Neu-trino		>35	0	0	1/2	1/2	Observed
Positron	Part of atoms	0.51	1	0	-1/2	1/2	
Electron Anti-Neu-trino	Radioactive decay product	0	0	0	1/2	1/2	
Anti-Muon		106	1	0	-1/2	1/2	
Muon Anti-Neu-trino		0	0	0	1/2	1/2	
Anti-Tau		1,784	1	0	-1/2	1/2	
Tau Anti-Neutrino		>35	0	0	1/2	1/2	

Fig. 34. List of Leptons and Charges

Quark Fermions:

Particle	Function	Mass-Energy Charge MEV/C^2	Electric Charge	Color Charge	Weak Isospin Charge, T^3	Intrinsic Angular Momentum (Spin)	Comment
Up Quark	Nucleon constituent	5	2/3	R,G,B	1/2	1/2	Indirect Observation
Down Quark	Nucleon constituent	9	-1/3	R,G,B	-1/2	1/2	Indirect Observation
Charm Quark		1,400	2/3	R,G,B	1/2	1/2	Indirect Observation
Strange Quark		170	-1/3	R,G,B	-1/2	1/2	Indirect Observation
Top Quark		174,000	2/3	R,G,B	1/2	1/2	Indirect Observation
Bottom Quark		4,400	-1/3	R,G,B	-1/2	1/2	Indirect Observation
Up Anti-Quark	Nucleon constituent	5	-2/3	AR,AG, AB	1/2	1/2	
Down Anti-Quark	Nucleon constituent	9	1/3	AR,AG, AB	-1/2	1/2	
Charm Anti-Quark		1,400	-2/3	AR,AG, AB	1/2	1/2	
Strange Anti-Quark		170	1/3	AR,AG, AB	-1/2	1/2	
Top Anti-Quark		174,000	-2/3	AR,AG, AB	1/2	1/2	
Bottom Anti-Quark		4,400	1/3	AR,AG, AB	-1/2	1/2	

Fig. 35. List of Quarks and Charges

The unit for mass-energy charge in these lists is derived from the $E = mc^2$ equation from special relativity ($m = E/c^2$). EV stands for electron-volt, a small unit of energy; M stands for mega (million).

$1\ MEV/c^2 = 1.783 \times 10^{-21}$ grams

Units of mass-energy charge are often written just as MEV or GEV (G stands for giga, billion) instead of MEV/c^2 or GEV/c^2 because physicists are generally too lazy to write out the whole thing.

Gravity and weak force charges have only one type of charge each: mass-energy charge for gravity and weak isospin for the weak force. Both forces are strictly attractive; they only pull objects together.

Electric charges for electromagnetic or Coulomb forces come in two types that we call positive and negative because they neutralize each other (like in the neutron described earlier). Electrostatic forces can either attract (pulling objects together) or repel (pushing objects apart) depending on the relative charges:

Positive charge repels positive charge.
Positive charge attracts negative charge.
Negative charge attracts positive charge.
Negative charge repels negative charge.

Color charge for the strong nuclear force has six types of charge: three types of charge for matter particles and three types of anti-charge for antimatter particles. The strong force is strictly attractive, like gravity, and it takes combinations to balance, or neutralize, the strong force:

All three charges neutralize the strong force.
All three anti-charges neutralize the strong force.
One charge and its anti-charge neutralize the strong force.

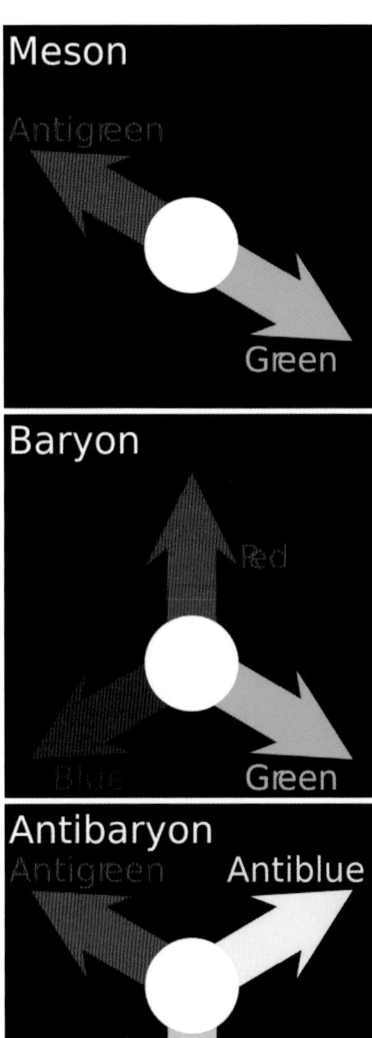

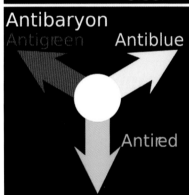

Fig. 36. Color Charges

Color charge got its name (Murray Gell-Mann again) because the balancing of charges acts very much like colors that blend together to make white light. The charges are called red, green, and blue after primary colors that combine to make white. Anti-charges are drawn as cyan, magenta, and yellow in the figure above, but they are called anti-red, anti-green, and anti-blue so physicists don't have to remember the color mixing charts.

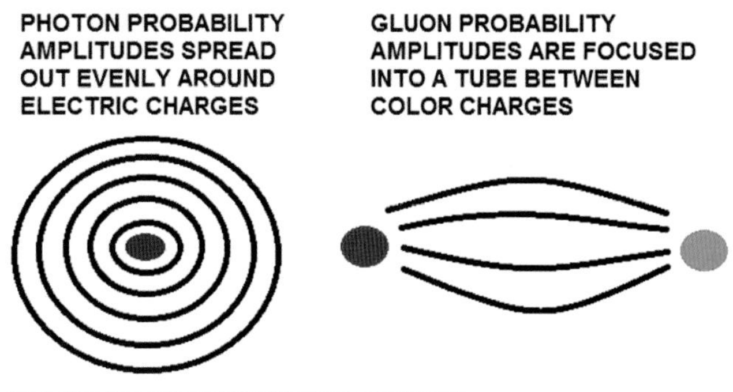

Fig. 37. Strong Force Is Focused

The nuclear strong force between quarks containing color charge does not decrease with distance, as gravity and electromagnetic forces do. It starts at zero for quarks right next to each other and increases as they get further apart. The force increases to about 2200 pounds (on a single particle!) and then stays at that value no matter how much further apart the quarks get.

The strong force behaves in this unusual fashion because the gluons that carry the strong force have color charge themselves. The photons of the electromagnetic force, by contrast, do not have electric charge. Because they do not interact (apply forces) with each other, photon probability amplitudes mostly spread out evenly in all directions. Gluon probability amplitudes do have color charge and do attract each other, so they stay focused in a narrow tube between other particles with color charge.

Quarks are never found alone; they are always found in combinations that neutralize the strong force. This is the case for two reasons. One reason, of course, is that the force between them is so strong. It never decreases to leave them free to wander around like leptons do.

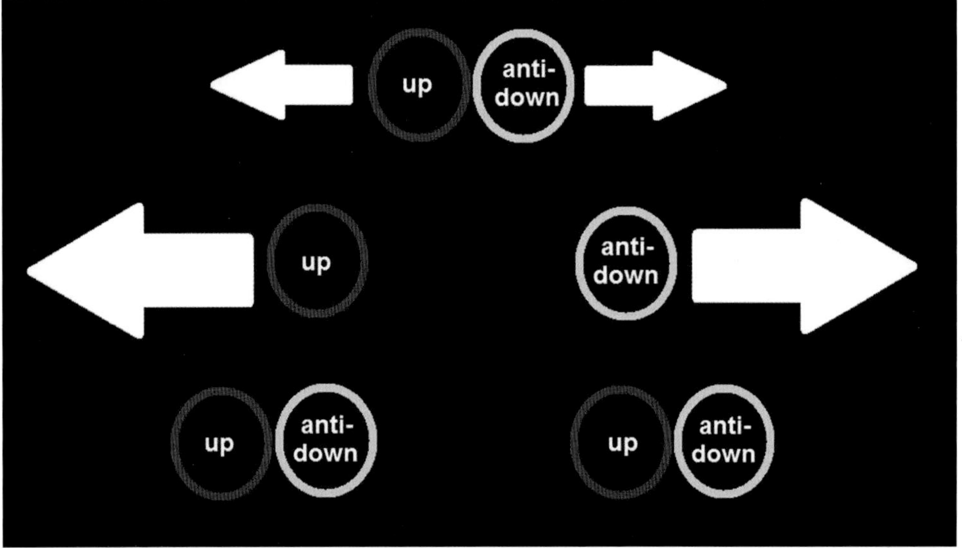

Fig. 38. New Quarks From Energy

The other reason has to do with energy. Remember that energy is work, force applied over a distance, and that quarks, like all particles, are energy. If a physicist does manage to pry two quarks apart, it takes a lot of work to do that, which increases the potential energies of both quarks. When the potential energies get high enough to match the rest energy of the quarks, two new quarks will pop into existence and neutralize the strong force again. (The quark creation process is called hadronization.) Remembering our quantum mechanics, the mathematically correct description of this is that would be that work done on the system to separate the quarks increases potential energy enough to induce two probability amplitude standing waves with the properties (charges) of quarks.

Technically and mathematically, the strong force is a long-range force like electromagnetism or gravity. But since quarks will always be created to neutralize it, it never actually acts over any distance very much greater than the diameter of a proton or neutron.

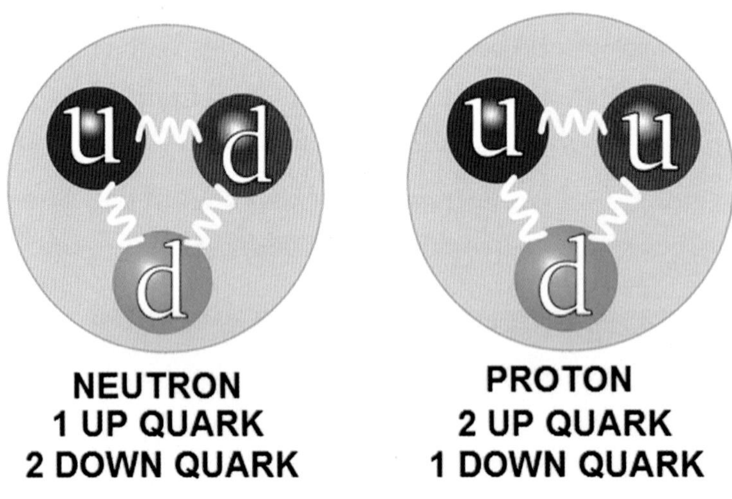

Fig. 39. Neutron and Proton Composition

Quarks are always found in combinations that neutralize the strong force. Particles made of quark groups are called hadrons. Because there are three types of charge combinations that neutralize the force, there are three types of particles composed of quark groups (hadrons). Three quarks with red, green, and blue charge make a baryon. Protons and neutrons are baryons; each is a group of three quarks. Three anti-quarks with anti-red, anti-green, and anti-blue charges make an anti-baryon. A quark and an anti-quark with red and anti-red, green and anti-green, or blue and anti-blue charges make a meson.

Color charges on quarks can change from red to green to blue, and they do change constantly. I mentioned earlier that there are eight types of gluon, the strong force exchange boson. Gluons differ in the way they change color charges when they interact with quarks. One type of gluon does a red-green shift, another type does a blue-green shift, and so on. Quarks change color charge whenever they emit or absorb a gluon (which happens constantly). Quarks can group into many different kinds of meson and hundreds of different baryons and anti-baryons.

When physicists first started studying particles, they called the enormous, bewildering number of different hadrons the "particle zoo." Early on, they thought that the composition of matter would turn out to be pretty simple. When they actually found hundreds of shifting particles instead, it caused confusion and uncertainty until Murray Gell-Mann (and others) made it all understandable again with the eightfold way and quark theory.

> *"The finder of a new elementary particle used to be rewarded with a Nobel Prize, but such a discovery now ought to be punishable by a $10,000 fine."*—Willis Lamb in his acceptance speech for the 1955 Nobel Prize, recounted by Bruce Schumm in *Deep Down Things*

The attentive reader may have noticed a small problem with our speculation that cropped up a couple of paragraphs back. Mesons are quark group (hadron) particles that combine a quark with an anti-quark in the same particle. Remember that the Feynman-Stueckelberg interpretation has antimatter particles traveling backward in time. If Feynman-Stueckelberg is physically correct, then it might be challenging to explain how two quarks traveling in opposite directions in time can possibly stick together to form a particle. We'll go into that later when we get to atomic nuclei; it turns out to be simpler than you might think. In fact, quarks have to be able to form forward time/backward time groups (mesons) in order to have atomic nuclei stick together at all.

Interactions

The mathematical description of the behavior of particles focuses on the interactions between them: on the exchange, the emission, and the absorption of bosons. Because the objects involved for an average particle interaction (two fermions and some number of bosons) are all in quantum state, the mathematics used are necessarily quantum mechanics. The probability amplitude (Ψ) for the system is a list of complex (x + yi) terms that each describes a possible state of the system. The result of the interaction will end up being predicted as a probability distribution that is based on a superposition and interference of all of the possible ways the particles in the system can interact.

For example, fermion A can emit a boson that is absorbed by fermion B, or the boson can be emitted by B and absorbed by A. The direction of the boson exchange is one of the possibilities for the system and has to be added into the mix in order to get the right answers. But the list does not stop there. There can be a boson passed from A to B and a boson passed from B to A. Or two bosons passed from A to B. Or two bosons passed from B to A. Or three bosons, or four bosons. The list of possibilities is literally endless.

In the discussion of Ψ in the quantum mechanics section, I mentioned that the mathematics for quantum mechanics gets really difficult when the number of objects in the system increases, because the number of possibilities expands so rapidly. For a system of one object with continuously variable attributes (like position or momentum), the probability amplitude includes an infinite number of terms: for two objects there are infinity^2 (that's not a correct math term, by the way; I just made it up); for four objects (two fermions exchanging bosons in two directions, for example) the mathematics would be infinity^4. Luckily, the two directions of boson exchange (A to B and B to A) can be considered separately, so physicists only have to add up 2 × infinity^3 terms to describe a single boson exchange (dodged a bullet there).

The point here is that doing the mathematics for something as physically simple as a boson exchange is really difficult, even for people as talented as physicists. The math was hard enough that it really slowed down the development of theories in particle physics. In fact, what Stueckelberg and Feynman were working on when they developed the backward time concept for antimatter was a simplified technique for organizing the mathematical equations so that particle physics calculations would be easier to do.

I hope it does not come as a complete surprise that what they ended up doing was representing their mathematical descriptions in a special version of the Cartesian coordinate system. Although Stueckelberg originated the idea, Feynman did the final work that made the approach really usable. Therefore, the graphical representation they developed is called a Feynman diagram (figure 40, next page).

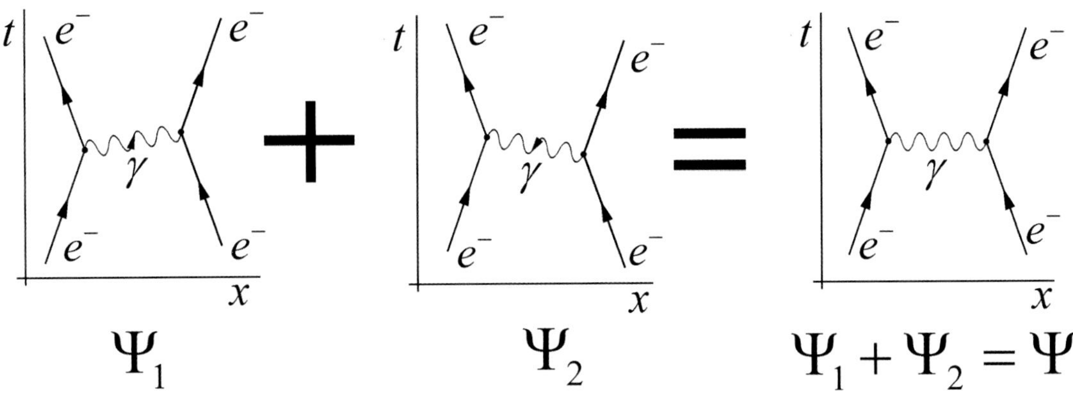

Fig. 40. Feynman Diagrams of Photon Exchange Between Electrons

A Feynman diagram is drawn in spacetime coordinates. What that means is that one axis represents time, labeled "t"; and the other represents space, labeled "x." Fermion probability amplitudes (those of quarks and leptons) are represented by straight line arrows. Photon, Z, and W boson probability amplitudes are represented by wavy lines. Gluon probability amplitudes are represented by spirals.

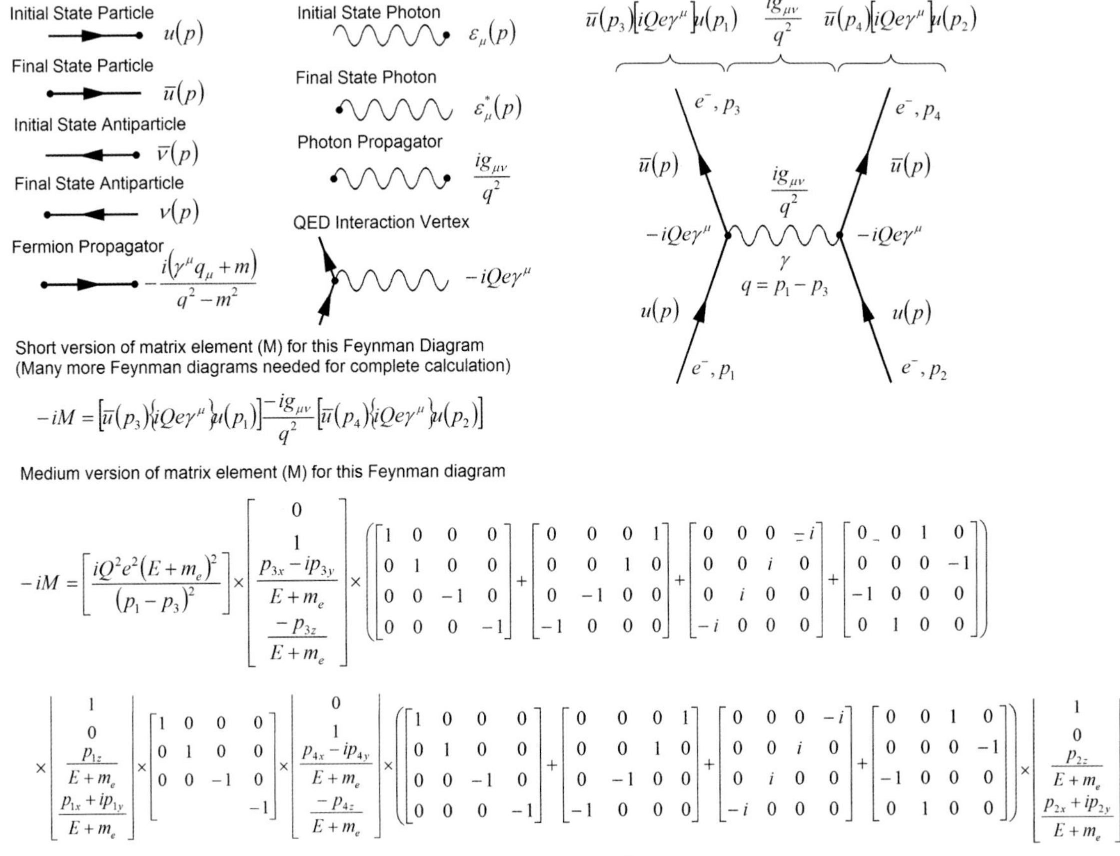

Fig. 41. Feynman Diagrams Represent Mathematics

The key thing that makes Feynman diagrams work for particle physics is a set of rules for drawing the arrows, and in particular, rules for the intersections of the arrows (which are called interaction vertices). One of the rules required for the whole thing to work is that the arrows for antimatter particles (representing the mathematics) have to be drawn in the negative time direction (pointing downward in the diagrams above).

The rules for the intersections (interaction vertices) are partly based on conservation laws. Conservation laws mean that some physical quantities do not change in the quantum state particle interactions that are represented by interaction vertices. The kinds of particles that leave an interaction vertex may not be the same as the ones that came in, but conservation laws (almost) always hold. At least, they (almost) always have.

I have already mentioned a couple of conserved physical quantities, momentum and mass-energy charge. Here is the whole list (from Wikipedia) of physical conservation laws:

Conservation of linear momentum
Conservation of angular momentum (includes particle "spin")
Conservation of mass-energy charge (gravitational force)
Conservation of electric charge (electromagnetic force)
Conservation of color charge (strong nuclear force)
Conservation of weak isospin (weak nuclear force)
Conservation of probability density (abstract quantum mechanics quantity)
Conservation of charge/parity/time conjugation (CPT) symmetry (particle decay)
Conservation of Lorentz Symmetry (indistinguishable inertial frames)[1]

A few additional quantities are conserved in particle decay interactions. I left them off of the above list because they have no known physical meaning. At our current level of knowledge, they are more like bookkeeping entries in the calculations.

The "almost" qualifier for the conservation laws is due to Heisenberg uncertainty. Complementary attributes can (and do) violate conservation for short intervals that are based on the Heisenberg uncertainty relations. Here are those relations again:

1 "Conservation Law." Retrieved c. 2014 from https://en.wikipedia.org/wiki/Conservation_law.

$$\Delta x \Delta p \geq \frac{h}{4\pi}$$

$$\Delta E \Delta t \geq \frac{h}{4\pi}$$

x = position
p = momentum (= m × v)
h = Planck's constant
π = ratio of the circumference of a circle to its diameter
E = energy
t = time

One of the effects of Heisenberg uncertainty is that conservation of momentum can be violated for short distances and conservation of energy can be violated for short times. More about that later.

Emmy Noether's Theorem

There is a bit of theoretical physics relating to conservation laws that I want to share here. This is part of the mathematical viewpoint offered by modern physics, a viewpoint that might lend credence to the speculation that our world might have a mathematical basis.

In 1918, mathematician Emmy Noether published a proof for the following theorem:

> *Any differentiable symmetry of the physical action of a system has a corresponding conservation law.*

In physics, the term *symmetry* means, among other things, something that does not change. What Noether's theorem means is that for any physical event that does not change, there must be a corresponding conservation law. In order for an experiment in physics (or any physical event) to have the same results in two different locations or times, some related physical process must be enforcing the same behavior in both locations. In our spacetime, it is the conservation laws that force physical events to behave in consistent ways whenever and wherever they happen.

Remember the complementary particle attributes from the section on Heisenberg uncertainty?

> Position is complementary to linear momentum.
> Orientation is complementary to angular momentum.
> Time is complementary to energy.

It turns out that those same pairings apply for Noether's theorem:

> In order for physical events to happen the same way at different positions, linear momentum must be conserved.
>
> In order for physical events to happen the same way in different orientations, angular momentum must be conserved.
>
> In order for physical events to happen the same way at different times, mass-energy charge must be conserved.

A Mystery of Quantum Mechanics

> *"We describe the Universe by combining fields to form a Lagrangian density L[ϕ(x)]. Our canonical quantization process often allows us to quantize these fields leading to a Universe pictured as a vacuum operated on by field operators like* □$_p^{\dagger}$*. The excitations of the vacuum that the field operators produce are particles and antiparticles."*—Lancaster and Blundell, *Quantum Field Theory for the Gifted Amateur*

There is some debate in the physics community about the implications of the mathematics for quantum field theory. The story we just went through with particles exchanging bosons associated with each of the four forces is a very common way for physicists to describe the process of momentum exchange interactions (forces). Despite the strangeness imbued by violations of energy conservation, the story has a comforting sort of normalcy to it, a reassurance of reality (once one is accustomed to it).

Yet, in a very fundamental way, the story of forces caused by the physical exchange of bosons is dead flat wrong. Remember that our goal is to understand how this world works, not just to slide through the physics as painlessly as possible. Explaining the flaws in the boson exchange model is going to require that we go fairly deep into the details of the mathematics of quantum mechanics. Dear readers, this section may be a challenge to follow, but the aspect of quantum mechanics described here is important. It tells us something very basic about the true nature of our universe.

One part of the speculation offered throughout this book is that our universe might have a mathematical basis. What follows is, in my opinion, a strong argument in favor of a mathematically based reality.

(The argument in this section is an abbreviated version of the much more complete description given by Jonathan Allday in *Quantum Reality, Theory and Philosophy*. For readers interested in a better, much more thorough description, I strongly recommend his very excellent book.)

The probability amplitude function for a particle is a sum of terms that describe the possible states for the particle, with a factor for each term that is a sort of complex (x + yi) square root of the probability that the particle will be in that state if it is measured. A state for a particle is a specific set of values for location (x, y, z, ict), orientation, and momentum/energy (p_x, p_y, p_z, E/c). The range of possible states and the values for their complex coefficients will depend on the physical surroundings of the particle. As was mentioned before, for an electron in a hydrogen atom, the possible states are spherical harmonics, as shown in the figure at the right.

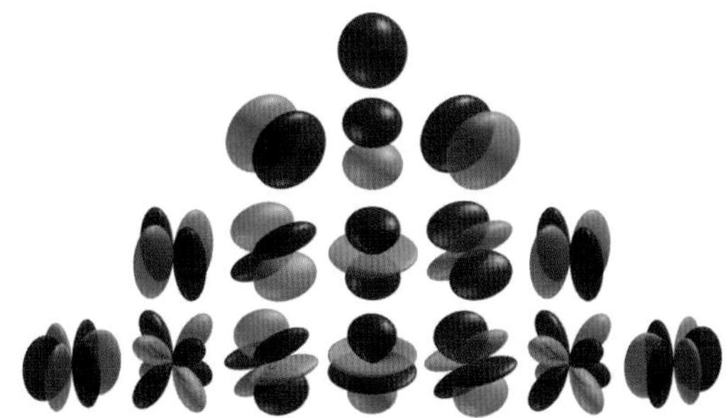

Fig. 42. Spherical Harmonics

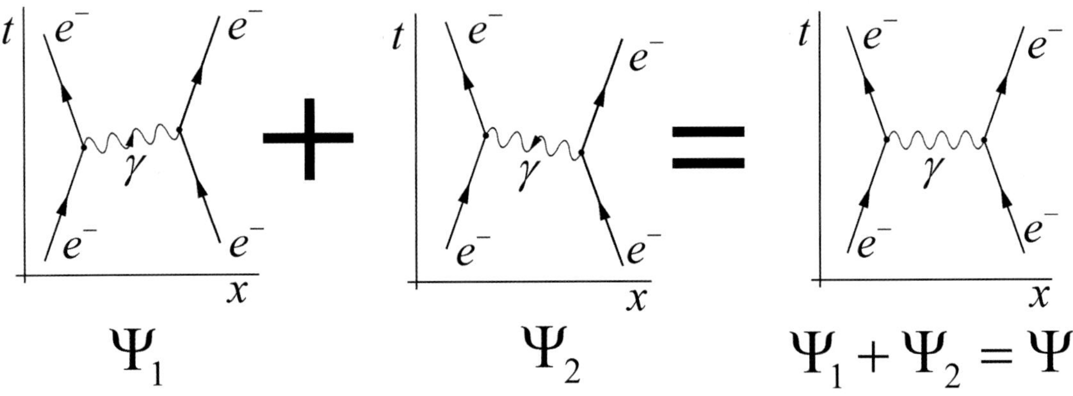

Fig. 42.1. Feynman Diagrams of Photon Exchange Between Electrons

For the much simpler case of two electrons repelling each other, as in the Feynman diagram (Fig. 42.1), some of the possible states can be represented as shown in the diagram on the right. The idea of the diagram is that this system (two electrons repelling each other) can be thought of as some

x

$\Psi_1(x,y,z,t)$	γ	$\Psi_1(x,y,z,t)$	γ
$\Psi_2(x,y,z,t)$	γ	$\Psi_2(x,y,z,t)$	e- γ γ
$\Psi_3(x,y,z,t)$	e- γ	$\Psi_3(x,y,z,t)$	γ
$\Psi_4(x,y,z,t)$		$\Psi_4(x,y,z,t)$	
$\Psi_5(x,y,z,t)$	γ γ γ	$\Psi_5(x,y,z,t)$	γ γ γ
$\Psi_6(x,y,z,t)$	e- γ	$\Psi_6(x,y,z,t)$	
$\Psi_7(x,y,z,t)$		$\Psi_7(x,y,z,t)$	e-
$\Psi_8(x,y,z,t)$		$\Psi_8(x,y,z,t)$	

t

number of particles that occupy available probability amplitudes. The two e^- symbols represent the electrons. The squiggly y symbol is the lowercase Greek letter gamma, which is the standard symbol for a photon. The distribution of particles in the available probability amplitudes shifts as the particles are affected by the interaction and their momentums and energies change. Notice the time and space axes as well.

The diagram shows two electrons and some number of photons, which may or may not be involved in the force interaction. One rule for this type of system representation (called a Fock state after the Russian physicist Vladimir Fock, who originally developed the idea—we should all banish those unseemly thoughts from our minds immediately) is that there can be only one electron per Fock state (available probability amplitude) because electrons are fermions and are subject to Pauli exclusion. There can be as many photons in each Fock state as we like, because photons are bosons and are not affected by Pauli exclusion.

Fock state representation can be handy because, like Feynman diagrams which help us keep track of the number and kinds of operators, they help us keep track of the numbers and kinds of terms in the probability amplitude functions (Ψ), especially in systems that have multiple particles like our sample here. But Fock states can be counted in a couple of different ways. We'll call one way the particle tracking approach, and we'll call the other way the state population approach.

In the particle tracking approach, particles are considered to be distinct objects that "move" from state to state. In this case, the condition shown on the left side of our Fock state diagram would actually represent several distinct states of the system. The particles would have identities like electron A and electron B, and there would be two electron states (either electron A in state 3 and electron B in state 6, or electron B in state 3 and electron A in state 6), plus many states for the various combinations of photon distributions.

In the state population approach, the particles are all identical. No one can tell electron A from electron B. There is only one Fock state for the condition on the left side of the diagram: the one with one photon in state 1, one photon in state 2, one electron and one photon in state 3, etc. In the particle tracking approach, particles, like electrons, are (mathematically) distinct objects. In the state population approach, particles are (mathematically) not distinct objects at all; they are more like bookkeeping markers within states.

During the early development of quantum mechanics, there was a bit of a struggle to figure out how it could be used to derive mathematical models that matched observations of the real, physical world. One day, Indian physicist Satyendra Nath Bose (both bosons and Bose-Einstein condensates are named in his honor) was giving a lecture intended to demonstrate the difficulties involved by showing that quantum mechanics produced an incorrect equation for a particular experimental result. (In this case, the distribution of photon frequencies for black body radiation.) To his embarrassment, after working through the derivation he arrived at the correct, experimentally derived equation.

Knowing that there had to be a mistake in there somewhere, he went back through his lecture notes and discovered he had erred in counting up electron states. At that point, he asked the right question: Why would a mistake in counting electron states produce a correct answer?

After some effort, Bose discovered that one reason quantum mechanics calculations had not been working was that physicists had exclusively been using the particle tracking approach to count up particle states. Only the state population approach to counting particle states works to produce accurate mathematical models of real-world physical behavior.

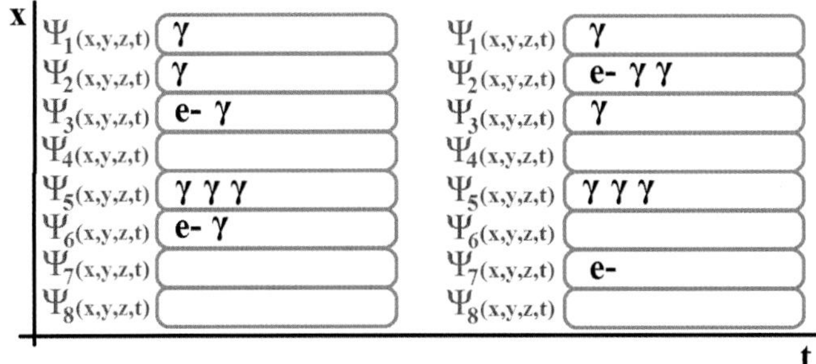

The common description given earlier, of momentum exchange interactions as particles emit and absorb bosons, implies that there exists a boson probability amplitude that physically moves from one particle to the other particle. In our Fock state diagram for the two-electron system, for example, it would imply that:

a photon comes into existence in state 6,
the photon moves to state 5 while the electron in state 6 moves to state 7 in obedience to conservation laws,
the photon continues through state 4 to state 3,
where it meets the electron in state 3 and vanishes,

changing the momentum and energy of the state 3 electron,
which then moves to state 2.

As clean as it sounds, however, the process described above does not physically happen. Mathematical models based on the above behavior do not accurately describe what physicists are able to measure in experiments. Rather, what does work is a process described by mathematics in which the exchange of momentum and/or energy between the state 6 electron probability amplitude and the state 3 electron probability amplitude is accompanied by the subtraction of a photon probability amplitude from state 6 and the addition of a photon probability amplitude to state 3 (or vice versa). The mathematics tells us that photons definitely do not move from electron to electron, passing through the positions in between. They disappear from and appear in spatially separated quantum states.

The message of quantum mechanics is that the objects that we think of as particles and material really exist as probability amplitudes. They only become the kind of things we think of as material when our conscious minds interact with them by measurement, perception, or choice.

As we have so far described the behavior of particle probability amplitudes, it may seem as though they act kind of like tiny little billiard balls. But Bose's discovery tells us that probability amplitudes do not act like billiard balls. They do not have trajectories; they do not move from position A to position B, sequentially occupying the positions in between. They do not have any kind of individual existence. Particle probability amplitudes disappear here and appear there. These disappearing and appearing particles have similar values of attributes like position, orientation, momentum, and energy because the similarity is enforced by conservation laws.

It is all very mathematical. It's almost as if the fundamental elements of our existence are not particles at all, but are quantum states: as if the particles are just bookkeeping entries in a ledger of quantum states.

As we continue, I will still describe particles as if they are some kind of real objects for the same reason that everyone, including almost all physicists, describes them that way: it makes the whole thing a lot more familiar and easier to understand. But we should all keep tucked away in the backs of our minds that they really aren't. Reality is nothing like we think it is.

Fundamental Particle Sizes

The theories, or mathematical models, of particle physics describe the behavior of particles: they describe what particles do, not what particles are. Until they are detected, the particles are all in quantum state with behavior described as superposition and interference of probability amplitudes. As I mentioned earlier, nobody knows what the physical reality is for quantum mechanics generally, and that is still very much true for particles.

One of the things that particle physicists *are* able to measure, this time in particle accelerators, is the diameters of objects. Diameters are often described as a charge radius, because what is actually measured is a volume that is influenced by charges. (Think of the diamond nucleus we discussed earlier.) Particles that are groups of fundamental particles, such as atomic nuclei, baryons like protons and neutrons, and mesons, all have a measurable charge radius. The fundamental particles themselves (quarks, leptons, and bosons) do not have any measurable radius.

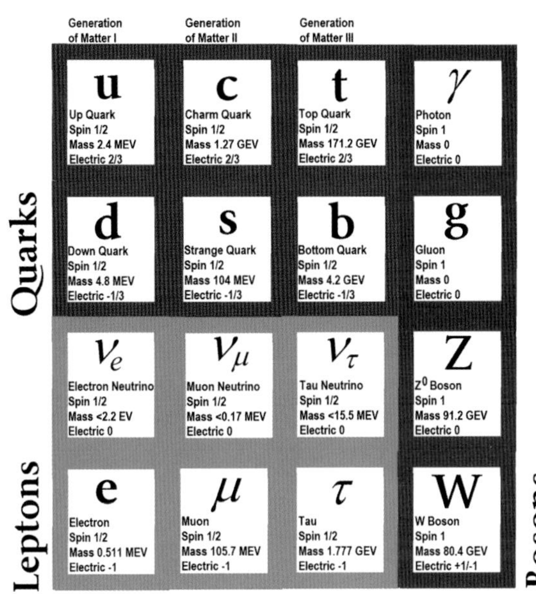

Fig. 43. Fundamental Particles of the Standard Model

Remember the de Broglie relationship between the wavelength of a quantum state object and its momentum:

$$\lambda = \frac{h}{mv} = \frac{h}{p}$$

λ = wavelength
h = Planck's constant
m = mass
v = velocity
p = momentum (= m × v)

In order for physicists to be able to "see" an object in a particle accelerator, the particle wavelengths must be smaller than the object. The reason that physicists want to build bigger and bigger particle accelerators (aside from the paychecks) is so they can push particles faster (generating greater momentum, p) so that the wavelength will get smaller and they can "see" smaller stuff.

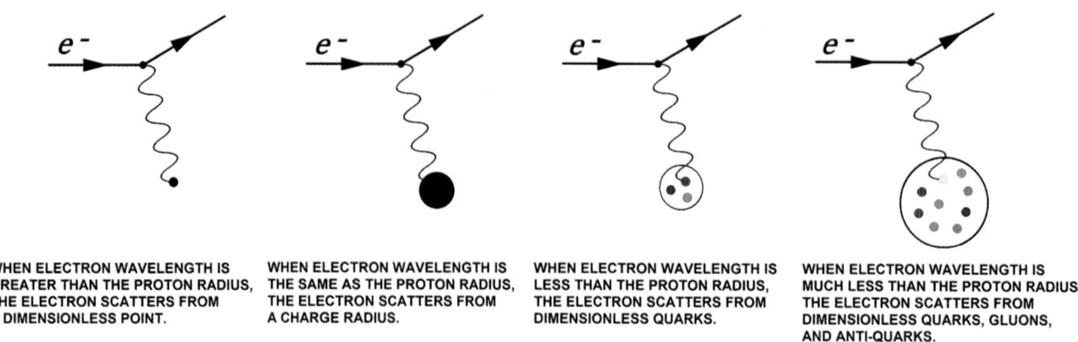

e⁻
e⁻
e⁻
e⁻
WHEN ELECTRON WAVELENGTH IS GREATER THAN THE PROTON RADIUS, THE ELECTRON SCATTERS FROM A DIMENSIONLESS POINT.
WHEN ELECTRON WAVELENGTH IS THE SAME AS THE PROTON RADIUS, THE ELECTRON SCATTERS FROM A CHARGE RADIUS.
WHEN ELECTRON WAVELENGTH IS LESS THAN THE PROTON RADIUS, THE ELECTRON SCATTERS FROM DIMENSIONLESS QUARKS.
WHEN ELECTRON WAVELENGTH IS MUCH LESS THAN THE PROTON RADIUS, THE ELECTRON SCATTERS FROM DIMENSIONLESS QUARKS, GLUONS, AND ANTI-QUARKS.

Fig. 44. Scattering Changes as Electron Energy Increases.

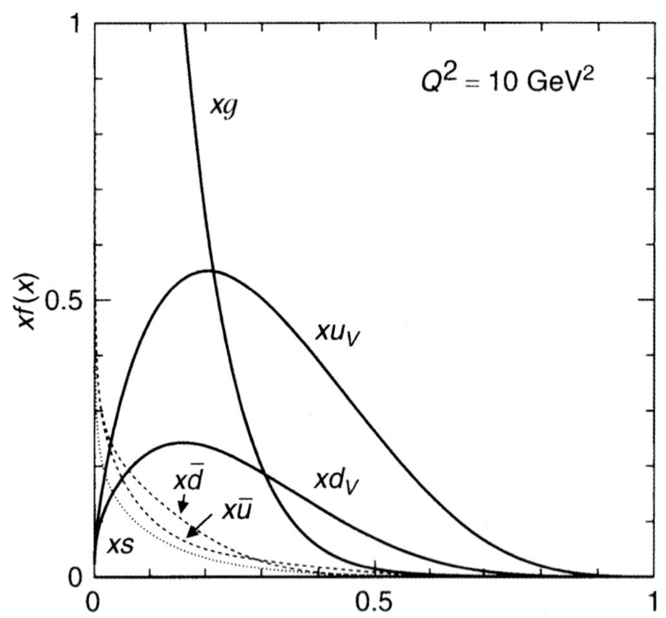

Fig. 45. Proton Particle Distributions

At low electron energy (lower momentum = longer wavelength) the proton "looks" like a dimensionless point charge. At higher energies (higher momentum = shorter wavelengths) the proton starts to "show" a measurable radius. When the electron wavelength is smaller than the proton radius, the electron scatters by interactions with the individual quarks.

The physical existence of quarks was confirmed in 1968 when the Stanford Linear Accelerator (SLAC) was able to produce particles with wavelengths less than 10^{-15} m. At that wavelength, the "image" of a proton shifted from that of a single point charge to an "image" of a group of smaller charges (the quarks).

At the present time, particle accelerators can "see" objects with diameters of 10^{-18} m, about 1/1000 the size of a proton. At that resolution, the fundamental particles all still look like point charges, with no discernible size.

Earlier, I mentioned that hadron (quark group) particles often exist as mixtures of fundamental particles called statistical ensembles. A proton, for example, is usually considered to be a hadron with two up quarks and one down quark, but the quarks constantly fluctuate into other types of particles.

The figure to the left (figure 45) shows a measured distribution of fundamental particles for the average proton with its radius on the horizontal axis. Xu_v and xd_v are the distributions for the up quark and down quarks. Xg is the distribution for the gluon strong force interaction bosons. Xd and xu with the bars over them are distributions of anti-down and anti-up quarks. Xs is the distribution of strange quarks.

One comment, for accuracy: I use the terms "see" and "image" in the description above because they are useful ways to describe the results of particle accelerator experiments. Particle accelerators don't actually produce anything that anyone but a particle physicist would recognize as an image. The data are actually the statistical distributions for directions, energies, and types of scattered particles. The mathematical models that make up the standard model of particle physics are mostly used to predict scattering distributions, interaction probabilities, and particle decay rules.

The mathematics of the standard model treats the fundamental particles (quarks, leptons, and bosons) as if they are all dimensionless points. This is not only because they "look" like points in particle accelerator experiments; it is also because the mathematics of the standard model do not work if they are *not* dimensionless points.

In the early development of the mathematics for particle physics, Heisenberg, Dirac, and others tried to develop mathematical models for fundamental particles that were blobs instead of points; none of them worked. The only "objects" that have worked so far are the dimensionless (0 dimension) points in the standard model, and one dimensional "strings" (in string theories and M theory—though these only "sort of" work).

Either way, the only objects that work for the physics—that match what we see in the world—are mathematical abstracts; not anything that anyone might ordinarily think of as a "real" "object."

Spontaneous Interactions Decrease Energy

Fundamental particles decay, changing from one type of particle into other types of particles in interactions that are given a "direction" in time by mass-energy charge. In the chart for fundamental particles, quarks and leptons are divided into three generations of matter. Equivalent particles (particles in the same horizontal row) for each generation have the same color charge, electric charge, and weak isospin charge, but the mass-energy charge increases. The generation II charm quark has a higher mass-

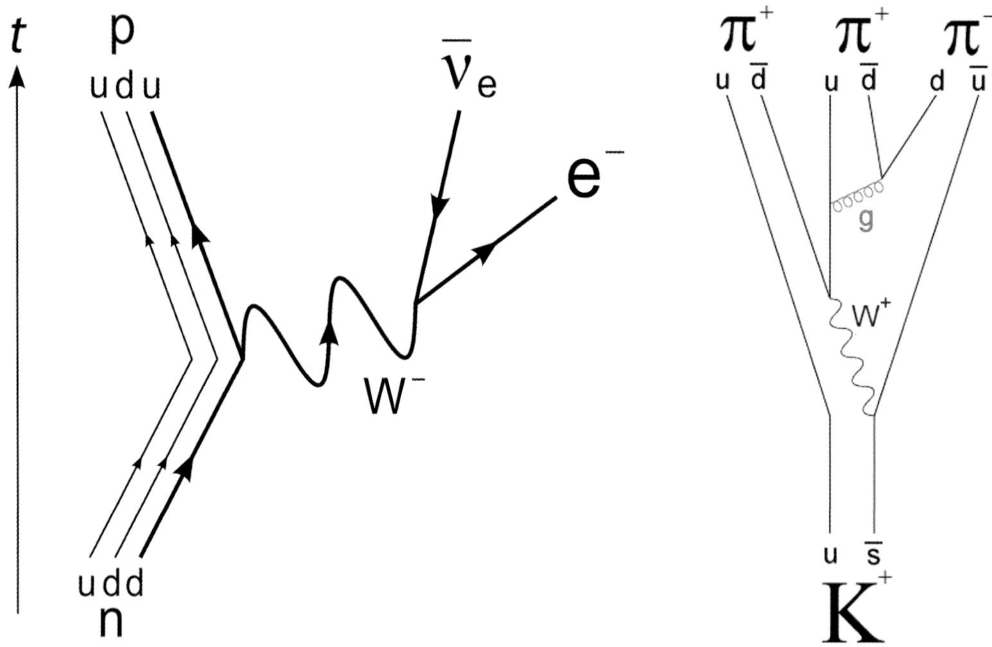

Fig. 46. Particle Decays, Free Neutron, and Kaon

energy charge than the generation I up quark, and the generation III top quark has a higher mass-energy charge than either the charm quark or the up quark.

In the long run, energy is always conserved in particle interactions, but the individual objects often change form. Objects with higher mass-energy charge spontaneously decay into objects with lower mass-energy charge. Objects with lower mass-energy charge will only morph into higher charge objects if energy is supplied to the interaction (in a star, for example, or by a particle accelerator).

Because of the spontaneous decay of higher mass-energy particles into lower mass-energy particles, the world we live in is almost entirely made up of generation I particles: up quarks and down quarks that compose neutrons and protons, electrons, and electron neutrinos. Generation II and generation III particles only occur in stars and particle accelerators. Even there, they quickly decay back into generation I.

All of the natural physical events we observe in the world do pretty much the same

	Generation of Matter I	Generation of Matter II	Generation of Matter III	Bosons
Quarks	**u** Up Quark, Spin 1/2, Mass 2.4 MEV, Electric 2/3	**c** Charm Quark, Spin 1/2, Mass 1.27 GEV, Electric 2/3	**t** Top Quark, Spin 1/2, Mass 171.2 GEV, Electric 2/3	γ Photon, Spin 1, Mass 0, Electric 0
Quarks	**d** Down Quark, Spin 1/2, Mass 4.8 MEV, Electric -1/3	**s** Strange Quark, Spin 1/2, Mass 104 MEV, Electric -1/3	**b** Bottom Quark, Spin 1/2, Mass 4.2 GEV, Electric -1/3	**g** Gluon, Spin 1, Mass 0, Electric 0
Leptons	ν_e Electron Neutrino, Spin 1/2, Mass <2.2 EV, Electric 0	ν_μ Muon Neutrino, Spin 1/2, Mass <0.17 MEV, Electric 0	ν_τ Tau Neutrino, Spin 1/2, Mass <15.5 MEV, Electric 0	**Z** Z^0 Boson, Spin 1, Mass 91.2 GEV, Electric 0
Leptons	**e** Electron, Spin 1/2, Mass 0.511 MEV, Electric -1	μ Muon, Spin 1/2, Mass 105.7 MEV, Electric -1	τ Tau, Spin 1/2, Mass 1.777 GEV, Electric -1	**W** W Boson, Spin 1, Mass 80.4 GEV, Electric +1/-1

thing. Driven by the strong force, quarks combine into the structures of atomic nuclei. Nuclear structures have different mass-energy charges because of differences in potential energy. Nuclear fusion in stars, fission in reactors, nuclear bombs, and radioactive isotope decays are all produced by nuclear structures with higher mass-energy charge spontaneously changing into different nuclear structures with lower mass-energy charge.

Electron probability amplitudes are pulled into standing waves around atomic nuclei by the attraction of the electric charges of the protons in the nucleus. Different standing waves have different energies. All of the light we see is made of photons that are emitted when electrons spontaneously change from higher energy standing waves to lower energy standing waves.

Electrons can form standing waves around more than one atomic nucleus. Shared electron standing waves bind atomic nuclei into the structures that we call molecules. Different molecular structures have different energies. Changes in molecular structures (we call them chemical reactions) that decrease internal energy can happen spontaneously. Energy must be supplied for chemical reactions that change lower energy molecular structures into higher energy molecular structures.

Quantum Particle Possibilities

Quantum mechanics calculations for particle interactions are always a sum of all the possible ways an interaction could occur. The net probability amplitude for an event is a superposition and interference of all of the individual probability amplitudes for the possible states of the system.

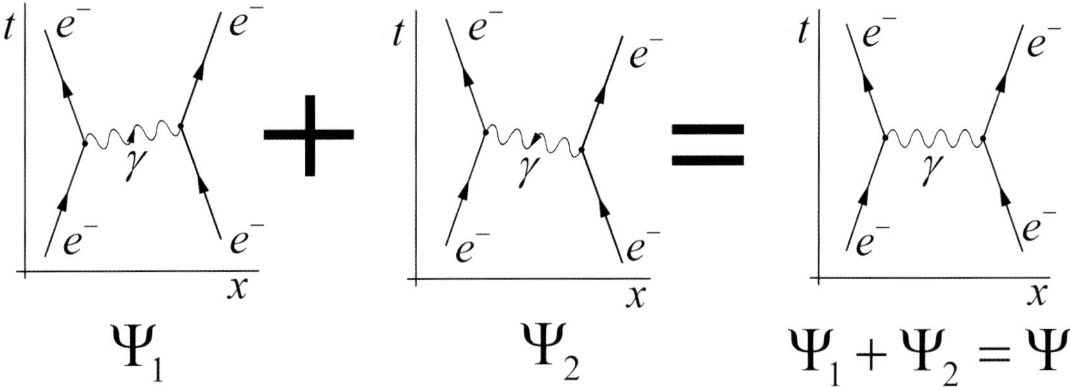

For a single particle interaction, the calculation is not represented by a single Feynman diagram; rather, the calculation is the superposition and interference of all of

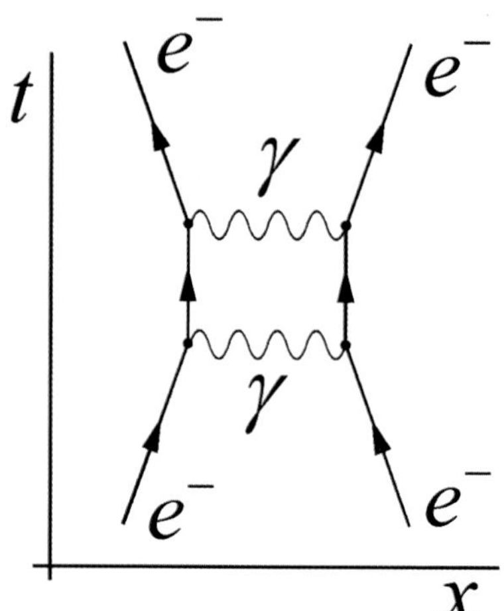

the Feynman diagrams that represent all of the possible ways the interaction could happen.

Calculations for photon interactions between electrically charged particles, for example, must include not only AB and BA directions of photon exchange (shown above), but also the possibilities for two photon exchanges, three photon exchanges, and so on.

Fortunately for physicists, calculations for photon interactions where approximate results are good enough (which is almost all real-world calculations) only need to deal with a relatively few Feynman diagrams. While there are theoretically infinite variations for photon exchanges, the probability of each variation decreases rapidly as the number of interaction vertices increases. For photon interactions, each additional interaction vertex decreases the probability of the interaction happening in that way by a factor called the fine structure constant:

$$\alpha = \frac{e^2}{2\varepsilon_0 hc} \cong \frac{1}{137}$$

α = fine structure constant
e = electric charge of an electron
ε_0 = electrical permittivity
h = Planck's constant
c = velocity of light

The usual calculations for photon interactions only need to consider a few interaction vertices because the effects of additional vertices are so very small. However, physicists occasionally spend the time to do more accurate work. The theoretical calculation for the magnetic field for an electron was originally done by Paul Dirac. Later measurements found that the calculation was incorrect by 0.1%. A more detailed calculation, with all of the Feynman diagrams having up to seven interaction vertices, agreed with the measured value to twelve decimal places. The calculation took several years.

Photon interactions are relatively simple to calculate, because photons do not have any electric charge. Calculations for gluon interactions and the strong force are much more difficult, because gluons do have color charge for the strong force.

The probabilities for Feynman diagrams with more interaction vertices don't decrease for gluons the way they do for photons. In one of the proofs for quantum chromodynamics (the mathematical model for the strong force), the physicists doing the calculation needed to demonstrate that over fifty thousand terms of equations all canceled out. T'Hooft and Veltman managed to demonstrate this in 1972 by developing a computer program to do the algebra for the cancelations.

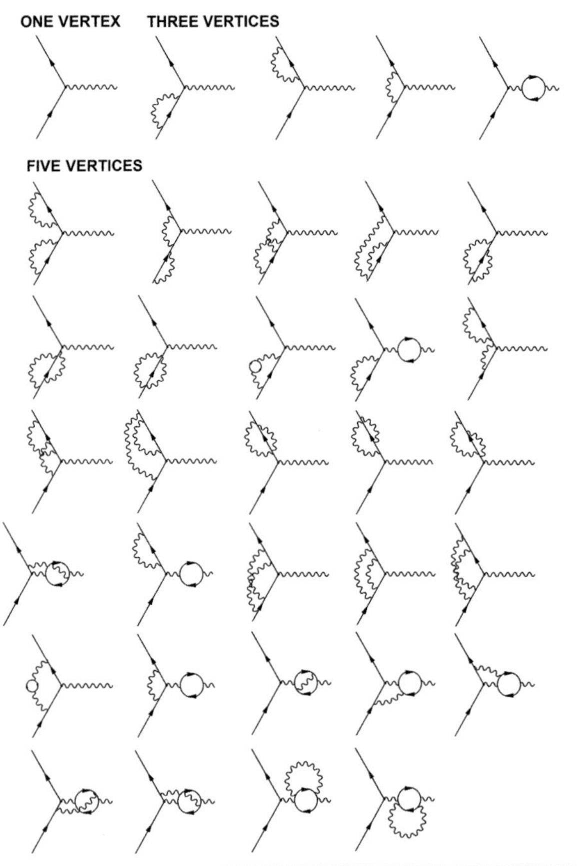

Fig. 47. Feynman Diagrams for Electron Magnetic Moment

Virtual Particles

In the basic photon exchange between two electrons, the photon (γ) is described as a virtual particle. It is considered to be virtual because it exists only for a short time; there is no photon at the beginning or the end of the process. Particles that persist over extended time, by contrast, are called real particles.

Any particle can be either real or virtual. Virtual particles can become real if there is enough energy available to provide the necessary rest mass. For example, real (not virtual) photons are emitted by electrons that change from higher energy spherical harmonic standing waves to lower energy standing waves. The photons that carry momentum for electromagnetic forces, however, are mostly virtual.

Ψ_1 + Ψ_2 = $\Psi_1 + \Psi_2 = \Psi$

This is probably a good time to remember that we are talking about quantum state particles here. Quantum state particles are not stuff; they are not what we think of as solid matter. They are waves of probability amplitudes. We are not really talking about immaterial stuff, or immaterial stuff changing into material stuff. What we are talking about are probability amplitudes that are changing the way they vibrate from one kind of possibility wave to a different kind of possibility wave.

Neutron Quark Structure

$Charge = \frac{2}{3} - \frac{1}{3} - \frac{1}{3} = 0$

Quark mass = 12.2 Mev

Measured mass = 939.6 Mev

$Spin = \frac{1}{2} - \frac{1}{2} + \frac{1}{2} = \frac{1}{2}$

Proton Quark Structure

$Charge = \frac{2}{3} + \frac{2}{3} - \frac{1}{3} = 1$

Quark mass = 9.6 Mev

Measured mass = 938.3 Mev

$Spin = \frac{1}{2} - \frac{1}{2} + \frac{1}{2} = \frac{1}{2}$

Fig. 48. Neutron and Proton Composition.

Some time back, I mentioned that the properties of neutrons and protons are time averages of the properties of different generations of quarks. Here is what that means.

A proton is a quark group with two up quarks (mass energy charge = 2.4 MeV/c^2) and a down quark (mass energy charge = 4.8 MeV/c^2). The rest mass of a proton (938.3 MeV/c^2) is considerably larger than the sum of the quark masses (9.6 MeV/c^2).

There are two reasons for the additional mass. One of them is special relativity. Remember that when objects move fast, their mass (mass-energy charge) increases. Because the change in momentum produced by strong force interactions is so high (2200 pounds per particle), quarks captured by the strong force are accelerated to really high speeds. The quarks in the average proton don't just sit around; they move at significant fractions of the speed of light (tens to hundreds of thousands of miles per hour). Most books that show atomic nuclei generally show the protons and neutrons as stationary balls all stuck together. That is not accurate; it is much more accurate to think of an atomic nucleus as a quark blizzard. Protons and neutrons are really just the form that quark groups take when we knock them out of atomic nuclei. Quark groups inside atomic nuclei constantly move and shift.

The other reason the rest mass of a proton is so high is fluctuations. The real up quarks (2.4 MeV/c^2) continuously fluctuate into virtual charm quarks (3270 MeV/c^2) and virtual top quarks (171,200 MeV/c^2). The real down quarks (4.8 MeV/c^2) continuously fluctuate into virtual strange quarks (104 MeV/c^2) and virtual bottom quarks (4200 MeV/c^2). The mass that we measure for a proton is thus partly a time-based average of the real and virtual quark masses.

The attentive reader should be calling foul here. Quark fluctuations require huge changes in mass-energy charge for the quarks. If energy is supposed to be conserved, where does all that energy come from? It doesn't actually come from anywhere. The answer is that, as I mentioned in the discussion of conservation laws, energy is only conserved in the long run. Energy is allowed to vary for short times within the limits of the Heisenberg uncertainty relation for energy and time:

$$\Delta E \Delta t \geq \frac{h}{4\pi}$$

E = *energy*
t = *time*
h = *Planck's constant*
π = *ratio of the circumference of a circle to its diameter*

Virtual particles depend on Heisenberg uncertainty for their existence. All particles require some energy in order to exist. Photons and gluons do not have rest energy (their mass-energy charge is zero), but they do have some energy as an attribute. Photons have energy proportional to their frequency (what we see as color). Gluons have potential energy because they have color charge and are subject to the strong force. The W and Z bosons for the weak nuclear force have mass energy charge, so they require much more energy to exist than photons and gluons.

Because they violate the rules of energy conservation, virtual bosons can only exist for brief amounts of time (limited by the Heisenberg uncertainty relationship for energy and time). Because they can only exist for brief times, they can only travel limited distances. The weak force only operates over short distances (basically inside atomic nuclei) because the large amount of energy required for the rest mass of W and Z bosons means that their maximum time limit is really tiny and they can't travel very far.

The same limitation applies to the version of the strong force that binds protons and neutrons into atomic nuclei. Gluon exchanges, the direct strong force, only happen inside quark group particles, inside protons and neutrons. Neutrons and protons don't exchange gluons; they continually swap quarks to exchange momentum and hold atomic nuclei together. Quarks, however, are always bound into quark groups by the strong force. No quark can ever wander around by itself, so the quark exchanges are always a two-way swap. No proton or neutron can ever have fewer than three quarks, so the two-way swap must always include one forward-time matter quark and one backward-time antimatter anti-quark. The two quarks simultaneously leave/arrive at one quark group and simultaneously arrive/leave from the other quark group.

Particles that combine a quark and an anti-quark are called mesons. Combinations of up and down quarks and anti-quarks are called Pi mesons. Pi meson exchanges inside atomic nuclei are called the residual strong force. Pi mesons that are exchanged for the residual strong force are always virtual particles. They have rest mass, so the range of the residual strong force is very short for the same reason that the range of the weak force is short: virtual Pi mesons can only exist for tiny amounts of time.

As shown in the figure, Pi meson exchanges can (and do) shift the quark compositions of the particles that exchange them, changing protons into neutrons and neutrons into protons. The total numbers of protons and neutrons always stay pretty much the same, but individuals change identities constantly.

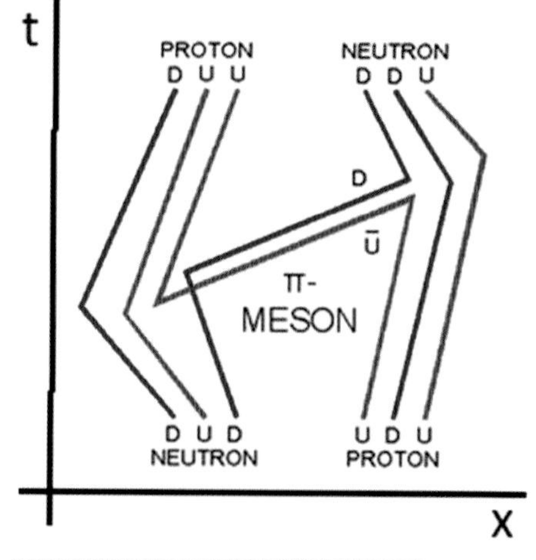

Fig. 49. Quark Exchange in Atomic Nuclei

I hope it has become apparent that atomic nuclei are very busy places!

Back in the original description of Heisenberg uncertainty, I mentioned that uncertainty has to be a fundamental characteristic of quantum state particles; it is not just an inaccuracy of measurement. This is what that statement means: quantum state particle attributes, like energy and time, have to really exist as probability distributions in order for the forces that hold our universe together to operate. Without fundamental, real uncertainty to allow the existence of virtual particles, this universe would literally fall apart.

There is a term in physics for virtual particles that temporarily violate energy conservation; they are referred to as being "off mass shell." The phrase is also used as a kind of insult in the physics community. It is applied to physicists who propose really goofy theories. I hope it is not surprising that the phrase could (accurately) be used here to describe many parts of this speculation in physics and theology. Some of us derive satisfaction from being off mass shell.

Theology from Particle Interactions

> *"In the beginning God created the heaven and the earth. And the earth was without form, and void; and darkness was upon the face of the deep. And the Spirit of God moved upon the face of the waters. And God said, Let there be light; and there was light. And God saw the light, that it was good: and God divided the light from the darkness. And God called the light Day, and the darkness he called Night. And the evening and the morning were the first day. And God said 'Let there be a firmament in the midst of the waters, and let it divide the waters from the waters.'"*—Genesis 1:1–6

This, I think, is a good time to take a short break from physics and do a little theology. We are most of the way down the rabbit hole here; there is only a little further to go.

Consider light. Light plays a pretty sizable role in Scripture. According to Genesis, before light was created, the earth was without form and void. After light was created and sorted out, the creation began to take on substance and form.

Consider light illuminated by particle physics. Particle physics informs us that light is photons. Particle physics also informs us that photons are much more than just visible or invisible light. Photons are the electromagnetic forces that bind atoms into the structures we think of as stuff. Crystals, minerals, and rocks all exist because of photons. Molecules, substances, and chemical reactions all happen because of photons. Photons are the glue that holds the atoms of our universe together to make stuff.

If we make a slight extension to include all of the bosons in a broader concept of light, then, in an allegorical sense, atoms themselves can also be thought of as held together by light.

So Scripture is compatible here with particle physics. Before matter and substance can exist, there must be light.

Vacuum Fluctuations

Fluctuations are changes in the properties of quantum state particles, which as we have seen, can change the identity of those particles. Quarks can fluctuate into different quarks. Electrons can fluctuate into other leptons. And as it turns out, the mathematics of particle physics also predicts that force exchange particles (bosons) can fluctuate into structural particles (fermions).

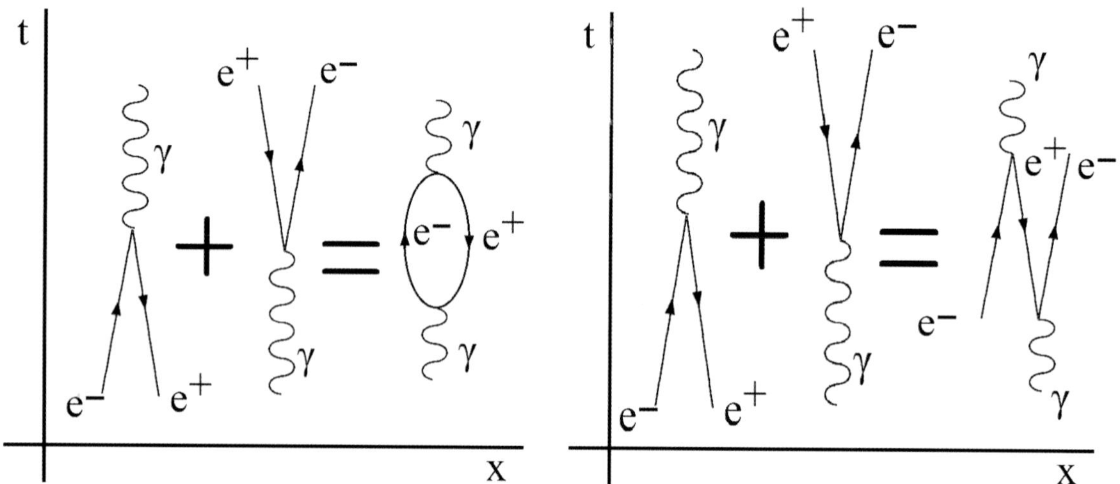

Fig. 50. Pair Annihilation and Creation

The Feynman diagrams on the left side of the figure show the interactions that allow the transitions from bosons to fermions and back to bosons. The Feynman diagrams on the right show differing points of view on what this means.

Boson fluctuations will now take us into an area where the Feynman-Stueckelberg interpretation for antimatter plays a role. Specifically, the interpretation affects our *story* about what is actually happening.

The consensus view of the physics community is that Feynman-Stueckelberg is only a mathematical convention. Antimatter particles don't really go backward in time. So the official story is that bosons can fluctuate into pairs of fermions, and pairs of fermions can fluctuate into bosons. Pairs of fermions, one matter and one antimatter, are always required for conservation of charges. The left Feynman diagram in the figure represent the standard interpretation.

Boson fluctuation into a fermion and an anti-fermion is called pair creation. Fermion pairs that fluctuate into bosons is called pair annihilation. Tying the two together creates a neat little circle that is called a vacuum fluctuation. In vacuum fluctuations, the fermion pairs are considered to be virtual particles; they exist only temporarily.

The deviant view (hence, my favorite one), that Feynman-Stueckelberg is physically real, gives a slightly different picture. The interactions are the same and the mathematics are the same, but the particles don't always tie up into neat little circles, and they are not necessarily virtual. If antimatter particles really do travel backward in time, then the boson-fermion interactions aren't necessarily creations and annihilations. They may also be time reversals (just as they appear to be in the Feynman diagram).

The story according to Feynman-Stueckelberg vs. the official story of annihilation and creation is really more of a quibble than a major disagreement. Pair creation and annihilation can still happen in Feynman-Stueckelberg: they are just not necessarily the entire story. The implications of the two differing viewpoints are minor for the consequences of vacuum fluctuations (our current topic). When we get to cosmology, we may find their differing implications are a greater concern.

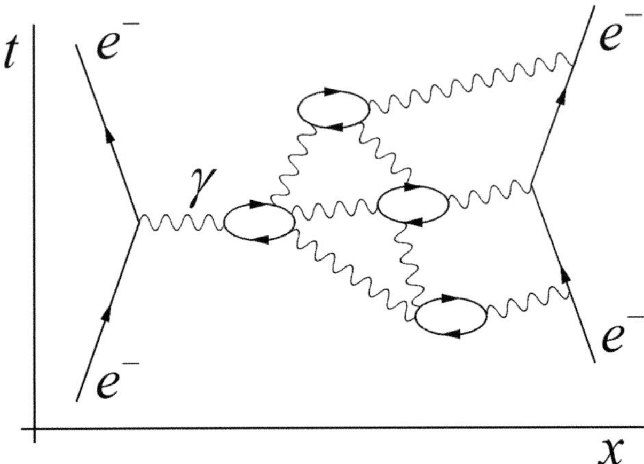

Fig. 51. Photon Vacuum Fluctuations

Vacuum fluctuations complicate the calculations for photon exchanges. The problem is that even though the fine structure constant (1/137) decreases the probabilities for Feynman diagrams with more interaction vertices, there is no limit on the number of different ways that boson-fermion interactions can occur.

We need a little bit of mathematics here to get an accurate picture of what happens in quantum mechanics calculations. Sums of an infinite number of terms are a common feature of the mathematics used in physics calculations (especially in quantum mechanics); they are called infinite series. Infinite series have been used in mathematics since the ancient Greeks (Archimedes used an infinite series in his estimate of the value of π). Some infinite series work well and give useful answers; the mathematics terminology for this is that the value of a series (the sum of all of its terms) converges to a finite result, a useful number. Other series are described as diverging, meaning that the sum increases to infinity. Small differences in the terms of an infinite series can swing it from converging (giving useful answers) to diverging (giving useless, infinite answers).

The infinite series of Feynman diagrams for straight photon exchanges (one photon, two photons, three photons, etc. ad infinitum)—with no vacuum fluctuations involved—produces a convergent infinite series: a sum of terms that adds up to an answer that represents a valid probability distribution (a positive number less than 1).

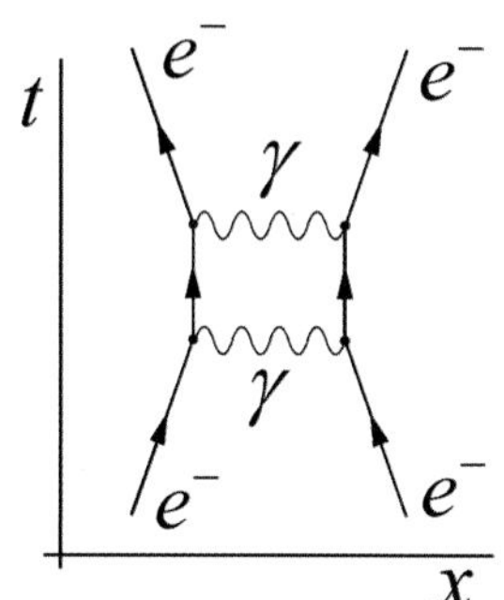

The infinite series of Feynman diagrams for photon exchanges with vacuum fluctuations included, on the other hand, never converges to a useful answer. They always diverge to infinity.

The divergent effects of vacuum fluctuations were first identified in the 1930s by Jordan, Born, Heisenberg, and Dirac (the guys who, along with Schrodinger, first developed quantum mechanics). The sensible thing to do, of course, was just to ignore vacuum fluctuations. Quantum mechanics calculations were producing results that were unlocking the secrets of the universe in a very real way. Nuclear power, laser beams, semiconductor physics to make integrated circuits: these all came out of quantum mechanics. Quantum mechanics provided answers everywhere. Mysteries that physicists had seen in their measurements and experiments for centuries tumbled like dominos.

The problem was, the calculations weren't quite right. The answers were close enough to yield working results, but they were just a little bit off. Earlier I mentioned that Dirac's calculation of the magnetic moment for an electron

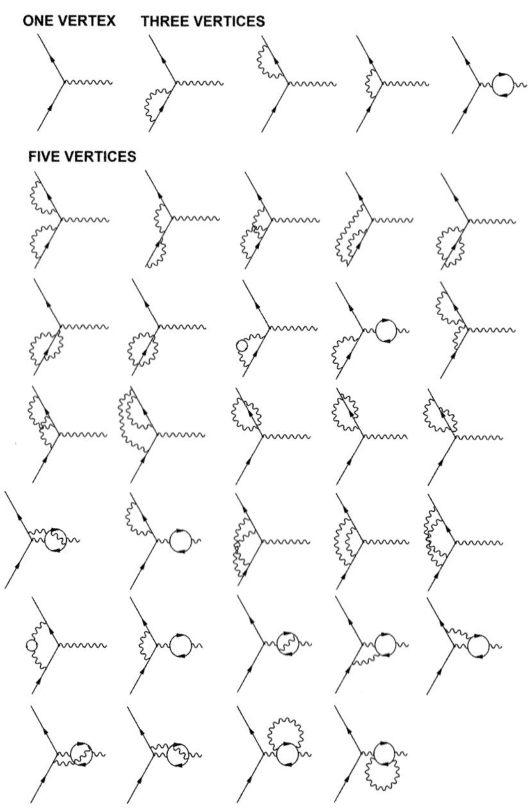

Fig. 51.2.
Feynman Diagrams for Electron Moment

was wrong by 0.1 percent (1/1000). That kind of tiny error was common.

It turns out that vacuum fluctuations have to be included in order for us to get the right answers. Looking closely at the Feynman diagrams for the calculations that finally gave the correct result for electron magnetic moment, you can see that several of them include vacuum fluctuations (the circles, figure 51.2, previous page).

Stueckelberg, Feynman, Schwinger, Tomonaga, and Dyson showed how to include vacuum fluctuations in quantum mechanics in the late 1940s when they developed a mathematical approach called renormalization.

The trick is to realize that what we can see and measure is not the individual little photons and electrons. Because we are so large ourselves, all we can really see is the big picture. Vacuum fluctuations form a cloud of virtual photons and electrons around the real photons and electrons (see figure 51.3). In the same way that the protons and neutrons we measure are summations of the real quarks plus heavier virtual quarks, the electrons and photons we measure are the summations of both real and virtual particles.

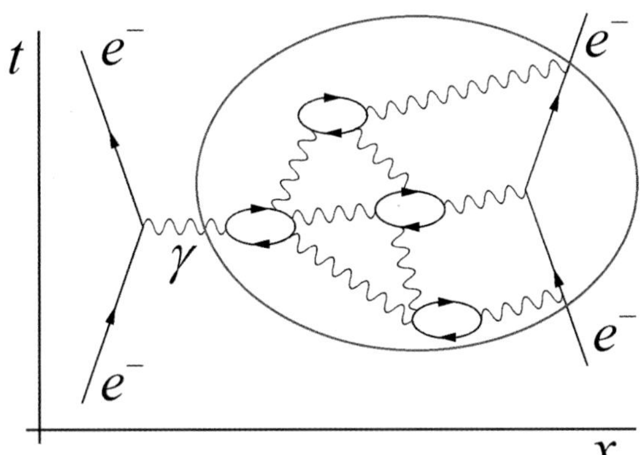

Fig. 51.3. Renormalization groups vacuum fluctuations.

Mathematically, when the divergent series that describe photon exchanges with vacuum fluctuations are added together in larger groups, enough terms from different series cancel out that the sum of infinities goes back to being a nice convergent probability distribution.

Earlier I mentioned that t'Hooft and Veltman did a proof in 1972 that required cancelling out over fifty thousand terms in Feynman diagrams. The proof they were working on was a demonstration of renormalization for gluon/quark vacuum fluctuations. They were successful, by the way.

There is some experimental support for the real, physical existence of vacuum fluctuations. The fundamental interaction, pair creation (or time reversal), is predicted by theory and was first observed in the

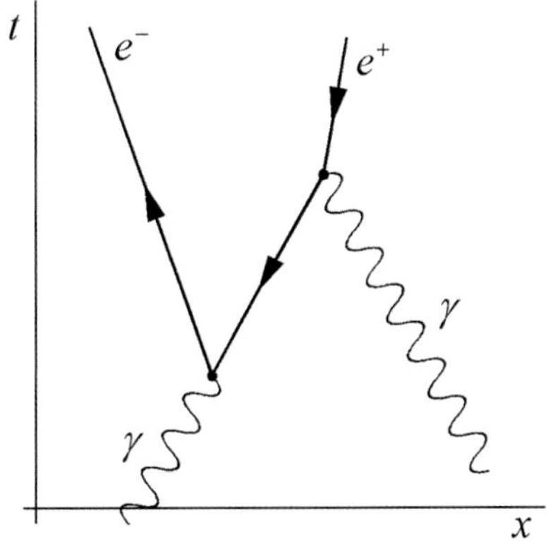

Fig. 52. Electron Pair Creation

particle accelerator at SLAC in 1995 by Melissinos. As shown in the figure, real (not virtual) pair creation requires two photons in order to preserve energy and momentum conservation.

Hendrik Casimir did a calculation in 1948 that predicted a small attractive force between two conductive metal plates when they are very close together (<0.0001 inch or so). Casimir's original calculation was done based on Van der Waal's forces (not really relevant here), but later calculations attributed the force to vacuum fluctuations. The Casimir Effect was experimentally confirmed in 1996 by Lamoreaux with the value predicted by Casimir.

Another proof for vacuum fluctuations is based on a behavior that is common for clouds of electrically charged particles; it is called charge screening. In our big world, we often see molecules and atoms form clouds of charged particles. Molecules that dissolve in water frequently break up into smaller bits; that's part of what dissolving is. The little bits often keep numbers of electrons that don't match the numbers of protons in their atomic nuclei, so they often have a net positive (too few electrons) or negative (too many electrons) electric charge. Atoms or molecules with electrical charge are called ions (a cute little name: "i" is the physics symbol for electric current; "on" is a suffix that means particle). Chemical ions dissolved in water move and flow in response to electric fields. Electroplating, for example, is done by putting an electric charge on an object so that it will attract chemical ions to come and bond to its surface.

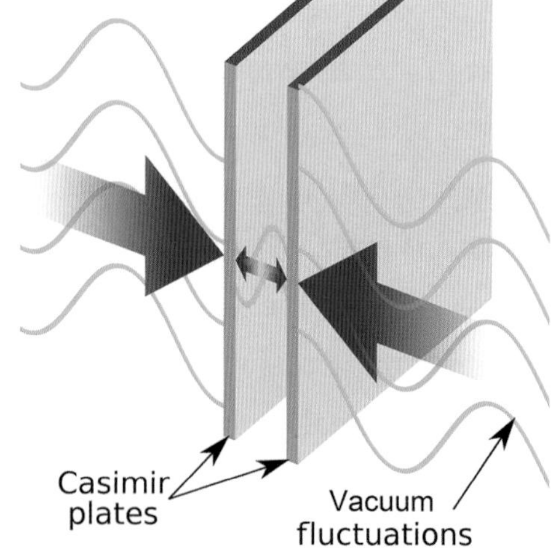

Fig. 53. Casimir Effect

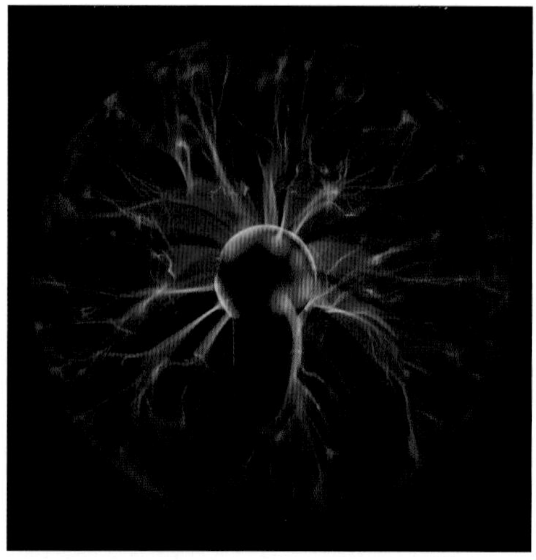

Fig. 54. Plasma.
Illustration © 2004 Luc Viatour.
Reprinted under CC BY-SA 2.5.

Ions also happen in gases under certain conditions (low pressure and strong electric fields); ions in gases are called plasma. In neon signs and fluorescent lights, the stuff that produces the light is plasma.

When particles with electrical charges are

free to move or flow in response to an electric force field, they always move to cancel out the field; the field diminishes or disappears as if the charge were hidden behind a screen. If clouds of charged virtual particles physically exist, and if they do surround real charged particles, they would be expected to behave in the same way. They would screen the charge of the real particles so the net charge of the cloud is less than the charge of the actual real particle (called the bare charge). We measure the net charge, not the bare charge.

Physicists have tested the behavior of charges using the de Broglie relationship between particle momentum and the wavelength of the probability amplitude:

$$\lambda = \frac{h}{mv} = \frac{h}{p}$$

λ = wavelength
h = Planck's constant
m = mass
v = velocity
p = momentum (= m × v)

Electric charges for electrons do increase in particle accelerators as the wavelengths of colliding probability amplitudes get smaller at higher speeds. The smaller wavelengths "see" less of the cloud surrounding the real particles, so there is less screening for the charge. The physics term for this behavior, where we see increasing electric charge at smaller wavelengths, is charge running.

The description above mostly refers to electrons and electric charge. However, electric charge is not the only charge that runs; the same is true for other particle charges. Color charge and weak isospin charge also run, but they decrease in strength as colliding particles are accelerated to higher momentum and shorter probability amplitude wavelength. Unlike photons, the bosons that mediate the strong and weak nuclear forces carry the charges for their forces, so the total charge decreases as the cloud gets smaller.

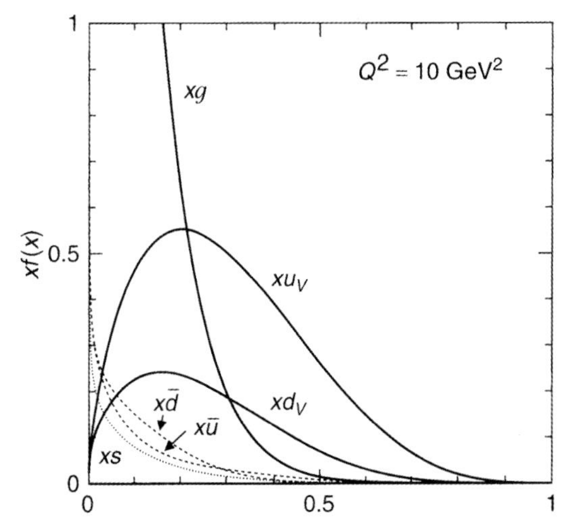

Fig. 55. Proton Fundamental Particle Distributions. Copyright © 2013 M. Thomson. Reprinted with the permission of Cambridge University Press.

The figure to the right shows measured distributions of fundamental particles as a function of radius for protons. The data is derived from particle accelerator experiments for collisions between high energy electrons and protons. Remember that, when the kinetic energy of the electrons gets high enough that their de Broglie wavelength is much smaller than the proton, the electrons start to collide with the fundamental particles that make up the proton. In the figure, xu_v and xd_v are the distributions for the up and down quarks, xg is the gluon distribution, and xs is the strange quark distribution (strange quarks are there because the up and down quarks fluctuate into higher mass quarks). The xd and xu distributions with lines over the d and u are distributions for anti-down and anti-up antimatter quarks. The antimatter quarks are thought to be there because of gluon-quark vacuum fluctuations.

The mathematical techniques of renormalization can be used "backward" to try to estimate what the value of the bare electrical charge for an electron is. The answer is that the bare charge may be infinite (the mathematically infinite charge is called a Landau pole). Recall that charge is a measure of how often a particle emits and absorbs the momentum exchange bosons associated with a particular force. Infinite electrical charge implies that each electron continuously emits and absorbs infinite numbers of photons.

Mathematically, an infinite cloud of (possibly) infinitely charged electron probability amplitudes (possibilities), each emitting and absorbing (possibly) infinite numbers of photon probability amplitudes, with half of them negatively charged electron possibilities moving forward in time and the other half negatively charged positron possibilities moving backward in time (and appearing to have positive charges because the movie runs backward), with one extra negatively charged electron probability amplitude moving forward in time to imbalance the cloud, produces—after all of the infinite interactions are added up and canceled out—exactly the momentum-changing behavior that physicists measure for one electron in what we call the real world.

As it goes for electrons, so it goes for all of the particles and forces that make up our existence.

The mathematics of particle physics and vacuum fluctuations inform us that there is no such thing as empty space in our universe. It is completely filled with a swarm of virtual fermions and bosons that continuously flit in and out of existence. We don't see them because, like neutrons, they are exactly balanced between positive and negative, particle and antiparticle. What we experience as matter is a structure built of small, local imbalances in the swarm of particles.

Dear readers, that is the reality in which we live, and move, and have our being.

"That they should seek the Lord, if haply they might feel after him, and find him, though he be not far from any one of us: for in him we live, and move, and have our being; as certain also of your own poets have said, For we are also his offspring."—Acts 17:27–28

Theology from Vacuum Fluctuations

"In the beginning God created the heaven and the earth. And the earth was without form, and void; and darkness was upon the face of the deep. And the Spirit of God moved upon the face of the waters. And God said, Let there be light; and there was light. And God saw the light, that it was good: and God divided the light from the darkness. And God called the light Day, and the darkness he called Night. And the evening and the morning were the first day.

"And God said, Let there be a firmament in the midst of the waters, and let it divide the waters from the waters. And God made the firmament, and divided the waters which were under the firmament from the waters which were above the firmament; and it was so. And God called the firmament Heaven. And the evening and the morning were the second day."—Genesis 1:1–8

"And God said, Let the waters under the heaven be gathered together into one place, and let the dry land appear: and it was so. And God called the dry land Earth; and the gathering together of the waters called he Seas: and God saw that it was good."
—Genesis 1:9–10

Here again, we will speculate about how Genesis 1 and modern physics might fit together. Most of what is presented here won't come up again; I simply wish to demonstrate how flexible both modern physics and Genesis 1 can be.

When I was first learning modern physics, vacuum fluctuations and renormalization were my favorite part—the part where I started to seriously consider how all of physics might mix with Scripture. The apostle Paul tells us in Acts that we live, and move, and have our being in God. So there is a sense in which, when the measurements and mathematics of physics get closer to the fundamentals of how this world works, we might be getting closer to glimpsing some part of the substance of God. It should be enormously satisfying to a believer that, at the most fundamental levels of structure, the mathematics of quantum mechanics and particle physics all start spinning into infinities. It was to me.

One of the terms physicists occasionally use to describe vacuum fluctuations is the Dirac Sea. Physicists originally proposed the concept of an infinite sea of particles (and zero-point energy) as a justification for the negative energy solutions to the Klein-Gordon and Dirac equations describing quantum mechanics and relativity. It's also a pretty good description of the picture of reality we get from vacuum fluctuations: an endless sea that fills every part of our universe, even the vacuum of space, with infinite swarms of virtual probability amplitudes waiting for the energy to become real.

The suggestion here should be pretty obvious. In one possible interpretation of Genesis 1:1–8, the term "waters" might be referring to the Dirac Sea of virtual particles. If our earlier guess that the term "light" in Genesis 1:3 might refer to the boson exchanges that produce forces is anywhere near correct, there could not possibly have been any physical water present in spacetime before light was made. There would not have been any strong force to bind quarks into atomic nuclei or electromagnetic force to bind electrons to nuclei and atoms to atoms to form molecules like real, physical water.

Genesis 1:6–8 describes a separation of the "waters" by an expanse into waters above and below. In one interpretation, the rest of the creation story focuses on the waters below the expanse, the part of spacetime where we live; the waters above the expanse drop out of the picture. If the two waters separated by the expanse of heaven actually are something like the Dirac Sea, it would imply that there is another part of spacetime than the part where we live, a part that we cannot see. Something like this does show up in the rest of the Bible in the form of the division between our physical world and the spirit world. According to Scripture the spirit world exists; other creations of God (not us) live there, but we cannot see it. (At least, we cannot see it without the help of someone who knows a lot more about physics than we do.)

The theory of charges and force exchange bosons offers a suggestion of how a separation of the virtual particles of the original Dirac Sea might possibly have worked. In the description of forces, I mentioned the solar neutrino flux. Huge numbers of neutrinos generated in the sun pass through the entire earth with little or no effect because they have very small charges and do not interact often with the very tenuous stuff (golf balls a mile apart) that we call solid matter. If we happened to be surrounded by other particles that have other charges and respond to other forces, we would never know it. Our earth could be passing through the center of a spirit world star right now, and we would never see the light or feel the heat and pressure.

The waters in Genesis 1:9–10, which "gather together" to reveal the dry land, definitely seem to be the wet kind of water—but a couple of interesting nuances can be projected into the description if one happens to be a shameless opportunist. If the term "waters" can also refer to the Dirac Sea, we may employ another interpretation of how waters can gather together to reveal dry land: cosmology and geophysics tell us that the gasses of space are gathered together by gravity to form planets, which also fit the description "dry land."

The other, slightly odd part of the description in Genesis 1:9–10 is that in the world we see around us, waters are also gathered together into seas by gravity. The implication is that there may have been no gravity, or different gravity, before the waters were gathered together.

General relativity tells us that spacetime is malleable; it can be bent, stretched, and twisted by mass-energy charge. Physicists naturally assume that the bending of spacetime is caused by the presence of mass-energy charge (and there is substantial observational confirmation of that viewpoint). The interesting thing here is that Scripture always speaks of events related to gravity, like the location and extent of seas, in terms of boundaries that are set by God. So is spacetime bent by mass-energy charge—or do particles with mass-energy charge congregate where spacetime is bent?

That's a rhetorical question; I don't have an answer. But there is something in standard big bang cosmology that may indicate the scriptural description is more accurate, at least for the stretching part. Shortly after the big bang (another place in physics, by the way, where the math all goes infinite), when all of the matter in what would become the universe was concentrated in a tiny, hot ball of unstructured energy, still too hot to form particles, spacetime started to expand. This does not mean that the matter in spacetime moved apart because of the explosion of the big bang. It means that spacetime itself stretched; real physical distance suddenly appeared between positions that had just been right next to each other. The volume of spacetime first expanded by a factor of roughly 10^{78}; the matter of spacetime effectively moved faster than light. Objects with mass-energy charge cannot move through spacetime faster than light, but spacetime itself can apparently move much faster.

The 10^{78} factor sounds impressive, but that first, rapid expansion was from something smaller than a proton to something about the size of a grapefruit; just enough to keep the big bang from collapsing into a big black hole. But our universe has continued to expand. Most of the huge distances between stars and galaxies now are due to spacetime expansion, not to the movement of the material. The "edge" of our universe is currently estimated to be expanding at about three times the speed of light.

Astronomical observations indicate that spacetime is still expanding; at least, it was when we last looked. The closest galaxies that show definite evidence of receding from us because of the expansion are 33 million light years away; the light from them that we see now shows what they were doing 33 million years ago. Most of the astronomical observations that indicate spacetime expansion go much further away and far longer ago than that (out to several billion light years away and several billion years ago).

By calculation, astronomers have deduced that a universe with an even distribution of stars (which ours is not—our stars are grouped into galaxies that are a long way apart) would not have any night. Although there would be less light from more distant stars, there would more of them within view. The entire sky would shine with the same brightness as the sun, and the earth's surface would be far too hot for us to live on it. Also by calculation, the same thing happens in the centers of galaxies, where the stars huddle together for warmth. Planets like our earth, with our kind of life on them, must be in the outer parts of galaxies (as we are); the centers are far too hot for us.

Without the continuing spacetime expansion after the big bang, it would not be possible for any of us (or any other living thing that we know of) to live on the surface of the earth.

> *"And God said, Let there be light; and there was light. And God saw the light, that it was good: and God divided the light from the darkness."*—Genesis 1:3–4

Fig. 56. Our Galactic Center
The Planet, the Galaxy and the Laser
© 2007 by Y. Beletsky, ESO.

> *"It is he that sitteth upon the circle of the earth, and the inhabitants thereof are as grasshoppers; that stretcheth out the heavens as a curtain, and spreadeth them out as a tent to dwell in."*—Isaiah 40:22

Accounting in Particle Interactions

Before we allow ourselves to take flight in further theological speculation, it's time to take a closer look at some math. Once again, it is not really necessary to memorize the details of complex number operations and group theory that will be shown here, but it will be useful for you to have a feel for how abstract mathematics play a role in the operation of our world. Part of the speculation to come may strike you as a few steps beyond goofy; I hope that an appreciation of the mathematics will help to retrieve the suggestion back from total insanity to mere implausibility. Once again, I am indebted to Bruce Schumm in *Deep Down Things*; as usual I recommend his very excellent book for anyone interested in a fuller explanation.

Particles derive their identity, the type of particle that they are, from the values of their properties. Some properties have already been mentioned: electric charge, color charge, weak isospin charge, and mass-energy charge. Other properties for particles exist as well. Some properties have a known relationship to a physical characteristic of the particle: electric charge, color charge, and weak isospin charge relate to how often the particle exchanges bosons with other particles. For other properties of particles, the relationship to physical characteristics is unknown; we do not know enough about what particles really are and how they function to completely figure out why particle properties do what they do. The generic name in physics for particle properties that (mostly) do not have a known physical basis is "internal symmetry spaces."

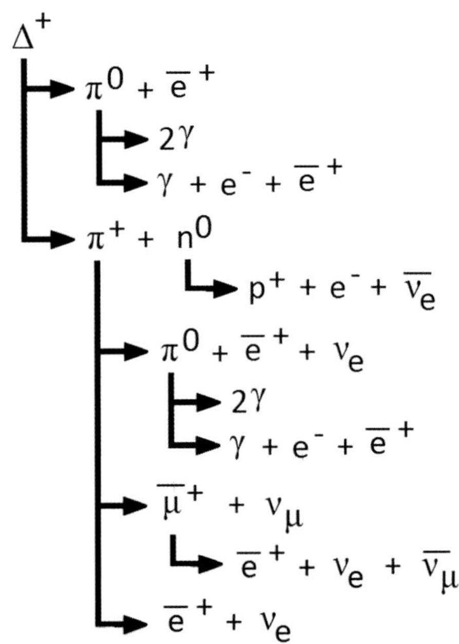

Internal symmetry properties are mostly derived from particle decay sequences. An example is shown in the figure on the previous page.

I mentioned earlier that the fundamental particles (quarks and leptons) come in three generations. Generations II and III have higher rest mass than generation I particles. If you recall, generation II and III particles always spontaneously decay (fluctuate) into generation I particles because generation I has the lowest energy.

As shown in the figure to the side, generation I particles that have higher energy structures also spontaneously decay into particles with lower energy. The delta+ baryon (quark group) particle shown has the same quark composition as a proton, but its structure is different, with higher energy. Proton rest energy is 938 Mev/c^2, while delta+ rest energy is 1239 Mev/c^2.

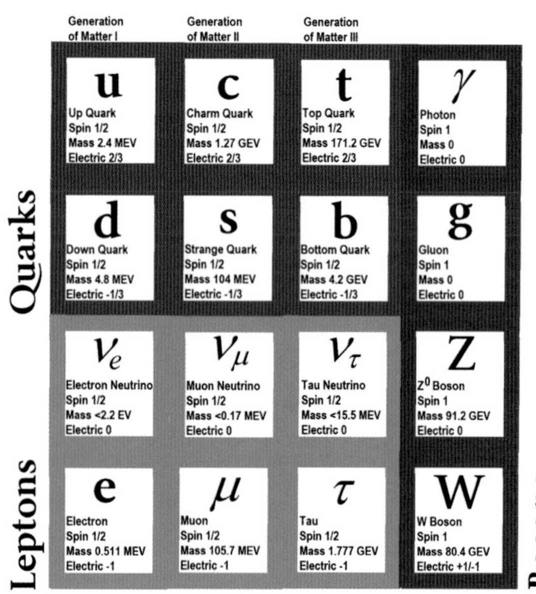

The black bars and arrows in the figure show the spontaneous decay pathways. Usually one particle decays into two or more lower-energy particles. Multiple arrows on a vertical bar indicate that the particle can decay in more than one way. A small horizontal bar over the particle symbol indicates an anti-particle. The *u*'s (up quarks) and *d*'s (down quarks) in parentheses show the quark composition for baryon (three quarks) and meson (quark and anti-quark) hadron (quark group) particles.

The stable particles, which have nothing with lower energy to change into, are photons, electrons, protons (the only stable quark group), neutrinos (both generation I electron neutrinos and generation II muon neutrinos), and their anti-particles.

Physicists partly use particle accelerators to produce higher energy particles so they can watch them decay. The mathematical models that together form the standard model of particle physics were partly derived from observations of particle decay sequences. What the models partly predict are the allowed decay interactions (some possible decays are never observed), with the probabilities of interactions and different decay pathways.

Internal symmetry spaces (particle properties with no known physical basis) are basically accounting rules that had to be added to the math models in order to derive the decay sequence behavior that physicists saw in cosmic rays and particle accelerators.

Here are the conservation laws mentioned earlier in the discussion of particle interactions:

Conservation of linear momentum
Conservation of angular momentum (includes particle "spin")
Conservation of mass-energy charge (gravitational force)
Conservation of electric charge (electromagnetic force)
Conservation of color charge (strong nuclear force)
Conservation of weak isospin (weak nuclear force)
Conservation of probability density (abstract quantum mechanics quantity)
Conservation of charge/parity/time conjugation (CPT) symmetry (particle decay)
Conservation of Lorentz Symmetry (indistinguishable inertial frames)

Here are some of the internal symmetry quantities:

Baryon number
Lepton number
Intrinsic angular momentum (spin)
Strong isospin
Strong hypercharge
Weak isospin
Weak hypercharge

We already saw some of the internal symmetries in our set of conservation laws. Some of them now have a known physical basis. Weak isospin, already mentioned, relates to the exchange rate for the W and Z bosons that carry the weak nuclear force. Baryon number was originally derived before Murray Gell-Mann's quark model; it turned out to be the number of quarks in a particle.

Intrinsic angular momentum, nicknamed "spin," plays a major role in particle behavior. It features units of angular momentum, the equivalent of linear momentum (p = mv), that applies to spinning objects. Individual particle spins have to be added into the calculations for larger objects (atoms and molecules) along with spinning motion to conserve angular momentum.

One odd thing about spin is that angular momentum usually involves something moving in a circle around a center—but fundamental particles do not have any dimensions. There is no part of them that can move around a center, because every part is at the center.

Spin is quantized: each type of particle always has a specific value of spin. Particle spins only show up as integer numbers of a basic unit that is called, oddly enough, spin 1/2 (spin can be 0, 1/2, 1, 3/2, 2, and so on). Quantized values might imply that some kind of standing wave behavior is associated with the thing we call spin, but the physical details are unknown.

Particle spins can be in different "directions" (like angular momentum), but the different directions (called spin up and spin down) are also quantized and don't really relate to a physical direction. I mentioned earlier that two electrons, for example, can only occupy the same probability amplitude standing wave in an atom if they have different spin directions. The delta+ baryon mentioned above has the same quark composition as a proton (uud), but it has a different behavior and a different rest energy (mass) because the spin orientations are different. In a delta+, all three quarks have the same spin orientation, so it has a net spin of 3/2 (1/2 + 1/2 + 1/2). The proton, on the other hand, has one quark with the opposite spin direction, so it has a net spin of 1/2 (1/2 + 1/2 − 1/2): the up quarks have down spins and the down quark has up spin, for example.

Particles with different values of spin behave in very different ways. Back in the discussion of the Feynman-Stueckelberg interpretation for antimatter, I mentioned that several different corrections were made to the quantum mechanics Schrodinger equation to adapt it to Einstein's relativity. The Klein-Gordon equation applies only to the behavior of spin 0 particles; the Dirac equation applies only to the behavior of spin 1/2 particles (quarks and leptons are spin 1/2). Another equation, the Proca equation, describes the behavior of spin 1 particles (photons, gluons, and W and Z bosons are all spin 1).

Pauli exclusion, the quirky behavior of probability amplitudes that keeps them physically separated so that we can have solid material, only applies to particles with half-integer spin (1/2, 3/2, 5/2, etc.). Particles with integer spin (0, 1, 2, 3, etc.) can clump together, with large numbers of particles effectively occupying the same tiny little space; physicists call clumps of integer spin particles "Bose-Einstein condensates." Atoms have net spin values that are the sum of spins and spin directions for the fundamental particles that join together to form them. Atoms also behave according to their net spin value: atoms with net integer spin can form Bose-Einstein condensates (in the proper, very difficult-to-achieve conditions). Atoms with net half-integer spin cannot form Bose-Einstein condensates because they are separated by Pauli exclusion.

Deuterium, an isotope of hydrogen with one neutron in the nucleus in addition to the proton, has integer spin (making it a boson) and is not subject to Pauli exclusion. Deuterium seems to be able to form a very dense kind of material: a four-inch cube of condensed deuterium would weigh about 130 tons (most deuterium is much, much lighter).

Strong hypercharge and strong isospin both played a crucial role in the development of the quark model of particle structure. Murray Gell-Mann noticed that when particle properties were graphed in Cartesian coordinates with isospin (I_P) values on one axis and hypercharge (Y) values on the other axis, the particles fell into neat little groups of eight that he called octets. Hence his name for the precursor to quark theory: "the eightfold way." He eventually developed quark theory because he also noticed that the shapes of the octets were characteristic of graphs for an abstract mathematical construct called an SU(3) Lie group (pronounced Lee).

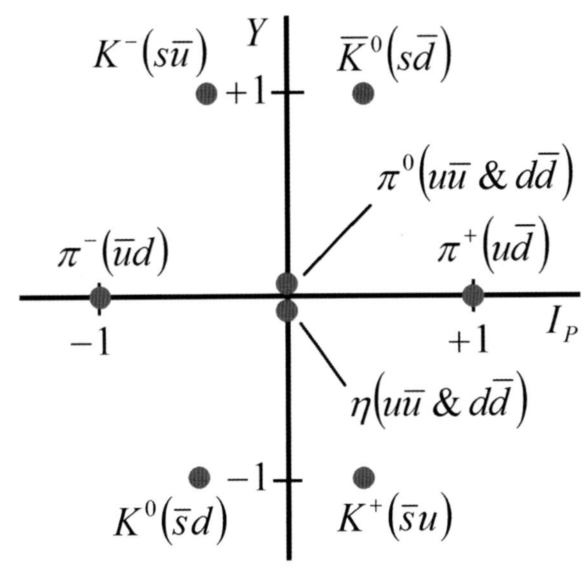

Fig. 57. Particle Octet of the Eightfold Way

Abstract Mathematics in Particle Interactions

Many people who study difficult subjects like mathematics and physics share a common experience: as the material slowly sinks in, they occasionally encounter episodes where it just does not make any sense to them. The logic is not apparent, the implications are obscure, the homework is impossible. Many of us experience an overwhelming sense of frustration that halts anything that might resemble rational thought.

To acquire the low level of skill in those subjects that I used to enjoy, one has to learn to put the frustration aside and keep plugging away. People who go on to become theoretical physicists and mathematicians, in addition to having lots of talent, actually like that sensation. They (especially the mathematicians) love puzzles; the harder the better.

Mathematicians develop mathematics just for the fun of it. As physicists work to develop mathematical theories to describe the behavior of our world (also mostly for the fun of it), they often end up using tools that were developed by mathematicians fifty to a hundred years earlier.

This is the case with Lie groups. Mathematician Sophus Lie proposed and developed the theory of Lie groups in the 1870s. A "group" in mathematics is a set of numbers with an associated operation. To be a group, the numbers and operation must meet a short list of rules:

- The set must be closed: applying the operation to any two members of the set must produce another member of the set (x*y = z, x, y, z all members).
- The operation must be associative: (x*y)*z = x*(y*z).
- The set must have an identity element: applying the operation to the identity element and any other member will give the member (i*x = x).
- Every member (x) of the set must have a corresponding member (x′) that will produce the identity element after the operation (x*x′ = i).
- Commutivity (x*y = y*x) is optional; it is not required for a group.

Lie groups are a special category of groups that have infinite numbers of members in their sets that can be produced by a finite number of operations. For Lie groups, the operations that produce the members of the set are called generators. For our discussion of particle physics we will only need three Lie groups: U(1), SU(2), and SU(3). U stands for unitary, SU stands for special unitary; the number relates to the number of dimensions in the group.

U(1) is a Lie group that includes all complex numbers (x + yi) with a length equal to 1 (unit length). The operation for U(1) is the multiplication of two complex numbers.

Remember that complex numbers can be shown on Cartesian coordinates as an arrow at some angle if one of the coordinate axes is designated as the imaginary axis. The angle between the arrow and the x-axis is called the phase.

It turns out that multiplication of two complex numbers, each with a length of 1, produces another complex arrow with a phase equal to the sum of the phases of the multiplied numbers. In Cartesian coordinates, multiplying complex numbers looks the same as rotating them. U(1) can be described as the set of unit complex numbers with the single operation (generator) of one dimensional rotation (rotation about one axis).

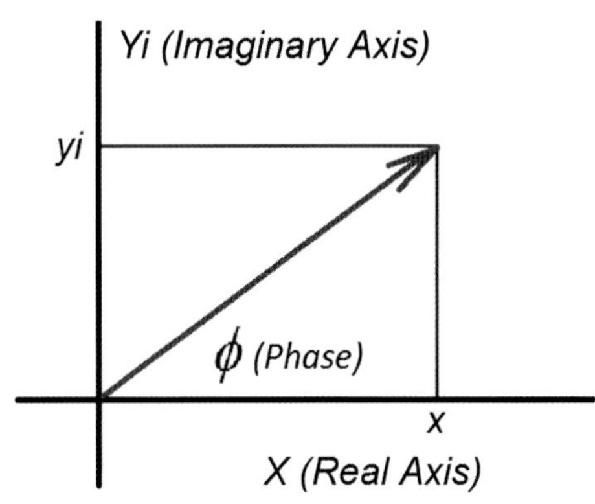

SU(2) is the set of complex numbers of unit length with the operation of two sequential rotations about two different axes. SU(3) is the set of complex numbers of unit length with the operation of three sequential rotations about three different axes. I would love to be able to draw figures to show how all this works, but that would be beyond my skill level. Rotations in one complex direction are shown in two dimensions, like in the figure above. Rotations in two complex directions would require a four-dimensional figure. Rotations in three complex directions would require a six-dimensional figure.

The generators (operations) are also different for rotations in complex directions. Rotations in two complex directions (about two complex axes) require three generators. Rotations in three complex directions require eight generators.

SU(2) and SU(3) also have what is called an algebra. The algebra for each is a set of rules that predict how the results will change if the rotations about complex axes are done in a different order.

So far, this discussion of groups and Lie groups is all just abstract mathematics. So what does all of this have to do with particle physics? Hint: quantum mechanics is all about complex numbers.

In 1954 physicists C. N. Yang and R. L. Mills pointed out that the Schrodinger equation was even more wrong than had been thought. As we saw, the Schrodinger equation is the energy balance that describes the way probability amplitudes (Ψ) change over time:

$$E\Psi = T\Psi + V\Psi \text{ (Total energy = Kinetic energy + Potential energy)}$$

is the shorthand version of the Schrodinger equation.

The full-length version is this:

$$\frac{ih}{2\pi}\frac{\partial}{\partial t}\psi(x,y,z,ict) = -\frac{h^2}{8\pi m}\nabla^2\psi(x,y,z,ict) + V(x,y,z)\psi(x,y,z,ict).$$

We'll be using a medium-length version here, with the Cartesian coordinate variables for functions not shown:

$$\frac{ih}{2\pi}\frac{\partial}{\partial t}\psi = -\frac{h^2}{8\pi m}\nabla^2\psi + V\psi$$

The Schrodinger equation is going to be getting a lot longer in this section, and it won't fit on the page with the full version.

The Klein-Gordon, Dirac, and Proca equations mentioned earlier used Einstein's relativity to extend the Schrodinger equation to work for objects traveling at high velocities (like particles in cosmic rays and particle accelerators). What Yang and Mills noticed was that the Schrodinger equation wasn't even accurate for objects moving at low speeds.

The probability amplitude (Ψ) assigns complex number values to points in space. Theoretically, the probability amplitude is infinite in space; it assigns a complex number value to every position in the universe. Remember that complex numbers (x + yi) can be represented in Cartesian coordinates as an arrow at some angle (called the phase). Remember also that the calculation of probabilities in quantum mechanics depends only on the product of the complex number and its complex conjugate: (x + yi) × (x − yi) = $x^2 + y^2$, the length of the arrow. Phase only plays a role in the superposition and interference of the terms of the probability amplitude, not in the calculation of probabilities.

Again, theoretically, if the phase of one of the complex number arrows for the probability amplitude somewhere in the universe changes for some reason, the phases for the complex numbers for every other point in the universe instantaneously change to corresponding values. Or, as a physicist would say, the probability amplitude displays global phase invariance.

Yang and Mills proposed that the Schrodinger equation needed some corrections to reflect the way things happen in the real world. To be compatible with Einstein's relativity, which tells us that nothing material moves faster than light, phase changes should only move from point to point at the speed of light. This implies that the Schrodinger equation should be corrected to be compatible with local changes in phase as well as global changes. In physics terms, the Schrodinger equation needs to include local phase invariance as well as global phase invariance.

Yang and Mills first added a term to the Schrodinger equation to allow local changes of phase for the electromagnetic force:

$$\frac{ih}{2\pi}\frac{\partial}{\partial t}\psi = -\frac{h^2}{8\pi m}\nabla^2\psi + qA\Psi + V\psi$$

In the new term, q is a factor, a number. A is some function—actually A(x, y, z)—that is selected to change the value of the kinetic energy term (the first term on the right, with the upside-down triangle) to correct the values of phase so that they conform to the light speed limitations of relativity. The next step is to figure out values for the factor, q, and the details of the function, A, that will give the right answers. It turned out that q needed to be the electric charge, and the function A(x, y, z) needed to be the electromagnetic potential energy function.

Mathematically, the qA(x, y, z) correction term mostly changes the phase of complex numbers assigned to points in space by the probability amplitude function Ψ(x, y, z, ict). Since phase changes can be thought of as rotations of the complex arrows, the action of the correction term looks a lot like the action of a U(1) Lie group. There is only a casual resemblance in the example I gave here for the Schrodinger equation—but the Schrodinger equation is not compatible with relativity and is therefore not true. When the same type of correction is applied to the real, accurate quantum mechanics equations (the Klein-Gordon, Dirac, and Proca equations), the similarity gets a lot stronger.

The fundamental role of Lie groups in the operation of our world becomes unmistakable when the same correction to slow down changes of phase to the speed of light is also done for the weak nuclear force and the strong nuclear force.

Probability amplitude functions that describe systems with weak force interactions must conform to the rules for the Lie group SU(2). Mathematically, the number of correction terms needed in the Schrodinger equation in order for it to be compatible with local phase changes for weak force interactions is three, the same as the number of generators for SU(2). The generators and the algebra for SU(2) play a role in the derivation of the allowed interaction vertices for weak force interactions. SU(2) describes rotations around two complex axes. For the weak force the two axes are the complex values of the probability amplitude (the same as U(1) rotations for electromagnetic force interactions) and the internal symmetry space called weak isospin (the same as the weak force charge).

Probability amplitude functions that describe systems with strong force interactions must conform to the rules for the Lie group SU(3). Mathematically, the number of correction terms needed in the Schrodinger equation to be compatible with local phase changes for strong force interactions is eight, the same as the number of generators for SU(3). The generators and the algebra for SU(3) play a role in the derivation of the allowed interaction vertices for strong force interactions. SU(3) describes rotations around three complex axes. For the strong force, the three axes are the complex values of the color charge.

Dear readers, this is an instance where physics steps across the boundary between a reasonable, natural world and one that might be fundamentally mathematical.

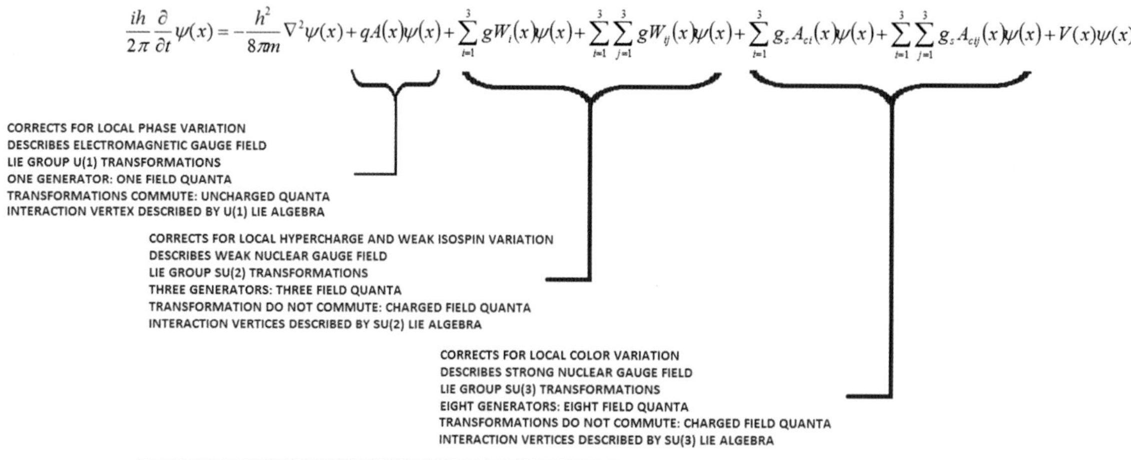

Fig. 58. Simplified Schrodinger Equation Corrected for Speed of Light

Figure 58 shows a simplified representation of the corrections to the Schrodinger equation to limit Ψ phase changes to the speed of light. It is not the actual equation; it's really just a picture of how the corrections operate. Please don't try to build a nuclear fusion reactor at home using this equation; it wouldn't work and might be dangerous.

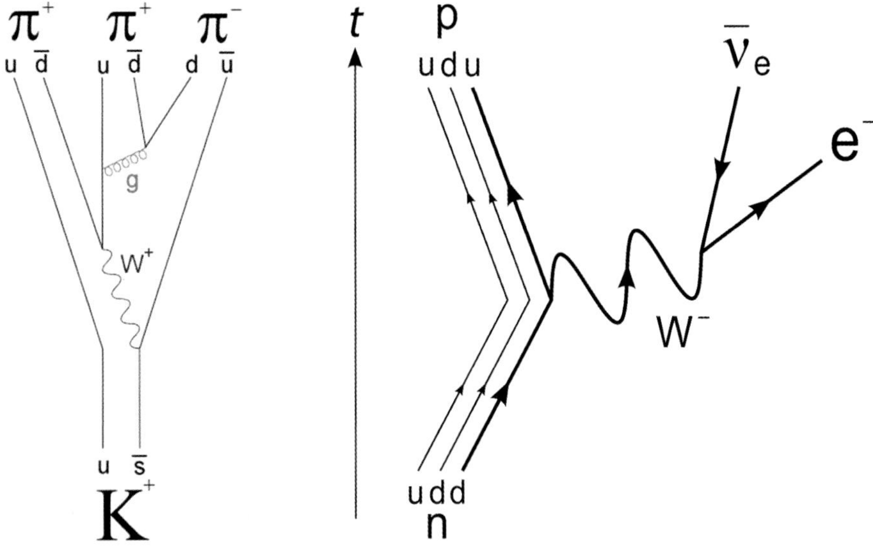

Fig. 59. Particle Decay Feynman Diagrams, Kaon and Free Neutron

The figure above shows Feynman diagrams for two typical particle decays: for a kaon (a meson: quark + anti-quark) and for a free neutron (a baryon: three quarks).

Particle decay series are built up of a sequence of interaction vertices. Each interaction vertex in a particle decay usually has a pair of fermions (structural particles) and a boson (a force momentum carrier). A particle decay is generally two interaction vertices that involve four fermions and one boson. Particle decays are referred to as electromagnetic decays, weak force decays, or strong force decays depending on which type of boson is involved. All of the very complex decay sequences we see in particle physics are composed of mixtures of a relatively low number of allowed interaction vertices. It is similar to the hundreds of quark group particles (hadrons) that turn out to be mixtures of just six quarks. Interaction vertices have to be compatible with conservation laws, but the vertices that are observed to happen in experiments are also compatible with Lie group algebras.

All of the allowed particle decay interaction vertices that happen in nature are theoretically derived using the Lie group algebras for U(1), SU(2), and SU(3). Electromagnetic decays obey the algebra for U(1): there is only one allowed vertex, the vertex with two charged fermions (usually electrons) and a photon (anti-electrons still count as electrons, they just move backward in time). All observed weak force decay interaction vertices correspond to the terms for the Lie group algebra of SU(2). Observed strong force decay interaction vertices match the terms of the Lie group algebra for SU(3).

There is one more little bit to cover before we are (finally) done with modern physics. That is the missing piece of mass (and mass-energy charge). The quantum mechanics equations are supposed to be energy balances, but none of the versions I have shown so far include the largest part of energy: the particle rest masses. If we really want to try to model the way things happen in the real world, our equations really should include rest masses.

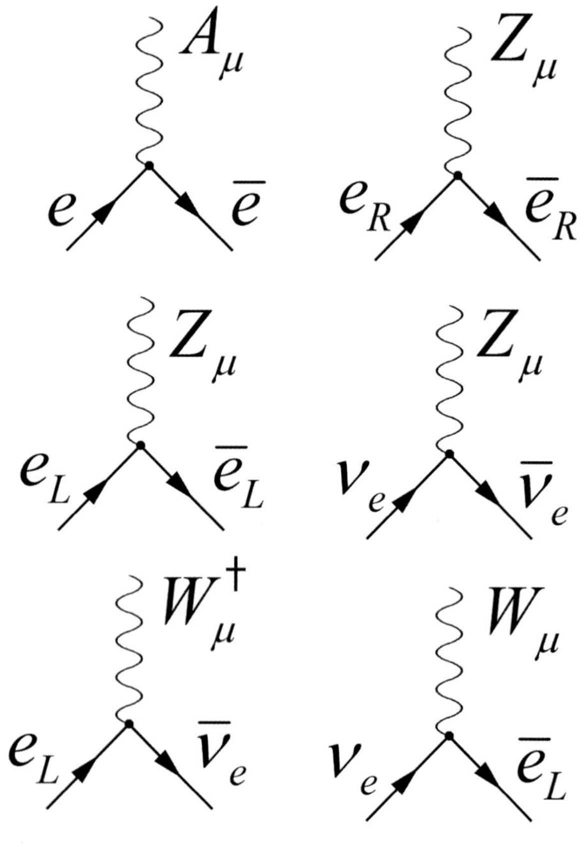

Fig. 60. Electromagnetic/Week Force Interaction Vertices.

Mathematically, it is pretty easy to add in the rest masses of the various particles. Unfortunately, when physicists did so for the modified equations proposed by Yang and Mills, the equations all stopped working. They no longer gave answers that matched events that we see in the world. In order to tweak quantum mechanics to get it working again, physicists had to add several more correction terms. Just as the Yang-Mills correction terms (Yang-Mills gauge theories, as they are officially known) describe the interactions of forces, the new correction terms described a new kind of interaction and a new boson. Half a dozen different physicists proposed the same mass corrections pretty much at the same time, but only one of them, Peter Higgs, predicted the existence of the new boson particle—so he got most of the credit. The new interactions are called Higgs fields, and the new boson is called the Higgs boson.

Higgs fields and the Higgs boson describe the behavior that we call inertial mass. Remember Newton's second law of motion:

$$F = \frac{dp}{dt}$$

F = force
p = momentum (= $m \times v$)
$\frac{d}{dt}$ = derivative operator with respect to time (t) (rate of change per unit time)

When forces push on objects, the objects only change their speed in proportion to their mass-energy charge. When the same force pushes on an object with twice the mass, it only changes speed half as much. One way to think of inertial mass is to say that objects resist changing speed; the more mass they have, the more they resist changing speed. What quantum mechanics tells us is that the reason objects do this is that they are held back by Higgs boson exchanges with stationary Higgs fields.

At the time I am writing this, data from the Large Hadron Collider project at CERN in Europe has recently confirmed the physical existence of the Higgs boson. This constitutes an experimental verification of all of the various theories that together make up the standard model of particle physics.

So, What's It All Mean, Mr. Natural?

So, that's the physics. We have, finally, reached the bottom of the rabbit hole—the place where we can see the truth of how our world functions. At least, as much of the truth as we know. I hope it has become apparent that we don't actually know how it all works. We know quite a bit about what it does, but next to nothing about how it actually works or why it does things the way that it does.

The next step in our speculation is to build a worldview, a story about how the world might work; a story about what the world possibly *is.* With worldview in hand, the final step will be to compare our worldview to what our Lord tells us about his creation in Scripture to see how it all fits together.

Physics advances in a cloud of theories; there are often many proposals for how things might work. Experimentation plucks a theory from the cloud and imbues it with the validity of natural law. To the best of my knowledge, the physics presented so far is completely compatible with both theory and experiment. But we are about to leave the reassurance of experiment behind and venture into parts of the cloud where there is no certainty to guide us, where any guess is as good as any other.

The world view coming up next is just a guess among other guesses. It is also possible to compose alternative world views out of other guesses that are just as likely as the rather odd perspective that I am going to propose. The point, the theme of this whole book, is that it is possible to build a world view based on modern physics that is compatible with Scripture. Creationists have struggled for years now to fit Scripture and physics into the same philosophical package. They have had a lot of victories (mostly due to some very sloppy science by evolutionary biologists and paleontologists), but, in my opinion, they have not been able to win the debate. I am suggesting here that one reason they have not won might be that their focus has been on resolving Scripture with classical Newtonian physics. Classical physics will probably never fit Scripture . . . because classical physics is not true. It is only an approximation, and an approximation that is in many ways just plain wrong.

Another possible reason for this mismatch between physics and Scripture is that classical physics is pretty much settled. It does not include a lot of nooks and crannies in our knowledge that might allow a fit with Scripture. Modern physics, on the other hand, has huge chasms where we are still ignorant of the truth. There could be an experiment or theoretical breakthrough at any time that validates decoherence theory or M theory and which would compel a complete reevaluation of compatibility with Scripture. But it hasn't happened yet. To the best of my (limited) knowledge, there is nothing in modern physics that conflicts with the descriptions of creation in the Bible—or anything in the Bible—when it is all viewed from the proper perspective—no matter how odd that perspective may be.

A Quick Summary of Reality

The world that we see is an illusion. The world that we touch, hear, taste, and smell is a "real" world, but what we *see* is a temporary, insubstantial projection derived from the "real" world but utterly unlike it.

What we see is produced by classical state particles. We see photons with localized, definite values for their attributes that trigger single, individual sensors in our eyes. When the sensor signals are all added together in our brains, they produce sharp, clear images. What we touch, hear, taste, and smell are quantum state particles. Our senses of touch and hearing rely on Pauli exclusion to produce the solidity that we feel and the vibrations in the air that we hear. Pauli exclusion is solely a property of quantum state particles. Taste and smell depend on chemical reactions. Chemical reactions depend on the interactions of electron probability amplitudes that are pulled into standing waves by the potential energy fields of atomic nuclei; localized classical electrons do not form standing waves and do not participate in chemical reactions.

The world as it truly is is insubstantial. Even classical particles are composed only of energy, a kind of stored force. Quantum state particles don't even have energy; they have a possibility function, a probability amplitude (Ψ) that will produce a value of energy if they are localized, but quantum state particles themselves have no energy. The vast majority of quantum state particles are virtual; they exist only for brief, fleeting moments and then vanish.

Our knowledge of the world is mathematical. We can only see particles in the classical state; we can only measure the illusion, never the "real" world. All that we know about how our existence works is a projection of mathematics. And it's not a sensible mathematics; it's a strange, abstract mathematics that bears no relationship to anything that can be counted. The heart of the calculation is the probability amplitude function Ψ, a function composed of the superposition and interference of waves of possibilities—possibilities that can only be described by complex $(x + yi)$ numbers that are themselves figments of a mathematician's imagination.

Particles, the fundamental objects that compose our existence, obey a strange mathematics of their own:

- they go backward and forward in time as the positive and negative solutions for a square root;
- they continuously change their essence in patterns dictated by accounting rules and the rotations of complex numbers about complex axes in complex coordinates;
- they are not single particles at all; they are described mathematically as slightly imbalanced clouds of virtual probability amplitudes that flit in and out of existence;
- they do not have any kind of individual existence; they can only be counted by their populations in quantum states.
- Entanglement information passes between particles faster than light; particles "remember" past (and future) encounters and correspond about current events using a mysterious medium of communication that cannot possibly be a part of the world we know.
- Strangest of all is the (possible) relationship of localization—the (alleged) transition of particles from quantum state to classical state—to conscious choice. Apparently, the world literally, physically changes solely in response to the thoughts and decisions of our minds.

Please remember that we have not started with the guessing part yet. All of the above is a summary of the science: science that has been speculated as hypothesis, given specific definition by the mathematical models of theory, and proven by experiment to be as demonstrably true as anything that we know of can be.

As we delve now into our guessing game, we are going to make the whole thing as simple and direct as we can. The result may be really strange (though not as strange as quantum mechanics itself), but the process that will lead us to the result is, I think, a straightforward extension of the sensible and familiar. We are going to retreat to the comfort and familiarity of our classical world and put the "reality" of modern physics into the only environment in all of our practical experience where such an odd thing could possibly exist.

02

Speculation in Computation

"In the beginning was the Word, and the Word was with God, and the Word was God. The same was in the beginning with God. All things were made by him; and without him was not any thing made that was made. In him was life; and the life was the light of men. And the light shineth in the darkness; and the darkness comprehended it not."
—John 1:1–5

From here on, we are, for the most part, going to be leaving the science behind us. I don't mean we are going to leave physics behind; I mean that we are going to venture into a speculative world where the nitty-gritty details of how things actually work are unknown. Science is suggested by hypothesis, defined by theory, and tested by experiment; it includes ideas that any reasonable person should accept as at least provisionally true. (Of course, as we have seen, scientific conclusions have an unfortunate habit of being superseded by other hypotheses, other theories, and other experiments.)

For a number of reasons, as we examine now the intersections of creation, reality, and Scripture, our speculation must move beyond the science, beyond the part of physics that is proven. One reason has already been mentioned many times: our speculation is going to be about the fundamental nature of our world, and that is a thing that science does not know.

Another big reason is philosophical, a matter of perception about what our world can plausibly be. The goal is to study the relationship, the fit, between modern physics and Scripture. In order to do that, it is going to be necessary, for the sake of exploration, to construct a worldview that accepts Scripture as being literally and completely true. That is a very difficult exercise (pretty much impossible, actually) for nonbelievers to do: for them, it is difficult to construct a body of logical deduction based on premises that are both hard to understand and counterintuitive when they are understood, and it is even more difficult to justify spending the time (hundreds of hours), concentration, and effort required to develop mathematical models for a physical worldview that any sane, rational person can plainly see is impossible.

From their perspective, anyway.

According to polls, 80 to 85 percent of physicists are nonbelievers. One practical result of that very large majority is that the culture of the physics community—its consensus of values and viewpoints, its notions of what is reasonable and what is nonsense—is rooted in a natural world where God and his action in creation are impossible. There are not very many developed cosmological theories (mathematical models) that are based on a scriptural worldview. Actually, as far as I have been able to tell, there aren't any. To accomplish our goal, then, we are going to be compelled to just make one up.

We should find this situation rather liberating.

A World of Bits and Qubits?

> *"The conventional view is that the universe is nothing but elementary particles. That is true, but it is equally true that the universe is nothing but bits—or rather, nothing but qubits. Mindful that if it walks like a duck and quacks like a duck then it's a duck, from this point on we'll adopt the position that since the universe registers and processes information like a quantum computer and is observationally indistinguishable from a quantum computer, then it is a quantum computer."*
> —Seth Lloyd, *Programming the Universe*

> *"And fear not them which kill the body, but are not able to kill the soul: but rather fear him which is able to destroy both soul and body in hell. Are not two sparrows sold for a farthing? And one of them shall not fall on the ground without your Father. But the very hairs of your head are all numbered. Fear not therefore, ye are of more value than many sparrows."*—Matthew 10:28–31

As the alert reader has probably already guessed, I am going to suggest here that the fundamental operation of our "reality" is computational. Please understand that I am absolutely not suggesting that we exist in a neural interactive simulation like the Matrix in the Wachowskis' 1999 movie. Our bodies (probably) aren't lying in hydroponic nutrient baths, and there (probably) aren't any killer agent programs that zip around acting as jailers (we'll just ignore the descriptions of demons in Scripture for now).

What I am suggesting is that we might be living in a reality where the quantum behaviors of fundamental particles (quarks, leptons, and bosons) are the results of a computational process very similar to what we do in our computers. The classical part of our reality, the part that we can see, derives from that quantum behavior the way the physics says it does.

As wacky as this may sound, the physics we've just waded through should demonstrate that it's possible. And in fact, it's under consideration by others more proficient than myself. It is, I think, ironic that the proposal that we might live in some kind of a computer model seems at first glance completely absurd to people who are not experts in the fundamentals of reality, while the experts themselves speak of it as being a very real possibility. For example: computer scientists and particle physicists Seth Lloyd (2006, *Programming the Universe*) and Stephen Wolfram (2002, *A New Kind of Science*) have argued that our world is computational. Physicist Paul Davies discusses a computational reality in *The Mind of God* (1992) and attributes the concept to Ed Fredkin, Tom Toffoli, and Frank Tipler. Philosopher Nick Bostrom published a paper in 2003 called "Are You Living in a Computer Simulation?" (*Philosophical Quarterly*, Vol. 53, No. 211, 243–255) examining the likelihood that our world (actually our universe) is a numerical simulation. One of his conclusions is that it is theoretically possible to make a computer capable of performing such a simulation using technology that is currently envisioned (assuming that it eventually works). It would take a computer the size of a planet (nicknamed a Jupiter brain), but it is possible. Physicists Silas Beane, Zohreh Davoudi, and Martin Savage released a paper in 2012 called "Constraints on the Universe as a Numerical Simulation" (arXiv:1210.1847v1 [hep-ph] 4 Oct 2012), where they start developing a mathematical model of numerical simulation in order to derive predictions that can be tested experimentally.

The actions of computers are enormously flexible; with a few practical limitations, anything that can be imagined can be modeled in a computer. The possibilities in a computational environment form a very large tent, one that can comfortably hold both modern physics and Scripture.

I mentioned some ways back that theoretical physicists will write papers about any bizarre idea that pops into their heads; it's part of the physics game to explore all possibilities. While the books and papers mentioned above, and others in the same vein, may or may not be serious science, they do illustrate that a computational reality is not outside the realm of the possible.

From the physics side, the basic list of reasons our reality might have a computational basis is the same as the summary of reality given a couple of sections back:

- The stark difference between statistical quantum behavior and localized classical behavior,
- The mere existence of two radically different kinds of physical behavior,
- Quantum state particles that exist as a superposition of possibilities,
- The insubstantial composition of the stuff we think of as solid,
- The insubstantial composition of a space and time that stretch and twist,
- Quantum entanglement that, although it can be measured, cannot possibly have a physical existence in any way that we can presently understand,
- Fundamental classical particles that are dimensionless point charges,
- Mathematically abstract particle interaction rules,
- Virtual particles that violate energy conservation in their brief existence,
- Mathematical descriptions that must be based solely on the numbers of particles in quantum states, where particles can't possibly have any individual existence at all (by the way, this aspect of our reality would dramatically simplify the mathematics of a computational model, if it is a computational model, by the enormous reduction in the number of permutations that need to be evaluated for multi-particle quantum systems),
- And, above all, the (possible) relationship between localization and conscious minds.

There is one other science story I'd like to add to help show why many physicists consider it possible that our reality might have a computational basis. The story begins during the Napoleonic Wars (1803–1815) between France and Great Britain. At the time, the breakthrough military technology that could potentially tip the balance of victory to one side or the other was the steam engine. French and British physicists worked diligently to develop theories of the operation of steam engines to help improve the size, power, and efficiency of the hot, smoky things. French physicist Nicolas Carnot and others developed thermodynamics, a mathematical model describing the relationship between heat, work, and mechanical motion that is still frequently used today in many fields. (Thermodynamics also turned out to be extremely useful for the analysis of chemical reactions, for example.)

Later, as part of the debate over the atomic nature of matter (settled by Einstein in 1905), three men named James Maxwell (1859), Ludwig Boltzman (1870s), and J. Willard Gibbs (1884) developed a group of mathematical models called statistical mechanics. Statistical mechanics uses the probabilities for the motions of large numbers of atoms to try to derive the behavior that we see in the big world. In particular, statistical mechanics was used to try to derive the behaviors described by thermodynamics based on the kinetic energies of individual atoms and molecules. One of Boltzman's results was his H theorem, which approximately described the behavior called entropy in thermodynamics. Entropy limits the amount of heat energy that can be converted to mechanical work and helps determine the time "direction" of chemical reactions.

Later still, in 1948 electrical engineer and mathematician Claude Shannon developed information theory to describe the transmission of messages over telegraph, telephone, and teletype wires. One of the mathematical models he developed described the limits for the amount of information that could pass through noisy, real-world electrical cables. He showed the derivation to fellow mathematician John von Neumann, asking von Neumann if he had any suggestions for a name.

Von Neumann answered, "You should call it H."

Shannon replied, "H? Why should I call it H?"

Von Neumann: "Because that's what Boltzmann called it."

You see, one of the reasons many physicists consider it a possibility that our reality might be computational is that Claude Shannon's information equations pop up all over the place in physics, not just in statistical mechanics.

One of the deep questions in physics: Why does the world that we see and measure behave in ways that can only be accurately described by abstract mathematics?

Feynman's answer: "Nobody knows, but we keep finding out interesting things that way."

The suggestion I am making here is an extension of the Copenhagen perspective ("the physics is what the math says it is"). Maybe the reason the world behaves mathematically is that the world really is mathematical.

The computational model suggested as a possibility here would use mathematical calculations to determine the behavior of matter in our world, for example: the distribution of particles in probability amplitude quantum states; quantum interactions between particle probability amplitudes; probability amplitude fluctuations; probability amplitude standing waves that form the structure of matter; et cetera, et cetera, et cetera. In short, it would use mathematical calculations to implement quantum mechanics and the standard model of particle physics that form the basis for all of the nuclear and chemical processes that we see as the real, material world around us.

The model would also use mathematical equations to calculate the behavior of spacetime described by special and general relativity, the motions and accumulation of matter in response to gravity, and the big bang cosmology that formed matter into galaxies, stars, and planets.

Mathematics that can calculate the physical behavior of our world can, with modest modifications, conceivably calculate other behaviors—behaviors that are not limited by the standard model and relativity. Behaviors, for example, like those described as miracles in Scripture.

Please remember that this is just a story; an exploration of what may be. There is no scientific proof that our reality is essentially computational. Yet the science does not rule out the possibility, and that is the point; a computational reality is one of many viable realities. Your humble author does think that this reality is a computational model, but your humble author is not numbered among the very wise.

There are, I think, two persuasive reasons to accept the bizarre notion that our reality might be computational, but they are from Scripture, not from physics. Physics only allows the possibility.

First, it seems likely that a creation made by God would be fundamentally mathematical. Any large project that we do routinely requires mathematical analysis and modeling before the actual work begins. For something like this creation, an enormous amount of planning and analysis would likely have been involved in setting up the physics, chemistry, and biology that make up our universe even before the actual work of creation began.

For us, the only way to accomplish that kind of detailed anticipation would be by mathematical modeling (usually on a computer). Of course, our limitations do not apply to God; he may have done (or be doing) something completely different. But mathematical modeling is a possibility. And mathematical modeling would require that the fundamental behavior of creation be mathematically predictable—as it is.

As I mentioned earlier, only in a computer do the behaviors described by relativity, quantum mechanics, and the standard model of particle physics fit with our classical intuition of what is common, what makes sense. Only in the flexibility of a computational reality that is not bound by classical physical law is it reasonable to imagine that such an odd collection of theories could be verified by experiment. Computational models are the only "physical" environment where we have been able to generate quantum behavior "from scratch." No experiment has ever been done that duplicates quantum behavior with a physical apparatus. We can build experiments that observe the quantum behavior of the world we live in, but we can't physically produce quantum behavior ourselves.

Looking from a comfortable armchair, general relativity, quantum mechanics, and the standard model of particle physics don't really fit into a reasonable natural world. For that matter, neither do many of the events of Scripture. But much like the physics, the events of Scripture suddenly become very reasonable in a computational reality that is not bound by physical law. There would be nothing "supernatural" about them:

Creation ex nihilo by speaking into existence?

A change in energy attributes to shift virtual particles to reality.

Changing a staff into a snake?

A copy and paste.

Parting the Red Sea?

A change in position attributes.

Fire from heaven?

A small adjustment of momentum attributes.

Shadows that move backward?

The sun stopping in the sky?

A shift in the local curvature of spacetime.

Raising the dead?

A simple restore.

Feeding the masses?

Copy and paste again.

Etc.

As long as physics allows the possibility that our reality has a computational basis, that the behavior of matter may not be limited to the equations of physics, there will never be anything in science that can contradict any miracle or prophecy in the Bible in any way. Any judgment of what is possible should be based on the freedom of the computational environment, not bound by the prison of modeled physical laws. For right now, with our current state of knowledge about the physics of our world, a computational reality is a viable alternative. It is arguably one of the more likely alternatives.

The second, and to me most persuasive, reason is that, regardless of the final form of God's creation, there is a place for a computational "reality" in the process. If one accepts the heretical notion that the creation was (or is) a kind of project, the result of a process of conception, development, design, and implementation, then it is not unreasonable that there should be a part of the project where different approaches are tried out to see what works best (development) and where final details are worked out (design). For us, the easiest and most common way to develop and design a complex project is with computational modeling: first comes the computational model, then the implementation of the real project.

> *"Heaven and earth shall pass away, but my words shall not pass away."*
> —Matthew 24:35

> *"For as the new heavens and the new earth, which I will make, shall remain before me, saith the Lord, so shall your seed and your name remain."*—Isaiah 66:22

Before we get all caught up in the possibilities of computational reality, we should keep in mind that even computers have a few restrictions and qualifications. The first restriction is pretty basic: digital computers, the kind we use now, are not capable and never will be capable of modeling quantum behavior on anything but the very tiniest scale. Our computers simply do not have the ability to keep track of the infinite list of possibilities that are embodied in a probability amplitude (Ψ).

Fortunately for our speculation, other kinds of computers might exist. I mentioned earlier that Nick Bostrom and others have estimated that computers based on technology that is currently thought to be possible do have the physical capability to model our universe. One of the items currently in development is known as a quantum computer. Quantum computers do have the capability for modeling quantum behavior; indeed, they cannot avoid it. The qubits mentioned in the title of this section are quantum bits, the basic element of information in quantum computers.

Another qualification relates to the nature of a computational world. The discussion of computational reality so far assumes that the computations are directed by intelligence, by God. It is not necessary that there be a directing intelligence in a computational world; it is possible to conceive of a reality that behaves in a computational way but does so mechanically, naturally, with no intelligent actors. A naturally computational reality is just another physical possibility among many possibilities and not particularly relevant to our speculation. But there is one interesting thing about it: follow the logic, and it ends up in the same place as our creation made by God. More about this later.

Finally, let's look at the issue of reality in a computational environment. Philosophers, physicists, and cosmologists occasionally amuse themselves by discussing the notion that we live in a computational model. They do so at conferences, in papers, and in books. One of the objections occasionally applied is that a computational reality is inherently fake, phony, a sham—not a reality at all. Any computational inhabitants (like us, if we are in such a reality) are not real, not actual persons.

Given this, it is likely easier for believers to seriously consider the notion that we might live in a computational model. For a nonbeliever, an inhabitant of a wholly natural and material world, the idea that we are computational models instead of material beings (whatever that really means) could be a serious disappointment. For a believer who accepts being a creation, something made, the difference in status between a computational model and some kind of breathing physical sculpture should not be all that important. Personally, if the choice is between existence as a computational model and no existence at all, I'll choose the bits and qubits every time and be grateful for the opportunity.

Next, if this universe is a computational model, it's a really nice computational model. It would not be wrong to call the computational models we make pale, inadequate imitations of reality, but God's creation is vibrant, bountiful, and indistinguishable from any imaginable reality. Before studying modern physics, I was completely fooled (and probably still am). Terms like *fake, phony,* and *sham* simply do not apply to the richly detailed world we see around us, however it was made.

Moreover, the notion that this creation, computation or not, is in any way less than real is not compatible with what Scripture tells us. The Bible holds that we are body, mind, and spirit. Our bodies will pass away when this creation ends (and probably sooner, for most of us), but mind and spirit are eternal. Being eternal, they are far more real than any short-lived, insubstantial, "material" body could ever be.

Lastly, Christ died for us. According to the Scripture in John 1:3, this creation was made through him. He would know better than anyone else how real or fake it was and is (and will be). Knowing the nature of creation, he chose to be born and live as one of us and to be tortured and killed to atone for our transgressions and provide us with a path to fellowship with him and with the Father. It is hard to picture him doing that for an existence that is anything less than real and true in every important way.

Theology from a Developmental Model

> *"Rejoice in the Lord always: and again I say, Rejoice. Let your moderation be known unto all men. The Lord is at hand. Be careful for nothing; but in every thing by prayer and supplication with thanksgiving let your requests be made known unto God. And the peace of God, which passeth all understanding, shall keep your hearts and minds through Christ Jesus."*—Philippians 4:4–7

I mentioned earlier that the notion of a developmental precreation before the final creation might be considered heresy. It is heretical, certainly; it conflicts with the omniscience of God. The whole idea is derived from an anthropomorphized God; a God reduced to something resembling human capabilities.

Guilty as charged, your honor.

I submit, however, that there may be some extenuating circumstances and a couple of reasons to consider the suggestion anyway.

First, remember that what I am proposing here is a creation where all of time simultaneously exists. In a sense, this may all be happening in an instant of time in the mind of God. It may only seem like long times are passing to us because we are in it.

Second, it's just a story. There is no claim of revealed truth here (nor, necessarily, any truth at all). The mechanism of creation probably isn't anything like what we do and think, in computers or anywhere else. But computers are something that we do (sort of) understand, and as Feynman said in answer to the question of why reality obeys abstract mathematics, we may find that we learn some interesting things by looking at creation in this particular way.

Moreover, the idea of a design-and-development phase isn't a reduction of God's capabilities if he simplified this part of creation as a matter of choice, out of consideration for us. There logically needs to be some point in creation where the details are worked out about how it is all to be done, what it will all look like, and how it will all work; the only odd part of the viewpoint suggested here, I think, is that *we* might be participating in that part of the process.

One of the arguments that advocates of atheism use to discredit the notion that our world is a creation made by God is the plain fact that it is imperfect. Viruses, disease pathogens, genetic defects, crippling injuries, the pervasive cruelty of a natural world composed of predators and prey, pain, suffering, hatred, injustice, corruption, crime, and war are all held up as examples of things a loving, omniscient God would never make (as if any of us could do as well, let alone better). While that logic may hold for a finished creation, it does not hold for a developmental precursor to a finished creation.

If this world is developmental, and if our conception of what a loving, omniscient God would do is anywhere near accurate (but good luck with that; his thoughts are higher than our thoughts), then all of those unpleasant things won't be present in the final creation. One reason they won't be there in the final creation is that they *are* here in the developmental creation—here where the pernicious effects and the root causes can be plainly seen so they can be weeded out of the final product.

One purpose of a developmental simulation (when we make them) is to try things out to find what works and what doesn't. In order to do that, things that probably aren't going to work still have to be done; sometimes the results can be surprising.

There are also parts of this creation that *do* work. Some of what does work might be in the finished creation because it was tried here first. Chocolate (ever tasted baker's chocolate? who knew?), pizza, beer, wine, cheese, sourdough toast, pasta, chips, fruit, vegetables (except zucchini), hot tubs, hammocks, cool breezes on a hot day, warm sunshine on colder days, spring water, forests, mountains, streams, swimming holes, downhill skiing, sailing, Harley Davidson motorcycles, soccer, music, etc.; all the many pleasures of God's generous providence that are just as much a part of development as sprained ankles, brain tumors, and sore backs.

Perhaps some of the aspects of creation that need to be worked out have to do with us: personalities, behaviors, relationships, and societies that will suit us in the final creation.

Perhaps God has generously given us an opportunity to participate in the process: an opportunity to help shape the final creation, an opportunity to make the creation partly ours as much as it is rightly his.

> *"And ye have forgotten the exhortation which speaketh unto you as unto children, My son, despise not thou the chastening of the Lord, nor faint when thou art rebuked of him: for whom the Lord loveth he chastiseth, and scourgeth every son whom he receiveth."*—Hebrews 12:5–6

Besides trying things out, there is another reason to do a developmental test run before the main event: they are very handy for stress testing. Project computer models get hammered as a normal part of any development process: they are stretched, bent, twisted, heated, frozen, dunked in water, struck with large heavy objects, turned upside down, and shaken. They are subjected to every unpleasant condition that the design team hopes will never happen to the real thing in order to expose flaws and weaknesses—to make the final project stronger.

Perhaps we are a part of a development. Maybe we are also being evaluated. If so, it would not be unreasonable to put us in a challenging environment, one where we could be exposed to conflict, suffering, and temptation in conditions where we could plausibly convince ourselves that we are alone and unobserved. A world where we could, if we tried, convince ourselves that God does not exist and that there will not be any consequences for whatever we can get away with. In that case, a developmental model would have to look like a natural world (unless one looked very closely).

There is one final characteristic of developmental models to be considered: the more accurate they are, the better their results are going to be. In order to get the very best results—for the final project to be very good—the developmental simulation has to be nearly perfect, almost indistinguishable from the real thing.

Computers and Quantum Computation

Coming up next is a brief presentation of the basics of two aspects of computation: computer architecture (why different parts of a computer go in particular locations) and quantum computation. The physics of computers will play a minor role in the speculation: the practical requirements for computer architecture, especially parallel computers, will be a factor in the speculation about Genesis 1. Quantum computation and the quantum nature of our reality will be a major factor in the final speculation about the nature of this world.

The significant feature of computer architecture is that the physical arrangement of the parts of a computer will depend on the task it is intended to do. Physical structure mostly depends on the required flow of information and the type of calculation that will be done.

The other important bit (pun intended) is that the modeling of quantum physical behavior (like our reality) is extremely difficult to do on a digital computer like the ones that we mostly use. The difficulty of quantum physical modeling has already been mentioned; the presentation in this section will show some of the details about how quantum modeling has to be done and why it is so difficult.

Computer Architecture

One of the foundations of modern computing was proposed by mathematician Alan Turing in 1936. He described a very simple, imaginary computer called a Turing machine. The Turing machine is not actually used to make our computers, but the idea is extremely useful for doing calculations about computers and computing. A Turing machine has the basic elements required for doing any kind of computation, and so any kind of calculation or computation that can actually be done on a computer can be modeled using the elements of a Turing machine. As long as a physical computer has all of the elements of a Turing machine available (called Turing complete), it is capable of doing any calculation or computation that can be done on any Turing complete computer.

Mathematical models based on Turing machines are also used to identify the many kinds of calculations that cannot be done efficiently, or at all, on digital computers—modeling quantum behavior, for example.

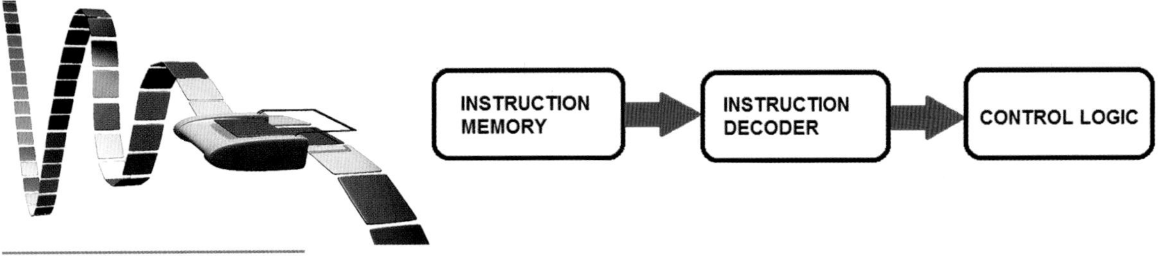

Fig. 61. Turing Machine

A Turing machine is very simple: it has a tape with symbols written on it, a symbol reader that reads one of the symbols on the tape, and a set of rules for performing actions (like moving the tape) based on the symbol. In terms more applicable to practical computers: a Turing machine includes an instruction memory, an instruction decoder, and control logic that acts as directed by the instructions.

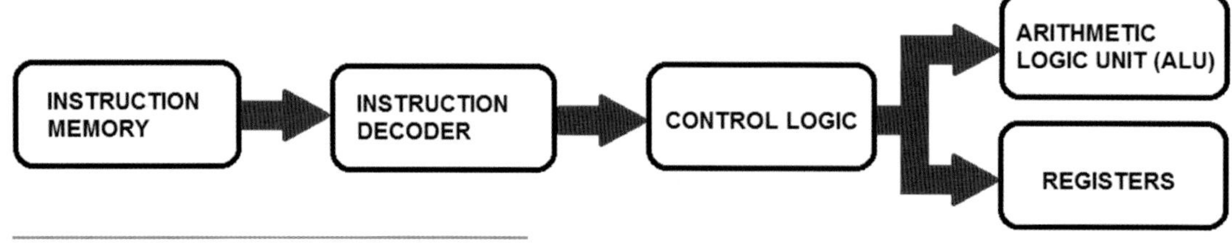

Fig. 62. Elements of a Computer CPU

We can make the step from an imaginary Turing machine to a real computer by adding two more elements: registers and an arithmetic logic unit (called an ALU). The symbols that our computers (mostly) work with are just numbers. Computer memories store numbers. Computer programs are lists of instructions, where each instruction is just a number in memory; a program is just a list of numbers. What computers and computer programs do is move and change the values of numbers in memory. The numbers that computers move and change are called data.

Both data and instructions are just numbers in memory. The only difference between them is how they are used by the computer.

Registers are places in a computer to store the value of one number. Different registers store numbers as instructions, as addresses (the physical locations of numbers of interest in memory), and as data.

The arithmetic logic unit, as its name suggests, is the part of a computer that does arithmetic. It adds, subtracts, multiplies, and divides numbers in data registers.

The addition of registers and an arithmetic logic unit transform the simplistic, imaginary Turing machine into a realistic computer, a central processing unit or CPU.

The diagram on the next page (figure 63) shows the architecture, the physical organization, of a Zilog Z80 microprocessor. The Z80 was a popular microprocessor for personal computers back in the 1970s before IBM gave the personal computer market to Intel and Microsoft in 1981. The Z80 is a relatively simple processor; modern microprocessors are far more complex.

Over on the left in the diagram are the control logic and instruction decoder. The

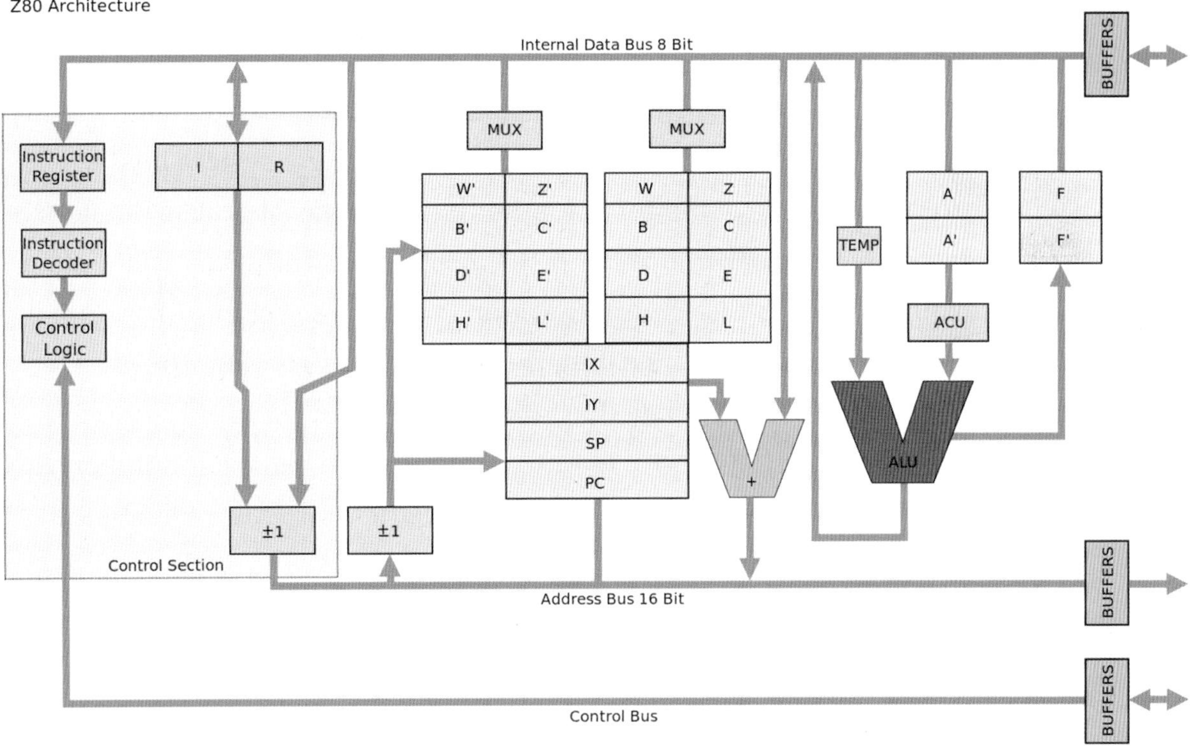

Fig. 63. Z80 Microprocessor (CPU) Block Diagram

instruction memory from the basic diagram has been replaced by an instruction register, because the Z80 uses the same memory (not shown) for both instructions and data. The only difference between instructions and data is what processor registers they are put in; both are just numbers.

The boxes with one or two letter names are registers. The I and R registers shown next to the instruction register, for example, store the address of the current instruction. The ±1 box below the instruction address registers means that the instruction address is increased by 1 when it is used to get the next instruction from memory.

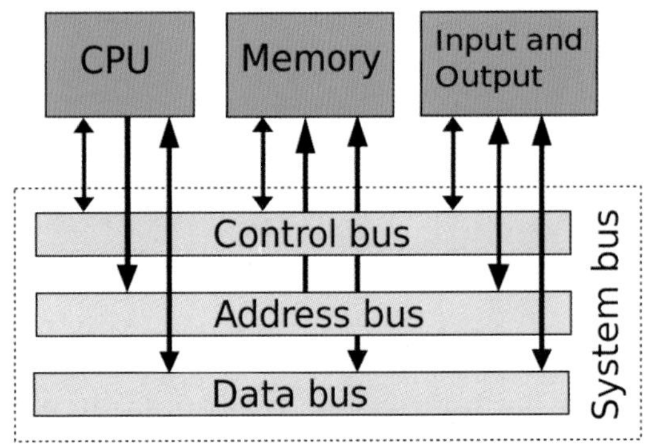

Fig. 64. Von Neumann Architecture.

The arithmetic logic unit is the red V-shaped block. MUX (multiplexer) boxes are switches that control which register each number is stored in. Buffers are groups of registers that temporarily store numbers going to and from the outside world.

The Z80 microprocessor, a very small (hence the "micro" in the name) central processing unit (CPU), is an example of the Von Neumann computer architecture. In the Von Neumann architecture, the CPU converses with the outside world through three pathways called the control bus, the address bus, and the data bus. Together, these are called the system bus. The Von Neumann architecture has a single system bus.

We will be going into some detail for computer bus pathways because the flow of information between the parts of a computer is the most critical influence that dictates the physical structure of computers. Communications pathways and information flow will also be a significant factor in the interpretation of Genesis 1 coming up later.

A bus is a communications pathway that connects different parts of a computer so they can pass numbers back and forth. In our computers, the values of numbers are represented by electrical voltages on wires. A typical electrical structure for a bus is shown in the diagram below.

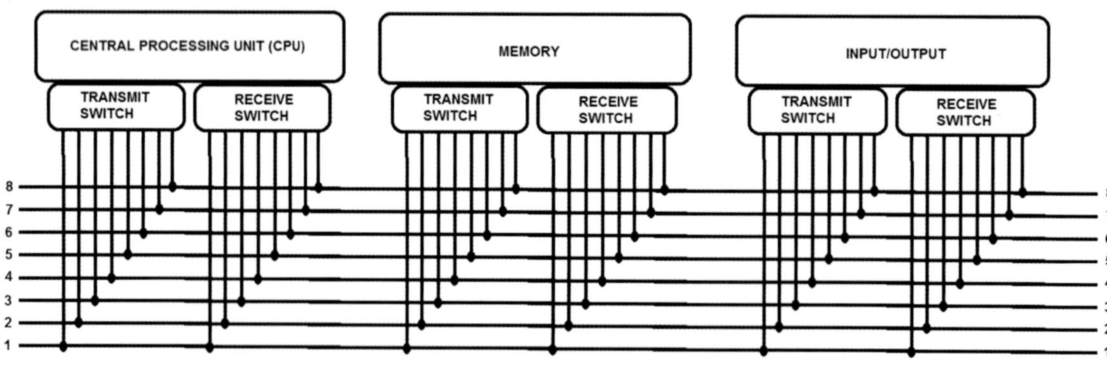

Fig. 65. Bus Electrical Diagram

The bus shown has eight wires to carry electrical voltages, so it would be called an 8-bit bus, like the 8-bit data bus on the Z80 microprocessor. The 16-bit address bus for the Z80 would have sixteen wires but would otherwise be much the same. Registers and other memory locations that store numbers are basically switches that connect to +5 volts or 0 volts (usually). Transmit switches in the diagram above connect the bus wires to the outputs of the memory switches; receive switches in the diagram connect to electronics that set the positions of the memory switches.

One of the main tasks the CPU does in a computer is control the flow of information on the various bus pathways. All of the buses are party lines, with many different potential talkers and listeners; the word *bus* is from the Latin *omnibus,* meaning "for all."

As an example, the following steps might be used by a CPU to get an instruction from memory:

> First, the CPU specifies the address, the location in memory, for the instruction by putting the address value onto the address bus. For a CPU like the Z80, where the address is twice the size of data, the CPU would load two (8-bit) data values into an address register (16-bit) and open the transmit switches that electrically connect the address register to the address bus (this sets the voltages on the bus wires to the levels specified by values of the bits in the address: 0 volts for a 0-bit value; 5 volts for a 1-bit value).
>
> The CPU would then use the control bus to ask memory for a value. To begin, all devices connected to the control bus except the CPU would only have receive switches open to the control bus. The CPU puts a number on the control bus to tell the memory that the next number is a command for the memory. Memory responds with a number on the control bus to inform the CPU that it is ready, willing, and able to serve. The CPU then puts a number on the control bus that tells the memory to send a number value.
>
> Responding to the command, memory opens receive switches to "read" the values on the address bus. Memory opens transmit switches for the memory location specified by the address to the data bus. The CPU then opens the receive switches for the instruction register to get the value from the data bus. If the command were to store a number value, memory would use receive switches to copy the value on the data bus to the location specified by the number on the address bus.

CPU actions are done in clock cycles. A single CPU is basically able to perform one simple action per clock cycle. A microprocessor clock speed of 2 GHz means that the CPU is performing two billion simple actions per second. Different CPU actions can take different numbers of clock cycles: simple actions like copying a number from the data bus to a register take one cycle; complex actions like getting an instruction from memory can, as described above, take many cycles. In modern processors, arithmetic actions like addition or multiplication usually take one or two clock cycles.

Each bus can only pass one number in one direction between one pair of computer elements at one time. Moving information on the buses is the slowest thing a

CPU does; a simple CPU like the Z80, doing a numerical calculation, might spend 80 percent of its time moving data on the buses and only 20 percent actually doing the calculation.

Efforts to improve the performance of computers mostly focus on increasing the speed of information flow on bus pathways or reducing the amount of information that flows on the various bus pathways.

One way to increase the speed is to put more information on the bus. Modern microprocessors use a 64-bit data bus. Even at the same clock speed (much faster now than they were back in the 1970s), a modern processor would move data eight times as fast as the old Z80 with its 8-bit data bus. The Z80 required four data transfers from memory to put a single 32-bit floating point number into registers (floating point numbers are decimals like 3.141592653). A modern microprocessor can move floating point numbers two at a time.

Another way to increase speed is to make the bus wires shorter. Electrical voltage signals move on wires at about 95,000 miles per second, but even at that speed a modern microprocessor would have to wait for several clock cycles to send and receive a message from a memory located on the other side of a circuit board. The length of CPU clock cycles is limited by the amount of time it takes to move electrical signals from one part of the CPU to another. Signal delay time is called latency in computer design. One of the main reasons modern microprocessors have higher clock speeds than the old Z80 is that modern CPU circuits are smaller and closer together.

Modern microprocessors usually have more than one set of buses (control bus, address bus, and data bus) to get numbers from memory. A Harvard architecture CPU, for example, has two system buses that each access different memories, one bus for data and one for instructions (figure 66, to the right).

Another way to make computations faster is to reduce the time that it takes to read or write numbers to and from memory.

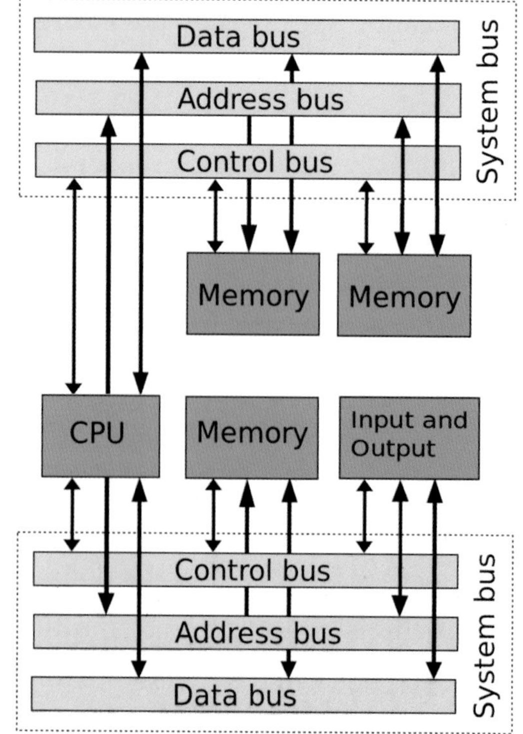

Fig. 66. Harvard Architecture

One of the fundamental rules of computer design is that small memories are fast and large memories are slow.

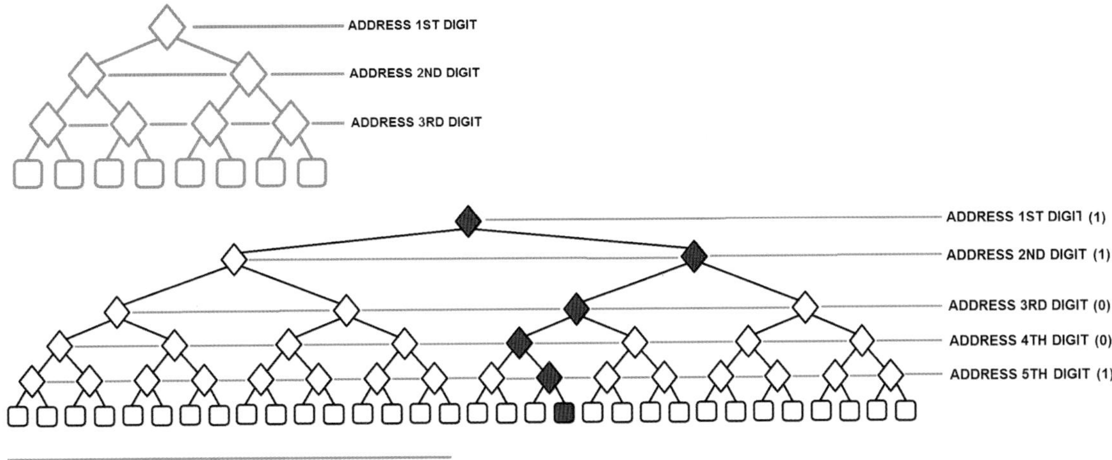

Fig. 67. Memory Address Switching

Computer memories (except for disc drives) can be organized as in the diagram above. Banks of switches (diamonds in the figure) are set by the numbers in the address to provide an access path to each memory location (rectangles in the figure) that stores a number. Smaller memories have fewer switches and shorter addresses; larger memories have more switch banks and longer addresses. It physically takes more time to get electrical signals from larger memories than it does from smaller memories, partly because the wires are longer and partly because it takes more time to set the switches in the correct positions. (Remember that for a modern 64-bit memory, each one of the diamonds in the figure represents sixty-four physical switches.)

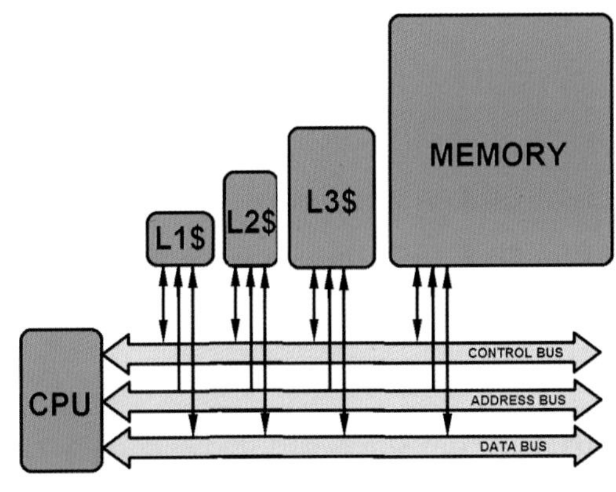

Because smaller memories can respond faster, modern computers have a chain of memories (called levels—L1, L2, L3 in the figure) with smaller memories close to the CPU and larger memories further away. The smaller memories are called caches ($ in the figure). Level one cache memory (L1$) is used for the most frequently needed data, L2$ the data next most frequently used, and so on.

Parallel Computers

The architecture of a particular computer can depend on the type of computation being done. Some types of computations, such as most scientific computing, commercial transactions for large companies, and—the most lucrative computation of all—computer video games are relatively simple calculations that are carried out again and again on very large amounts of data. One of the ways to do faster computations for these types of problems is to divide up the data and do the calculations in multiple CPU processors at the same time.

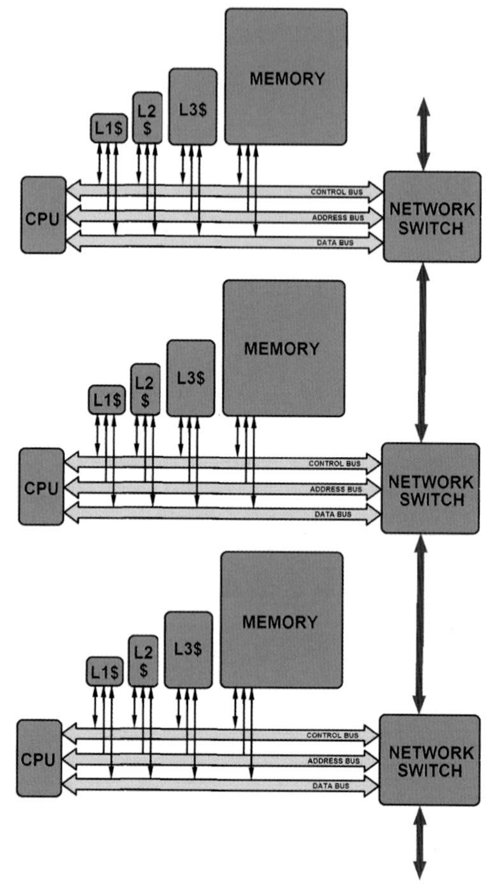

The figure at right shows a simple example of several processors, each with its own memory, that are linked together by a communications network in an architecture that is called a parallel computer. The communications network is used to divide up the data, to pass results between processors when they need to share data at the boundaries of the data divisions, and to make sure that all of the processors are working on the right things at the right times (synchronization).

The links between switches for each processor in a communications network are very similar to the bus pathways that are used inside the CPU: they pass one number at a time between two linked switches. Information passing between processors that are not near each other must pass from switch to switch to switch as it travels through the network.

Passing information over longer distances can take a (relatively) long time and slow down the performance of an entire group of processors. Parallel computer architectures use different layouts of switches and links (called a network topology) to try to reduce the time required to move information as much as possible.

Figure 68 on the opposite page shows some different ways of arranging communications links (the blue bars) between processors (the gray spheres) in a parallel computer communications network. Simplest is a one-dimensional (1-D) network with

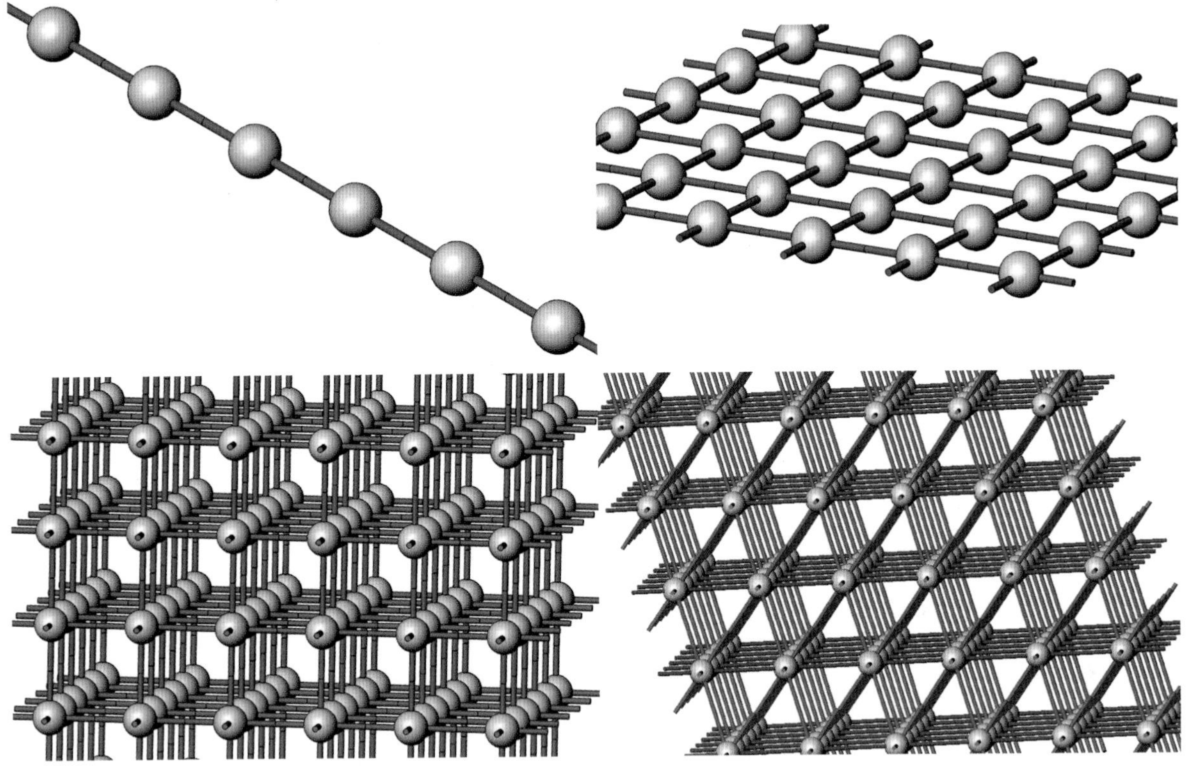

Fig. 68. Network Topologies, 1-D, 2-D, 3-D, and 4-D Grid.

processors arranged in a line. Some of the first supercomputers, which used a parallel architecture in the 1980s with a few tens of processors, would use a two-dimensional grid topology. Modern parallel supercomputers with up to 60,000 CPU processors mostly use a 3-D grid arrangement.

The 4-D arrangement is just included to show that it is possible to extend network topologies to higher numbers of links between switches. No current parallel computers use a 4-D grid network topology.

A Little Theology from Computer Architecture

The physics of computer architecture will play only a minor role in the speculation about Genesis 1 later in this book, but it's important to remember that the flow of information and the type of computation being done affects what physical arrangement is best to use. In terms of our computational speculation, computers that model rocks or stars would be arranged differently than computers that model bacteria, whales, and elephants (or us).

If anyone is interested in a betting pool, your author would like to place a small wager ($1, your author is not financially courageous) that the parallel computer network that models our physical reality (if there is such a computer) uses a four-dimensional network topology with processor nodes that model probability amplitude interaction vertices. Just a guess.

Quantum Computation

> *"What other problems can quantum computers solve more quickly than classical computers? The short answer seems to be that we don't know. Coming up with good quantum algorithms seems to be* hard." —Nielsen and Chuang, *Quantum Computation and Quantum Information*

The easiest way to explain quantum computation is by explaining how it is different from classical computation. So this explanation will start with some more nitty-gritty details of how binary computers work.

There are many ways to make computers. Binary, two-state computers, with numbers (0 and 1) represented by groups of on or off signals, are the most common type. Other kinds of computers can use more than two states. A four-state computer, for example, might use different voltages to represent the numbers 0, 1, 2, and 3 and do base 4 mathematics instead of base 2.

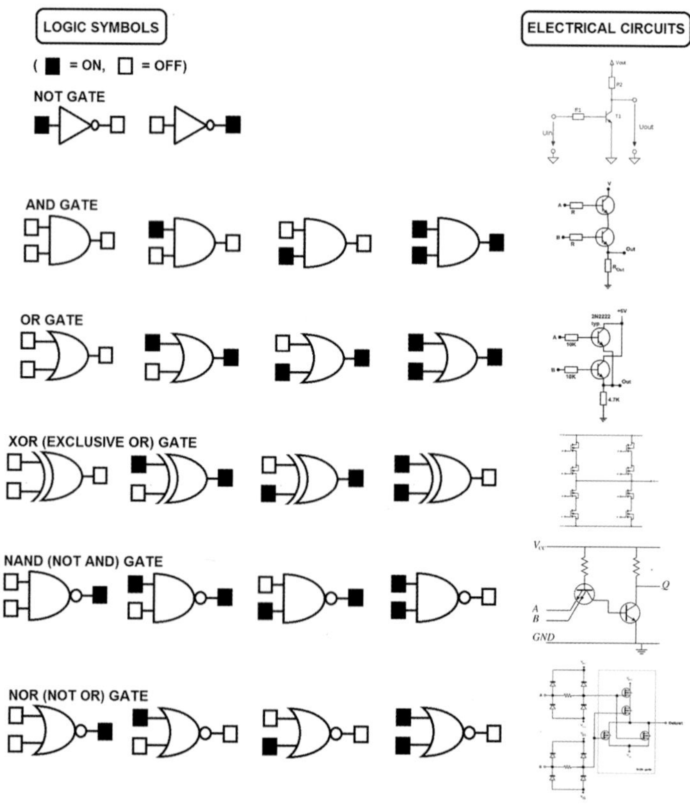

Fig. 68.1. Logic Gates

It is also possible to make analog (continuously variable) computers with infinite states. Multiple state computers and analog computers are both theoretically more capable than binary computers; they can do calculations to solve problems faster than binary computers can. But only theoretically. In the real world, where wires are noisy, binary computers work the best because, as Claude Shannon derived mathematically in 1948, the most efficient way to transmit information on a noisy real-world line is with binary electrical signals that use all of the available voltage for each bit of information. Shannon's information theory applies to the bus pathways inside the CPU and to all of the wires in an electronic computer.

Binary computers, multi-state computers, and analog computers are all based on classical physics: the results they produce are exactly determined by the data and the programs they run.

In the same way that the architecture for processors is based on the imaginary Turing machine, the detailed operation of binary computers is based on the idea of logic gates.

Logic gates use one or two binary (on or off) inputs to determine the state of a single output. Some common logic gates, and some electronic circuits that could be used to make logic gates, are shown in the diagram on the previous page (from Wikipedia). Our computers mostly use electronics to make logic gates. Early computers used mechanical relays instead.

To make computers, logic gates are combined in groups called logic gate arrays, or combinatorial logic. In modern computers, most of the parts of a CPU—the instruction decoder, the control logic, the arithmetic logic unit, and others—are made of logic gate arrays. The diagram to the right (based on graphics from cpuville.com) shows the logic gate arrangement for an 8-bit adder that would be a part of an arithmetic logic unit.

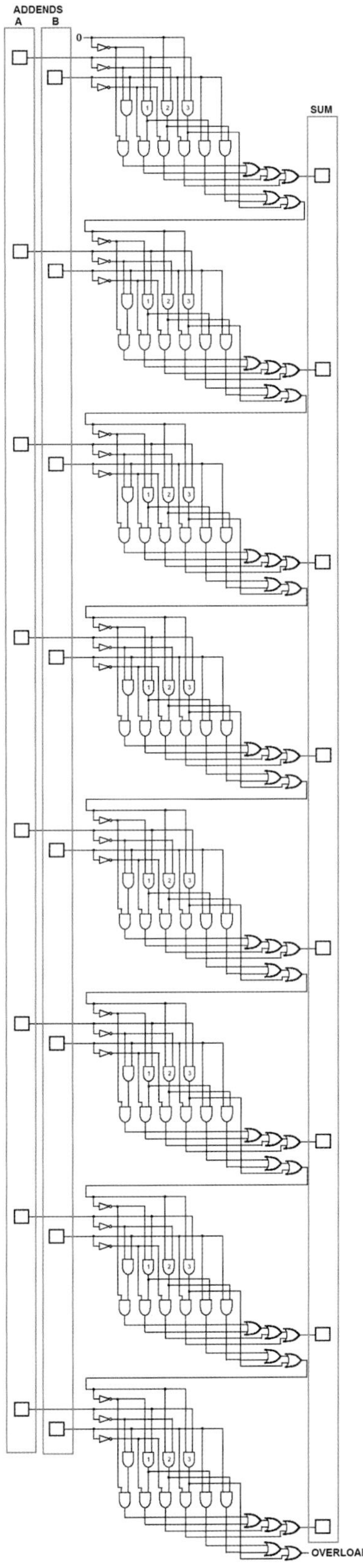

Fig. 68.2. Gate Array for 8-Bit Adder
Adapted from *Adder Gate Array*, circa 2014, www.cpuville.com, © 2004 by Donn Stewart. Reprinted with permission.

To use the adder, two numbers to be added would be loaded into the addend registers A and B. The resulting sum could be read a few clock cycles later after the gates all have a chance to arrange themselves.

It is possible to make logic gate arrays that will produce practically any binary result from any binary input. The instruction decoder in a CPU might be a logic gate array that opens or closes switches based on the binary composition of the instruction. An instruction to load a value from the data bus into a register, for example, would be a binary input to a logic gate array whose output for that particular input opens the read switches that connect the register to the data bus. Different input sequences (i.e. different instructions) would each have different outputs from the gate array, all of which perform different operations in the CPU.

What is the point of all this? Just this: the values of the outputs from logic gate arrays in binary computers are exactly determined by the arrangements of the logic gates in the various gate arrays that together make up the CPU. In philosophical terms, the behavior of binary computers is deterministic. In physics terms, the results of computations on binary computers are classical, completely determined by how the computation is done.

The basic unit of information in a binary computer is a *bit,* short for *binary digit.* As was mentioned before, a bit is either on or off. The basic unit of information in a quantum computer is a *qubit,* the quantum mechanics version of a classical bit. Remember that, in quantum mechanics, a physical system is described by a probability amplitude (Ψ) that is a list of all of the possible states of the system and the associated possibilities for each state. Possibilities in quantum mechanics are always complex numbers that can be multiplied by their complex conjugates to give probabilities. Also remember that when an object like a qubit is in the quantum state, it actually exists as a distributed probability amplitude, not as a localized classical object (according to the Copenhagen interpretation).

The mathematic description of a single qubit in quantum state is written:

$$|\Psi_1\rangle = (x_1 + y_1 i)|0\rangle + (x_2 + y_2 i)|1\rangle$$

The straight line and arrow notation is used in quantum mechanics to describe the states of a system. The straight line and right arrow above is called a ket, and it describes the list of states. The equation above means that the probability amplitude Ψ for a single qubit is the superposition of the states 0 and 1, where the 0 state has the possibility ($x_1 + y_1i$) and the state 1 has the possibility ($x_2 + y_2i$).

As long as the qubit is not used to produce a readable result, it remains in quantum state as a superposition of the possible states (0 or 1 for a single qubit). When one of us decides to read a result, each qubit localizes to a particular value, either 0 or 1. The probability that the value of the qubit will be 0 is the product of the possibility for the 0 state and its complex conjugate: $(x_1 + y_1i) \times (x_1 - y_1i) = x_1^2 + y_1^2$. Similarly, the probability that the qubit will provide a result of 1 is $x_2^2 + y_2^2$.

The mathematic description for a two-qubit word in a quantum computer would be:

$$|\Psi_2\rangle = (x_1 + y_1 i)\,|00\rangle + (x_2 + y_2 i)\,|01\rangle + (x_3 + y_3 i)|10\rangle + (x_4 + y_4 i)\,|11\rangle$$

As with the single qubit, each possible state of the two-qubit word has its own possibility. For a two-qubit word, there are $2 \times 2 = 2^2 = 4$ possible states. As was mentioned before, the mathematics for quantum mechanics gets really difficult when the number of objects in the system increases above 2. The same sort of thing happens in quantum computation. Here is the mathematic description of a 32-qubit word, not quite as long as the 64-bit word length used in modern binary microprocessors; a 32-qubit word has $2^{32} = 4{,}294{,}967{,}296$ possible states:

$$|\Psi_{32}\rangle = (x_1 + y_1 i)\,|00000000000000000000000000000000\rangle + \cdots$$
$$\cdots + (x_{4,294,967,296} + y_{4,294,967,296} i)\,|11111111111111111111111111111111\rangle$$

The probability amplitude for a 32-qubit word has over four billion terms. A 64-qubit word would have more than 10^{19} complex ($x + yi$) possibilities in its probability amplitude.

I mentioned earlier that it is not practical to model the behavior of quantum state physical systems on our binary computers. This is why. A binary model of a quantum state system that is approximated by 64-bit floating point numbers would have to keep track of the values of 10^{19} complex possibilities for each number that represents some feature of the system. Computer models of physical systems frequently require millions or billions of 64-bit floating point numbers. A binary CPU would have to store 10^{30} or so numbers in memory and move 10^{19} floating point numbers (or more) over the data bus to do even a simple addition. Don't try to hold your breath while waiting for results.

Physical computer models with 64-bit accuracy for each floating point number are average. They produce results that give useful information, but they generally do not accurately model real-world physical behavior, not even classical physical behavior. Critical models that need more accurate results might use 128-bit floating point numbers (10^{38} probability amplitude terms) or 256-bit floating point numbers (10^{77} probability amplitude terms—and we just ran out of particles in the universe on which to store numbers). Quantum computers (if and when we figure out how to make them) would be able to do those kinds of calculations routinely.

Quantum computers would use quantum wires and quantum logic gates to do computations in the same sort of way that binary computers currently use electrical wires and electrical logic gates. The big difference between classical and quantum binary computers—the reason that quantum computation may be so much more powerful than classical computation—is that quantum logic gates do not change the value of the qubit. A qubit in quantum state does not have a value to change. Rather, quantum logic gates change the values of the complex ($x + yi$) possibilities. A 64-qubit quantum logic gate array, if we ever manage to make such a thing, would be able to change the values of all 10^{19} possibilities for a 64-qubit word in just a few clock cycles. The values of all 10^{19} possibilities can effectively be stored in just sixty-four qubits.

Because they would be able to manipulate huge amounts of information with just a few logic gates and clock cycles, quantum computers are theoretically capable of doing some types of calculations enormously faster than digital computers. The alert reader may have noticed that word "theoretically" popping up again. Like multiple-state and analog computers, quantum computers have a fundamental problem: they can store and manipulate huge amounts of data very efficiently, but they can never show it to us. It all remains hidden.

Why? Because when results are read for a quantum computer calculation, the probability amplitude for the qubits localizes to one binary number. In other words, qubits act exactly like particles do. All the information in the distribution of possibilities effectively vanishes when one of us chooses to read a result. It is tempting to wonder whether the quantum information was ever really there at all, but, just like particles, the values of the binary numbers that show up as the results of quantum computations can only be explained with quantum information and quantum mechanics. If the same calculation is done many times, the results form a distribution, as predicted by the probability amplitude for the qubits. Calculations on quantum computers do not generally provide specific answers; they provide a distribution of numbers that is close to the answer.

In some types of calculations, distributions of answers would still be much better than the much longer times required for equivalent digital computations. Mathematicians have been able to figure out a few practical applications for quantum computers: factoring large numbers into primes, searching huge amounts of data, and modeling the quantum behavior of the real world. The number is small because, as mentioned in the quote at the start of this section, the mathematics for quantum mechanics is really difficult to do.

Scientists are interested in more efficient information searches and modeling real world (quantum) behavior, but the big money now driving the development of quantum computers is the possibility that they could be used to factor large numbers into primes very quickly. Many of the encryption schemes that are used today to secure military and diplomatic communications and financial transactions are based on finding prime numbers that can be multiplied together to produce very large numbers. In other words, it looks as though quantum computers will be very good at breaking codes.

For our speculation in this book, the noteworthy feature of quantum computers is just that they would have to manipulate huge amounts of information in order to do even the simplest computations. Complex, real-world quantum calculations would be extremely difficult to do on any kind of classical physics computer that we know of. Modeling real-world quantum behavior is completely beyond our current capability.

One other little interesting point before we move on. We are currently trying to figure out how to build quantum computers, and at the moment, it looks as though we will likely succeed in time. But the quantum computers that we are perhaps close to making *use fundamental particles as qubits;* they rely on the quantum behavior of our world to work. And we still don't know how or why the fundamental physics of our world is quantum mechanics—nor do we have any idea at all of how to produce quantum behavior in any reasonable sort of physical world. As I mentioned earlier, the only physical environment where we are currently able to reproduce quantum behavior is in computational models.

Requirements of Creation

"The overall problem of habitable zones is highly nonlinear. It will require considerable computational power to perform the required Monte Carlo simulations and long temporal integrations. Its solution will require continued advancements in astrophysics, geophysics, climatology, and biology." —Guillermo Gonzalez, "Habitable Zones and Fine Tuning" in *The Nature of Nature*

So what are the developmental and design issues that would likely need to be addressed in preparing for a project like creation? In this section, we'll list some of these issues in order to see whether the universe and the world around us fit with the notion that our reality might be an intelligently designed, developmental computational model. If it is, one thing we would expect to see is that it is an efficient model: that it achieves the goals of the project, identifying the needs of creation, without a lot of wasted time and energy. Our universe should be just enough, and maybe a little more, than is necessary to do the job.

Surprisingly, an enormous amount of work has been done by physicists, astronomers, cosmologists, astrobiologists, and astrophysicists over the years on this very subject. It is one of the hotly debated topics in science because it is a major point in the ongoing debate between believers and nonbelievers over the role and existence of God in this world—a debate that has been going on for several hundred years. Wikipedia has some articles on the subject; some of the generic topic names include *anthropic principle, fine-tuned universe, circumstellar habitable zone, galactic habitable zone,* and *cosmic habitable age* (this one is not in Wikipedia yet). Books on the subject (and sources for some of the information in this section) are:

- *The Accidental Universe*, 1982, Paul Davies. A relatively short introduction to the physics of creation.

- *The Anthropic Cosmological Principle*, 1986, John Barrow and Frank Tipler. This is a serious tome, probably more than most would actually want to know about fine-tuning.

- *New Proofs for the Existence of God*, 2010, Robert Spitzer. A very readable summary of some of the arguments regarding the physics of creation.

- "Habitable Zones and Fine Tuning," Guillermo Gonzalez, in *The Nature of Nature*, 2011, edited by Bruce Gordon and William Dembski. A very nice, short, but comprehensive presentation of fine-tuning. *The Nature of Nature* is a large compendium of scientific papers on the subject of creation, mostly from an Intelligent Design perspective, including history, philosophy, physics, biology, etc.

Because this is a topic of debate, many of the issues mentioned in this section are disputed; the scientific validity of some things said here is questionable. But I am going to mention these uncertain issues anyway, because uncertainty is good enough for speculation. We are not trying to establish a truth here—nobody knows enough to do that. We are just trying to explore a possibility.

The other reason for this list is to try to give an impression of how much work would be involved in making something with the size and complexity of this creation—to perhaps, provide some reassurance that a developmental computational model might be useful.

As with most of the science that has already been presented in this book, it is not necessary for you to memorize the list; the goal is only for you to get a feel for what would be involved in producing something like creation. Flipping through the pages of this section with a comment like, "Wow, that's a lot of work!" is really all that's needed.

The major issue, of course, is that the observed universe is really big and looks like it has been around for a long time. There are an estimated 170 billion galaxies in the part of the universe that we can see. The furthest galaxy we can see (Z8 GND 5296) was thirteen billion light years away the last time we saw it (thirteen billion years ago); it is probably about forty-two billion light years away by now. Small galaxies have ten million stars. Really big ones have 100 trillion stars. Ours has about 400 billion stars.[1] The estimated age of our universe, the time since the big bang, is 13.8 billion years.

Looking around at our universe we might ask: was all of that really necessary?

But when we look at the requirements for a stable biome, for the kind of environment that can develop and support the variety of life that we see here on earth, the answer is yes, it probably was all really necessary.

---

1 "Milky Way." Retrieved c. 2014 from https://en.wikipedia.org/wiki/Milky_Way

The Basics

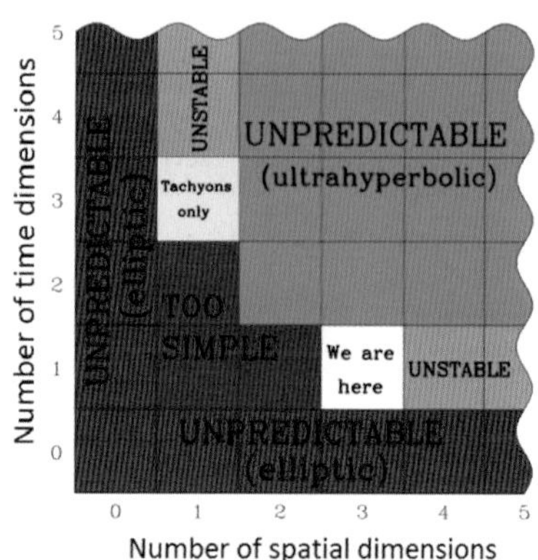

Fig. 69. Other Spacetimes

- **Spacetime.** Creation needs to have a place where everything can happen. A spacetime with three spatial dimensions and one time dimension (like ours) turns out to be convenient for life. With other dimensions:
    - Electromagnetic fields don't work.
    - Protons and electrons are unstable.
    - Planetary orbits are unstable.
    - Conservation laws do not produce predictable physical behavior.
- **Matter.** It would all be pretty boring with nothing in it. To have matter, creation requires:
    - Conservation laws (including the quantum mechanics equations) and Pauli exclusion.
    - Quantum mechanics properties and attributes.
    - Quantum mechanics probability amplitudes (Ψ).
    - Fundamental particles with distinctive properties.
    - Particle interaction vertices with U(1), SU(2), and SU(3) Lie group interaction rules.
    - Electric, color, weak isospin, and mass-energy charges.
    - Electromagnetic, strong nuclear, weak nuclear, and gravitational forces.
    - Higgs fields and Higgs bosons.
- **The right start.**
    - A big bang with the right expansion rate relative to the strength of gravitation and the weak nuclear force turns out to be ideal for the world we need. "Expansion rate" refers to how fast distance increases between stationary objects as spacetime stretches and expands. Physicist Paul Davies estimates that:
        - A slower expansion rate or stronger gravitation and weak nuclear force (by one part in 10^{40}) would have collapsed into a big crunch before now.
        - A faster expansion rate or weaker gravitation and weak nuclear force (also by one part in 10^{40}) would have dispersed matter too quickly to form galaxies.

- A big bang with low entropy is likewise important. Entropy is the measure of energy available for nuclear and chemical reactions (among other things); increasing entropy (or decreasing energy) is required for stars to burn and living organisms to live. The universe would need low starting entropy to have active stars for a long time.
  - Mathematician Roger Penrose calculated the probability of the observed low entropy of our universe after the big bang as one chance in ten raised to the 10^{123} power (1 with 10^{123} zeroes after it, a very large number).
- A big bang with the right amount of variation in the distribution of mass-energy (one part in 100,000) is likewise necessary for us to exist. According to astronomer Martin Rees, a smoother distribution would not condense into galaxies, and a more uneven distribution would form a few giant galaxies that are too turbulent to form solar systems with planets.

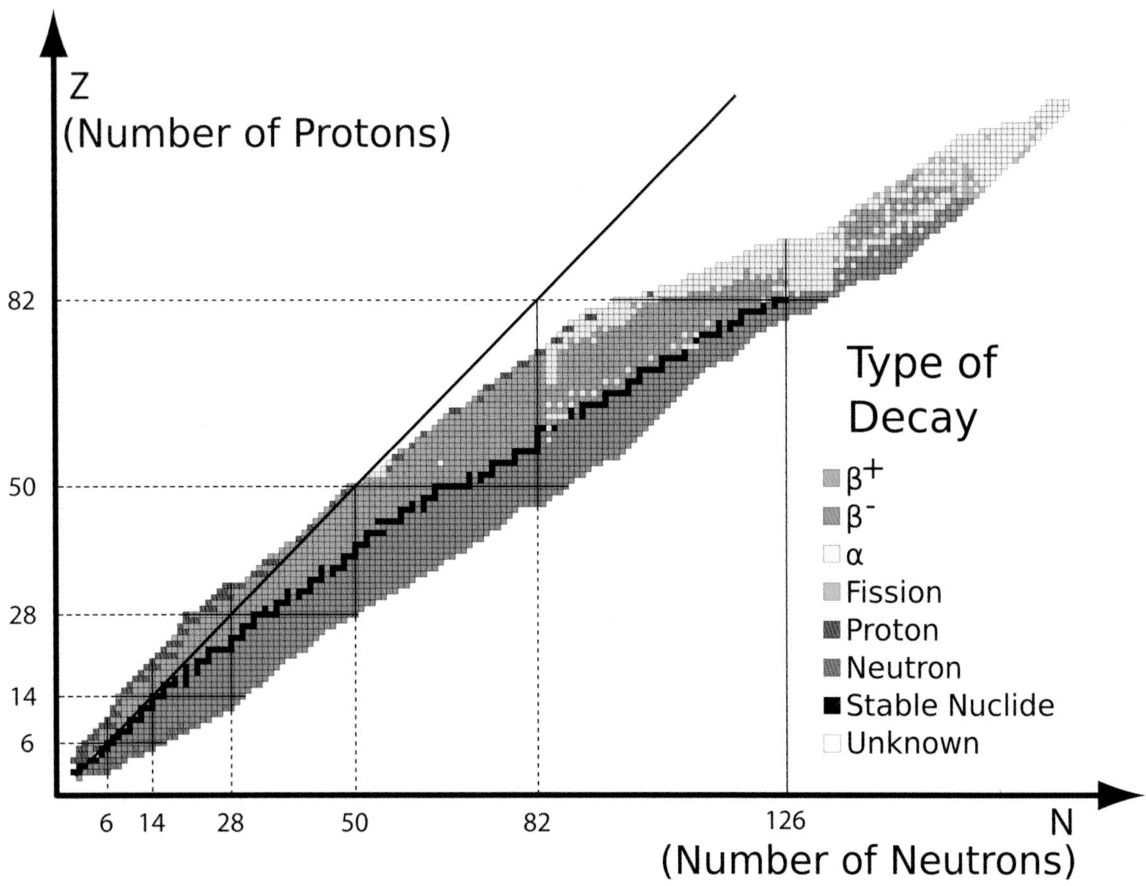

Fig. 70. Table of Nuclides—Elements with Stable and Unstable Isotopes

- **Chemistry: elements and energy.** Matter not only needs to be here, it needs to interact. Chemistry requires:
  - Atomic nuclear structures with different electric charges (elements). Figure 70 on the previous page shows the nuclear structures (assemblies of neutrons and protons) that can stay together long enough for us to see them. Isotopes are different nuclear structures with the same number of protons (same chemical element). Colored isotopes are unstable (radioactive); black isotopes are stable (not radioactive). As far as we know, all unstable isotopes spontaneously decay into stable isotopes (usually a different element). Most (not all) isotope decays are weak force interactions.
- Atomic nuclear structures with differing mass-energy charge to allow spontaneous, high-energy structural changes (nuclear reactions). In the next figure (figure 71, below), the steep drop in mass-energy charge for the small atomic nuclei (hydrogen, helium, and lithium on the left) is the basis for the nuclear fusion reactions that provide the energy for smaller, younger stars (like ours). Solar energy provides most (not quite all) of the chemical energy used by living organisms. The low point (energy minimum) for iron (Fe) stops nuclear fusion reactions before everything just burns up.
  - The small dips in energy for carbon (C) and oxygen (O) mean that fusion reactions will produce relatively large amounts of carbon and oxygen, which turns out to be really handy for us. Carbon-based chemical structure is the most versatile type of chemical structure, and oxygen-based metabolism is the most efficient style of metabolism, available to make living organisms.

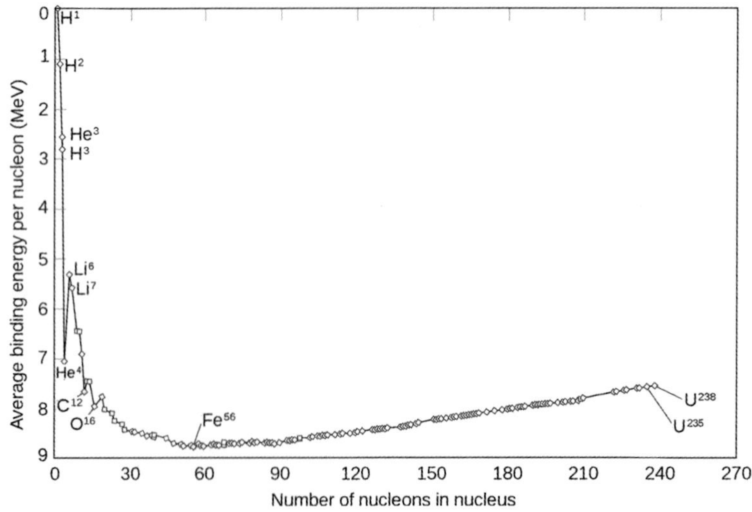

Fig. 71. Nuclear Binding Energies

  - Physicists Fred Hoyle and William Fowler noticed that structural resonances (particular values of energy that can easily form nuclear structure, similar to the specific values of energy that shift electrons between atomic orbitals) in the carbon 12 and oxygen 16 atoms allow plentiful formation of carbon and oxygen in stars. If the carbon resonance were 4 percent lower, carbon would not have formed. If the oxygen resonance were 0.5 percent higher, all of the carbon would have become oxygen.
- A big bang that produced mostly hydrogen (75 percent) and helium (25 percent) so that there is plenty of fuel for stars to burn for a long time. The initial composition of matter after the big bang is strongly influenced by the relative strengths of the strong nuclear force and the electromagnetic force:
  - Brandon Carter estimates that if the nuclear strong force were 2 percent stronger than it is, there would have been no hydrogen; matter would have been all helium and heavier elements (no small stars, no water).
  - He also estimates that if the nuclear strong force were 2 percent weaker than it is, there would have been only hydrogen; no heavier elements would have formed.
- Nuclear reactions in stars that produce larger nuclear structures (heavier elements with higher charges). Production of heavier elements is called nucleosynthesis; two particular kinds of nucleosynthesis are the alpha process (shown in the figure below) and neutron capture for elements heavier than iron (Fe).

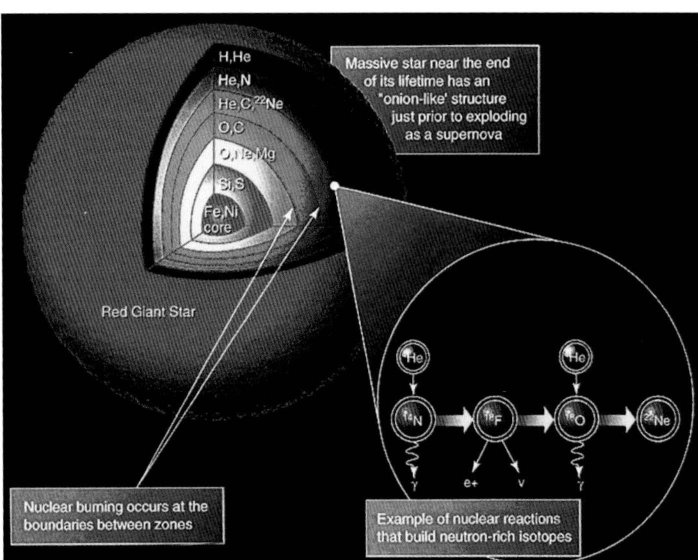

Fig. 72. Nucleosynthesis, the Alpha Process

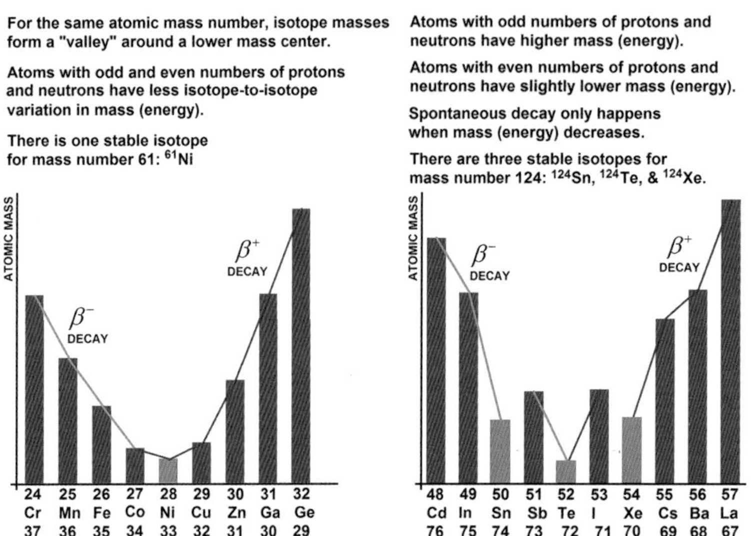

For the same atomic mass number, isotope masses form a "valley" around a lower mass center.
Atoms with odd and even numbers of protons and neutrons have less isotope-to-isotope variation in mass (energy).
There is one stable isotope for mass number 61: ^{61}Ni
ATOMIC MASS
β⁻ DECAY
β⁺ DECAY
24 25 26 27 28 29 30 31 32
Cr Mn Fe Co Ni Cu Zn Ga Ge
37 36 35 34 33 32 31 30 29
Atomic number (# Protons) above element name
Number of neutrons below element name
Mass number (protons + neutrons) = 61
Atoms with odd numbers of protons and neutrons have higher mass (energy).
Atoms with even numbers of protons and neutrons have slightly lower mass (energy).
Spontaneous decay only happens when mass (energy) decreases.
There are three stable isotopes for mass number 124: ^{124}Sn, ^{124}Te, & ^{124}Xe.
ATOMIC MASS
β⁻ DECAY
β⁺ DECAY
48 49 50 51 52 53 54 55 56 57
Cd In Sn Sb Te I Xe Cs Ba La
76 75 74 73 72 71 70 69 68 67
Atomic number (# Protons) above element name
Number of neutrons below element name
Mass number (protons + neutrons) = 124

Fig. 73. Isotopes with less mass are stable.

- Stable nuclear structures that occupy local minima for mass-energy charge (local minimum means that isotopes with fewer or more neutrons have higher mass-energy charge and are unstable and radioactive); local minima form the stable isotopes. It would be much harder to make living organisms with radioactive materials.

Fig. 74. Tycho's Supernova, observed 1572

- Exploding stars, novae and supernovae, to distribute heavier elements out into gas clouds that condense into planets. Novae and supernovae are caused by the pressure of neutrinos generated in the core on the outer layers of the star. Neutrino pressure depends on the strength of the weak nuclear force.
  - Paul Davies estimates that if the weak nuclear force were slightly stronger, neutrinos would be bound in the core and would not develop the pressure required for a nova or supernova.
  - If the weak nuclear force were slightly weaker, neutrinos would pass through the outer layers more easily, and the pressure required for explosion would not develop.

- ◦ Galaxies to concentrate material so that gas clouds with heavier elements (produced by supernova) can recombine into solar systems.
- ◦ Galaxies that are old enough to have formed and distributed heavier metallic elements and to have given radioactive isotopes time to decay into stable elements that can form the chemistry for living organisms (the time required for this whole process is estimated to be about ten billion years). Our galaxy, the Milky Way, probably has one of the highest (ninety-eighth to ninety-ninth percentile) metallic element concentrations in the universe that we can see.
- ◦ Electron probability amplitudes that are pulled into standing wave patterns around charged atomic nuclei. Electron probability amplitudes form standing waves both around atomic nuclei and between nuclei to bind atoms into molecules.
- ◦ Molecular structures with a distribution of heat and entropy values (Gibbs free energy) that allow spontaneous structural changes (chemical reactions).

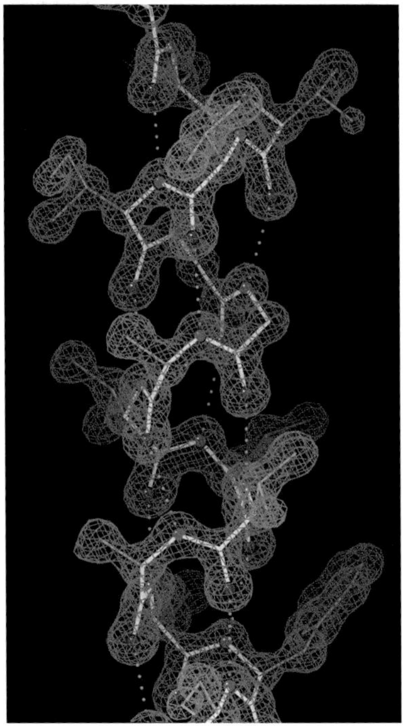

Fig. 75. Electron Density Map for a Protein Helix

A Nice Neighborhood

- The right location in the galaxy.
  - ◦ A part of the galaxy that has few supernovae. Supernovae produce a lot of radiation, which can be harmful to life on nearby planets. Some of the worldwide extinctions in the fossil record may have been caused by a nearby supernova. Supernovae tend to be more common in the central parts of galaxies where there are many more stars.
  - ◦ Metals formed by supernovae accumulate faster in regions of high supernova occurrence. Mineral planets (like ours) and life (like us) require plenty of metals. At the present time, about 10 percent of the stars in our galaxy are close enough to the galactic center to have enough metals and far enough out to have few nearby supernovae.

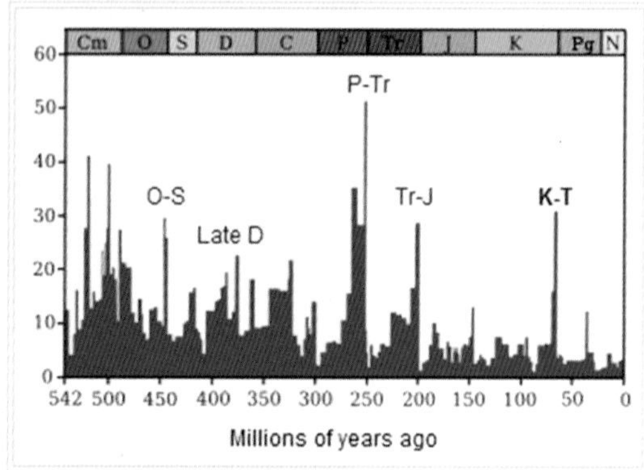

Fig. 76. Fossil Extinctions

Fig. 77. Galaxy NGC-6744 (Like Ours)
Wide Field Imager view of a Milky Way look-alike, NGC 6744 © 2011 by ESO. CC-BY 3.0.

- Gravitational effects of nearby and passing stars, more common closer to the center of the galaxy, destabilize the orbits of comets and cause more comet impacts on inner solar system planets.
- The arms of spiral galaxies (like ours) are (probably) density waves that rotate about the galactic center at a different rate than the stars. Star density, gas cloud density, and radiation levels are much higher inside the arms than between them. Our solar system rotates around the galactic center at very nearly the same rate as the arm waves (so we seldom cross them) and is currently located midway between two arms in a low-density region.

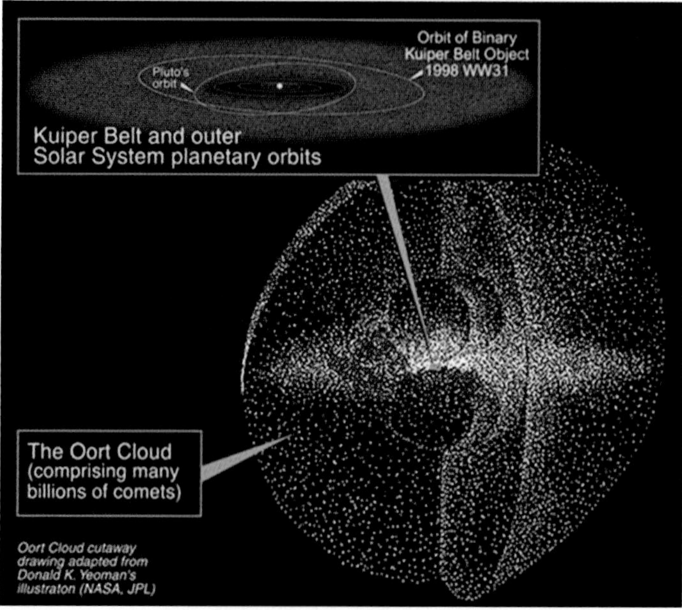

Fig. 78. Local Comets (Called the Oort Cloud)

- A planetary orbit that has relatively few major large meteoroid impacts, which disrupt global temperature distributions. This implies that a low density of asteroids in the solar system is handy; most of the meteorites that strike the earth are debris from asteroid collisions.
- A planetary distribution with at least one largish planet between the earth and the asteroid belt (Mars in our case) to reduce the incidence of asteroid debris and comet collisions on the earth.
- No giant planets (like Jupiter) in the inner part of the solar system. They disrupt the formation of smaller planets (like ours). About 10 percent of stars that have been observed to have planets at all have giant planets close to the star.
- A solar system configuration that produces the right amount of surface water. Solar system condensation computer models predict that water will mostly form icy debris further out from the sun than the earth's orbit (~2.5 times as far). The size and orbits of planets in the vicinity (Mars, and especially Jupiter) strongly influence how many ice body orbits degrade so that they can be captured by the earth.

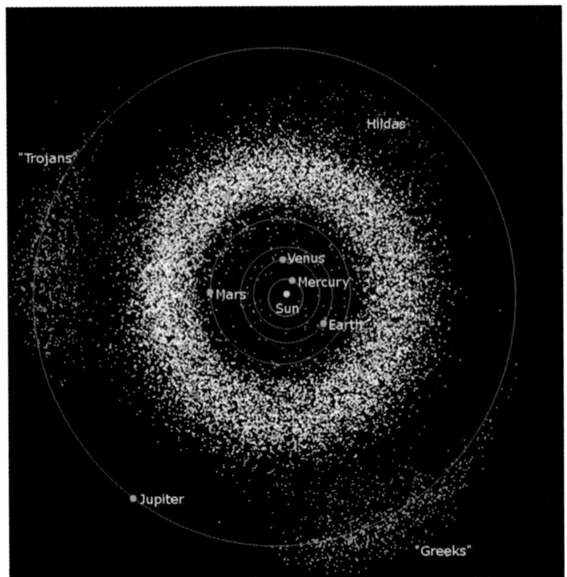

Fig. 79. Asteroid Belt

- The right size and kind of star.
    - The size of the star influences the amount of surface water on inner planets; smaller stars tend to have planets with less water.
    - Star size (mass) affects the sizes and distributions of planets that condense to form the solar system. Stars very much smaller than our sun may have smaller rock planets and no giant planets at all (meaning less or no surface water).
    - A star with stable heat output. Even small variations in heat (light) output

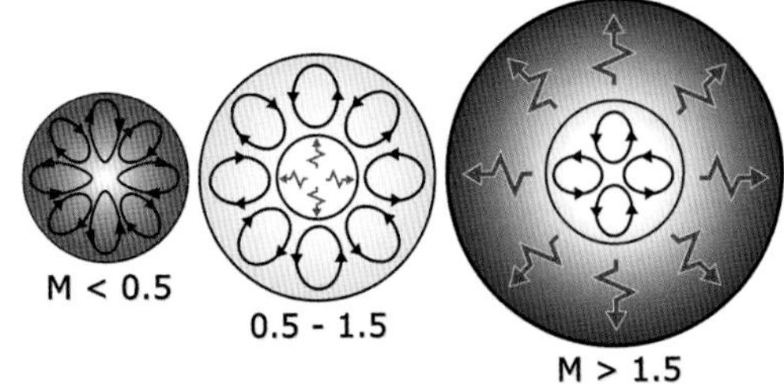

Fig. 80. Stellar Convection

can cause large changes in planetary surface temperatures; the earth has been through periods when all water was completely frozen and periods when there were no ice caps at all. Our sun has unusually low optical variability for a star of its size and age.

- The burning process in medium-sized stars (like ours) depends on convection (circulation of material inside the star) to maintain a relatively stable burn rate (stable energy output, required for stable surface temperature on the earth). Convection behavior depends, in part, on the relationship between the strengths of gravitation and the electromagnetic force.
  - Physicist Paul Davies estimates that if gravity were slightly weaker or electromagnetism slightly stronger, only red dwarf stars would have stable burn rates.
  - If gravity were slightly stronger or electromagnetism slightly weaker, only blue giant stars would have stable burn rates.

A Nice Place to Live

- A planet to maintain an atmosphere. The planet needs to be large enough to keep gases from escaping into space (Mars is too small) and needs to have about the right amount of gas (Venus, smaller than Earth, has an atmospheric pressure ninety times as high).
- Planetary orbit in the liquid water zone. To maintain surface temperatures that allow liquid water on the surface, a planet's distance from the star has to be within a relatively narrow range (0.95 to 1.2 times as far as Earth for our star, according to computer models). Higher temperatures may cause runaway greenhouse effect (water vapor is a much stronger greenhouse gas than carbon dioxide). Lower temperatures may result in runaway glaciation (ice ages that never end). Large amounts of surface water (like Earth's) reduce the range of temperature variations, so the planetary liquid water zone partly depends on the amount of surface water as well.
- Prograde rotation (planetary rotation in the same direction as the planet's orbit). Core mantle resonances for planets with retrograde rotation (rotation direction opposite of orbit) generate heat that significantly increases volcanic activity on the surface (like Venus).

- Optimum conditions for photosynthesis. High oxygen concentrations are pretty much required for large multicellular organisms (like us). Oxygen has to be continuously replenished, mostly by photosynthetic plankton. A high oxygen concentration requires an optimum environment for plankton photosynthesis:
    - Large areas of the planet surface covered with water.
    - High concentrations of plankton nutrients in the water.
        - The right ratio of continent to ocean area. The right total amount of surface water compared to the height of large geologic features (continents).
        - Continents with water-soluble mineral structures. Soluble continental materials are produced by denser mantle material that mixes with water at the surface and is then re-melted inside the mantle. The planet has to have a liquid core to allow recirculating flow, plate tectonic flow at the surface, and lots of surface water to make continents.
    - Relatively fast planetary rotation to limit the daily variation in surface temperature. Plankton as a group can tolerate large variations in temperature, but individual plankton have limited tolerances for temperature changes. Optimum temperature range for photosynthetic bacteria, for example, is 72–108°F.
    - A single large moon to stabilize the planet's axial wobble. Planets with no moons or smaller moons can have rotational axes that wobble up to ninety degrees (which has a severe impact on surface temperature distributions). The earth's axis of rotation has only wobbled a few degrees (23.4° +/− 1.3°).
    - A star with the right color (yellow dwarf for us). Photosynthesis is not as efficient with the light produced by red dwarf stars, for example.

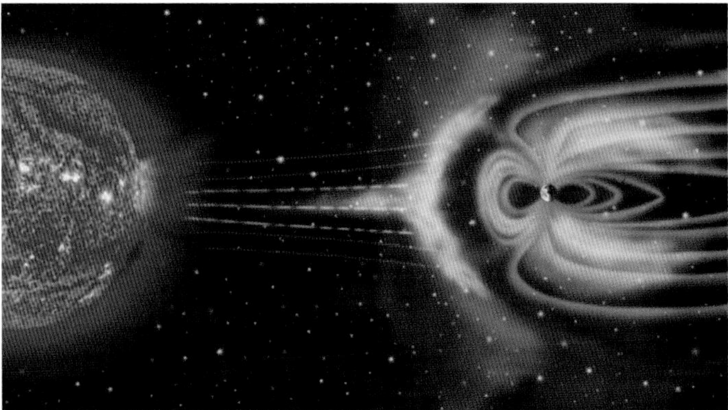

Fig. 81. Earth Magnetic Field Protection

- A planet with a magnetic field generated by a liquid iron core and rapid rotation to reduce cosmic ray and solar wind radiation. Part of the reason Mars has so little atmosphere is that it has no magnetic field to protect gases from cosmic ray and solar wind impacts. The sun also has a magnetic field that helps to shield the inner solar system from galactic cosmic rays.
- A planet with an acceptable value for axial tilt (23.4° for Earth). Smaller axial tilt would probably cause much larger ice caps (no summer to melt them), and possibly, permanent ice ages. Larger axial tilt would produce much more severe weather and large surface temperature variations (much hotter summers, much colder winters).
- A solar system with low orbital eccentricities for its planets (the change of distance between the planet and the star as it orbits). Large changes in the distance to the star cause large surface temperature variations. The eccentricities of other planets (especially Jupiter) affect the eccentricity of Earth, which currently varies 0.00–0.04). An orbit for Jupiter with a large enough eccentricity (>0.15) would destabilize the orbits of smaller inner planets (no Earth at all; it would have fallen into the sun long ago).

Life

Everything we've seen so far, the physical environment, is the easy part of creation. Even with its complex, abstract mathematics and intricate relationships between spacetime, particle properties, and forces that conspire to produce our world, the creation and operation of life is a far more difficult case. We can (sort of) deal with the mathematics of spacetime, forces, and individual particles, although we still don't really understand atomic nuclei and molecules all that well. But the mathematics of life are completely beyond our current capabilities.

We are getting to the point where we can mostly understand how life works. We can construct computational models based on our observations of critters that will predict the behavior of other biological systems. We can even tinker with the critters themselves (really simple ones, anyway) by mixing and matching bits and pieces. But we are currently unable to predict the chemistry and structure of organism molecules based on the physics alone. We can't design biological systems from scratch, let alone conceive the possibility of life based on chemistry in the first place or figure out how to do it, as God has evidently done.

The following is a very tiny list of the highlights of the mechanics of life, just enough (I hope) to get a feel for how life works. We'll start with the basics of protein chemistry and build up to embryonic development and fossil history. Among other things, I hope to show why Intelligent Design is a reasonable perspective for understanding the biological world.

Biology also provides us with some of the best answers for why creation is the way it appears to be. Why is time so very long and space so very large? One way to look for an answer to those questions is to look for the most difficult, challenging aspect of this creation, the part that would most likely be the main purpose of a developmental creation. In my opinion, that's *life,* in particular the genetic mechanisms needed for biological adaptation.

For me, molecular biology was the best part of creation to study—it is truly one wow after another. If you wish to read more, the entries for biology in Wikipedia tend to be very well written and informative, unlike the physics entries (which I found to be generally useless). The basic information is also available in any textbook on protein chemistry and molecular biology. I used *Proteins, Structure and Function* (2005) by David Whitford and *Molecular Biology of the Cell* (2002) by Bruce Alberts, et al. For a good presentation of the mechanisms of biological adaptability, I recommend *Evolution: A View from the 21st Century* (2013) by James Shapiro. The debate over whether this world occurred naturally or was created hinges on a few key issues. Adaptive mechanisms (the ways that organisms adapt to environmental changes) are, in my opinion, one of these. Others include the DNA modification processes and the configuration of protein sequence space.

- Proteins are the molecules that make living organisms operate. Many other chemical molecules are used in the operations of organisms, but proteins are the fundamental parts that make it all work. Nearly all actions or behaviors of living cells happen because proteins make them happen.

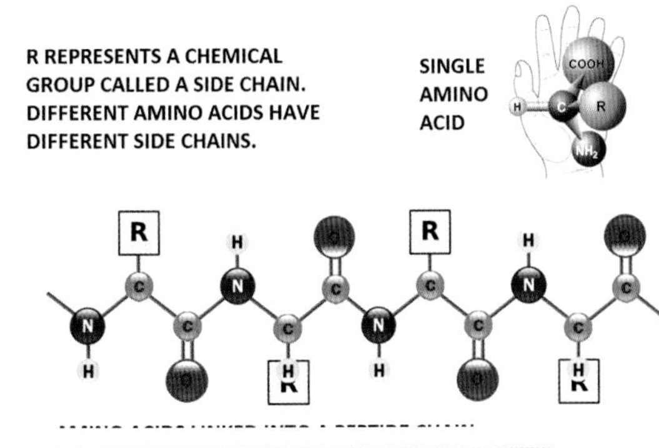

Fig. 82. Amino Acids and Peptides

  - Proteins are made of linked chains of twenty or so different kinds of amino acids. The generic name for chains of amino acids is peptides. Not all peptides are proteins.

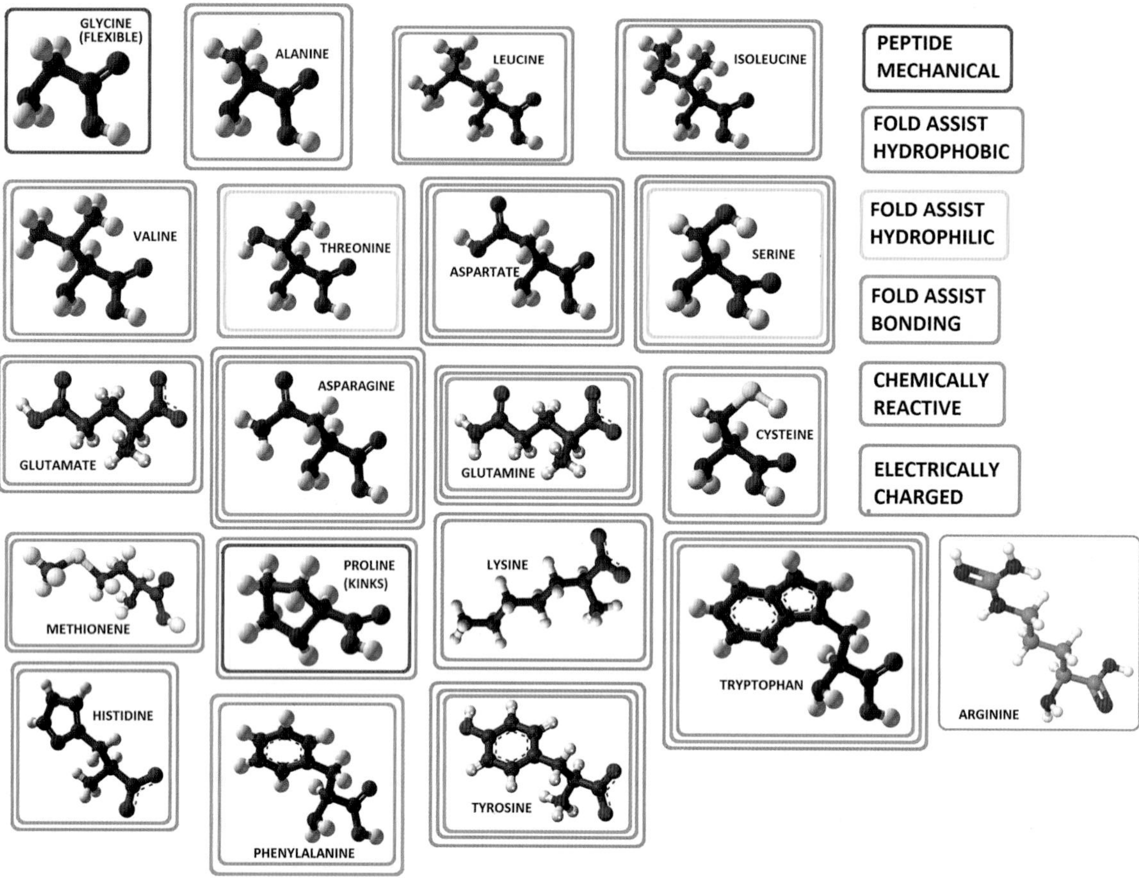

Fig. 83. Biological Amino Acids, Ball and Stick Models.

- Proteins are peptides that have a unique, three-dimensional folded structure and perform biological activity.
- Amino acids have a variety of functions in proteins.
  - Some amino acids affect the mechanical shape of the peptide backbone that links side chains together. Some are flexible, some kink the backbone, and some allow the normally stiff backbone to twist.

Fig. 84. Space Fill Representation of a Protein (Chymotropsin, PDB ID 2CGA) Showing Atom Positions

- Some amino acid side chains help guide the peptide chain into the folded protein shape.
- Surrounding water molecules pull hydrophilic (water-loving) side chains to the outside and push hydrophobic (water-fearing) side chains to the middle of the peptide tangle. (Biology happens in water.)
- Bonding side chains align specific sections of the peptide chain to form the unique 3D structure.

- Chemically reactive side chains make and break chemical bonds of target molecules affected by proteins.
- Charged side chains act with protein structure to bind target molecules and other proteins. Proteins form three-dimensional jigsaw pieces with charges located in matching hills and valleys to bind other molecules. To bind a target molecule, a protein must have a socket exactly shaped to fit the molecule with charged side chains located next to the oppositely charged atoms on the target. To bind to another protein, each protein must have a complementary shape and charge distribution at the binding site (hills match valleys; positive charge matches negative charge).

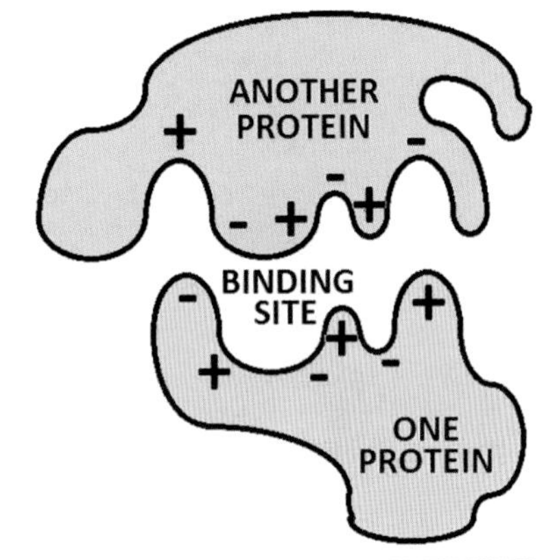

Fig. 85. Protein–Protein Binding

- Protein structure (also called folding) is described with four "levels" of organization:
  - "Primary structure" refers to the list of amino acids in the peptide chain. In the figure, each amino acid is

HUM	WHA	HUM	WHA
G	V	K	
L		K	
S		G	
D	E	H	
G		H	
E		E	
W		A	
Q		E	
V		I	L
L		K	
N	H	P	
V		L	
W		A	
G	A	Q	
K		S	
V		H	
E		A	
A		T	
D		K	
I	V	H	
P	A	K	
G		I	
H		P	
G		V	I
Q		K	
E	D	Y	
V	I	L	
L		E	
I		F	
R		I	
L		S	
F		E	
K		C	A
G	S	I	
H		I	
P		Q	H
E		V	
T		L	
L		Q	H
E		S	
K		K	R
F		H	
D		P	
K	R	G	
F		D	
K		F	
H		G	
L		A	
K		D	
S	T	A	
E		Q	
D	A	G	
E		A	
M		M	
K		N	
A		K	
S		A	
E		L	
D		E	
L		L	
K		F	
K		R	
H		K	
G		D	
A	V	M	I
T		A	
V		S	A
L		N	K
T		Y	
A		K	
L		E	
G		L	
G	A	G	
I		F	Y
L		Q	
K		C	

Fig. 86. Comparison of Human and Whale Primary Structure for Myoglobin

represented by a letter; myoglobin is a small (153 amino acids) protein that binds oxygen in muscles.

- "Secondary structure" refers to a few common physical configurations that are often found in proteins. Common shapes are helixes (the most common are called alpha helixes), where the backbone twists like a corkscrew; sheets (beta sheets are most common), where the backbone passes back and forth like threads on a loom; and turns, where the backbone bends through some specific angle. The peptide chain shapes are similar, but different proteins with similar secondary structures usually do not use the same amino acid sequences to make the structures.

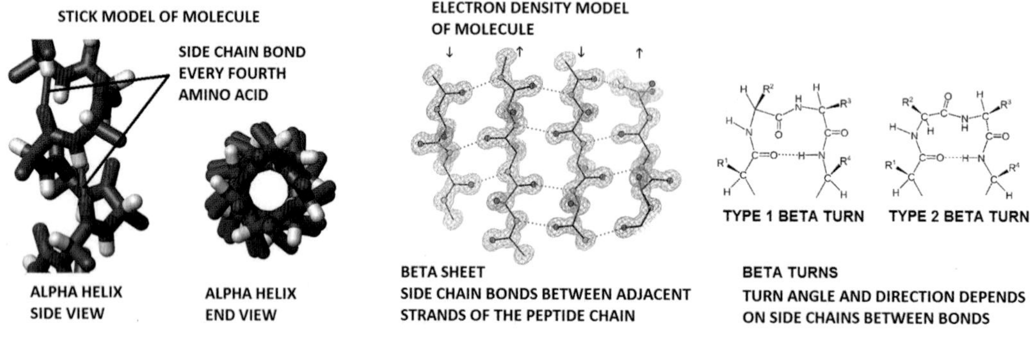

Fig. 87. Common Protein Secondary Structures Showing Side Chain Bonding

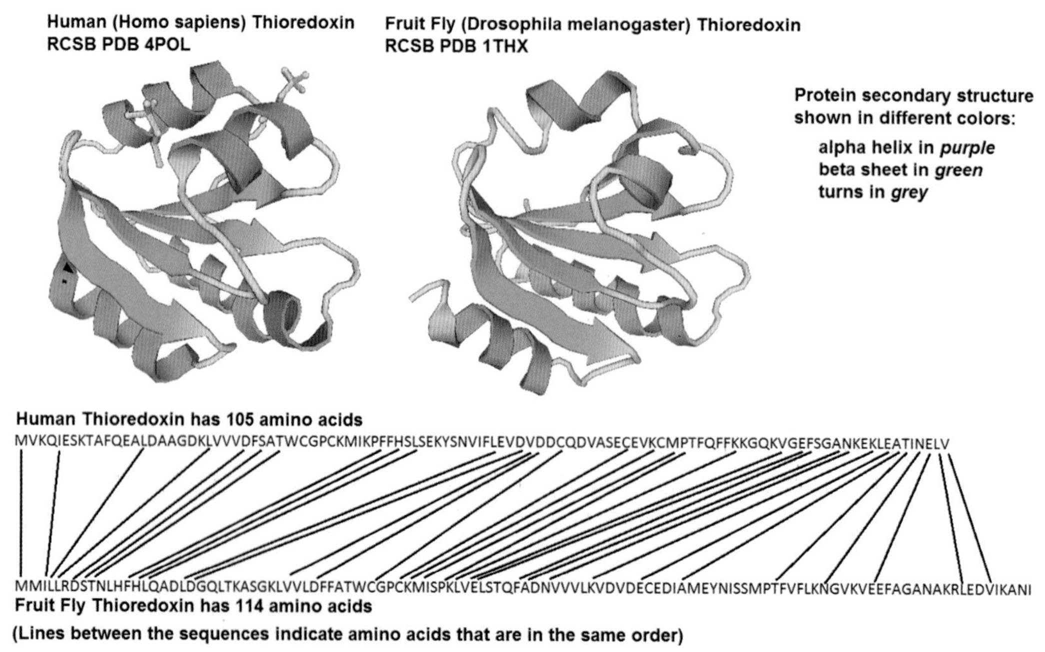

Fig. 88. Similar protein shapes usually have different amino acid sequences. Protein ribbon images from the RCSB PDB (www.rcsb.org), IDs 4POL and 1THX.

- "Tertiary structure" is the unique folded shape of a single peptide chain.

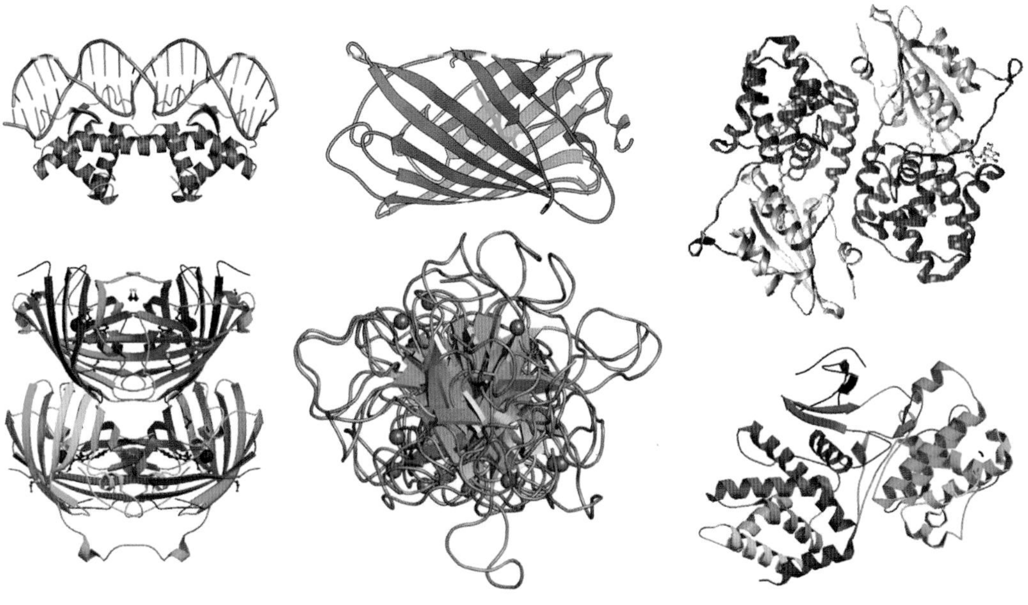

Fig. 89. Typical Protein Peptide Chain Structures

◦ Ribbon molecule models show peptide backbone structure:
  - Many proteins have quaternary structure; they are made of two or more peptide chains (called subunits) that bind together.

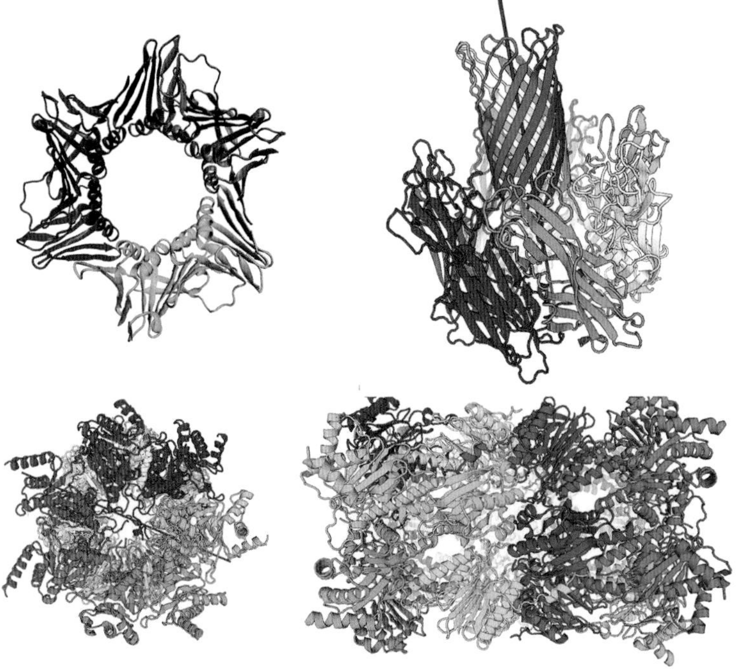

Fig. 90. Typical Proteins Made of Multiple Peptide Chains (Quaternary Structure)

- Each protein folds into a different 3-D structure, but the same protein (peptide sequence) always folds the same way in the same order, usually with secondary structures forming first and then bonding into the final shape.
- There are many different kinds of chemical bonds. The chemical bonds that form the peptide chain (covalent bonds) are much stronger than the bonds between side chains (Van der Waals and hydrogen bonds). Proteins are able to fold and unfold and change shape without breaking the peptide chain.
- Biological organisms together use millions of different proteins. (Proteins are generally different for each type of organism even when they do the same things; the human body is estimated to use 100,000 to 120,000 different proteins). How they all got here is the major issue in biological creation apologetics. An average bacterial protein has ~389 amino acids in a peptide chain. There are 20^{389} (= 10^{506}) possible peptide chains with that length. Biologist Douglas Axe has estimated that only one in 10^{77} peptide chains will have a tertiary folded structure at all. Far fewer will have the molecule binding and chemical activity that is common for biological proteins. Proteins that will functionally fit into the interlocking systems that form living cells are rarer still. (You can read one of Dr. Axe's papers in *The Nature of Nature.*)

- Chemical reactions that happen in living organisms are (almost always) done by proteins. Proteins that perform chemical reactions are called enzymes.

Enzymes act as catalysts for chemical reactions in organisms. A catalyst is a chemical that increases the rates of chemical reactions (reactant molecules change to product molecules), where molecules either combine into larger molecules, break apart into smaller molecules, or change to another molecule.

- Chemical reactions (not involving proteins) happen when reactant molecules collide and rearrange to form product molecules.
- Chemical catalysts (again, not involving proteins) work by reducing the amount of energy change required to rearrange reactant molecules. Chemical catalysts can typically make reactions 10–1,000 times faster than the reactions would be without a catalyst.
- Chemical reaction rates are also affected by the orientation of reactant molecules. Part of what determines a reaction rate is the chance that

the colliding reactant molecules will bump in the right places to form a molecular bond. Catalysts that bind reactants in the correct orientation can increase reaction rates 10,000,000 times.

- Protein enzymes normally combine molecules by capturing reactants (and filtering out other molecules), twisting them around to the correct orientation, binding them in positions to form the chemical bond, and placing a reactive side chain right next to the bond site to act as a chemical catalyst. The combination of orientation and chemical catalysis typically increases reaction rates by 100,000,000,000,000 (10^{14}) times.

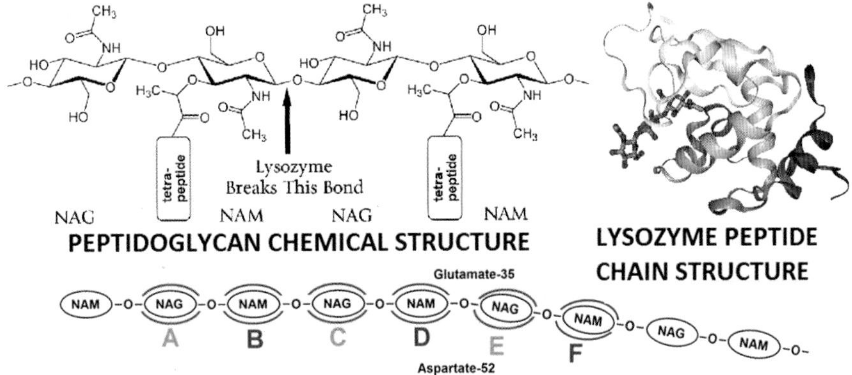

Fig. 91. Protein Enzyme (catalyst) Action

- Protein enzymes break molecules apart by capturing target molecules, twisting them around to fit the binding site, binding the molecule with a kink to stretch the bond that is to be broken, and placing a chemically reactive side chain next to the stretched bond to act as a catalyst to break the bond.
- Protein enzymes do chemistry atom by atom and molecule by molecule.

• All biological organisms use proteins to change the chemicals (and minerals) found in natural environments into the very specific chemicals they need to live.
  - Different proteins act one after another, changing natural chemicals atom by atom, in chains of actions called metabolic pathways.
  - Pathways for eubacteria and archea (two kinds of bacteria) are slightly different than for eukaryotes (a much larger cell with very different structure

than bacteria; we are made of eukaryote cells). All eukaryotes, from amoebas to mushrooms to us and redwood trees, use pretty much the same chemical steps with some differences in the particular proteins.

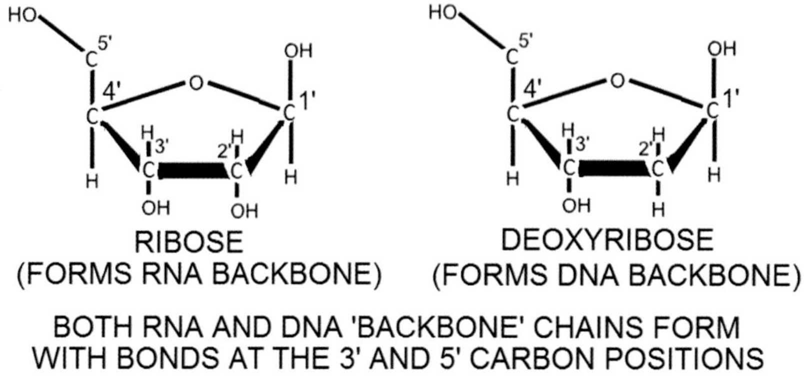

RIBOSE
(FORMS RNA BACKBONE)

DEOXYRIBOSE
(FORMS DNA BACKBONE)

BOTH RNA AND DNA 'BACKBONE' CHAINS FORM WITH BONDS AT THE 3' AND 5' CARBON POSITIONS

Fig. 92. RNA and DNA Chain "Link" Molecules

- DNA and RNA, as they are used in organisms, have a structure similar to the amino acid peptide chains that form proteins in that they have both a "backbone" chain and chemical side chains. Both RNA and DNA use only four side chains (instead of the twenty found in proteins) but are still capable of forming three-dimensional folded structures (like proteins) with bonding between side chains. With fewer side chains, RNA and DNA have the capability to act as orientation catalysts but cannot usually do the combined orientation and chemical catalysis that makes proteins such effective enzymes.

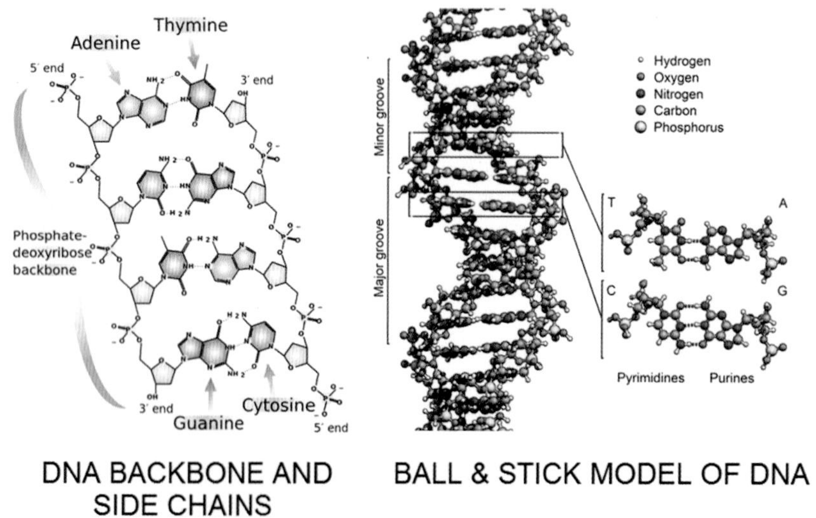

Fig. 93. DNA Chemical Structure

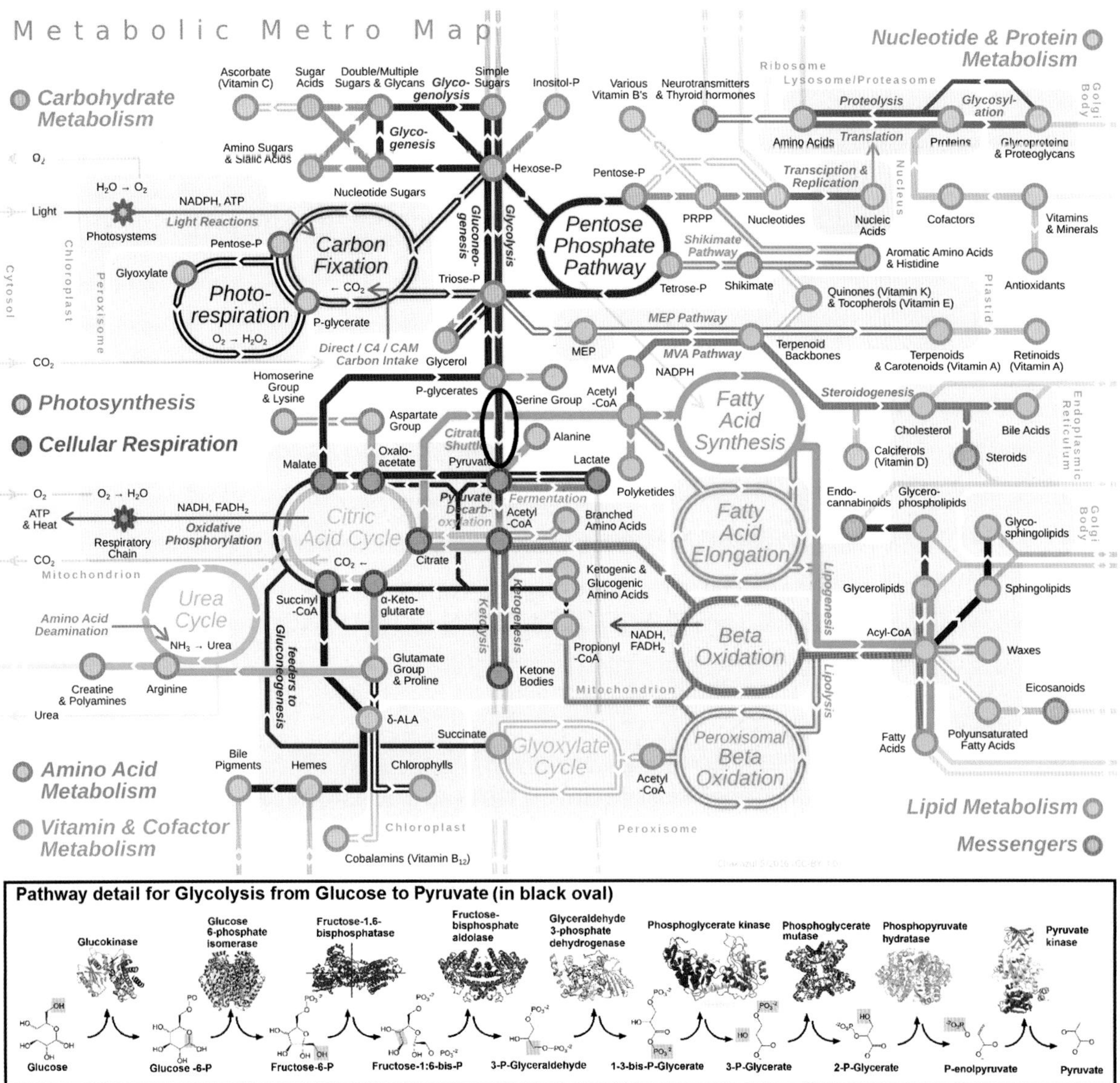

Fig. 94. Eukaryotic Metabolic Pathways

- Like peptide chains, the chemical bonds along the backbone chain (covalent bonds) are stronger than the bonds between side chains (hydrogen bonds) that form the folded structure. RNA and DNA can fold and unfold without breaking the backbone chain.
- Biological DNA uses four side chains: adenine, cytosine, guanine, and thymine (nicknamed A, C, G, and T). Adenine and guanine are longer molecules; cytosine and thymine are shorter. Adenine and thymine can bond together by forming two hydrogen bonds; guanine and cytosine can bond together by forming three hydrogen bonds. The combination of size and

number of bonds means that backbone chains can only be bonded together if the side chains are complementary: adenine must be paired with thymine; cytosine must be paired with guanine.

- Biological RNA uses three of the same side chains (adenine, cytosine, and guanine), but it substitutes uracil to bond with adenine instead of thymine.

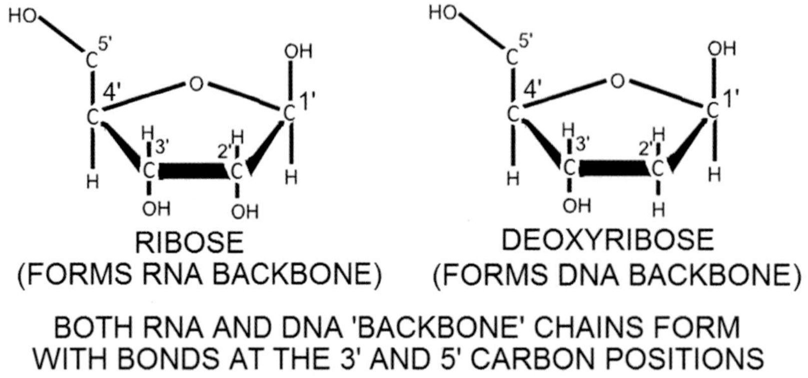

RIBOSE
(FORMS RNA BACKBONE)

DEOXYRIBOSE
(FORMS DNA BACKBONE)

BOTH RNA AND DNA 'BACKBONE' CHAINS FORM
WITH BONDS AT THE 3' AND 5' CARBON POSITIONS

Fig. 94.1. RNA and DNA Backbone Molecules

- Although DNA is capable of forming three-dimensional folded structures, as far as we know it is only used for the storage of prescriptive information in biological organisms. DNA is always present as paired strands that are complementary and inverted (every A has a T on the other strand, every T has an opposing A, every C has a G, every G has a C). Backbone direction is described using the bond site numbers 3′ and 5′. Paired DNA strands are always oriented opposite each other: a 3′ to 5′ strand is paired with a 5′ to 3′ strand.
- Each side chain pair (one on each strand) is called a base pair or nucleotide. Genetic information is measured in base pairs (nicknamed bp). The "housekeeping genes" the DNA that codes the fundamental operational parts of cells, are estimated to be ~250,000 bp in bacteria. There are lots more in eukaryotes; eukaryote processes tend to be more complex.
- Paired, complementary strands keep the DNA stretched out so that it can be "read" by transcription proteins.
- Biological RNA is used both for information recording strands (messenger RNA) and for enzyme and structural elements (similar to proteins but not as versatile).

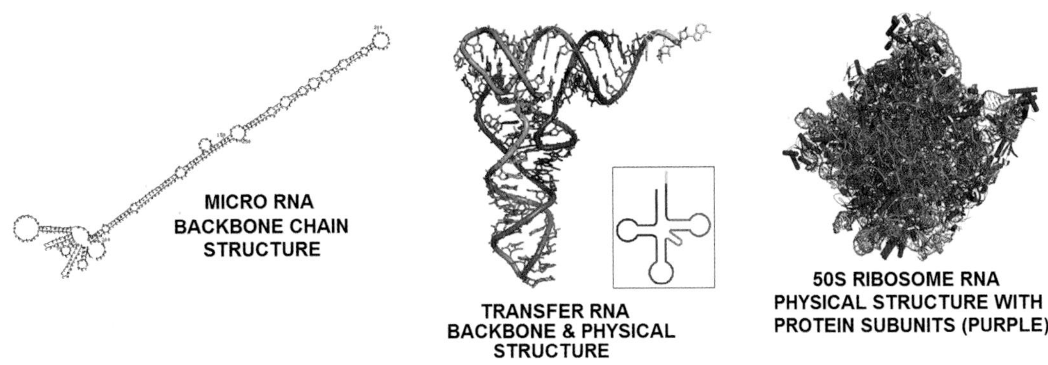

Fig. 95. RNA Folded Structures

- Bacterial DNA floats inside the cell as a ring (sometimes more than one ring). Bacterial DNA typically uses between 500,000 and 5 million base pairs.
- Eukaryote cells have lots more DNA, about five hundred times as much as bacteria on average. Single-celled eukaryotes (yeast, algae) have 10 million to 100 million base pairs. Multicellular eukaryotes (like us) have 100 million to 15 billion base pairs. Strangely, the winner for the most DNA is the salamander. We humans have an average amount of DNA for multicellular organisms, at 3.2 billion base pairs.
- Eukaryote DNA has to be packed in order to fit into cells.

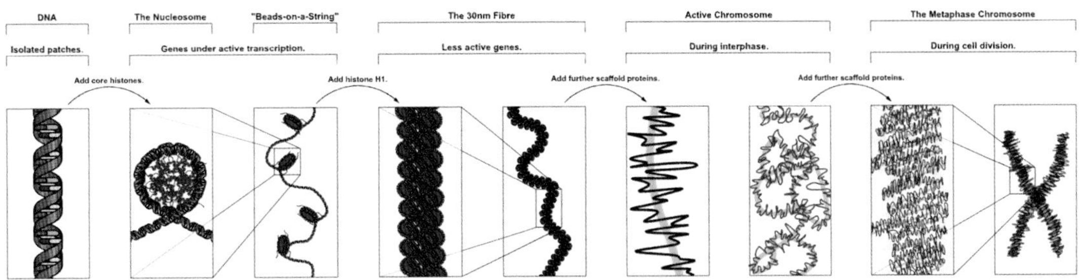

Fig. 96. Eukaryotic DNA Packaging

- Proteins read one of the DNA strands and manufacture a complementary RNA strand (messenger RNA, nicknamed mRNA) in a process called RNA transcription. Genetic information can be on either strand of DNA.
  - Bacteria use a 5-subunit protein assembly called RNA polymerase (nicknamed RNAP) to make messenger DNA.
    - A small protein key called a sigma factor bonds to a specific DNA

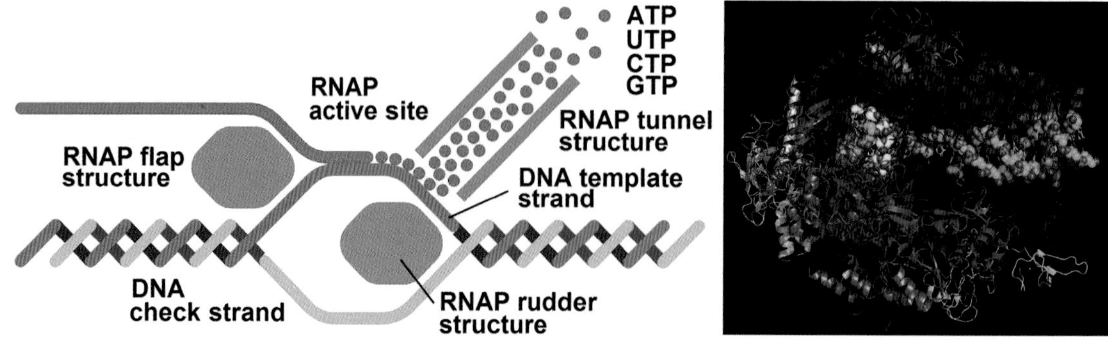

Fig. 97. RNAP Function and Structure. Rudder structure separates DNA template and DNA check strands. Tunnel structure gathers and filters RNA phosphates. RNA phosphates bond to template strand: ATP to thymine; UTP to adenine; CTP to guanine; GTP to cytosine. RNAP active site catalyzes phosphates to bond into RNA strand. Flap structure separates RNA and DNA strands.

sequence called a basal promoter. Different keys bind to different DNA sequences; bacteria make different amounts of specific keys to control relative amounts of proteins made from the DNA (and, therefore, to control the current structure of the cell). RNAP binds to the combination of DNA and sigma factor.

- RNAP separates the two DNA strands.
- RNAP filters ribose plus side chain molecules through a tube to bond to exposed DNA.
- RNAP catalyzes the ribose molecules to form backbone chain bonds.
- Ribose molecules shorten as they are bonded, pulling the DNA strand through RNAP at fifty base pairs per second.
- A cutting structure on RNAP slices off the RNA strand as the DNA is pulled along. The freed DNA strands recombine.
- The last part of the DNA sequence codes an RNA "hairpin" that folds as it leaves RNAP and jerks the RNA strand out of RNAP.

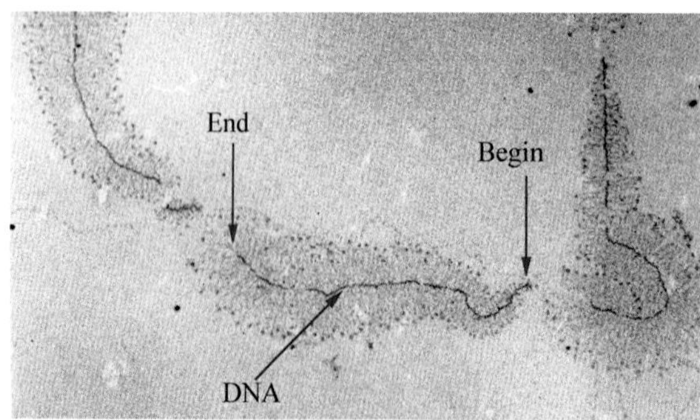

Fig. 98. RNA Strands on Bacterial DNA

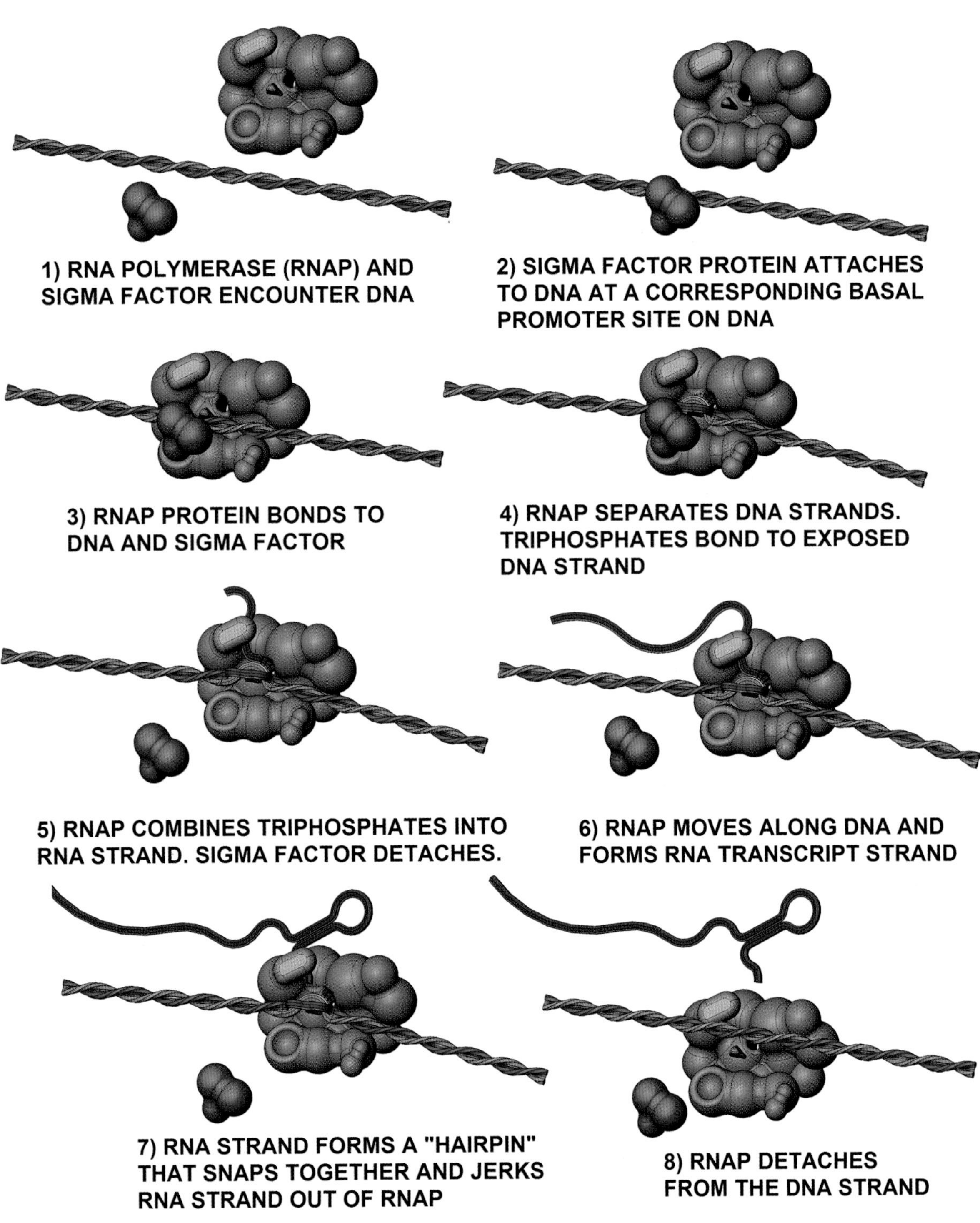

1) RNA POLYMERASE (RNAP) AND SIGMA FACTOR ENCOUNTER DNA
2) SIGMA FACTOR PROTEIN ATTACHES TO DNA AT A CORRESPONDING BASAL PROMOTER SITE ON DNA
3) RNAP PROTEIN BONDS TO DNA AND SIGMA FACTOR
4) RNAP SEPARATES DNA STRANDS. TRIPHOSPHATES BOND TO EXPOSED DNA STRAND
5) RNAP COMBINES TRIPHOSPHATES INTO RNA STRAND. SIGMA FACTOR DETACHES.
6) RNAP MOVES ALONG DNA AND FORMS RNA TRANSCRIPT STRAND
7) RNA STRAND FORMS A "HAIRPIN" THAT SNAPS TOGETHER AND JERKS RNA STRAND OUT OF RNAP
8) RNAP DETACHES FROM THE DNA STRAND

Fig. 99. Bacterial RNA Transcription

- Larger, more complex eukaryote cells use a large protein assembly (over one hundred subunits) to bind RNAP and start RNA transcription.

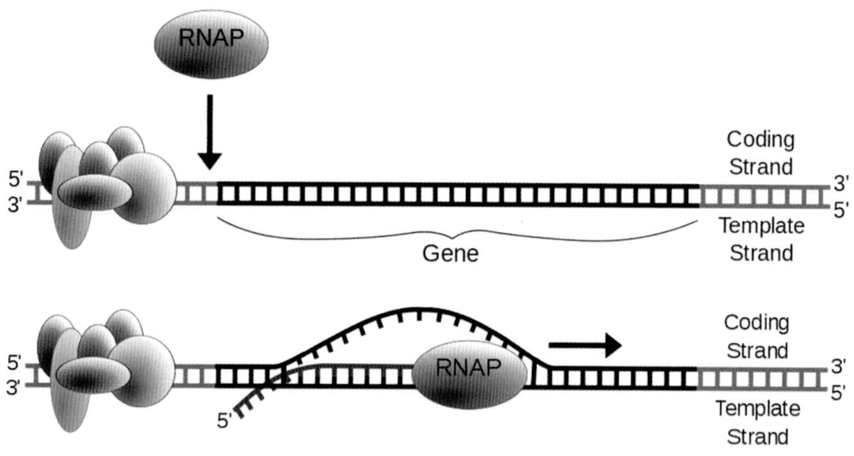

Fig. 100. RNA Transcription in Eurkaryotes

- Proteins are made by a large assembly called a ribosome. For bacteria this is three RNA and fifty-two protein subunits; for eukaryotes, it's four RNA and seventy-nine protein subunits.
    - The ribosome binds messenger RNA.
    - RNA structures called transfer RNA bind amino acids and are filtered in to bind to the messenger RNA by the ribosome.
    - Each transfer RNA (with a specific amino acid) binds to a specific sequence of three RNA base pairs called a codon.

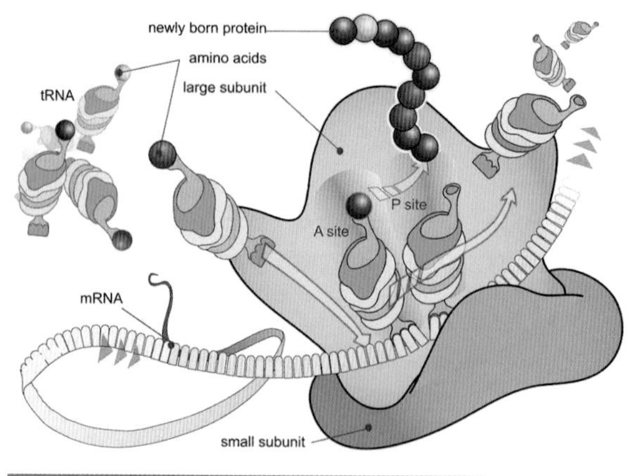

Fig. 101. Ribosomes Make Proteins

- DNA codons are complementary (T for A on RNA, A for U, G for C, C for G)
    - RNA (and DNA) codons specify amino acids according to a genetic code. With a few minor exceptions, all cells (bacteria, eukaryotes, and us) use the same genetic code. Stop codons halt protein synthesis by binding a release factor protein instead of a transfer RNA.
    - Most amino acids are specified by more than one codon, which, among other

features, allows flexibility in the RNA sequence to prevent messenger RNA folding.
  - Transfer RNAs hold amino acids in the sequence specified by messenger RNA.
  - The ribosome catalyzes amino acids to bond into a peptide chain and separate from transfer RNA. Bacteria build proteins at twenty amino acids per second; eukaryotes at two per second.
  - With no amino acid bound, transfer RNA changes shape and disconnects from the messenger RNA strand.

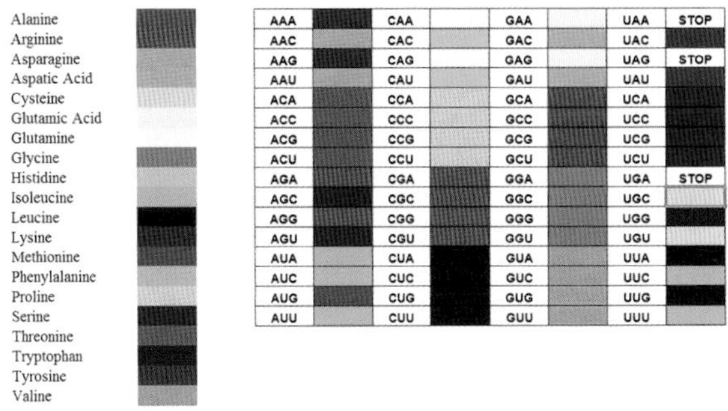

Fig. 102. RNA to Amino Acid Genetic Code

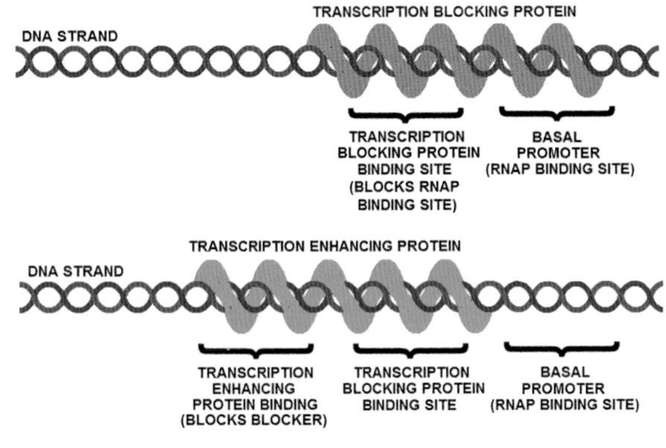

Fig. 103. Proteins Control Gene Expression

- RNA trancription can be allowed or stopped (a process called gene expression) by teams of proteins that bind to the DNA strand.
  - Transcription blocking proteins bind to DNA and obstruct the RNAP binding site.
  - Transcription enhancing proteins obstruct the binding of blocking proteins or make it easier for RNAP to bind to the DNA strand.
  - Blocking and enhancing proteins work together to control the presence and concentration of the proteins that make up a cell.
  - Cells make changes to accommodate different environments by using gene expression control proteins to change the proteins that are produced, which changes the structure of the cell. This is called cell specialization.
  - Cell reproduction, called binary fission in bacteria and mitosis in eukaryotes, happens as a sequence of stages and results in the cell splitting into two cells. Each stage involves different proteins that are expressed to carry out the actions for the particular stage; the process is controlled by a timed sequence of gene expressions.

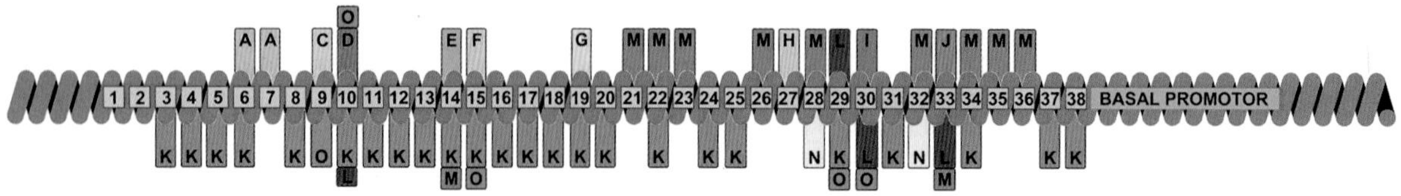

Fig. 104. A typical example of animal gene expression controls—protein binding in the regulatory region of the ENDO16 gene in the sea urchin Strongylocentrotus purpuratus. ENDO16 participates in embryo blastula and mid-gut development. The mapped regulatory region is 2200 base pairs of DNA 'upstream' of the basal promoter site that binds 14 proteins (A-O) at 38 binding sites. Proteins cover or block coverage of the basal promoter.

  - Embryo development in multicellular eukaryotes (like us) is controlled by gene expression proteins. Genes are expressed at different times in the process and at different locations in the growing organism to build specialized cells at the right times and in the right places. Put another way, this means the RNAP binding site is covered or uncovered and the RNA transcribed or not to develop a living organism like ourselves.
- Messenger RNA is spliced to form protein templates.
  - A gene is a DNA sequence from the RNAP binding site (basal promoter) to a transcription stop (a hairpin RNA sequence in bacteria, for example).
  - Eukaryote genes produce messenger RNA (actually called a pre-mRNA strand) that is a mixture of amino acid coding sequences (called exons) and non-coding sections (called introns).
  - After transcription, the pre-mRNA strand is spliced by an RNA and protein assembly called a spliceosome to produce the final mRNA strand (exons only).
  - Exons are mixed and matched using splicing control RNA and protein structures very similar to gene expression control. The process is called alternative splicing.
  - Eukaryote genes typically produce mRNA for more than one protein. The average is two to three different proteins per gene. Remember, a "gene" is a DNA sequence for a protein from transcription start to transcription end.
  - Our DNA codes an estimated 100,000 to 120,000 different proteins in about 25,000 gene sequences.
  - The DSCAM (Down syndrome cellular adhesion molecule) gene in the fruit fly Drosophila melanogaster is a record holder for alternative splicing: this

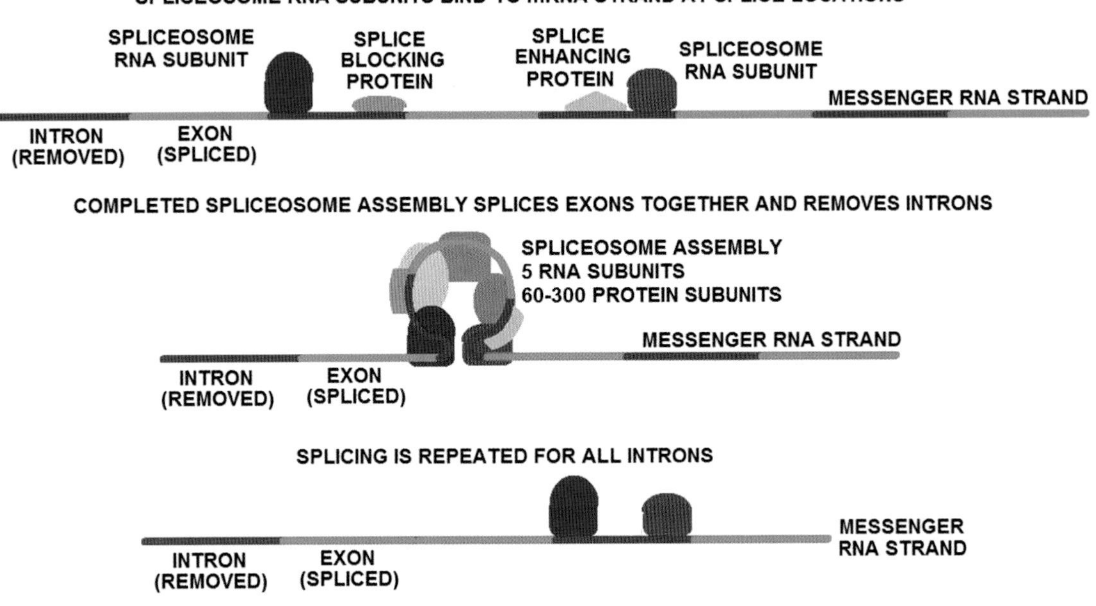

Fig. 105. Eukaryote Messenger RNA Splicing

one single gene can produce 38,016 different proteins.

- Gene expression (bacteria and eukaryotes) and messenger RNA splicing (eukaryotes only) are partly controlled by protein signaling pathways.
- Protein signaling changes gene expression (and therefore cell structure and chemistry) in response to internal cell events (mitosis and binary fission) and external conditions (nutrient concentrations, light levels for plankton, and signals—mostly proteins—from other nearby cells).
- Membrane proteins are embedded in the cell wall (and they only fold in the presence of that wall). The binding of an external signal protein or nutrient molecule on the outside of the cell changes the shape of the protein on the inside of the cell and binds or releases an internal signal protein.

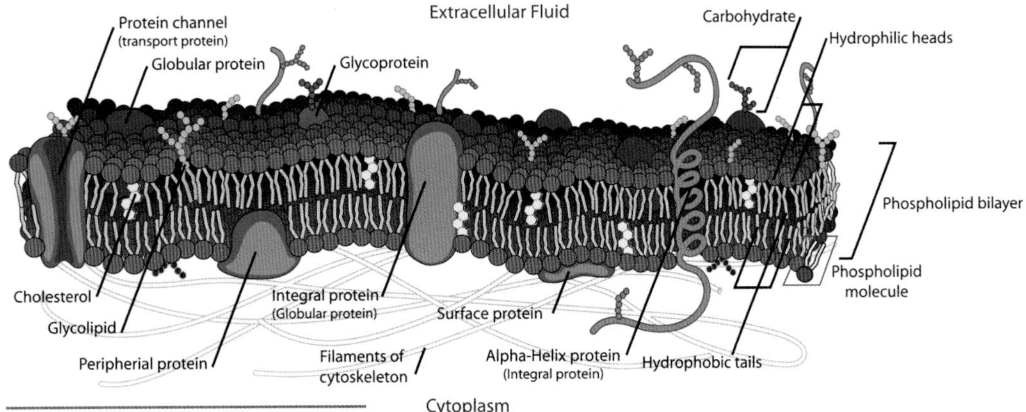

Fig. 106. Membrane Proteins

Signal Transduction Pathways

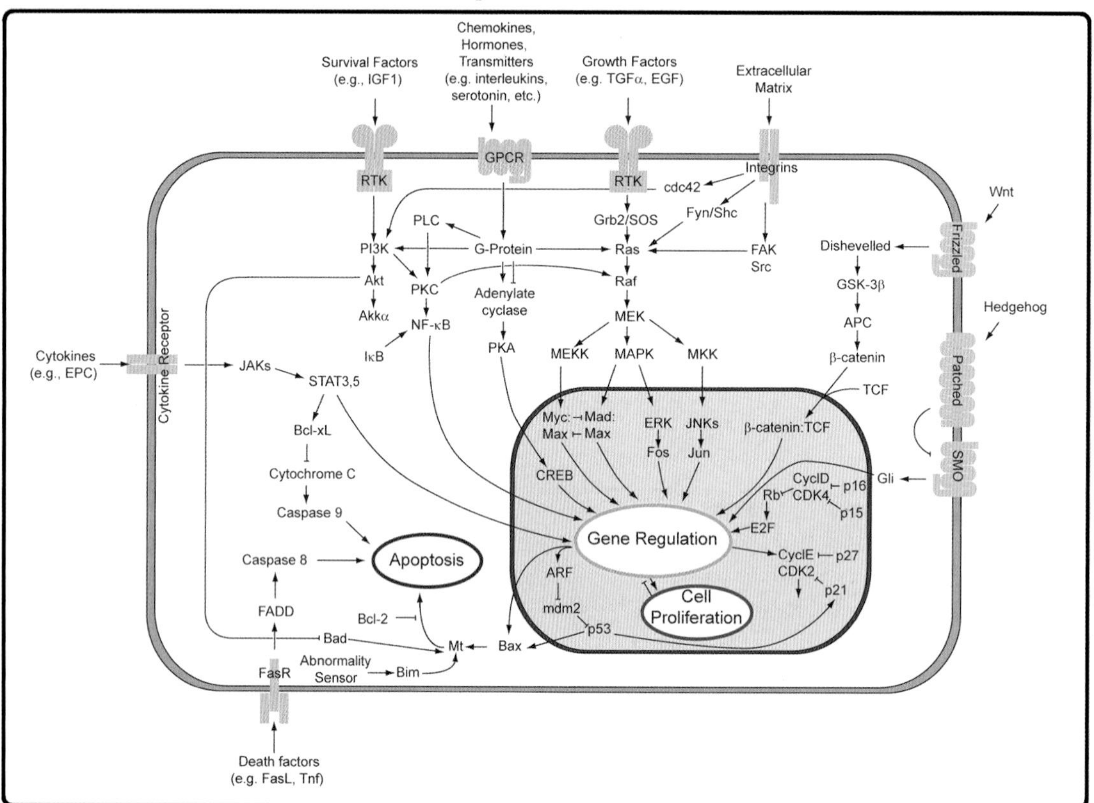

Detailed Examples:

P13K-Akt Pathway Activation

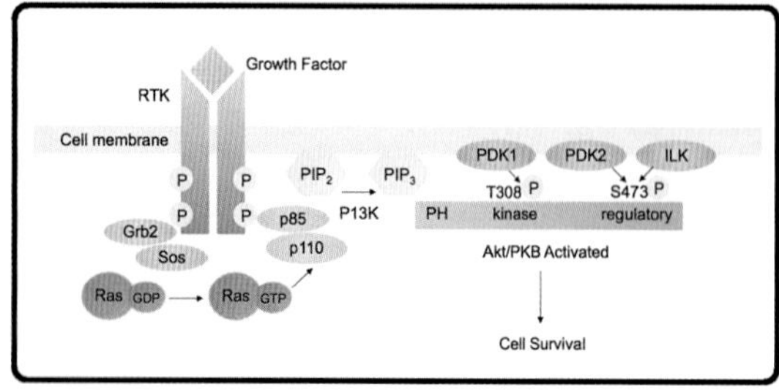

Role of Akt in Cell Cycle Regulation

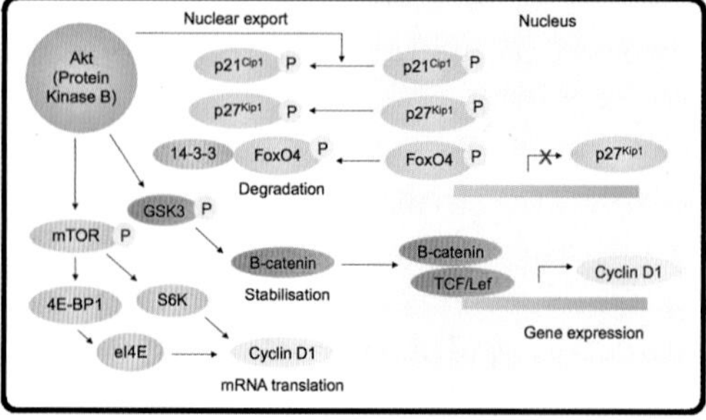

Role of Akt in Cell Survival

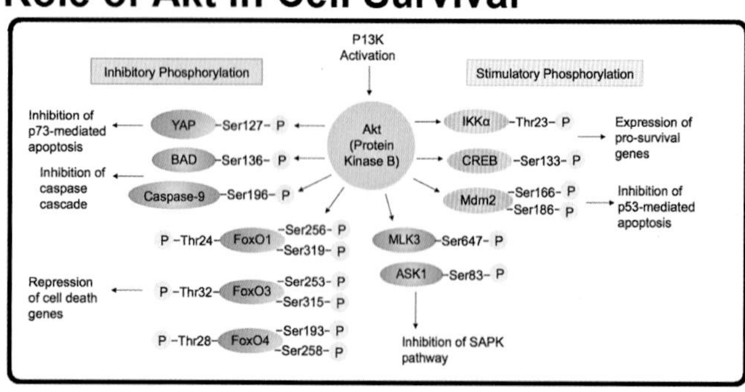

P13K-Akt Feedback Loops

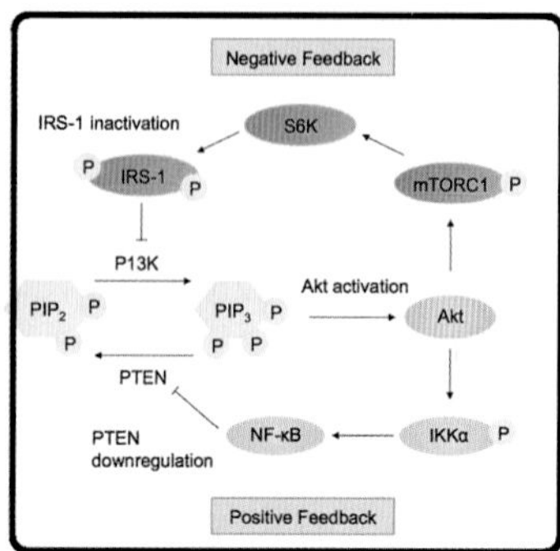

Fig. 107. Protein-based signaling pathways influence gene expression.

- Tubular membrane proteins called porins control the inward passage of nutrients and the outward passage of waste through the cell wall. Porins have internal structures that pass only certain molecules. Gene expression controls the number of particular porins in the cell wall, and therefore, the relative concentrations of nutrients inside a cell.

- All organisms require lunch; that is, chemicals to provide the materials they are made of and the energy they need to operate. Life on Earth is organized into intricate food chains (the biological term is trophic webs), with predators gobbling prey. At the bottom of all food chains are primary producers, organisms that extract materials and energy directly from rocks and sunlight.
- The number of critters needed to fill in a food chain depends on the relative sizes of predators and prey. There are lots of exceptions in special conditions, but the average predator is about ten times larger than the average prey.
- At the bottom of nearly all food chains (eaten by everybody and everything) are prokaryotes: bacteria and archea. Bacteria and archea look similar, but their internal chemistry and DNA sequences differ. Bacteria tend to be more numerous. Archea tend to do better in extreme environments: high

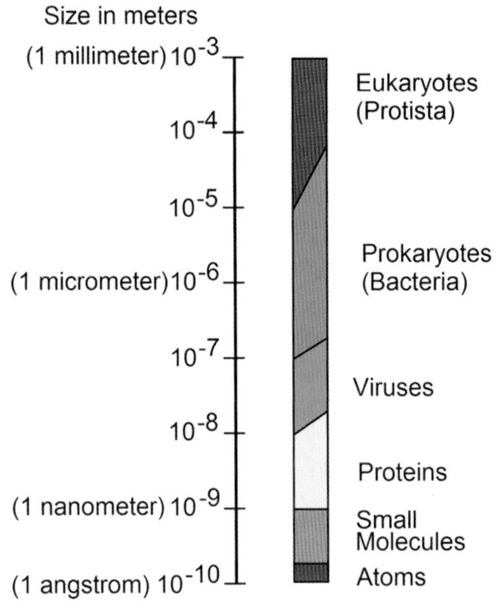

Fig. 108. Sizes of Single-Cell Organisms

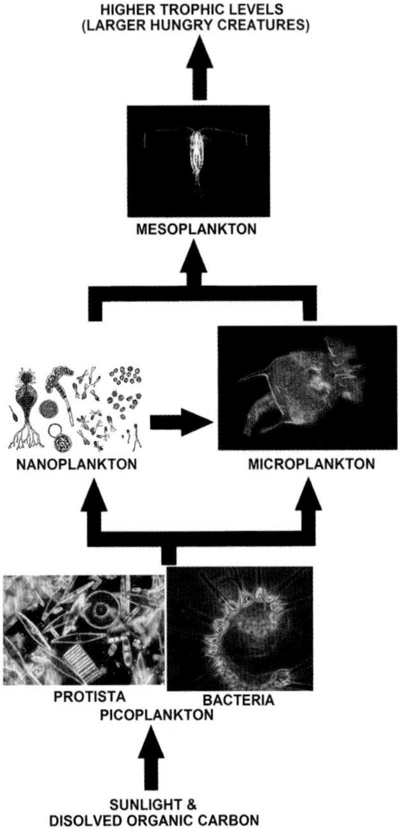

Fig. 109. Plankton Food Chain
Adapted from illustrations from Uwe Kils, a contributor to Alger, Frank Fox (www.mikro-foto.de), Gordon T. Taylor, and the NOAA Mesa Project.

temperatures or unusually high chemical concentrations.

- Prokaryotes are tiny. They are, on average, 1/100 the diameter of eukaryotes, the other cell type common on Earth. Eukaryotes are dramatically different from prokaryotes in structure, chemistry, and DNA. This means that the volume of prokaryotes is 1 million times smaller than eukaryotes.

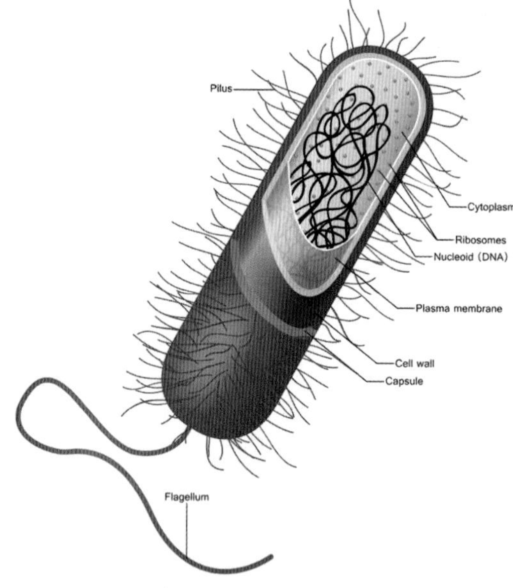

Fig. 110. Prokaryote Cell Structure

- Prokaryotes are tough. They thrive in environments where no other organism can live at all. Prokaryotes have been found living five thousand feet underground, in Arctic and Antarctic ice, and in boiling hot springs (100°C).
- Prokaryotes are extraordinarily adaptable. Microbiologists studied bacteria and archea for years by getting samples in natural settings and taking them back to the laboratory. They found roughly 9,300 prokaryotic species. After developing instruments capable of measuring DNA sequences for wild populations, they discovered that wild prokaryotes typically live in communities with tens of thousands of different species. The laboratory prokaryotes they had been studying were either extremely rare or could not be found at all in wild populations. What microbiologists had been studying were specialized prokaryotes adapted to sample containers.

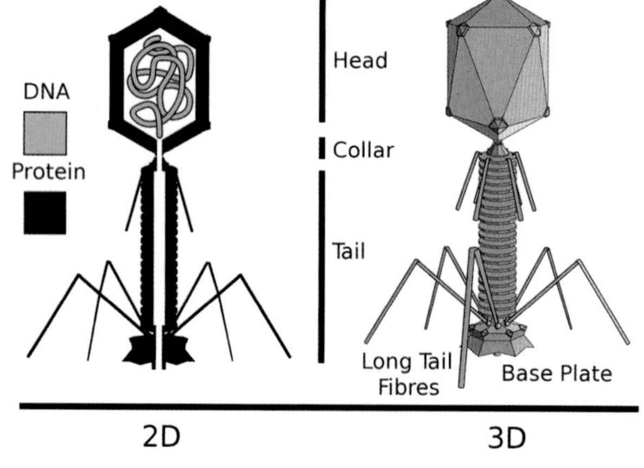

Fig. 111. Bacteriophage, Similar to Gene Transfer Agent (GTA)

- Prokaryotes adapt to environmental changes by shifting gene expression and by modifying gene DNA sequences. DNA sequence changes are partly done by swapping DNA fragments between species (called horizontal gene transfer). DNA is exchanged by direct contact, by releasing unprotected DNA fragments to be picked up by other prokaryotes, and by exchanging DNA fragments in protein cases called Gene Transfer Agents (nicknamed GTA). DNA fragments can be several genes, single genes, or gene fragments. All horizontal gene transfers are made to happen by proteins that cut out or copy DNA sequences and other proteins that read incoming fragments and splice them into existing DNA in appropriate locations. Prokaryote horizontal gene transfers are carefully controlled, not random.

- ◦ Wild prokaryote populations appear to shift species distributions, change species behavior by alternate gene expression, and form new species in response to changing environmental conditions.
- ◦ Because they are the primary producers, all life on Earth depends on prokaryotes. We would all die without them.

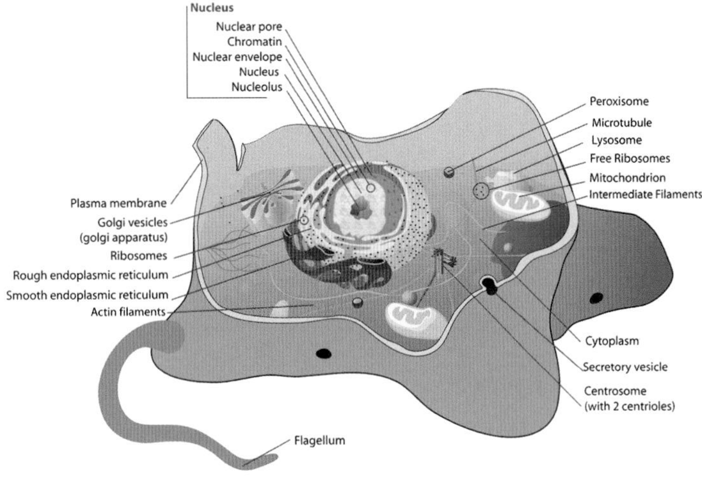

Fig. 112. Eukaryote Cell Structure

- Single-celled eukaryotes (mostly plankton) occupy food chain positions between prokaryotes and multi-celled organisms in the oceans (fish, in other words). Photosynthetic single-celled eukaryotes (algae, for example) are also the primary producers of atmospheric oxygen.
  - ◦ Eukaryotic cells are much larger than prokaryotes and use internal membranes to separate parts of the cell.
  - ◦ Eukaryotes maintain their shapes with an internal skeletal structure, the

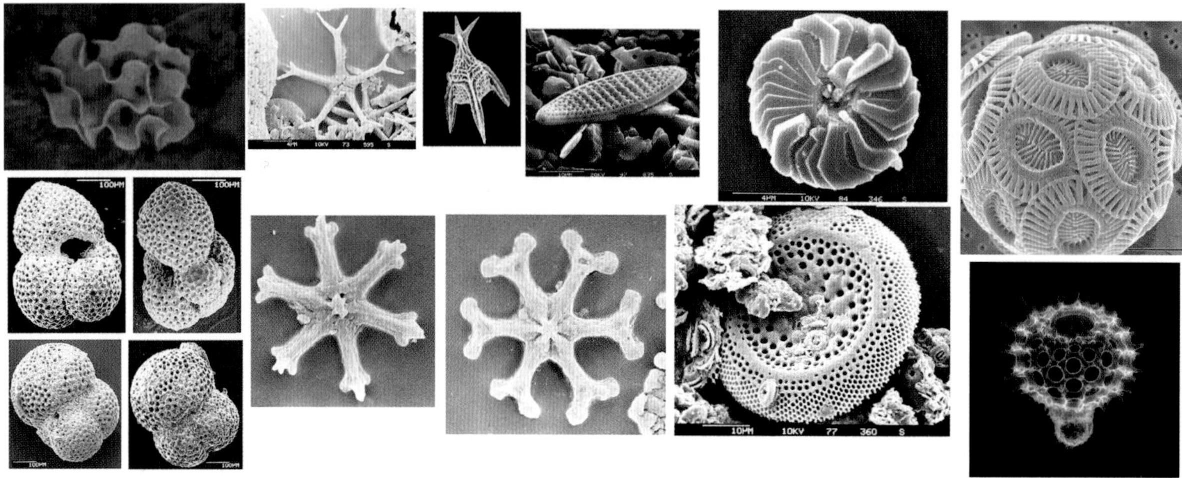

Fig. 113. Eukaryote Microfossils (Mostly Single-Cell Plankton)

cytoskeleton. Prokaryotes are mostly shaped by internal pressure (20–40 psi). Some single-cell eukaryotes also form hard outer shells, which leave fossils.

- Most eukaryote DNA and protein synthesis occurs in and around a cell nucleus that contains DNA. Some membrane-isolated structures (mitochondria and chloroplasts) include DNA and protein synthesis for some abundantly used proteins.
- Eukaryote proteins, including most proteins needed by mitochondria and chloroplasts, are delivered to their work sites by transport proteins that bind to address sequences and tow proteins along the cytoskeleton to the correct location. Prokaryote proteins drift (diffuse) to their assigned work locations; no addresses are required or present.
- Single-celled eukaryotes do horizontal gene transfers like prokaryotes do, but they do it on a much smaller scale. Eukaryotes have a much larger cell volume (1,000,000 times larger) available to store inactive DNA, and they tend to maintain libraries of alternate DNA sequences called transposable elements. Like prokaryote GTA, transposable elements (nicknamed TE) can be several genes, single genes, or parts of genes.
- Differences in DNA sequences between eukaryote species (both single cell and multicellular) tend to be different selections of active TE (transposable elements) in different locations.
- Eukaryote cells use different protein chemical chains (metabolic pathways) than bacteria, and they use them in different sequences to produce the

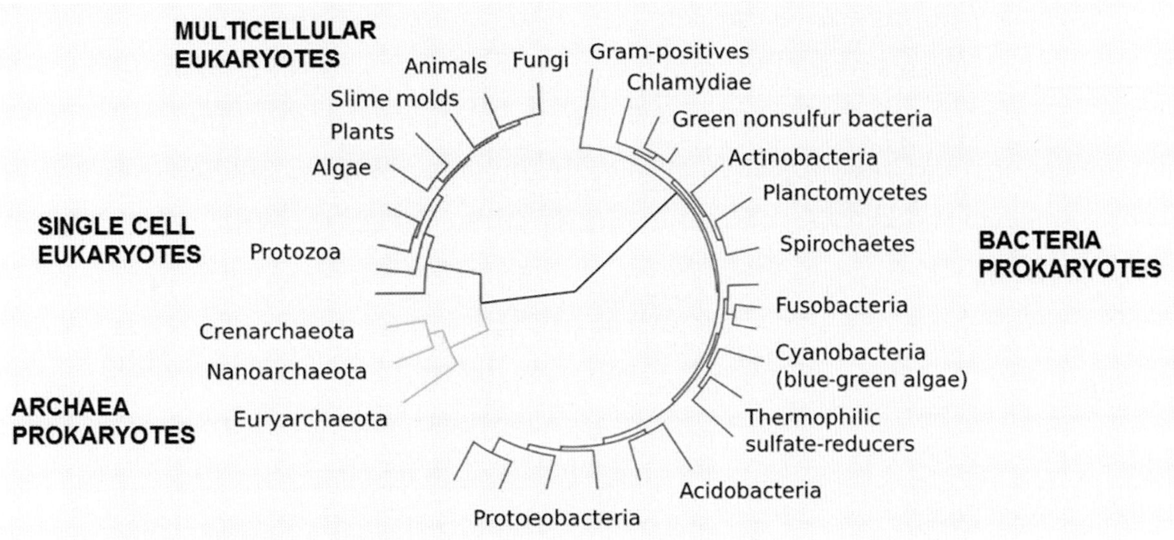

Fig. 114. DNA Sequence Similarities in Organisms

materials they need for structure and energy. The chemistry of archaea prokaryotes has more in common with eukaryotes than with bacteria prokaryotes.

- Many prokaryotes and single-cell eukaryotes specialize. They alter gene expression and therefore their structure and function based on signals from the external environment or on the needs of the moment.
- Cell specialization is the key attribute of multicellular eukaryotes. We exist as colonies of specialized cells, or organs, that all cooperate to survive as an organism.
    - Cell specialization is far more extreme in multicellular eukaryotes than in single-cell creatures. Individual cells from multicellular organisms are not usually able to survive on their own; they require the artificial environment formed by their companions to live at all.
    - Multicellular eukaryotes have much more DNA, which is able to store the information needed for numerous different types of cells and the extremely complicated gene expression rules that control cell structures and functions for different locations in the organism, different neighbor cells, and different times in the life of the organism. Multicellular eukaryotic cells have 100 million to 1500 million base pairs of DNA, compared to 500,000 to 100 million for single-cell creatures.

The following table is an estimated list of the numbers of specialized cells used by the earliest organisms for the animal types (phyla) that, according to the fossil record, have appeared on Earth. According to the fossil record, all animal types either did appear or could have appeared at roughly the same time: 542 million years ago, during an event called the Cambrian Explosion (from Valentine, 2004, *On the Origin of Phyla*, page 74).

Phylum	Number of Cell Types	Phylum	Number of Cell Types
Placozoa	4	Pogonophora	20
Porifera (Cellularia)	5	Chaetognatha	21
Nematomorpha	8	Gastrotricha	23
Cnidaria	10	Phoronida	23
Acanthocephala	12	Hemichordata (Pterobranchia)	25
Entoprocta	13	Bryozoa	30
Nematoda	14	Onychophora	30
Cycliophora	15	Brachiopoda (Articulata)	34
Rotifera	15	Nemertea	35
Gnathostomulida	16	Sipuncula	35
Kinoryncha	17	Arthropoda	37
Ctenophora	18	Mollusca (Polyplacophora)	37
Loricifera	18	Urochordata (Ascidiacea)	38
Tardigrada	18	Chordata (Cephalochordata)	39
Priapulida	20	Annelida (Polychaeta)	40
Echiura	20	Echinodermata (Crinoidea)	40
Platyhelminthes (Turbellaria)	20	Chordata (Agnatha)	60

- Different multicellular organisms mostly use cell types that are very similar. Eye cells are similar between species; gut cells are also similar in different species. The differences between animal types (phyla) are mostly in the DNA sequences—the binding sites for blocking and enhancing proteins or micro RNA that control gene expression and splicing. What makes a different organism is where particular specialized cells show up.

Multicellular organisms develop in many varied ways. The following description portrays a typical development sequence.

- Multicellular organisms begin development from a single cell (called a zygote) into large conglomerations of cells by dividing the zygote to produce more cells. This is called cell cleavage, and it results in a spherical mass of cells called a blastula. (When I say "large conglomeration," that is the truth: we humans have 37.2 trillion cells, according to Bianconi "An Estimation of the Number of Cells in the Human Body," *Annals of Human Biology*.)

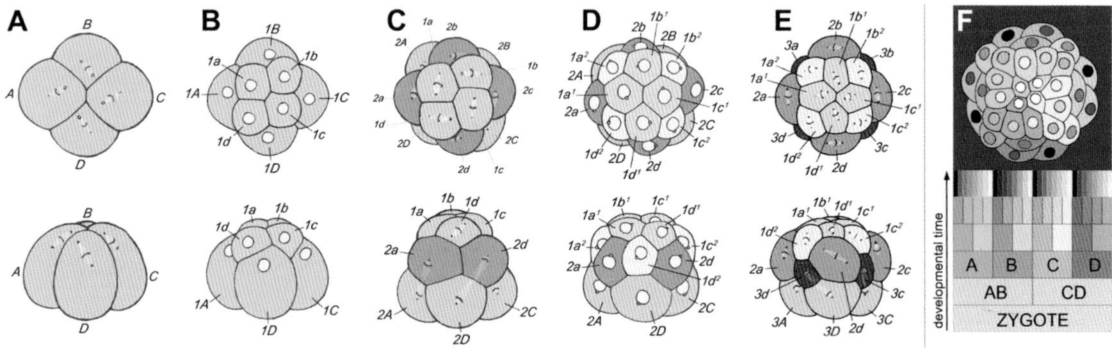

Fig. 115. Cell Cleavage in Embryo Development

  - The divisions during cell cleavage always occur at particular locations on each cell, because the proteins that change cell structure so that a cell will divide act on specific binding sites on the cell wall. The cells also bind to each other, with the membrane proteins that bind cells together also located at specific positions on the cell walls.
  - In the spherical blastula, each cell position always has the same division history: each cell "knows" its position by recording which "side" of each division it was on. Cell history is recorded by gene expression; for example,

an expressed protein can be its own expression enhancer so that it will always be expressed after it has been made once.

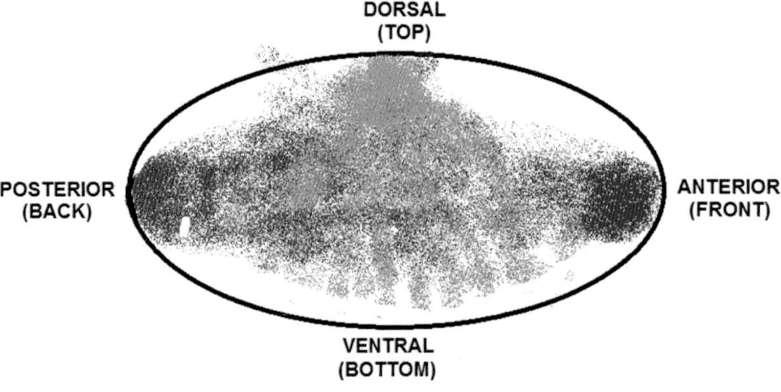

Fig. 116. Morphogen Proteins Signal Position

- Cell division continues to build a larger mass of cells.
- Cells at what will be the "ends" of the organism start producing signal proteins (called morphogens). Morphogen proteins are chemically unstable; they fall apart quickly, so there is a lower concentration for each morphogen further away from the cell that makes it.
- Morphogen concentrations are used to establish a coordinate system (actually similar to Cartesian coordinates) inside the mass of cells.

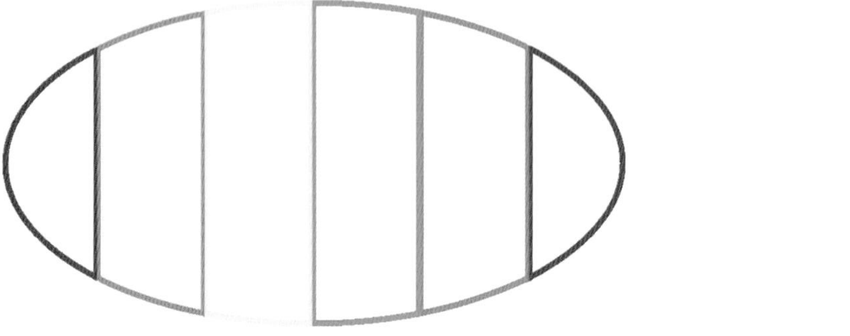

Fig. 117. Developing Embryo Sections Identified by Gene Expression

- The mass of cells is divided up into sections. Gene expression is used again to record the section each cell is in; the particular genes used to record section locations are called Hox genes (short for homeobox). Other genes record the position of each cell in its section.
- Cells continue to divide into more cells and use morphogen signaling proteins to create local "coordinate systems." The division patterns and

morphogen types and locations are different for each section and section position in the organism (they are also very different in different organisms). Cells eventually specialize (express a particular set of proteins that gives them a distinctive structure) into cell types (gut cell, muscle cell, bone cell, nerve cell, etc.) based on the history of divisions and locations stored by gene expression.

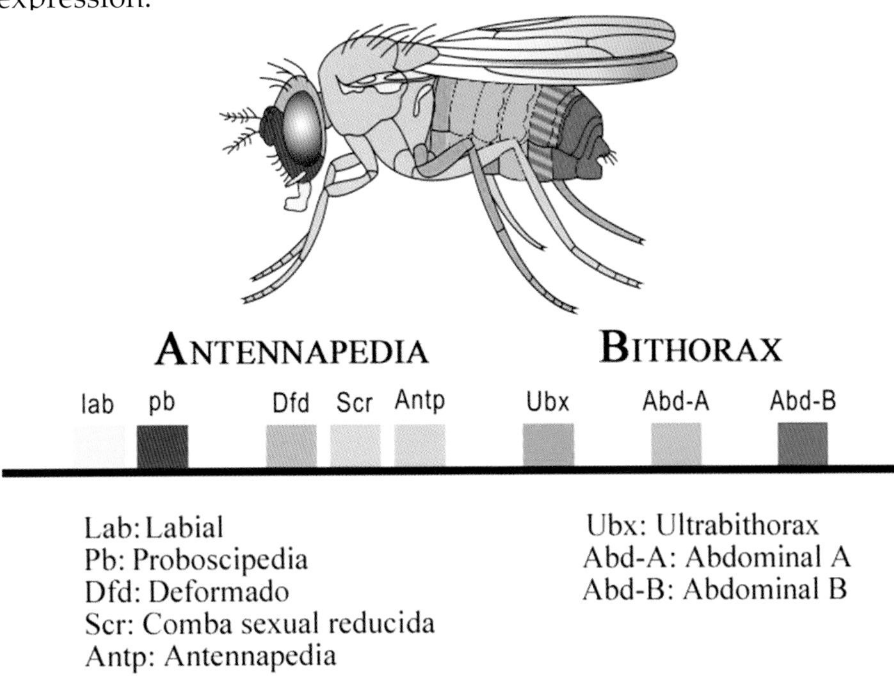

Fig. 118. Hox genes identify regions in organisms.

- Some of the genes used to record division and position history for each cell in a developing multicellular organism are highly conserved, meaning they are very similar (almost identical) for all multicellular organisms. Larger, more complex organisms use more of them. We have more Hox genes than a fruit fly, for example, but some of our Hox genes are very similar to the ones a fruit fly uses, even to the point of being recorded in similar positions in our respective DNA strands.
- The difference between types of multicellular organisms, between a fruit fly and a worm or a human being for example, are mostly found in what the cells at each position do in response to where they are. Gut cells, nerve cells, muscle cells, etc. appear at different locations in each different type of critter.

- Biologists divide animal multicellular organisms into categories with similar features or similar DNA sequences. (Features and DNA are mostly, but not always, related.) These categories are phylum, class, order, family, genus, and species. Phyla are separated by differences in the basic distribution of organs (called the body plan). Insects (phylum Arthropoda) have a very different internal organization than humans (phylum Chordata) do. There are currently about thirty-five animal phyla. The definitions tend to shift over time for some very interesting reasons.

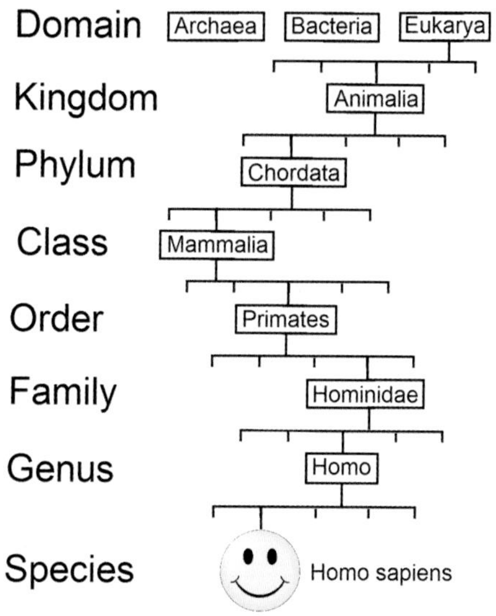

Fig. 118.1. Animal Categories

- The differences in animal shape and internal organization (body plan) are mostly the result of different correlations between expressed genes that record the position of cells in the organism and the expressed genes that determine the structure and function of each cell.
- The DNA protein coding sequence (gene) for every protein that plays a role in specialized cell structure or function must, in some way, have RNA polymerase and spliceosome blocking and enhancing sites that are keyed to signal proteins produced by the gene expression that records the position and history of every cell in the organism.
- Body plan features (legs, gut, eyes, muscles, etc.) usually require hundreds to thousands of specialized proteins and developmental sequences.
- As far as we know, most of the large differences between the millions of animal species on Earth were accomplished by the movement of DNA transposable elements in the genetic code. Horizontal gene transfer (as is seen in bacteria) also played a role, probably via viral infections. Other features of DNA coding are probably also related to the physical features of organisms (simple sequence repeats, for example), but the specifics of how they affect development are not yet known.
- As mentioned earlier, the animal phyla that we see today did appear or could have appeared suddenly in the fossil record during the Cambrian geologic period.
- There are numerous fossils that show the divergence of the original species in each phylum (original species are called stem taxa) into many, many different

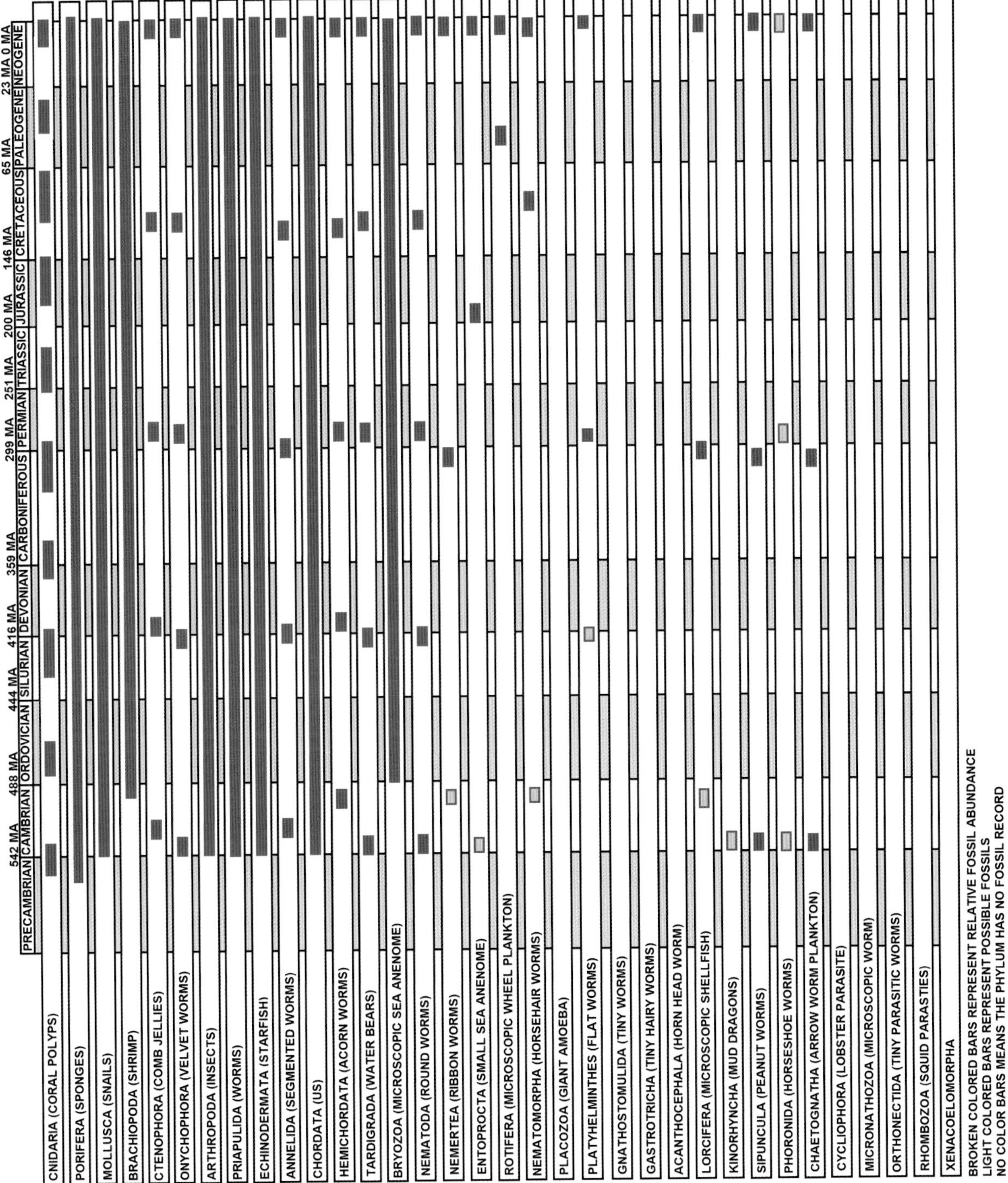

Fig. 119. Appearance of Phyla in the Fossil Record

species of animals; maps of these relationships are called fossil descent trees.

- There is no indication in the fossil record that any animal descent tree has ever crossed from one phylum into a different phylum.
- Early animal species changed into radically different species (to form classes,

orders, and families) faster and more often long ago than they generally do now. The early prevalence of more radical genetic changes is called "top down" evolution.

- Biologists today organize plants into divisions instead of phyla; there are about ten divisions of plant types.
- Plants use a development scheme controlled by local coordinate systems similar to that used by animals, but the relationship between the proteins expressed at each location and the consequent structure and function of the cells are very different for plants than they are for animals.

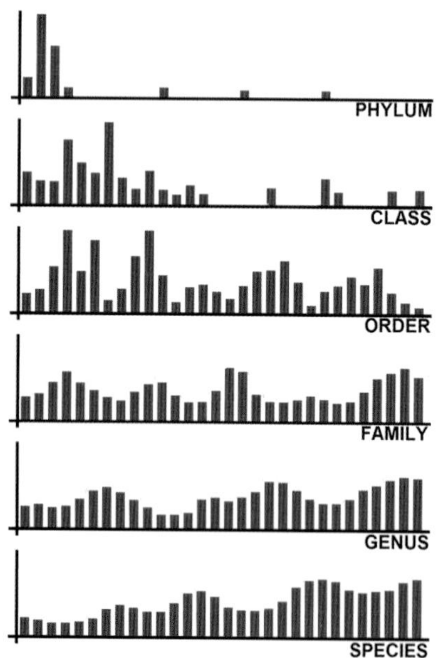

Fig. 120. Typical Pattern of Fossil Appearance through Geologic Time.

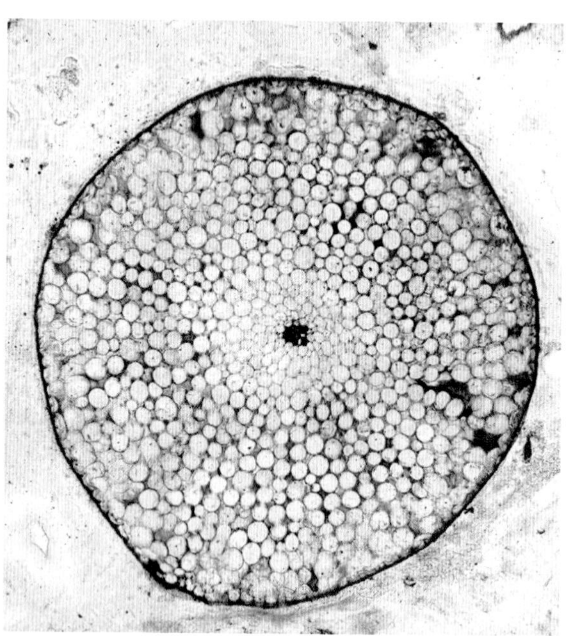

Fig. 121. Plant Fossil Stem Cross Section

- Plants appear in the fossil record after animals. By radiometric dating, animal phyla mostly appear in the Cambrian period about 542–488 million years ago. Plant divisions mostly appear in the Silurian period 443–416 million years ago and later (also determined by radiometric dating). Like animal phyla, plant divisions appear in the fossil record in a relatively short period of time, geologically speaking.

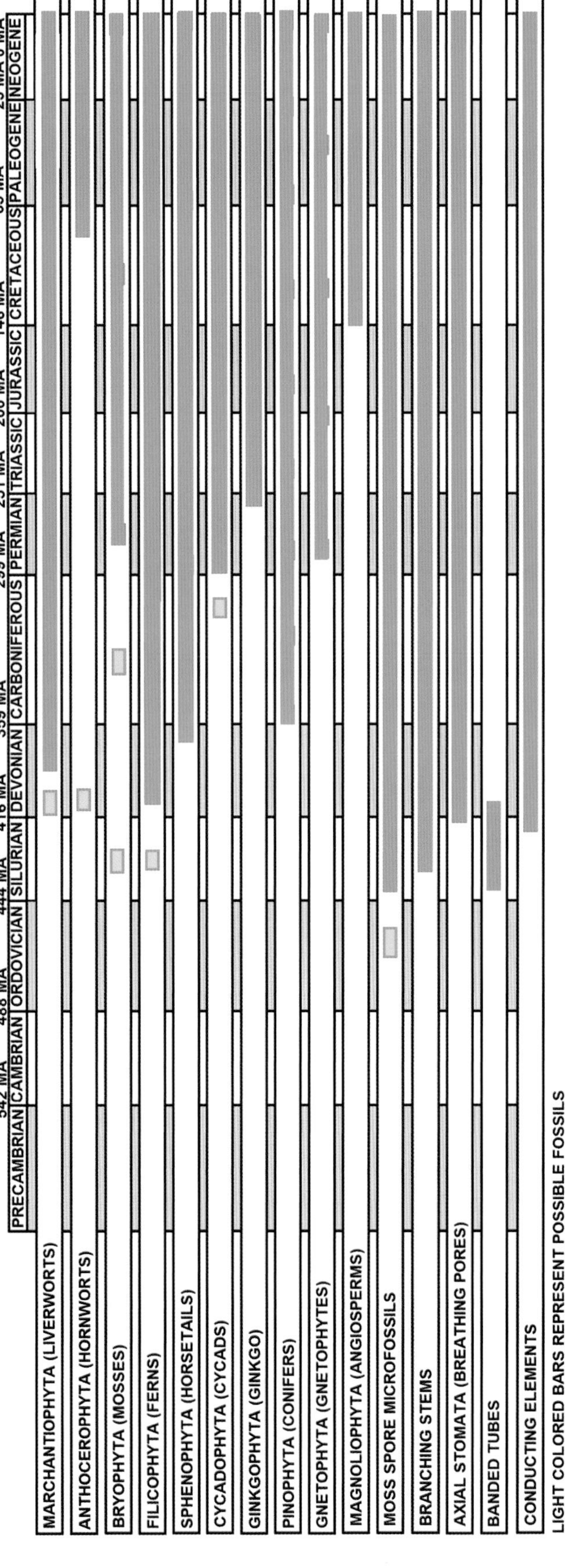

Fig. 122. Plant Fossil Division and Feature Appearance

Evolution in a Developmental Creation

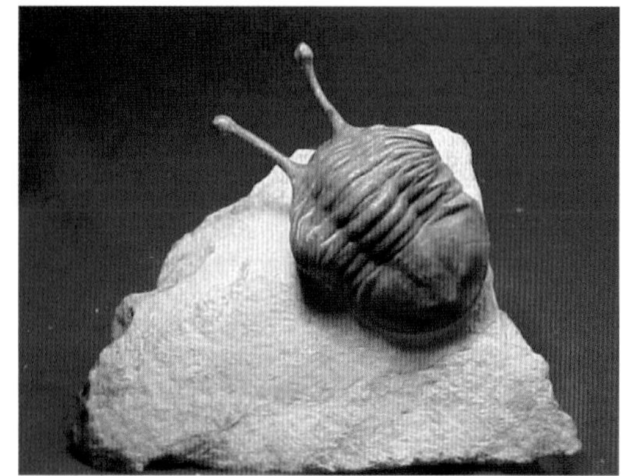

Fig. 123. Trilobite Fossil

Evolution, the changes in living organisms over time, is going to play a moderate role in the interpretation of Genesis 1 coming up. Because of the strong passions invested in the debate over evolution between creationists and naturalists, I wish to precede that interpretation with a brief explanation of the perspective on evolution that will be used. It would take a second volume to do a thorough presentation of the reasons why I treat evolution as I do here, so this will just be an overview.

People debate evolution on a foggy battleground with a rich variety of gradations and nuances of viewpoint. Three primary positions, where armies camp on small, fortified hills poking above the fog, will serve to illustrate the common boundaries of the debate: creationists who support a literal, classical physics interpretation of Genesis; naturalists who argue that our reality is wholly natural, without God or any type of supernatural creation act; and Intelligent Design guys who, oddly enough, base their positions on the observations and logical deductions of science and natural philosophy.

By the way, so that you can attempt to accurately judge bias in the following presentation, I am a Young Earth Creationist (I call it "scriptural literalism") with a twist of quantum mechanics—sort of a Young Spacetime Creationist.

Back to our three armies. On a bluff by the still waters amid green pastures are the Young Earth Creationists. They hold that the naturalists have distorted the science and natural philosophy involved to support naturalism. Their goal is thus to reexamine the science and natural philosophy—the basic factual observations—to see if the bare facts might be compatible with a six-day creation as described in Genesis 1 and a six thousand to twelve thousand year age of the earth, as derived from the genealogies of Genesis 5 and Genesis 11. (Specific times depend on the version of original Hebrew text used; there are at least two.)

On its classical physics face, the Genesis timescale is not long enough to allow for stellar development, the slow geologic disruption of the earth's surface, the slow formation of fossils buried in layers of sediment, or any kind of developmental process needed to produce the millions of living species that we see around us on this earth. Young Earth Creationists, therefore, have questioned the deductions of science and natural philosophy in astrophysics, geology, paleontology, and especially, evolutionary biology.

Over the years, the creationists have scored some significant victories. Rapid geologic processes are recognized (some are, some aren't), and rapid fossilization is accepted as possible (it is possible for an organism to fossilize in a few hours, but it doesn't happen often). These are currently consensus viewpoints in natural philosophy; the scientific work that supports those viewpoints was probably originally motivated by creationist criticism. Likewise, paleontologists have spent significant effort filling in gaps in the fossil record that were pointed out by creationists. In fact, much of the recent scientific work directed at deciphering the detailed mechanisms of change in genetic code might be motivated, at least in part, by a desire to refute creationists.

In all of this, what creationists have mostly done is to insist that natural philosophers prove their conclusions in some logical, scientific way. Creationist arguments can seem pretty goofy to people who are not aware of their motivation (or their scientific background), but I submit that, overall, the application of science to natural philosophy is a lot more solid for evolution now than it would have been without them.

On a stony crag dominating the battlefield, with a plentiful supply of pointy rocks to hurl at their opponents, are the naturalists. Naturalists hold that this reality is an entirely random, wholly natural place, with no God and, especially, no divine act of creation. They see the role of science and natural philosophy as deciphering how this reality naturally works and how it naturally came to be the way that it is. Currently, they have a rough idea of how the whole thing works and how it happened, and they have filled in some of the details to their satisfaction.

Naturalists generally do not regard the admitted gaps in observational support for their theories as counting against the truth of their position. They hold that the universe must have happened in some natural way, and in time, the details will be revealed. Meanwhile, the current naturalist theories (evolution, for example) are the best they have been able to think of, and therefore they must be at least provisionally true. Naturalists are often annoyed by the creationist notion that they really should prove their conclusions by theory and observation before they claim truth or scientific law.

Naturalists see themselves as defending the truth of science. Because it is literally impossible (for them) that their theories could be fundamentally wrong, any observation or scientific analysis that challenges the truth of naturalism must be defective. Any challenger, trained scientist or not, must be mentally or morally suspect and should not, as a matter of right, participate in the community of science and natural philosophy. Motivated by a sense of offended justice, naturalists tend to be vicious when crossed in scientific debate.

We'll skip the details of the naturalist theories for now. I suspect they are already known to all. Basically, naturalists hold that natural theories for abiogenesis, original descent, evolution, and speciation must all be correct; some of the details may be fuzzy, but that does not alter their fundamental truth. Because of their advantage in numbers, naturalists guard all the doors and hold all the keys in the scientific and natural philosophy community. They are the consensus.

Intelligent Design advocates have formed a (small) line of battle on a low rise in the field of truth, banners waving in defiance. The biological version of Intelligent Design holds that the vast diversity of living organisms in this world could not possibly have been the result of any remotely random process. They suggest that the earth was terraformed by person or persons unknown and was seeded with life that had been specifically designed to adapt in a hostile natural environment.

The Intelligent Design perspective on evolution is the one we will use in our Genesis speculation, so we'll go into some detail on it here.

Necessary differences in scientific approach divide theories of biological origin and development into four basic areas: abiogenesis, original descent, evolution, and speciation.

Abiogenesis

Abiogenesis (from Greek: "not life beginning") theories try to describe the transition from naturally occurring chemicals to living organisms. Abiogenesis theories so far proposed by naturalists have a couple of significant problems. While most types of chemicals used in living organisms can be produced in natural settings, no single location has ever been found that produces all of the required chemicals with the conditions needed for those chemicals to combine into the structures used in critters (i.e. high concentrations and a source of chemical energy to drive reactions). For example, the surface of the earth was, at the time life appeared here, exposed to unfiltered sunlight, with UV radiation intensities that break down organic molecules (UV light is frequently used in industry to sterilize surfaces). The oceans give protection from UV radiation, but they also dissipate chemicals. Bacterial cells have an internal pressure (called osmotic pressure) of roughly 30 psi, the same as a car tire, caused by the very high concentrations of chemicals inside living organisms. Without a strong cellular wall to contain the pressure and concentrate the chemicals, they die. In the case of abiogenesis, without a preexisting strong cell wall, they could never be born. Similar problems go on.

The major objection to abiogenesis, though, is based on statistical analysis. The sequences of amino acids in biological proteins must be extremely specific in order to take on the shape and function necessary for organic proteins. The same is true for DNA genetic sequences, which are used to build proteins. Because of the very long length of amino acid chains needed to form proteins (an average of 300–400 amino acids for bacteria; about a thousand for eukaryotes) the odds against randomly discovering functional protein sequences is much, much greater than astronomical. Doug Axe has estimated that roughly one in 10^{77} amino acid sequences could have any physical structure or chemical function at all. Far fewer would have the very specific structures required for the proteins that mostly make up living organisms. (See "Estimating the Prevalence of Protein Sequences Adopting Functional Enzyme Folds" in *Journal of Molecular Biology*, 8/27/04, 1295–1315.)

The following table shows an outline of a very inaccurate calculation of the number of protein coding gene sequences that could have been produced in the universe we know (no one knows enough to do an accurate calculation). This calculation is almost certainly *larger* than the real number could possibly be. It uses bacterial single gene replications because that is the fastest mechanism we know of for producing new amino acid sequences. Any nonliving process would be much slower. The calculation also assumes that genes will change in random ways every time they are replicated. No organism could survive if that were actually true; gene replication errors are usually rare in living cells (roughly one wrong DNA base pair per billion base pairs).

Description of Factor	Factor to multiply by	Net Number of Genes Made
Average number of genes in bacteria	3,768	3,768
One bacterial replication every five minutes is 105,120 whole genome replications per year for each bacterium. This times the number of individual genes is the number of individual gene replications per year for one bacterium.	105,120	3.961×10^{8}
There are an average of one million bacteria in each milliliter of ocean water. This is a typical number for surface water where the sun shines. Dark, deeper waters have lower populations. The product is the number of gene replications per year in one milliliter of ocean water.	1,000,000	3.961×10^{14}
This times the number of milliliters in a cubic mile gets the number of bacterial gene replications per year in each cubic mile of ocean water.	4.168×10^{15}	1.651×10^{30}
This times the volume of surface water on Earth gets the number of bacterial gene replications per year on Earth.[2]	3.19×10^{8}	5.27×10^{38}
This times the estimated number of stars in the universe (also from Wikipedia) gets the maximum possible number of gene replications every year in the entire universe. This assumes that there might be a life-bearing planet like Earth circling every star. There certainly aren't anywhere near that many.[3]	3×10^{23}	2×10^{62}
This times the age of the universe since the big bang gets the maximum possible number of bacterial single gene replications in all of the universe throughout all of time. This number is an upper boundary. There cannot possibly have really been anywhere near that many gene replications, or, the point of the calculation, different long amino acid sequences (peptides) produced by any natural process.	13.798×10^{9}	2×10^{72}

2 "Ocean." Retrieved c. 2014 from https://en.wikipedia.org/wiki/Ocean.
3 "Universe." Retrieved c. 2014 from https://en.wikipedia.org/wiki/Universe.

If the universe can only possibly have produced 2×10^{72} amino acid sequences, and only one in 10^{77} sequences can have any kind of structure or function, then our universe only has roughly one chance in fifty thousand of randomly producing even one single functional protein. One bacterium has, on average, 3,768 proteins, with physical structures that interlock and function with intricate teamwork. The odds of randomly producing a single living bacterium are roughly one chance in $50{,}000^{3{,}768}$. Or, since there can be more than one kind of bacterium, a trillion chances in $50{,}000^{3{,}768}$ (= one chance in $50{,}000^{3{,}756}$). Or a trillion trillion kinds of bacteria (one in $50{,}000^{3{,}732}$). Throw in as many trillions as you like; it doesn't change the numbers in any noticeable way.

The naturalist's go-to process, natural selection, is not random and is able to dramatically improve the odds. But natural selection can only choose among candidates—*and this universe does not have the statistical capability to randomly produce even a single viable candidate.*

One rebuttal made by naturalists, tacitly admitting the low probability of spontaneous life, holds that life may have happened at least once somewhere in the universe, and it just happens to have been here on Earth. That idea understates the odds against the kind of life we see. The statistical calculations do not indicate that the occurrence of life should be rare. They indicate that it cannot have happened randomly anywhere in this universe, or anywhere in a million or a billion universes just like it, even if time were a million or a billion times longer than it apparently has been.

Original Descent

Original descent is the idea that all of the living organisms currently found on Earth are descended from a single ancestral cell, probably a bacterium or something very like a bacterium. Original descent is essential to any natural theory of biological development for two reasons. The first is statistical. Even naturalists admit the very low probability that life could have happened by chance, so the idea that it could have happened more than once here on Earth is really hard to justify. (Though they do try. Naturalists deserve points for perseverance.)

The second, much stronger reason is observational. All life on Earth examined so far uses the same fundamental chemical organization. All creatures use double-stranded DNA to make RNA as a template for making the protein amino acid chains that do almost all of the work of living. All organisms use virtually the same three specific

CODON	AMINO ACID
AAA	LYSINE
AAC	ASPARAGINE
AAG	LYSINE
AAU	ASPARAGINE
ACA	THREONINE
ACC	THREONINE
ACG	THREONINE
ACU	THREONINE
AGA	ARGININE
AGC	SERINE
AGG	ARGININE
AGU	SERINE
AUA	ISOLEUCINE
AUC	ISOLEUCINE
AUG	METHIONINE
AUU	ISOLEUCINE
CAA	GLUTAMNE
CAC	HISTIDINE
CAG	GLUTAMNE
CAU	HISTIDINE
CCA	PROLINE
CCC	PROLINE
CCG	PROLINE
CCU	PROLINE
CGA	ARGININE
CGC	ARGININE
CGG	ARGININE
CGU	ARGININE
CUA	LEUCINE
CUC	LEUCINE
CUG	LEUCINE
CUU	LEUCINE
GAA	GLUTAMIC ACID
GAC	ASPARTIC ACID
GAG	GLUTAMIC ACID
GAU	ASPARTIC ACID
GCA	ALANINE
GCC	ALANINE
GCG	ALANINE
GCU	ALANINE
GGA	GLYCINE
GGC	GLYCINE
GGG	GLYCINE
GGU	GLYCINE
GUA	VALINE
GUC	VALINE
GUG	VALINE
GUU	VALINE
UAA	STOP
UAC	TYROSINE
UAG	STOP
UAU	TYROSINE
UCA	SERINE
UCC	SERINE
UCG	SERINE
UCU	SERINE
UGA	STOP
UGC	CYSTEINE
UGG	TRYPTOPHANN
UGU	CYSTEINE
UUA	LEUCINE
UUC	PHENYALANINE
UUG	LEUCINE
UUU	PHENYALANINE

DNA and RNA base-pair sequences (called codons) to specify particular amino acids in protein chains. (Eukaryotic mitochondria and a few bacteria have slight variations in genetic code, the codon to amino acid relationships.) And they all use similar chemical processing sequences with similar proteins to produce the essential chemicals needed to live (called metabolic pathways).

For these and other reasons, naturalists have assumed that original descent is how it all really happened. Remember, for them, this has to be true. Fortunately or unfortunately, depending on which side one is on, observations of the real world do not support original descent. A fossil record compatible with original descent would need to look like the diagram on the left below: fossil populations that start with a very few simple organisms and gradually branch out, adding more and more complex species over long periods of nearly continuous change.

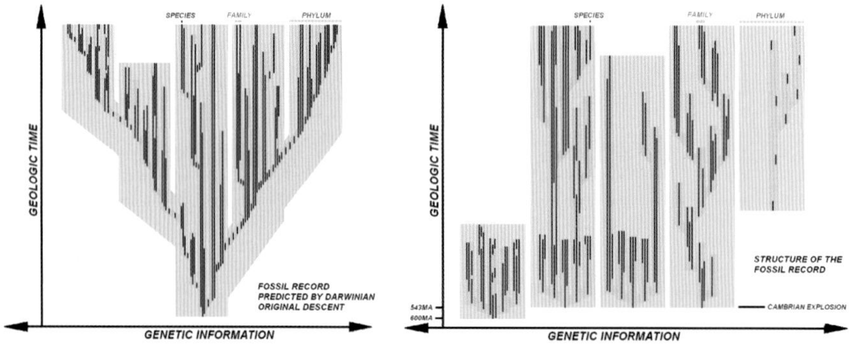

The actual fossil record for animals is more like the diagram on the right. New phyla appear suddenly as single or a few species and then rapidly branch out to form species in new classes, orders, and families. The term for this is "top-down evolution," meaning that "higher," more drastic physiological changes, happen early.

(The above diagrams, by the way, are just cartoons. They illustrate the concepts but are not based on any real, specific fossil data. It would be nice to present real data but circumstances make that difficult. Since the two diagrams present opposing views one of them would have to be a cartoon. Most existing tree of life diagrams conform to the consensus of the biological community and force the data into conformance with Darwinian evolution and original descent. Mainstream biologists are close to admitting that observations of life on Earth do not support Darwinian evolution or original descent, but they are not quite there yet. When they do change the consensus they will have to redo decades of papers and books because they refused to listen to a reasoned argument. It's really a bit of a tragedy.)

At this time, all or nearly all phyla could have appeared at roughly the same time (542 MA, the Cambrian Explosion; MA stands for mega-anna or one million years ago), and there are no lines of descent in the animal fossil record that cross between phyla.

The fossil record for single-celled organisms is older, but it is similar. The oldest definite fossils for bacteria are the Gunflint Iron Formation biota (1900 MA). The oldest definite fossils for eukaryotic Protista are *Bangiomorpha pubescens* (1200 MA). Both are very similar in appearance and capability to modern bacteria and Protista.

Evolutionary molecular biologists have made an exhaustive study statistically comparing the genetic DNA sequences for living creatures. They have produced descent trees based on similar DNA sequences that are like the diagram on the next page and that mostly match the tree of life produced by biologists and paleontologists studying physiological similarities. The most commonly cited molecular tree of life was based on the 16S (bacteria) and 18S (eukaryotes) RNA subunits in ribosomes.

Comparisons of other DNA sequences give different descent trees or no tree at all. Molecular descent trees are currently an "active area of inquiry" in biology as scientists try to account for chaotic relationships in DNA sequences. One of the current issues is horizontal gene transfer between species and kingdoms. Some DNA sequences seem to jump from branch to branch in the molecular tree of life without the benefit of intermediary

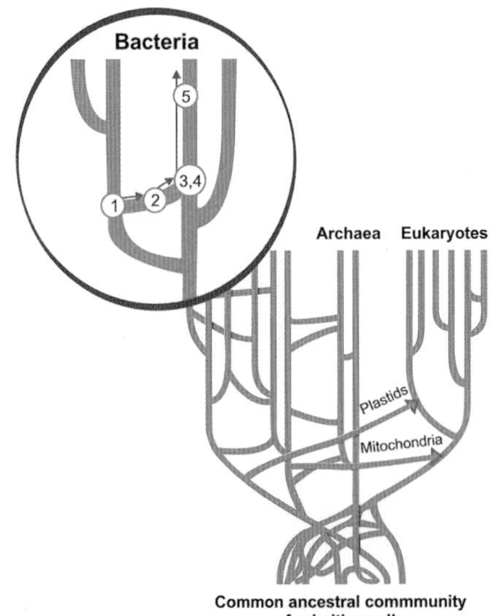

Fig. 124. Current Tree of Life with Horizontal Gene Transfer

species. Molecular biologists, firmly attached to naturalism, are guessing that early organisms passed bits of DNA back and forth as modern bacteria are known to do. In any case, the molecular evidence for original descent is foggy at best.

The final and strongest evidence against original descent is statistical, just as for abiogenesis. The amount of genetic information required for organisms does not increase smoothly with physiological complexity. It jumps. The two diagrams below (cartoons again) represent the necessary picture for original descent on the left and what actually appears to have happened on the right.

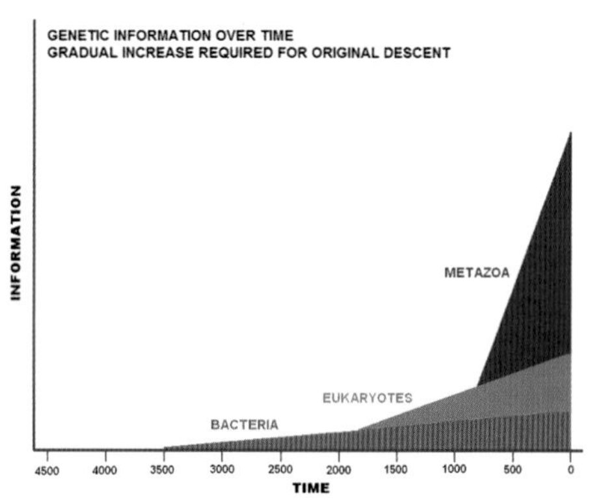

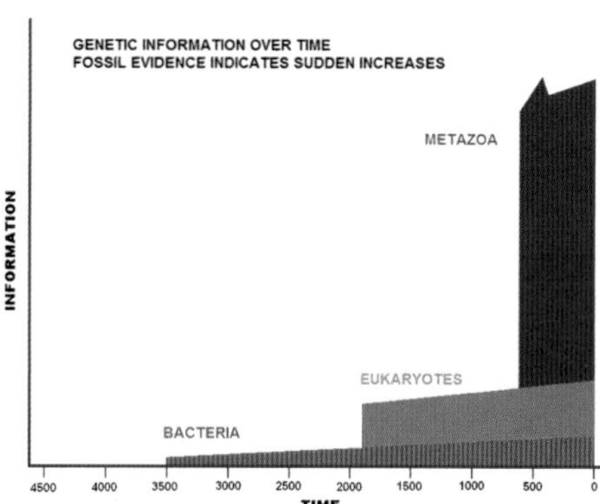

To examine the statistics more closely: Bacterial DNA typically has between 500,000 and 5 million base pairs. Single-celled eukaryotes (yeast, algae) have 10 million to 100 million base pairs, an average of twenty times more DNA than bacteria. Multicellular eukaryotes (like us) have 100 million to 15 billion base pairs, roughly fifty times as much DNA as single-celled eukaryotes (we have 3.2 billion base pairs of DNA; salamanders are the reigning genetic champions, with 15 billion base pairs of DNA).

Unlike abiogenesis, where candidate organisms cannot have inherited characteristics from previous generations, natural selection can theoretically play a major role in reducing the odds against the large jumps in genetic information associated with the origin of eukaryotes and multicellular animals. The fossil record, however, is moderately detailed for the appearance of both, and there is little or no observational support for gradual development. As was mentioned earlier, both single-celled eukaryotes and multicellular animals appear suddenly in the fossil record. Natural selection *could* theoretically have produced such large jumps in genetic content, but there is no conclusive observational evidence that it did—and there is nowhere near enough time (see the calculation for abiogenesis).

Evolution

Evolution is the change in inherited characteristics in biological populations over successive generations.[4] Darwin called it "descent with modification."

To examine this idea, let's first look at physiological evolution, the changes in bodily traits and features that paleontologists see in the fossil record and biologists see in living creatures. The scientific, observational support for physiological evolution, including origination of new species, genera, families, and so on—up to but not including phyla—is quite good. For the most part, that support is comprised of fossils.

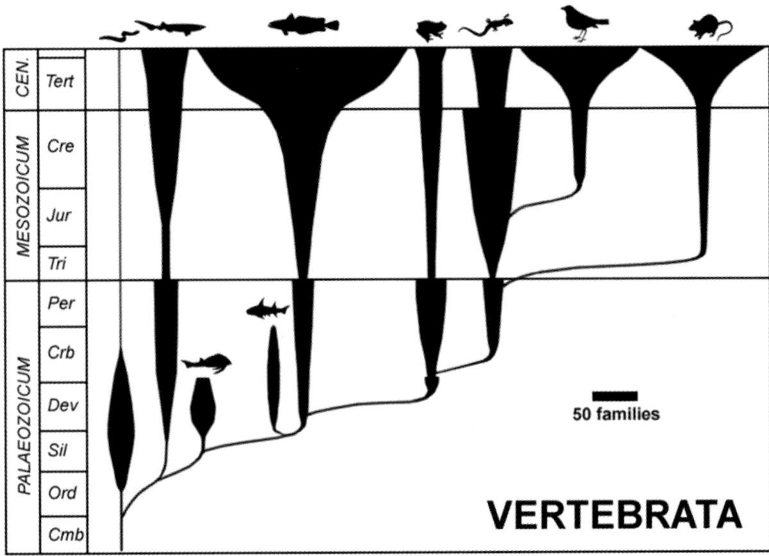

Fig. 125. Evolutionary Spindle Diagram Showing Relative Numbers of Families

Everyone agrees that physiological evolution of living creatures has occurred on Earth. Creationists have historically questioned the timing of physiological changes, but not whether they happened. Intelligent Design guys are okay with the millions and billions of years of geologic time proposed by naturalists, and they support physiological evolution. Naturalists vehemently insist that, since physiological changes have occurred, all of their other theories must be true as well.

Because there is general agreement, we won't discuss physiological evolution at any length here. Remember, though, that if one accepts the Feynman-Stueckelberg interpretation for time and antimatter as possibly true (as I do), there is not necessarily

4 "Evolution." Retrieved c. 2014 from https://en.wikipedia.org/wiki/Evolution

any conflict between the timescales of Scripture and the millions and billions of years of geologic and evolutionary time; it is perfectly logical to be a scriptural literalist and a physiological evolutionist at the same time.

Speciation

The real battle is in the area that I call speciation: the details of how physiological changes in bodily traits happen in molecular biology. From bacteria to salamanders, all of our bodies are made from the information stored in our DNA genetic codes. Any physiological change in an organism has to be preceded by changes in the genetic codes that control the construction and maintenance of that organism. The very existence of physiological traits in multicellular animals—traits like legs, eyes, wings, or lungs—must be preceded by the massive changes in DNA genetic sequences that are needed to make them. Naturalists hold that the changes occur gradually, piece by piece. Even so, the DNA that controls the construction of each physiological piece must be present in the genetic code before it can exist.

Creationists tend to favor special creation, the idea that each species or genus was individually made by God; there has not been enough time on a young Earth for any significant biological development. Naturalists support the Darwinian mechanism: an accumulation of random errors when DNA is copied for the next generation. The Intelligent Design viewpoint, based on observations in molecular biology, is that new physiological traits are the result of modular changes to genetic codes by a system that was designed in when the organisms were first made.

For interested readers, I found James Shapiro's 2011 *Evolution: A View From The 21st Century* to be a good synopsis of our current knowledge of evolutionary processes at the molecular level. Because our own capabilities are so limited, we sometimes tend to underestimate God's power (at least, I know I do). I think biological speciation may be one area where that is true. Based on our observations of life here on Earth, what God appears to have done is far more difficult and, to me, far, far more beautiful than simply the continuous, special creation of new species.

DNA genetic codes for bacteria, single-celled eukaryotes, and multicellular organisms (including us) appear to be modular. Segments of genetic code (called transposable elements) can be moved, traded with other blocks of code, or activated or deactivated to produce viable physiological changes in organisms. Transposable elements can be parts of genes (parts of proteins), whole genes, or groups of genes. They can also be the regulatory DNA sequences that control when genes produce proteins. The observed differences in genetic DNA sequences between closely related species are mostly due to the movement of transposable elements.

In multicellular creatures, genetic differences between individuals result from genetic recombination, the mixing of genes during sexual reproduction, and possibly, changes in the distributions of repetitive DNA sequences called simple sequence repeats (nicknamed SSR). Physiological features that can vary in size between individuals in a species might be controlled by SSR distributions. At this time there is an observed correlation between variable features and the distribution of SSR, but nobody knows yet how it works (or if the correlation actually indicates causation). Incidentally, the judicial identification of individuals by their DNA is done by counting distributions of simple sequence repeats.

Movements of transposable elements, genetic recombination, and changes in simple sequence repeat distributions do not happen randomly. Transposable elements do not move themselves; they are just bits of DNA. Instead, intricate systems of proteins cut, copy, and paste transposable elements into viable positions on chromosomes. There are probably address DNA sequences for each transposable element that indicate what it can be used for and which other bits of DNA it can be swapped with, but we don't really know the complete details (I'm just guessing about the addresses). The movement of genes during recombination is much the same.

The same is also true for simple sequence repeats. While there may be a roll of the dice involved in the final distribution of SSR for an individual, changes in SSR distributions are controlled by DNA-cutting-and-splicing proteins. Protein hands are rolling protein dice to choose the specific genetic code for each individual in a species.

I claim that modular DNA is a far more difficult creative mechanism than special creation because the odds of finding functional proteins (one in 10^{77}) and whole cells that can live (one in $10^{300,000}$ or so for bacteria; roughly one in $10^{60,000,000}$ for multicellular animals) have not changed or gone away. In a modular DNA system, most of the possible combinations of groups of DNA sequences must produce viable proteins and living cells. God had to deal with those incredible odds in order to make the system that we see.

Fig. 125.1. Trilobite Fossil

You may remember the cute little trilobite fossil at the start of this section. Here he is again, courtesy of Wikipedia. Trilobites were among the first species of the phylum Arthropoda that appeared around 542 MA in the Cambrian Explosion. Arthropoda are still around today; the phylum includes spiders, crabs, and insects. If the modular DNA concept is correct, and if, as the fossil record indicates, all of those creatures developed here on Earth, then it is likely the little guy who posed for that statue had enough variability built into his DNA genetic code to generate over 800,000 living species.

For readers who enjoy numbers, the odds calculation for trilobite DNA code that includes the adaptability to generate numerous new species would be something like one in $(10^{60,000,000})^{800,000}$. Numbers on that scale become almost meaningless. Personally, I prefer to just say that making those original, adaptable DNA codes was very, very difficult. This living creation is a magnificent achievement.

As we finally delve into Genesis, we will use the Intelligent Design perspective on the origin and development of life on Earth: the earth was seeded with life by God. The life he put here had enormous adaptability designed into it and, during the millions and billions of years of geologic time, developed into the millions of living species we see around us. Intelligent Design fits very well with the observations of science and natural philosophy, and it also fits very well with the idea of a developmental creation. It does not fit well with a typical Young Earth Creationist understanding of time—but because of the Feynman-Stueckelberg conception of time, we have already seen that there is no definite conflict between geologic time and the timescale in Genesis 1. The fit of geology into Scripture then becomes more a question of interpretation than any kind of conflict.

Many naturalists in the scientific community harbor a bitter resentment against Intelligent Design proponents; more passionate perhaps even than the annoyance and contempt they have for Young Earth Creationists. Personally, I found the attitude a little odd when I first encountered it. I was, at the time, still an atheist. Trained in physics, I found in Intelligent Design literature a proper, logical, scientific approach that is largely missing from the naturalist practice of evolutionary biology. Besides, for a long-time science fiction fan, the idea of the earth being terraformed and seeded with life struck me as just plain cool. No supernatural mysticism required.

The reasons for the naturalist hatred of Intelligent Design are still a bit of a mystery for me, but I do have some guesses. Intelligent Design guys tend to be believers. There are some doors in naturalist minds that just plain cannot be opened without the individual ceasing to be a naturalist; they are much the same doors that I had to open in order to make the transition from atheist to servant of Christ. For a naturalist, no matter how logical the deductions of Intelligent Design may be, and no matter how firmly based on the observations of science they are, Intelligent Design must be wrong. It cannot possibly be correct. The logic must be flawed; the observations *must* be wrong in some way.

One issue, perhaps, is that Intelligent Design is a step toward creationism. Just as the physics community originally resisted big bang theory because it was way too creative, the biology community has reflexively resisted Intelligent Design. Naturalist physicists, however, were eventually brought around to accept the big bang because of some fairly solid science. Despite the presence of the same in their field, naturalist biologists have not budged an inch.

Another possible reason for resistance, I suspect, is what the biological history of life on Earth tells us about whoever might have done the terraforming and seeding.

The jumps in biological information that conflict with original descent theories indicate that the earth was not seeded just once; it was likely seeded several times: first with bacteria and archea to condition the environment, next with single-celled eukaryotes to start building the food chains for larger, multicellular creatures. Animals then appear in several stages: Ediacaran fauna, sponges, and jellyfish come earlier, followed by the rest of the animal phyla in the Cambrian Explosion. Plants appear suddenly 100 million years or so later. The timespan from the first likely seeding (3400 MA or so for bacteria) to the last likely seeding (around 400 MA for plants or 140 MA for flowering plants) is around 3.0 to 3.3 billion years. I don't care what galaxy you're from; that's a long time to be working on a construction project.

The biological and genetic similarities among all of life that we have seen—the observations that make original descent a requirement for naturalists—would indicate that, if the life seeded here was designed as it appears to be, it was probably all designed using the same technology, the same modeling computations giving similar solutions to similar problems.

The technology used to design living organisms, if technology was used, is impressive. We would have to get ridiculously better at physics, mathematics, and computation to have any chance at all of doing anything similar. It is questionable whether we ever could attain the levels of skill and knowledge that might be on display in the life here on Earth.

One odd part about the terraforming scenario is that, as far as we can tell, whoever did the terraforming never came to live here. If we ever do terraforming projects in future, the purpose would almost certainly be to go and live on the planet when it's finished. We human beings, however, are most likely natives here. The observational evidence that *Homo sapiens* developed here on Earth is quite good. Paleontologists have found numerous fossils for both preceding species and early human beings. Our molecular biology and genetic code are almost identical to those of immediately preceding species (*Homo neanderthalensis*). Archeologists have found plentiful remains that show a slow expansion in both population and technology.

The list of suggestions for person or persons unknown that could reasonably do a thing like terraforming the earth the way it was apparently done is pretty short.

Choices in Creation

"The intrinsically statistical character of atomic events and the instability of many physical systems to minute fluctuations ensures that the future remains open and undetermined by the present. This makes possible the emergence of new forms and systems, so that the universe is endowed with a sort of freedom to explore genuine novelty."
—Paul Davies, *The Mind of God*

So far in this chapter we have mostly been discussing requirements for creation: things like the fundamental physics needed to build our universe, the earth's extraordinarily benign environment for life, and the basic operations of the same life. Those things are pretty much required for there to be a creation such as the world we see around us at all.

But at our current level of knowledge, just looking at the basic requirements does not provide compelling reasons why some parts of this creation are the way they are—that is, why they are the way we saw them to be back in our discussion of physics. In this section, we are going to look at some parts of creation that might be choices for God instead of requirements. Creation as a computational model could be done in many different ways. Some of them are much harder to do than others.

There are three aspects of this creation that might, I think, be choices; things that might have been simpler to do differently. One is the observation that this creation, if it is a computational model, looks like a Monte Carlo model. Another is the Feynman-

Stueckelberg picture of time, with past, present, and future all simultaneously existing. The third is quantum mechanics, a perceptual reality composed of possibilities. Whatever the reasons that influenced God to make creation in this particular way, they must have been very compelling—because they involved a lot of extra work.

Rolling Dice

A Monte Carlo computer model, named after the famous casinos in Monte Carlo, is one that is based on random choices. Any computational model will start with parameter values that describe the initial conditions (the state of the system being modeled at the beginning), perform calculations based on the initial values of parameters and the mathematics that describe the behavior of the system, and produce predictions of what the modeled system will do.

In a Monte Carlo model, the initial values of parameters are randomly chosen. Each parameter is assigned a probability distribution, random numbers are used to select a value for each parameter based on its probability distribution, and a single computation is done for the random group of parameters. The computation can be repeated many times with different, randomly chosen groups of initial parameters to develop a probability distribution for the behavior of the system.

Monte Carlo modeling is often used when there are too many possibilities, too many permutations of initial parameters, to run all of them. If you hear of an engineering system (like a building or an aircraft) described as having "one chance in a million of failing," it's a pretty good bet that the failure analysis was done with a Monte Carlo model. Monte Carlo techniques are often used when a model is complex, when the mathematics that describe the relationship between initial conditions and behavior are too hard for us to do exactly.

My first engineering job after college was a Monte Carlo analysis for the performance of a plastic cover used to seal an underwater missile launch tube. There were almost a hundred different parameters that significantly affected performance: dimensions of the tube, cover, and missile; gas pressures inside the launch tube and seawater pressure outside; the motion of the missile as it launched; the gases generated by the explosives that blew the cover off the tube; and many more. The model equations described accelerations and motions of the plastic cover, expansion of the gas bubble against seawater, and impact forces if the missile hit the cover on its way out.

The basic goal was to figure out if or how often the cover would break the missile during a launch. But there were too many initial variables with strong interactions, and the model equations were too difficult, to do an exact solution. The analysis was done by assigning probability distributions for each starting parameter, randomly picking values of initial conditions for each computation, and repeating the computation again and again to model a few thousand missile launches. The thousands of predictions were used to estimate a probability distribution that was then used to estimate the chance of a successful launch.

This creation looks like a Monte Carlo model. Consider:

- The distributions, ages, and compositions of stars and galaxies look random. At least, they match the predictions of the Monte Carlo models that we use to study such things.

- The compositions and physical behaviors of the solar system and the earth are compatible with random condensation from a gas cloud (we use Monte Carlo models to study this as well).

- The terrain features of the earth appear to be the result of random geological processes.

- The distributions and types of fossils that we find in sedimentary rocks indicate that physiological changes in organisms have been mostly random. Natural selection probably played a role, but most fossil descent relationships are more bushy than tree-like: many physiological differences were "tried," but only a few of them form the line of descent from the original creatures to the different creatures that we see today.

Again, we use Monte Carlo modeling to simulate natural, random processes when a mathematical model is too difficult to solve exactly, and sometimes, when it is not possible to get an answer any other way. Some mathematics problems simply cannot be solved; not because the math is too difficult or because we don't know how, but because there is not enough information available to define a solution.

We can only guess at the reasons that God apparently chose to make this creation a Monte Carlo model. (If, of course, it is a model at all.) It seems unlikely that the limitations of ability or perseverance in mathematics that motivate us to roll dice in computer models would be a consideration for him; he has amply demonstrated in his creation that he knows a lot more about mathematics, physics, and computation than we do (or than we likely ever will know). A Monte Carlo model of sorts might be a convenience for God because it is the easiest way to get results that look random: in this case, to make a creation that looks as if it might be a natural world. Personally, I suspect that one reason might have been artistic, a nuance of the experience: perhaps God wanted to be surprised.

Whatever the reasons, a Monte Carlo model of our physical universe with the scale and level of detail that we see in this creation would not in any way be an easy thing to create. A spacetime 92 billion light years in diameter with 14 billion years of time filled with hundreds of billions of galaxies, 10^{23} stars, and infinite swarms of virtual particles. And the physical model is the easy part.

Monte Carlo modeling for life is far more difficult. As we've seen, it would require the development of a modular construction scheme for proteins and organisms so that bits and pieces of DNA coding can be swapped around to produce different physiologies. We know enough about life to see that the construction of organisms is probably modular, but we have no idea how it all actually works. We don't know enough yet to be able to see the patterns of structure for proteins, cells, and organisms that would have to form a basis for a modular construction system.

As It Was in the Beginning, So It Is Now and Ever Shall Be

> *"This view is quite different from that of the Hamiltonian method which considers the future as developing continuously out of the past. Here we imagine the entire space-time history laid out, and that we just become aware of increasing portions of it successively."*—Richard Feynman, "The Theory of Positrons," 1949

As usual, there is some debate among philosophers regarding the nature of time (three things I have never seen: the eye of an ant, the foot of a snake, or any issue that philosophers do not debate). They mostly divide into supporters of the Hamiltonian perspective (the present develops continuously out of the past; called presentism in philosophy because only the present exists) or the Feynman-Stueckelberg perspective (the whole of spacetime is all laid out, and we only become aware of it successively; called eternalism in philosophy because all of eternity exists). My Genesis speculation, as should be evident by now, presents an eternalist perspective.

Presentists hold that only the present instant of time physically exists; the past and the future do not have any real, physical existence. There is no support in physics for presentism in any theory that has been verified by experiment. All verified theories at least imply that time is eternal, that past, present, and future all simultaneously exist. At our current level of knowledge, it is still possible that our reality is presentist. But it is scientifically more likely that it is eternalist. We probably really do live in a four-dimensional spacetime.

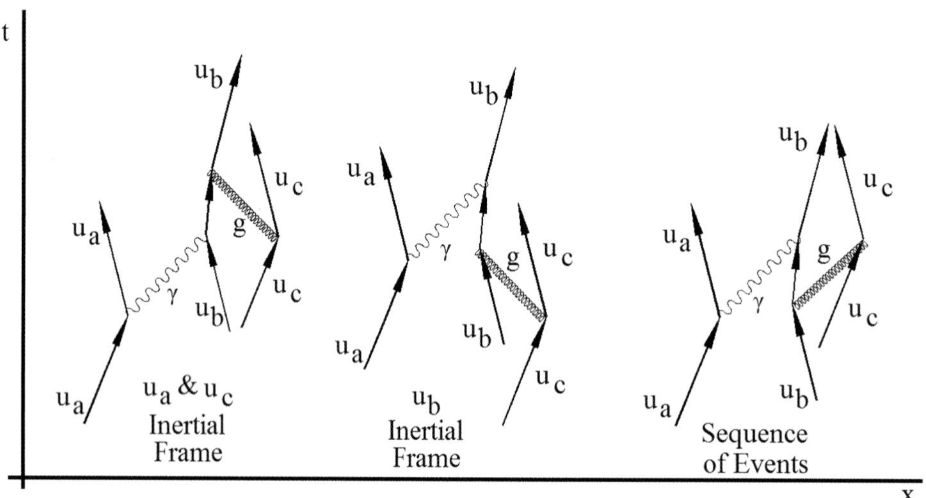

One of the implications of special relativity is that events that happen simultaneously in one inertial frame happen at different times in a different inertial frame; either "simultaneous event" can happen before the other, depending on the relative direction of travel. The Feynman diagram shows an exchange of bosons, a gluon and a photon, between up quarks. For two of the up quarks (u_a and u_c in the same inertial frame), the photon is exchanged first and the gluon second. For the other up quark (u_b), the gluon is exchanged first. Any candidate for our reality has to be able to accommodate a sequence of events like the one shown to the right in the diagram, where the gluon effectively moves "backward" in time. Backward time gluons are not a problem for an eternalist reality, where objects (especially bosons) can move any way they want in time. It is difficult to explain for a presentist reality where only one moment of time exists.

Mathematically, the lack of simultaneous events in special relativity means that it is not possible to identify a present instant of time for the universe to exist in. Because objects in the universe travel at vastly different speeds in all possible directions, any "present" can't be a nicely defined point. It has to be more of a big, squishy blob. For example, the furthest galaxy that has been seen by astronomers is estimated to be roughly 13 billion light years away. From our frame of reference, the photons from that galaxy took 13 billion years to get here. But photons travel at the speed of light. Both time and distance in their direction of travel are infinitely contracted (remember, the Lorentz contraction factor is $(1 - v^2/c^2)$, which is 0 when $v = c$) meaning that there is no distance for them, and time does not pass. From their own perspective, photons are born and die in the same instant of time and at the same location. Any "present" instant of time for photons from that most distant galaxy would be 13 billion years long for us.

The nature of time indicated by particle physics has already been discussed at considerable length in this speculation, so we'll skip it here. The point is that the physics abundantly supports eternalist time, not presentist time.

In spite of that, most physicists prefer presentism because of our own subjective experience that time passes moment by moment. It is apparently difficult to explain how our physical brains can possibly extract a presentist conscious experience from an eternalist spacetime in any natural way.

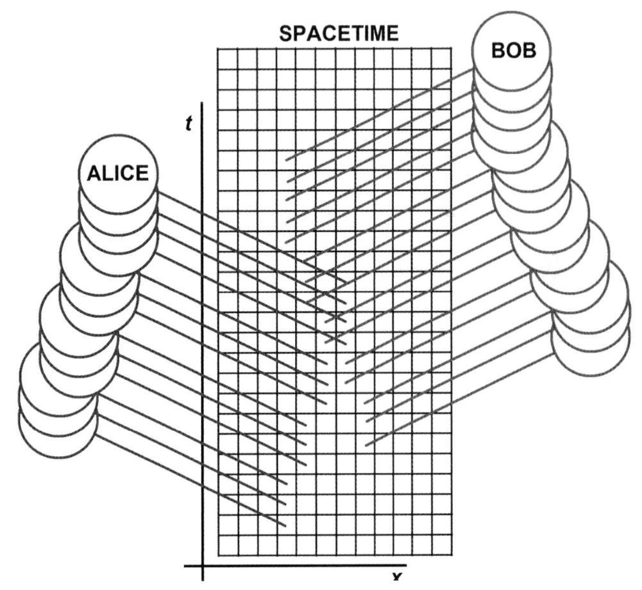

There is no such difficulty, of course, in the computational model used for this speculation. The parts of the model that form our consciousness would only need to extract perceptual information from a spacetime model of the physical world in a sequential, moment-by-moment way. A single spacetime model shared by all of our individual consciousness models would be, by far, the easiest way to maintain a common experience of reality—to make it so that we all see the same world around us (which we do).

There is a temptation here to claim that our presentist experience of a reality that is physically eternalist provides a logical argument for the existence of God and his creation. If there isn't a convenient natural explanation for an observation that *is* easily explained in a divine creation, then Ockham's Razor would urge us to logically support creation as the most likely alternative. William of Ockham (1287–1347) originally proposed the logical principle (*lex parsimoniae*—the stingy law, also called Ockham's Razor) that, in the absence of certainty, the choice among competing explanations should be the one that requires the fewest assumptions. The simplest story (technically, the simplest hypothesis) that provides an adequate explanation should logically be regarded as the one most likely to be correct.

Unfortunately, your author does not agree that a natural explanation for presentist experience is particularly difficult. The uncertainty in this issue arises from the fact that most of the mathematical equations that physicists use to describe real-world behavior are symmetric in time, meaning that they work equally well whether the objects involved travel forward or backward. That is why it has so far been impractical to set up an experiment to see if antimatter particles really do travel backward in time. There are two areas in physics that are not symmetric in time, that do have a preference: processes that involve changes in energy or entropy (a specific kind of energy) like nuclear and chemical reactions, and quantum processes with entanglement that evolve over time in accordance with the Schrodinger equation (and its relativistic derivatives). Most of the universe that we interact with is based on nuclear and chemical reactions, which are entangled quantum processes that involve changes in energy and/or entropy, and therefore it has a preferred direction in time. The processes that treat time as more of a guideline—i.e. the motions of individual particles—are mostly too small for us to see without very rare and expensive equipment.

Our bodies, and most importantly our brains, are based in chemistry and share a direction in time with the chemical reactions that let us live. Chemical signals from our senses meet in our brains to combine into our perception of now. Because it is all based on chemical reactions, our experience is a string of nows that is ordered in time. Our brains remember by chemically recording sensory perception, by storing moments of experience. Physiologically, we think by recalling groups of stored moments in some logical sequence. Thanks to scientific instruments that can generate images of brain activity, we know that when we are thinking, groups of memories flash on and off at roughly forty times per second. The process that we use to organize memories into thoughts is still a mystery, but it is not at all unreasonable that thought would make more sense if it shared the same direction of time used in individual memories.

As was mentioned before, our Genesis speculation uses an eternalist perspective for time. Simultaneous time fits very well with Scripture: it provides scientific support for the prophetic ability of the Father, and it allows an interpretation of Genesis 1 that is, I think, fully compatible with the observations of science.

On top of that, simultaneously existing time might be a convenience for a creation that is a developmental computational model, because it would probably be the quickest way to get results. Even with an eternal perspective, 14 billion years would be a long time to wait for the results of a computer model.

A presentist, sequential time model where time advances the way that we perceive it with a present that develops from the past and a future that isn't actually there at all, where all that really exists is now, would have to run continuously with each moment following the previous moment from beginning to end.

An overall model that is split into smaller, shorter time models might finish much more quickly. The 14 billion years that science tells us this creation has been here could, for example, be divided into 14 million models that handle one thousand years each. In that case, the whole development could all be done several million times faster, in a thousand years or so (technically, the time it takes to do the computations for one thousand years, which could be either more or less than the time that we perceive).

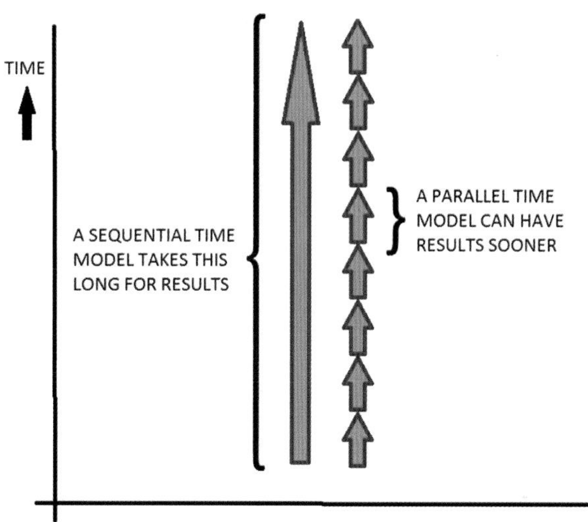

Looking a little more deeply at the issue, however, we can see a couple of problems that make the idea of parallel models much harder to actually do. One issue is that the total number of calculations required for creation does not change. The same total number of events happen in 14 million models of one thousand years each as happen in one 14-billion-year model. In order to actually reduce the time it takes to finish the model, then, it would be necessary to increase the rate that calculations can be done. In order to actually finish the computation in one thousand years or so, it would take 14 million computers, each with the capability of modeling our entire universe: 14 million or so Jupiter Brains, or, in keeping with the choice of astronomical names, a massively parallel Solar System Brain.

There are other difficulties with a simultaneous time model that might imply that creation requires far more computational capability than a mere little Solar System Brain. Two of the really hard parts are flexibility and continuity.

A Web of Possibility

> *". . . if God had wanted to put everything into the world from the beginning, He would have created a universe without change, without organisms and evolution, and without man and man's experience of change. But He seems to have thought that a live universe with events unexpected even by Himself would be more interesting than a dead one."*—Karl Popper, *Unended Quest: An Intellectual Autobiography (recounted in Wikipedia)*

As we've seen, creation appears to be a Monte Carlo model, and it also might use simultaneous time. In such a model, calculations for all of the various bits of model time happen at once, or nearly at once. In order to do calculations for the last bit of model time before the calculations for all of the preceding bits of model time are done, the conditions for the last bit of model time have to be either known or capable of being figured out before the model even starts. In philosophical terms, a simultaneous time model prefers to be deterministic, meaning that all events have been strictly determined by preceding events. Monte Carlo computational models usually only make random choices of parameter values for the conditions at the start of the model; the rest of the calculations for the model are set by the choices of initial conditions. Even Monte Carlo models are, for us, by and large deterministic.

The situation for creation is a bit more complex, because we are in it, and we appear to have this thing we call free will. Free will, if it is really free, introduces random choices into the middle of a model, not just in the initial conditions. There is some debate among both philosophers and theologians over free will. For philosophers, the question is whether our choices are free or only seem to be free, and are really compelled by preceding events. Philosophical doubt arises from the deterministic nature of classical physics, where the very specific states of particles are always the predictable result of preceding interactions with other particles. In theology, tension exists between the sovereignty of God and our use of free will: are our choices really free, or are they controlled by God?

This speculation will, as usual, take the simplest approach available—a sort of Copenhagen interpretation for human choice. In our own minds, it feels like we are making free choices. It looks as though the other people around us are doing the same. So, for the sake of speculation, our will is here assumed to be truly free; our choices truly independent.

If this creation is a simultaneous time computational model, it should have some way of accommodating both events and consequences that are random or unpredictable; there needs to be some flexibility in the model to allow alternatives to develop. One way for such a model to be flexible would be if the fundamental nature of the model were a web of possibilities, with actual results brought into existence as the model evolves. If unpredictable conscious minds (like ours) are involved, actual results could, in part, be drawn from among possibilities by the choices of those same conscious minds.

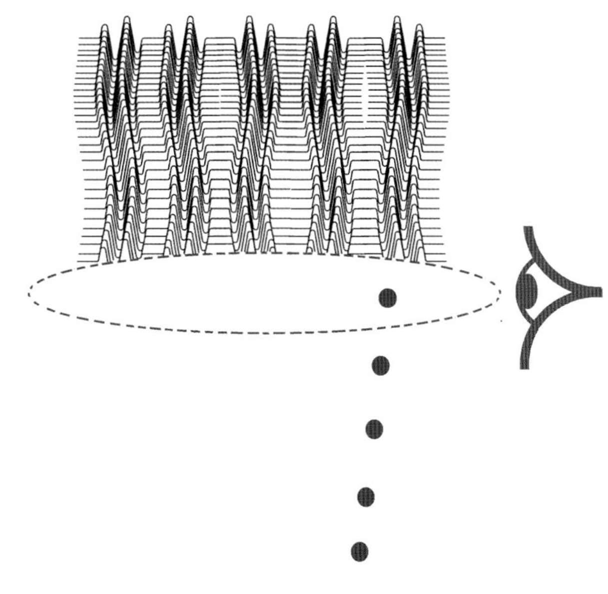

A physical reality made of possibilities?

Possibilities made "real" by the perceptions or choices of conscious minds?

This should be starting to sound familiar. It happens to be exactly the observed physical behavior that physicists describe with quantum theory, probability amplitudes, and localization. At least, it is a good match for the Copenhagen interpretation of quantum mechanics.

As has been stated, Copenhagen is only one possible explanation for the physical behavior described by the mathematics of quantum mechanics. The physical reality, the underlying reasons why matter behaves the way we see it behave, is unknown. It would be really nice to be able to claim that quantum mechanics proves that we are living in a simultaneous-time Monte Carlo computational model, a creation made by God, but we don't know nearly enough about physics to be able to make that claim. It is only a possibility. This is just speculation.

There is no doubt, however, that our reality does behave as described by the mathematics of quantum mechanics. It appears to be fundamentally uncertain, made only of possibilities. If this is a creation made by God as described in Scripture, then everything in it is here for a reason. If this is a creation made by God, he chose to use quantum mechanics to accomplish some purpose. One possible reason for basing our reality on quantum mechanics is to provide flexibility for a reality where all of time has a real, simultaneous physical existence. As was mentioned above, flexibility might be needed to allow us the independence of free will.

It's also tempting to claim that God made quantum mechanics to allow us genuine free will, but that would be a little self-absorbed. We are not alone in this creation. A flexible reality might also be handy to allow for novelty in physiological evolution. We might be more valuable to God than many sparrows, but that does not mean that sparrows have no value at all.

Scripture implies that some of us may still be living when (if) the big crunch happens at the end of spacetime. That may also imply that the big crunch will happen fairly soon. One of the things the fossil record tells us is that most species have limited lifetimes. If common species limitations apply to us, then our time on this earth may be limited.

If that is true, then we look like a kind of afterthought in this creation. We were apparently just popped in for the last few thousand years of a spacetime that stretches out for millions and billions of years.

I suspect that one of the main purposes for this (possibly) developmental creation is to provide a canvas for the picture of life provided by the (possible) modular genetic adaptive systems in bacteria, Protista, and multicellular organisms. Biological adaptability is, I think, the most challenging and wonderful feature of creation.

A requirement for the accommodation of biological flexibility also offers a possible answer for why quantum theory shows us a world with flexibility of events at the subatomic particle level. Biology happens atom by atom. A creation made to allow random combinations of genetic DNA, for example, would also have to be flexible atom by atom.

Causes and Effects

Another difficulty with a simultaneous time model is that time in creation, from our perspective (and as far as we know, from the perspective of everyone and everything in creation with us), is sequential. Events appear to happen one after another. For the three spatial dimensions of spacetime, objects, including us, can go in any direction. For the time dimension, we matter objects all only pass in one direction. We can travel at different relative "velocities," depending on what inertial frame we happen to be in, but only in the same shared direction. Meanwhile, all of antimatter (possibly) passes through time in the opposite direction. Events are probably even sequential for antimatter; they would just follow each other in an order that seems backward to us.

Although the continuity in time of our individual experience doesn't pose a real challenge for creation, there is another type of continuity that is a little more difficult to understand: the continuity across long periods of time between our ancestors, us, and our descendants.

The events of our individual experience are given a direction in time by the chemistry of our senses and our brains. In order to model sequential times when all times exist simultaneously and in order to provide the historical experience of time that progresses, the results of computation—the choices of possibilities that become real—have to be connected across time so that "later" events will be based on the results of "earlier" events. By the way, that is pretty much exactly how quantum entanglement works in the Copenhagen interpretation of quantum mechanics.

I think a small warning is appropriate here, before we proceed to the next step. So far, although we may not be accustomed to thinking about time in this way, our discussion has still been kind of linear: Scripture seems to imply that time passes for God, but his time is probably not the same as our time. Our sense of time is evidently derived from chains of moments that are picked, one after another, out of an eternalist spacetime. Both the guess about God's time and our own perception of time involve a logical order of events and consequences. Things that happen "later" are partly caused by "earlier" events, while "later" events have no effect whatever on "earlier" events. This concept of events and consequences ordered in time is called causality in physics and philosophy.

The trouble is that our notions of cause and effect may not be completely accurate in the kind of reality suggested in this speculation. At first thought, if spacetime is an eternalist web of possibility, there needs to be something that ties the bits and pieces of experience together to provide the historical continuity we all see. Somehow, even though they all exist at the same time, when Calvert and Schliemann excavated Troy, Hector and Achilles must already have fought and died; Agamemnon and the Greeks must have already sacked and burned the city.

In one of our computational models, we could maintain continuity using a technique called time sharing. When one ("later") thread of a computation needs information from a different ("earlier") thread, it stops and waits until the source thread is finished. If we apply that technique to our historical example of Troy, when Calvert and Schliemann started digging at the site of Troy, they would freeze until all of the Troy models had finished—until all the events of thousands of years had been decided. The problem with this picture is that Calvert and Schliemann are not alone in this creation. If they froze for a few hundred years, some of their friends and relations would probably notice (their creditors certainly would).

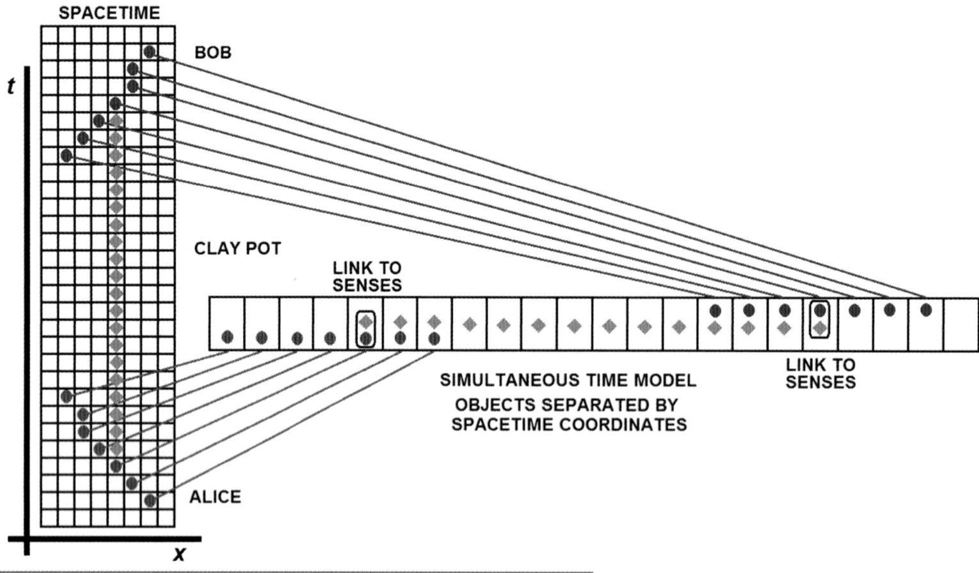

Fig. 126. Causality in a Simultaneous Time Model

The trick for trying to understand how this all works is, I think, to become unstuck in spacetime. I found the figure above to be very useful for building an image of how a simultaneous time model might work. The diagram illustrates a bit of historical continuity: Alice (red dots), a potter, makes a clay pot (brown diamonds) at some time in the past. Bob (blue dots), an archeologist, finds the pot and adds it to his collection. In between, the pot is used, lost, and aged by the nuclear and chemical reactions it is exposed to. On the left in the figure is a spacetime diagram of how those events would appear to play out in the world that we see. On the right is another sort of spacetime diagram, with time all compressed into a single instant: a simultaneous time model.

In an eternalist, Feynman-Stueckelberg sort of reality, all of the moments of Alice's life exist all at once. Each moment is separated from the others by its location in spacetime, but they all exist at once. All of the moments of Bob's life also exist all at once and share the same instant of "time" (not spacetime here) as all of Alice's moments of life; once again, Alice and Bob are separated by their positions in spacetime.

At one of her moments of life, Alice interacts with the physical world through her senses to change a part of it into a clay pot. Like Alice and Bob, the moments of the pot's existence all happen at once. One of those moments is the one where it is made by Alice; another is the moment that it is seen by Bob. "In between," the pot is aged by nuclear and chemical reactions that give it a direction in time, an "earlier" and a "later" that we see as cause and effect.

The point here is that causes and effects—causality—in an eternalist, simultaneous time reality, are not as rock solid as we would like to think; they're more like Jell-O. Since all objects, including us, would have all of their moments of being all at once, arrows of cause and effect could theoretically be drawn backward in time as easily as they are apparently drawn in the forward direction that we consider normal.

Incidentally, this perspective does not contradict observed science. Most of the mathematics used in physics works just as well backward in spacetime as it does forward. Again, the only physical processes that give a direction in time that we know of are reactions that depend on changes in energy (and/or entropy) and entangled quantum processes. When we make changes to the physical world, they, like nuclear and chemical reactions, normally involve work and changes in the form of energy. The kind of historical continuity we are discussing here is thus provided by physical objects, by changes to the physical world, by changes in forms of energy made by us during our lives. The changes that we make to the physical world only persist "after" we make them; they only exist for spacetimes with larger ("later") time coordinates.

Chemical and nuclear reactions also help provide the same direction of time for historical continuity that they do for our conscious thoughts. Remember the delayed choice quantum eraser experiment, where the detection of one member of an entangled photon pair could change an image made by the other member of the photon pair even if the kind of detection was chosen after the image was made. Except for the detections themselves, there were no energy-changing reactions in that experiment; the arrow from cause to effect could be (and was) drawn in either direction in spacetime.

What it all seems to boil down to is that our experience of passing time—both our subjective perception and the historical continuity provided by changes in physical objects—depends on an observed behavior in physics. Changes in forms of energy and changes in entropy (a particular kind of energy) only happen in one direction in time; the results of a change in energy only exist for "later" spacetime coordinates. It may be one direction for energy changes associated with matter objects (like us) and the opposite direction for energy changes associated with antimatter objects, but both matter and antimatter each only go one way.

This perspective is taking us back to the basics of quantum mechanics. Remember that the quantum mechanics equations that describe how systems change over time (the Schrodinger equation, the relativistic Klein-Gordon, Dirac, and Proca equations, and the Yang-Mills gauge theories) are all energy balances. They all describe changes in the forms of energy over time.

We have finally arrived at the basic question in the philosophical debate on the nature of time, the debate over eternalism versus presentism: why do some changes in energy only persist in one direction in time while others can go both ways?

It is tempting to claim a logical point for creation here in the natural vs created debate about our world, but that would really be bad form. We do not know enough about physics to be able to say much of anything definite or conclusive about the details of how our world works and why it behaves the way that it does, so there is no firm answer available on the naturalist side of the debate.

In the created computational world speculated in this book, the answer is pretty simple: the fast-running eternalist model was set up that way in order to create the feeling of passing time for the individuals and objects in it. That answer, though it makes perfect sense to believers, is very frustrating for the naturalists:

Naturalist: "There! Look at that! Why does it do that?"

Theologian: "Because that's the way God made it. As with all things, it was ordained before the beginning of time."

Naturalist: "But why?"

Theologian: "It's a mystery."

Because the modeling capabilities of a computational environment are so very wide, such an understanding of reality can include almost anything that can be imagined. Claiming that something is the way it observably is because that's the way it was programmed to be is only a tiny bit more definite than claiming mysterious divine intervention; it's an answer that isn't really an answer. For now, though, it's the best we can do. The versatility of computational modeling is the very reason I selected it as an allegory for our world in this speculation: it's the only environment that we know of that could logically support the physical behavior we observe. It is entirely providential that the same versatility can also hold the events described in Scripture.

Observations

Before we cast off at last into the heart of our Genesis speculation, I want to examine a few observations to fill in some corners for readers who are interested. The entire speculation of this book is based on the idea that our reality might be computational; that in some sense and in some way, everything that happens here, from virtual particle interactions to symphony orchestras, might be the result of some kind of mathematical calculation or some process that works out very much like a mathematical calculation. Of course, it could be that the fundamental operation of the world just happens to produce behaviors that look like the results of calculations, that it is all entirely natural. It could be that we are living in a computer model made and operated by a person or persons unknown, but who are not God (this is the possibility suggested by Nick Bostrom). Or it could be that we are living in a computational model of reality created by God.

For the rest of this section and for the speculation in theology coming up we will assume that we are living in a computational model of reality created by God. The other possibilities for a computational reality will be discussed in some detail after the interpretation of Genesis.

So, a few observations about a computational creation.

Simplicity

For us, a computational model would be, by far, the easiest way to make something like this creation (not that we actually could). It would be easier for us because the control of matter and the use of energy on the scale displayed here is far more difficult than jiggling some numbers in a computer, even jiggling a lot of numbers in a really huge computer.

The physical restrictions that apply to us don't exist for God. His power is without limit. But a computational model might still be the most efficient way to make a short-term, developmental creation, if that is indeed what we are living in.

The point is not to imply that God took any shortcuts with creation. He has surely made this world in whatever way best suits his purpose. The point is that the version of reality suggested here as a possibility is the simplest explanation currently available to us. If we apply the *lex parsimoniae*, Ockam's Razor, the relative simplicity of a computational model makes it logically the most likely version of reality to be correct.

Vision

Even if this universe is all "just" a mathematical model, the mathematics and the computational capacity involved are really impressive. But there is another aspect to this thing that is also impressive: God saw the atom of possibility for this vibrant, bountiful creation even though it was hidden in an ocean of dead universes full of burnt-out stars and useless DNA genomes that produce lifeless slime.

The tiny probabilities for the kinds of living organisms that we see here on Earth have already been discussed in the section on evolution in creation; I won't repeat that here. The section on the requirements of creation mentioned that the physical constants that define how our universe physically works, the masses of fundamental particles and the strengths of forces and charges, need to be very close to their observed values in order to have a universe with any kind of life in it at all.

The diagram above shows a type of graph that is called a fitness landscape or a fitness topology. For the present discussion, the idea is that horizontal positions in the diagram represent different combinations of physical constants, and the heights of the hills or depths of the valleys represent how friendly or hostile to life a universe with that particular set of physical constants would be. Some calculations in physics indicate that there may be other combinations of physical constants that could support life, other combinations that produce a hill on the fitness landscape. We do not currently know enough about physics, chemistry, and biology to be able to draw an accurate fitness landscape for the fundamental physical constants; the diagram above is just a cartoon to illustrate the concept. We do know, however, that our universe is on the top of a pretty high, sharp peak.

Our knowledge of physics is insufficient to tell us whether the physical constants for our universe can have different values or if the values of fundamental particle masses, charges, and the strengths of forces that we measure are the only possible values. The standard model of particle physics mostly describes behavior. Standard model equations use measured masses and charges to make their predictions; they have little or nothing to say about how the basic physics actually works or why physical constants have the values they do.

There are other theories in physics, however, that may contribute a little more insight.

The standard model is based on quantum mechanics probability amplitudes for particles that are dimensionless point charges. As has been mentioned, if particles are assumed to have three dimensions, standard model equations no longer produce accurate predictions of measured physical behavior. Because the particles are dimensionless point charges, the mathematics implies that particles can be closer together than the Planck length (1.6×10^{-35}m, the natural unit of length for quantum mechanics). General relativity predicts that the strength of the normally weak gravitational force increases at shorter distances and that particles with mass that are closer together than the Planck length will form black holes—very unhealthy for us if it actually happens.

String theories and M theory are mathematical speculations in physics that offer more of a description of how the really itty-bitty stuff might actually work. At this time, they are only speculations; they have not been able to make completely accurate predictions of observed physical behavior, and they have not been confirmed by experiment. But they have been able to provide some interesting insights. String theories have been used to predict the masses of fundamental particles purely by calculation (that, by the way, is a major accomplishment); and they have an explanation for why our universe is not one big black hole.

String theories (there are several of them) are based on the idea of quantum mechanics probability amplitudes of vibrating, one-dimensional strings. The objects that we "see," particles, are made of groups of interacting strings. The particle masses, charges, and interaction forces that we measure are determined by standing waves and quantized interactions between the strings.

The conflict between general relativity and quantum mechanics, the production of black holes at distances shorter than the Planck length, is resolved in a very simple way: the strings themselves are a little larger than the Planck length, so they can never get close enough to each other to collapse into black holes.

String theories have some characteristics that might seem a little odd. Remember that Stueckelberg and Feynman had to introduce the idea of negative time particles (antimatter) in order to get the versions of the Schrodinger equation compatible with Einstein's relativity to produce valid probability distributions. String theories have a similar problem: in order to calculate valid quantum mechanics probability distributions, string theories have to have nine dimensions of space and one of time: a ten-dimensional spacetime instead of the four-dimensional spacetime that we see around us. In string theories, we only *see* a four-dimensional spacetime because six of the spatial dimensions are folded into very tiny knots that occupy every point in our bigger spacetime. The physics terminology is that the six extra spatial dimensions are compactified at each point in spacetime.

Additionally, in order for the mathematics to work out, compactified dimensions have to be folded in very particular shapes that are called Calabi-Yau surfaces.

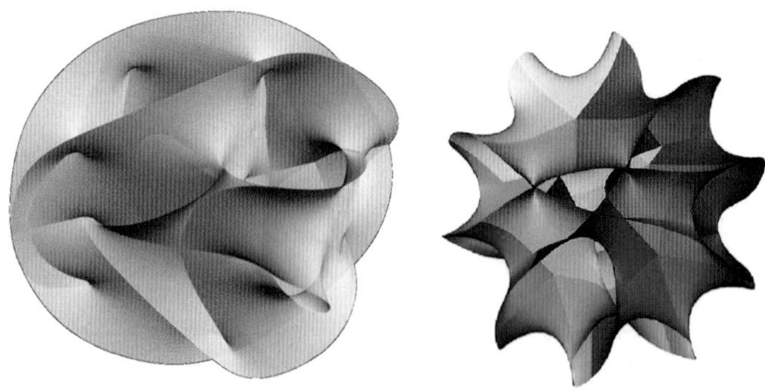

Fig. 127. Calabi-Yau Surfaces

Here we arrive at the source of some existential frustration for string theorists: the exact physical behavior of strings and the particles they form depends on the particular shape of the Calabi-Yau surfaces of the six compactified dimensions. Unfortunately, there are rather a lot of possible Calabi-Yau surfaces to choose from: about 10^{500} of them. String theories have not been able to perfectly reproduce observed physical behavior or make predictions that can be tested by experiment because the theoretical physicists developing string theories have not yet been able to find the right Calabi-Yau surfaces. String theories, at least so far, are like a huge banana split dangling in front of the theoretical physics community—and they can't quite reach it.

There are several (at least five) different string theories (mathematical models) that each describe different physical behaviors. M theory consolidates the various ten-dimensional string theories into a single mathematical model by adding a tenth spatial dimension (to make an eleven-dimensional spacetime) and treating strings as the one-dimensional projections of two-dimensional (mem)branes.

The theory is called M theory instead of membrane theory, and the structures that project strings are called branes instead of membranes, because membranes are mostly two-dimensional and branes mostly aren't. As I mentioned earlier, string theories and M theory can be a little odd.

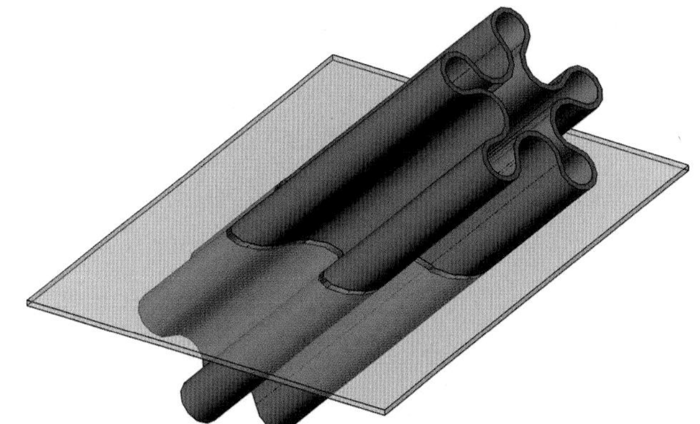

For interested readers, I found two books to be enlightening: *Warped Passages* (2005) by Lisa Randall and *The Elegant Universe* (1999 and 2003) by Brian Greene. *Warped Passages* also has a good description of general relativity and is exceptionally good at sharing the experience, the feel, of the mathematics. *The Elegant Universe* gives a more thorough description of string theories and is a bit easier to read.

String theories and M theory don't have any significant influence on the speculation ahead. The notion that our reality might be based on computations is allowed in physics partly because the fundamental objects of theories are all mathematical abstracts, not anything that seems physically real. If string theories were based on real physical strings (or branes) they might affect the viability of a computational reality, but they are not. String theories still use quantum mechanics and are based on probability amplitudes, the superpositions of possibility distributions, of one-dimensional strings (or higher dimensional branes). The math is a little weirder than the standard model, but it is still just math.

The relevance of string theory for this discussion is that the physical constants for our universe are likely to be variable and that there are an enormous number (about 10^{500}) of possible sets of values. That implication plays an important role in the version of the philosophical debate between a natural cosmology and a created cosmology. If this is a natural universe, how did it manage to stumble onto a combination of fundamental physical constants that is so very friendly to the existence of organic life?

Naturalist arguments in cosmology tend to propose mathematical models for our universe that are infinite in time or space and allow for enough variation in fundamental physics to randomly produce the comparative paradise that we live in: a bouncing universe that infinitely cycles between big bang and big crunch (physical constants might change for each bounce); a budding universe where the universe we can see is only one of very many pocket universes in a much, much larger multiverse (physical constants are different in each pocket universe); etc.

Cosmological Intelligent Design supporters tend to reply that the proposed cosmological models aren't big enough or old enough to find a low probability universe like ours. In the bouncing universe, for example, the model predicts that the mixture of matter and energy would change a little for each bounce. Astronomical measurements of the distribution of matter and energy in our universe indicate that it can't be more than about one hundred bounces old, not nearly enough to randomly find a statistically unlikely universe like ours.

To make this creation, God must have somehow seen this sliver of life, one set of physical constants among 10^{500} or so, that produced a universe capable of nuclear reactions, chemistry, and the intricate molecular machinery to bring the chemistry to life. Scripture tells us that the creation attests to the existence of God. There may have been easier ways to make creation, but at the edge of our knowledge of science, it's the statistical impossibility of the thing that most strongly argues for the existence of God.

Power

Back in the introduction, I mentioned that the study of creation led, for me, to a glimpse of God's power. That's what this whole book is really about.

Dear readers, I'd like to share a simple, quick little exercise that makes this all seem much more real to me. All it takes is a momentary, willful suspension of disbelief. One word of caution, though: if you prefer to keep a reasonably strong grip on reality, it might be best not to do this very often. I can advise from personal experience that it can become difficult to get back to the "real" world.

First, accept that the heavens and the earth are all made by God, from the tip of your nose to the furthest galaxy; every inch of space, every second of time, and every particle of matter are made by him. Second, accept that it is all made according to his will. The hordes of virtual particles that fill the universe, the light and heat of the stars, the solid earth under our feet, the drum of rain, the whisper of wind, the smell of spring, all of the living creatures with their billions and trillions of intricate cells that share this earth with us, all were conceived by him and made by him. Next, accept that this universe is here because he keeps it here; the stars burn because he makes them burn, the earth turns because he turns it, our hearts beat and our blood flows because he causes our muscles to work.

Finally, knowing what this creation is, turn away from this book and look at it.

03

Speculation in Theology

"The mystery of divine creativity is, of course, ultimately unknowable. The Genesis narrative does not seek to make intelligible what is beyond human ken. To draw upon human language to explain that which is outside any model of human experience is inevitably to confront the inescapable limitations of any attempt to give verbal expression to this subject. For this reason alone, the narrative in its external form must reflect the time and place of its composition. Thus it directs us to take account of the characteristic modes of literary expression current in ancient Israel. It forces us to realize that a literalistic approach to the text must inevitably confuse idiom with idea, symbol with reality. The result would be to obscure the enduring meaning of the text."—Nahum Sarna, *The JPS Torah Commentary: Genesis*

And now, at last, it is time to ignore the sound, sensible advice of every commentator and do some theology. All of the explanations of physics, all of the intricacies of this creation, and all of the descriptions of computation so far have been to support the ideas in this section. Here, we are going to try to match the physics and the computational speculation about how our world works to what Scripture says about the creation of our world in Genesis 1.

Remember, the interpretation presented here is just a story, just a guess. The reality of creation may or may not be at all like the possible reality suggested here. Nevertheless, we are going to take the previous speculation about the physical nature of our world and see how it fits with the series of events described in Genesis. We are going to attempt to craft a story that is compatible with both Scripture and modern physics. As was mentioned earlier, some parts of it (I think) fit really well. Other parts don't. This speculation is probably not the real answer, but it might illuminate some parts of the process of creation that are otherwise in shadow, or, as Paul said, seen through a glass darkly.

I will use a few pretty simple assumptions to construct the following interpretation of Genesis, the following story.

First assumption: Scripture is literally true. Every event mentioned in Genesis 1 happened exactly the way it is described.

There really isn't much choice about this one. It is hard for me to see the profit in any other way of approaching the task of comparing physics to Scripture. The whole point of this exercise is to resolve the apparent differences between them. It would be hard to be effective at that by first supposing that one of them is wrong or by picking and choosing bits that fit and leaving out ones that don't.

Even with such a demanding assumption, there is still quite a bit of flexibility available for interpretation. The description of creation given in Genesis 1 is sketchy. There is not a lot of detail to constrain speculation. The description also, as far as we know, uses terms that are illustrative rather than precisely defined the way physics jargon is defined. It paints a picture of creation rather than providing a detailed description. As with physics, there is still a lot of wiggle room for us to make up stories.

When approaching Scripture from a literal interpretive standpoint, one runs into a major problem having to do with translation. Genesis was originally written in (ancient) Hebrew. The many translations into English (or any other language) all suffer from the same problem: the correlations between the words and ideas of one language can be very different from those of another language. It's not just that the words have different meanings. The ideas that the words represent are often very different.

To avoid the translation issue as much as possible, the version of Scripture I am going to use here is the original Hebrew. As an example, here is Genesis 1:1:

Hebrew:	**Strong's Biblical Usage or Gesenius' Lexicon:**
re'shiyth	beginning, first, chief, choice part
elohiym	rulers, judges, divine ones, angels, gods
bara	to cut, to make by cutting, shape, fashion, create, make fat
eth	indicates next word is object
shamayim	sky, heaven
eth	indicates next word is object

erets	whole Earth, Earth with inhabitants, inhabited land, territory, ground

The Hebrew and the meanings of the Hebrew words are taken from the Blue Letter Bible, found at blueletterbible.org. For anyone interested in the details of translation, I highly recommend the Blue Letter Bible site. They have an enormous amount of information and just about the best organization of it (considering the task) that I have seen anywhere on any subject. I personally have found the details of translation very interesting; there is a depth and strength in the original Hebrew that, for me, doesn't really come across in most of the English translations.

The Hebrew on the left is Anglicized: the spelling is more like English than it technically should be. The meanings on the right are short synopses of the definitions given by Strong and Gesenius. One bit of warning: the short definitions were picked out from descriptions that sometimes go on for pages; there is, without doubt, a "slant" in the meanings given here that will tend to support my speculation. I've tried not to stray from the meanings presented, but there are many cases where the physical perspective of our speculation has an impact on the translation of the word.

Even for experts like Strong and Gesenius, there is often some guessing about the original meaning of ancient Hebrew words. Some words have changed their meanings over hundreds and thousands of years, and the original meanings must sometimes be deduced from the context they are used in and the meanings of similar words in other languages. There are a few cases (especially for "bara," more on this later) where a meaning that is derived from context changes because our perspective on what is being described will change as part of our speculation.

Second assumption: The science and natural philosophy that have been derived from what we see in the world around us are basically correct. The logic here is the same as it was for the first assumption: it would not be profitable to start a comparison of science and Scripture by assuming that one of them is wrong. Again, the whole point here is to try to resolve the differences, not to cover them up.

Third assumption: The Feynman-Stueckelberg interpretation of antimatter, and by implication, the block universe or eternalist theory of time, is correct.

> An aside for readers who cannot resist the temptation to jump straight to the end of a book to see how it all turns out: if you do not already know exactly what the preceding sentence means, I strongly recommend that you go back and read the section on physics before going any further. What comes next is not going to make any sense at all to a normal person with a strong grip on reality. A good dose of modern physics is vital for a proper doubt regarding the reality of this world.

Feynman-Stueckelberg and the eternalist universe imply that spacetime exists all at once and that it was created all at the same instant (the same "day"), from top to bottom, from back to front, from side to side, and from beginning to end. I mentioned way back in the introduction that Feynman-Stueckelberg is the key theory that unlocks the consolidation of Scripture and science (and natural philosophy). Right here is why that's true:

The largest stumbling block to resolving Scripture and science has always been the different timescales: the six days of creation set against the millions and billions of years of geology and cosmology. Feynman-Stueckelberg can be used to turn that stumbling block into smooth pavement.

According to the third assumption, Genesis 1 does not describe a sequence of events that happened chronologically in the way that we think of events as happening one after another in our time. Genesis 1 describes a sequence of changes to a spacetime that are each applied over all of spacetime, from beginning to end, to build this creation from the foundation up, layer by layer, with each later layer depending on the ones before it.

This "all at once, layer by layer" sort of viewpoint is necessary to resolve both the timescales and some differences in sequence between the scriptural description and what we see in the natural philosophy. For example, in Genesis 1 plants appear early in the creation, on day three. Animals appear later, on days five and six. In the fossil record studied by natural philosophers, however, animals appear first (542 MA in the sea, 425 MA on land), with plants showing up a bit later (423 MA for small land plants, 385 MA for seed-bearing plants, and 140 MA for flowering plants "yielding fruit"). All of the dates are radiometric, based on radioactive decay rates; it is possible that the actual dates may be off in one direction or another, but the sequence should be correct. (As a reminder, "MA" stands for "mega anna": one million years ago.)

With the Feynman-Stueckelberg view of time (all of time is simultaneously existing), plants could have been sprinkled into spacetime at whatever dates suited God's purpose. It was only necessary to put them into the creation before the animals so that the animals would have something to eat when they got here. Plants show up in the fossil record at roughly the same time as land animals, who would have needed something to eat. Early marine animals mostly ate prokaryotes and Protista that were already present in the oceans.

Fourth assumption: This creation is a computational model. This is actually more of a guideline; the first three assumptions are required for our speculation, but this one is really optional. There are some reasons to include it, but they are reasons of convenience, not reasons of necessity.

First of all, the assumption that this creation is a computational model eliminates (for the sake of the speculation) the notion that any of creation is in any way "supernatural." What we are attempting here is a comparison of true physics to true Scripture. In order to do that, we have to start by assuming that the Scripture is compatible with the physics and that the physics is compatible with the Scripture; the only reason to apply the term supernatural to any part of Scripture is that we don't understand the physics, not that Scripture is not compatible with the physics.

The notion that this "reality" is a computational model is a really handy tool for this attempt. It frees our minds. It allows us to measure the events of Scripture by what is possible in a computational model, not by what we think is possible in a physical world that is itself only a part of the model.

Next, the idea that this creation is a computational model is an application of Ockham's Razor. When we prepare for large, expensive projects, we often use computational modeling to help work out the details. We do this because it is the fastest, cheapest, and easiest way to explore the repercussions of what are often hundreds or thousands of choices in how the details may be done. It may be possible that a process similar in some ways to what we do in computers could be used by God—for similar reasons or for different reasons that are completely unknown to us. (Apologies for the vague statement, but I think it is important to remember that, with our current state of knowledge, we cannot legitimately step any closer to certainty.)

Finally, a computational model forms a pretty reasonable allegory for creation. It allows us to interpret the events described in Genesis 1 in ways that are (relatively) easy for us to understand, to use words and concepts from our world that can make creation more familiar. Remember, though, that a computational model is only an allegory; it is useful to help organize the interpretation, but it is (probably) not the whole truth.

Remember always that the parts of the interpretation coming up that look like allegory, like the story in the Scripture, should be assumed to be literally true. The parts that look like they are literally true, the descriptions of physics and computational activities, should be thought of as allegory—as just a story.

Genesis 1:1

"In the beginning, God created the heavens and the earth."

Hebrew:	Strong's Biblical Usage or Gesenius' Lexicon:
re'shiyth	beginning, first, chief, choice part
elohiym	rulers, judges, divine ones, angels, gods
bara	to cut, to make by cutting, shape, fashion, create, make fat
eth	indicates next word is object
shamayim	sky, heaven
eth	indicates next word is object
erets	whole earth, earth with inhabitants, inhabited land, territory, ground

In most English translations, Genesis 1:1 is rendered as a first, broad introduction, with additional details filled in later. It is tempting to think of this sentence that way, as a sentence that we skip over to get to the interesting part, but it is not. In this interpretation of Genesis 1, Genesis 1:1 is a key verse: a place where the physics interpretation fits the best. This is because the meaning of the Hebrew word *bara* may change in the light of physics. In particular, it may have a very different meaning if it is thought of as applying to a computational model.

Bara is mostly translated, based on the context, as "created," like it is in the KJV above. The literal meaning is the verb "to cut." This definition very reasonably morphs into "to create" through the notion of carving, of making something by cutting. Most of the uses of the word *bara* in Scripture relate to God making things and are translated as "create." A few, however, do not seem to have this meaning. Here are the uses that do not necessarily relate to God making things:

> *"But if the Lord make* [bara] *a new thing, and the earth open her mouth, and swallow them up, with all that appertain unto them, and they go down quick into the pit; then ye shall understand that these men have provoked the Lord."*—Numbers 16:30

> *"And Joshua answered them, If thou be a great people, then get thee up to the wood country, and cut down* [bara] *for thyself there in the land of the Perizzites and of the giants, if mount Ephraim be too narrow for thee."*—Joshua 17:15

> *"But the mountain shall be thine; for it is a wood, and thou shalt cut it down* [bara]*; and the outgoings of it shall be thine: for thou shalt drive out the Canaanites, though they have iron chariots, and though they be strong."*—Joshua 17:18

> *"Wherefore kick ye at my sacrifice and at mine offering, which I have commanded in my habitation; and honourest thy sons above me, to make yourselves fat* [bara] *with the chiefest of all the offerings of Israel my people?"*—1 Samuel 2:29

> *"Also, thou son of man, appoint thee two ways, that the sword of the king of Babylon may come: both twain shall come forth out of one land: and choose* [bara] *thou a place, choose* [bara] *it at the head of the way to the city."*—Ezekiel 21:19

> *"And the company shall stone them with stones, and dispatch* [bara] *them with their swords; they shall slay their sons and their daughters, and burn up their houses with fire."*—Ezekiel 23:47

With a little stretching (especially in Numbers 16:30 and Ezekiel 21:19), *bara* can be interpreted as "to cut" in all or most of the above uses. For example, where it is translated as "make yourselves fat" in the KJV, we might use the phrase "take a cut" to describe what they are doing.

My suggestion here is that *bara* still means "to cut" in Genesis 1:1 and in all of Genesis 1. Three different words are used in Genesis 1 when God is making something: *bara* (to cut), *amar* (to speak), and *asah* (to make). They are applied as follows:

	bara (to cut)	**amar (to speak)**	**asah (to make)**
Gen 1:1	ground and sky		
Gen 1:3		light (not sources of light, but the light itself)	
Gen 1.6		solid firmament dividing waters from waters	
Gen 1:7			solid firmament dividing waters from waters
Gen 1:9		water of the sky bound into dry land	
Gen 1:11		grass, edible plants, trees bearing fruit	
Gen 1:14		stars	
Gen 1:16			the sun and the moon
Gen 1:20		swarms of small creeping animals and birds	
Gen 1:21	large swimming animals and flying animals		

	bara (to cut)	amar (to speak)	asah (to make)
Gen 1:24		large and small animals that live on ground	
Gen 1:25			large and small animals that live on ground
Gen 1:26		mankind	mankind
Gen 1:27	mankind		
Gen 1:27	man and woman		

Bara is applied in Genesis 1 to three things: the whole of creation (the ground and sky), large swimming and flying animals, and us. Using the computational model assumption for interpretation, *bara* is applied to parts of creation that either require a lot of computational resources because they are very large (the ground and sky) or that may require a different type of network structure because the model has to produce the unpredictable behavior of conscious minds (large animals, and especially the most unpredictable part—us). For example, a linear, four-dimensional network might be appropriate for the basic spacetime model, while a neural network might work better for modeling conscious minds.

In our computers, we would use the term partition to describe the allocation of computational resources to a particular task. In a single core computer, the term would apply to a section of memory set aside for use by the task and to a slot in the time-sharing sequence. In a computational network, it would mean that some number of cores is dedicated to the task.

In any case, *bara* would be a much more appropriate word choice if Genesis 1:1 is describing the necessary first step in building a computational model than either *amar* or *asah*, the other choices used in Genesis 1.

So the interpretation of Genesis 1:1 is this: first, God partitioned (cut out, set aside) computational capability that would be used to model the sky and the earth.

Genesis 1:2

"And the earth was without form and void; and darkness was upon the face of the deep. And the Spirit of God moved upon the face of the waters."

Hebrew:	Strong's Biblical Usage or Gesenius' Lexicon:
erets	whole earth, earth with inhabitants, inhabited land, territory, ground
hayah	to be, to become, to come to pass, to exist, to happen, to fall out
tohuw	formlessness, confusion, unreal, empty, nothingness, wasteland, place of chaos, vanity
bohuw	emptiness, void, waste
choshek	darkness, obscurity, lightless
paniym	face, presence, person, surface, in front of
tehowm	deep waters, deep sea, abyss in sea, primeval ocean, abyss, the grave
ruwach	wind, breath, spirited (breathing quickly), spirit of man, Spirit of God
elohiym	rulers, judges, divine ones, angels, gods
rachaph	to be emotionally affected, to cherish (as parents toward children), to brood or hover as a bird over its nest
al	upon, above, over, in addition to, on the ground of, concerning
paniym	face, presence, person, surface, in front of
mayim	water

Although the sentence in English uses the word *earth (erets* in Hebrew), according to natural philosophy and science, the physical earth is not around yet at this point in Genesis 1. Geophysics informs us that the composition of the earth is compatible with gas condensation models for the formation of our solar system. In the computer models of solar system condensation (confirmed by observation), the relative concentrations of elements and the ratios of radioactive isotopes change with distance from the sun. The elemental composition and isotope ratios for the earth (and moon) which we see in nature are correct for our distance from the sun. Acceptance of the science implies that the physical earth cannot show up in creation until day four, when the stars are made (just a preview: this entire interpretation is going to be a little inconvenient when we get to the creation of plants on day three—but we'll cross that bridge when we come to it).

Following the physical interpretation of Genesis 1:1, Genesis 1:2 would be describing a (probably very large) computational environment that will later be used to model the earth and sky. It is noteworthy here that what will become the earth is described as a formless, empty, dark, large, and/or deep space. This is noteworthy because the earth is not like that anymore, while the sky (most of it) still is formless, empty, dark, and vast. In Genesis 1:2 the same is true of the earth.

Genesis 1:2 uses two words, *tehowm* (deep water) and *mayim* (water), that describe water or, possibly, fluids. Our physics term "fluid" includes both gas and water, anything that flows. Because acceptance of the science implies that there is not yet any physical earth present, or probably any physical water, the water terms used here are assumed to be illustrative, meant to convey an image rather than literally meaning physical water. So for the purpose of interpretation, *tehowm* and *mayim* will be assumed to refer to the computational space that has been cut out (partitioned) for the creation model.

If this is true, it implies that God perceives this computational space as looking like water, in that something (information?) flows in it. He perceives it as being very large (to justify the term *tehowm*) and having a defined, perceptual boundary that would merit the term *paniym* (face). The notion of a multidimensional network of computational cores fits pretty well into this image.

At this early point in the process of creation, the computational network has been prepared (or is being prepared). The hardware is ready, but it is not programmed yet; there is no organization to the flow of information that will later give the creation form, light, warmth, and what we perceive as substance.

Much of the preparation is probably already done here: the development of the mathematics for the standard model of particles and the forces that bind them together; the shaping of spacetime that will be gravity; the nuclear reactions to power the stars; and the chemistry that will become the earth, seas, and life, with its incredible complexity. At this moment, just before the real action of the creation starts, the Spirit of God pauses for a moment to savor the excitement and anticipation, to cherish what is about to happen—what he is about to bring into being.

There is a cute little play on words here, one of the bits that, for me, made researching the original Hebrew so enjoyable. Our spirit, the essence of our life, is later described as *nephesh,* as breath. Here in Genesis 1:2, the Holy Spirit is named *Ruwach Elohiym,* Wind of Gods—still a motion of air, but a little higher than a breath.

Genesis 1:3

"And God said, Let there be light; and there was light."

Hebrew:	Strong's Biblical Usage or Gesenius' Lexicon:
elohiym	rulers, judges, divine ones, angels, gods
amar	say, speak, utter
hayah	to be, to become, to exist, to come into being
owr	(noun) light everywhere diffused, light cast, not a source, daylight, light of sun, moon, stars
owr	(noun) light everywhere diffused, light cast, not a source, daylight, light of sun, moon, stars

Once again, the accepted science and natural philosophy implies that although the Scripture speaks of *light* here, no sources of what we think of as light will be present until the stars appear on day four. Scripture here agrees with the science: the light in Genesis 1:3 is described as *owr,* light itself, instead of sources of light (which would be *ma-owr*).

Instead, we will assume the light in this verse to be the light of particle physics, the boson exchange interactions that mediate the four forces and hold matter together. What is possibly happening here is that the computational space is being programmed with the standard model of particle physics: exchange interactions, vertex interaction rules, conservation laws, Yang-Mills gauge theories, particle properties and attributes, particle property fluctuations, vacuum fluctuations, and the Dirac Sea—the swarms of real and virtual particles that (we think) fill all of our universe. What is possibly being made here is spacetime itself, the fundamental foundation of this creation wherein everything else happens.

Although virtual and real particle swarms are possibly present here, there would still not necessarily be anything we would think of as matter. Matter, remember, is an imbalance in the swarms of particles; each matter particle is one extra matter probability amplitude in an otherwise balanced swarm of matter and antimatter probability amplitudes. As long as the swarms of particles are exactly balanced, with an antimatter particle for every matter particle, the whole thing would still look and act like a vacuum, like empty space.

Here in Genesis 1:3, then, the model is still empty, but with the standard model in place, it is ready for matter. Matter can now appear from "nothing" (*ex nihilo*) at the flick of a probability amplitude attribute value.

Genesis 1:3 contains the first appearance of the second of the three creative terms used in Genesis 1: *bara* (to cut), *amar* (to speak), and *asah* (to make). Light is *amar*; it is spoken into existence.

For the sake of interpretation, I'd like to suggest some tentative meanings for the three creative terms. These are just guesses; we'll try them on to see how they fit.

As we earlier saw, *bara* seems to be applied to parts of creation that require more than their fair share of computational resources, or else different resources—parts of creation that require a partition of some part of the possible network of cores.

Amar might apply to parts of creation that were worked out ahead of time and just needed to be programmed into the model.

Asah might refer to parts of creation that were worked out as part of the developmental model—that were made as a part of the creation process (at least, the part of the creation process that is described in Genesis 1.

Genesis 1:4

"And God saw the light, that it was good: and God divided the light from the darkness."

Hebrew:	Strong's Biblical Usage or Gesenius' Lexicon:
elohiym	rulers, judges, divine ones, angels, gods
ra'ah	to see, to perceive, to have vision, to be seen
eth	indicates next word is object

owr	(noun) light everywhere diffused, light cast, not a source, daylight, light of sun, moon, stars
kiy	that, for, because, when, since, surely
towb	good, pleasant, agreeable
elohiym	rulers, judges, divine ones, angels, gods
badal	to divide, to separate, to divide into parts, to make a distinction
beyn	between, among, in the midst of
owr	(noun) light everywhere diffused, light cast, not a source, daylight, light of sun, moon, stars
beyn	between, among, in the midst of
choshek	darkness, obscurity, lightless

At this point in the interpretation of Genesis 1 we have a computational model of spacetime filled with the standard model of particle physics that is apparently working very nicely. Way back in the introduction, I mentioned that the division of light and darkness in Genesis 1:4 probably referred to the spacetime inflation and expansion in the big bang cosmology model. Calculations by astronomers tell us that spacetime had to be stretched out: the nuclear fires in our stars burn so hot that there must be huge distances between them in order to make a world cool enough for us to live in.

We are accepting the science as part of our interpretation, and the big bang cosmology is an important part of it. Providentially for our speculation, the big bang fits very comfortably into Genesis 1:4. The big bang theory tells us that, according to mathematical models verified by observation, creation started out with all of spacetime contained in a single point, which then expanded out to the size that we see today—and is apparently still expanding. Or at least, it was expanding millions and billions of years ago when the photons of starlight astronomers see today left their respective stars.

The big bang cosmology tells us something about creation's past, and it fits very well with a Scripture that tells us that God stretched out the sky and separated the

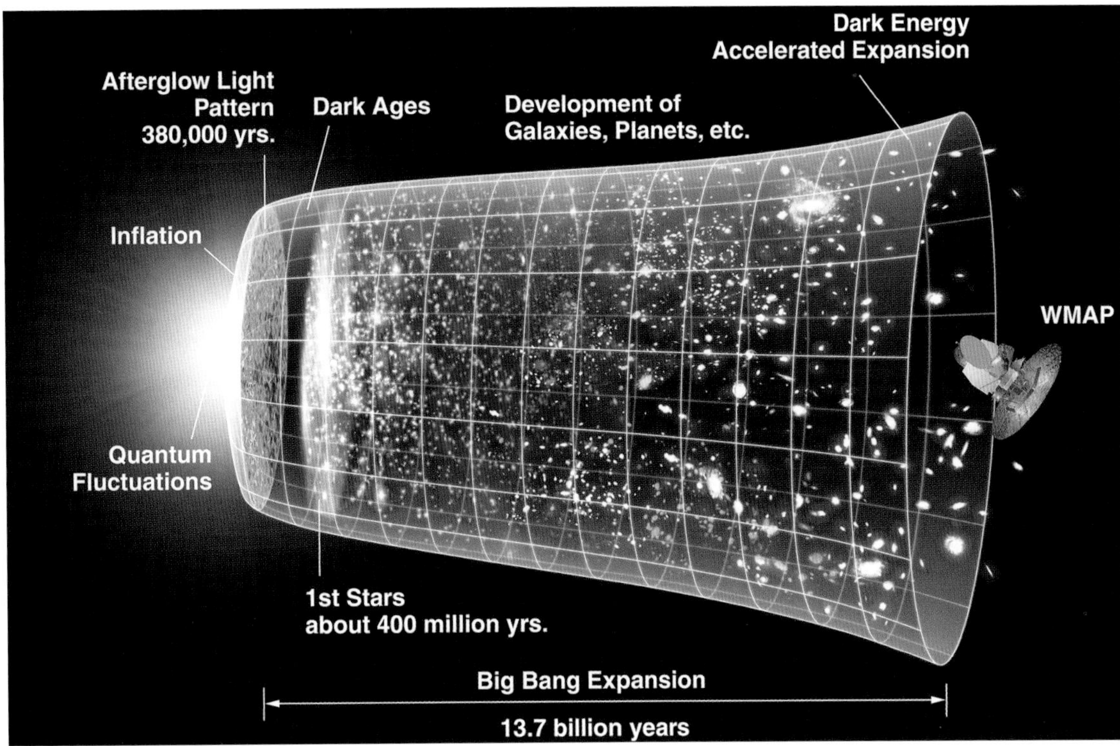

Fig. 128. The Standard Big Bang Cosmology

light from the darkness. But it does not have very much to say about our future, and it does not have a currently viable reason for why the big bang happened at all.

All of the major cosmology theories (that is, the mathematical models of cosmology) are future infinite; they all assume that the universe will go on poking along pretty much the way it is now forever. They are also all based on a Hamiltonian notion of a time that "develops continuously out of the past" (Feynman); they assume that all that really exists is now, that the past is over and done with, and that the future has not happened yet.

But the picture needs to be little different for this interpretation of Genesis 1, where we are assuming that the Feynman-Stueckelberg version of time—with a past that is just as real as the present and an existing, real future—is correct. If we are in a Feynman-Stueckelberg reality, our past is not infinite, the size of our universe is not infinite, and it seems pretty reasonable to infer that the future is probably not infinite either.

Big bang theory does not have a reason for the big bang. We don't know why it happened. The issue of *why* has been a struggle for the physics community; there are a number of cosmology theories (math models) based on the assumption of a natural world, but none of them have been conclusive yet. They propose reasons like a bouncing universe or epkyrotic brane collisions, but most of them conflict with observational data. Robert Spitzer does a nice job of describing various cosmologies in *New Proofs for the Existence of God: Contributions of Contemporary Physics and Philosophy* (2010).

The issue of why is an even bigger problem for an interpretation that assumes that we are in a computational model; in a computational creation made by God, there would certainly be a reason for something like the big bang. While we really don't know very much about physics, there are at least two possible reasons a computational big bang might be needed.

The first possible reason is that it speeds up the developmental model. Big bang expansion starts with matter (mostly low atomic number hydrogen and helium) concentrated into a dense, hot mass. It is possible that the nuclear reactions that produce higher atomic number elements (the metals needed for life) would happen faster under such conditions. A big bang expansion might produce metals quickly in the beginning and then expand to provide a cooler environment fit for life later on.

The second possible reason (more of a wild speculation, really) has to do with vacuum fluctuations. Remember that the interpretation of vacuum fluctuations can shift a little if Feynman-Stueckelberg is assumed to be true. The Feynman diagram below and to the left represents the consensus, Hamiltonian view of the physics community: virtual particles in vacuum fluctuations are always created as pairs and annihilate as pairs, so the fluctuation clouds always stay nicely balanced.

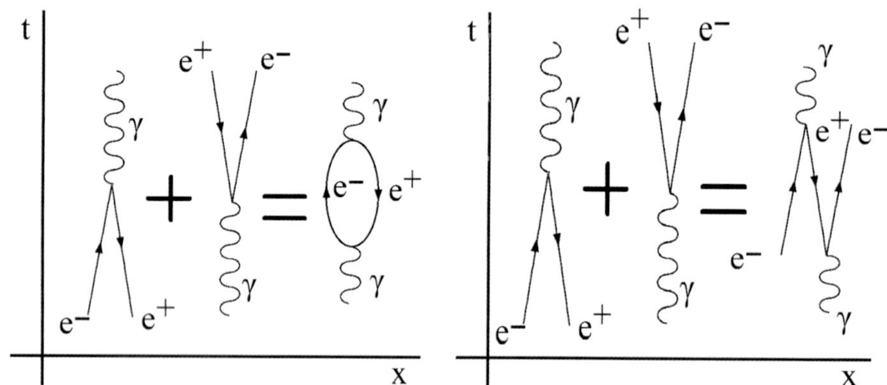

Pair creation and annihilation absolutely do happen; they have been observed in experiments many, many times. But if Feynman-Stueckelberg is considered to be correct (as we do), then the Feynman diagram above and to the right, showing time reversals instead of pair annihilation and creation, can also happen.

Dr. Feynman often said that, in quantum mechanics, anything that can happen does happen. One of the things that can happen is shown in the Feynman diagram below, showing a particle "trapped" in time by photons.

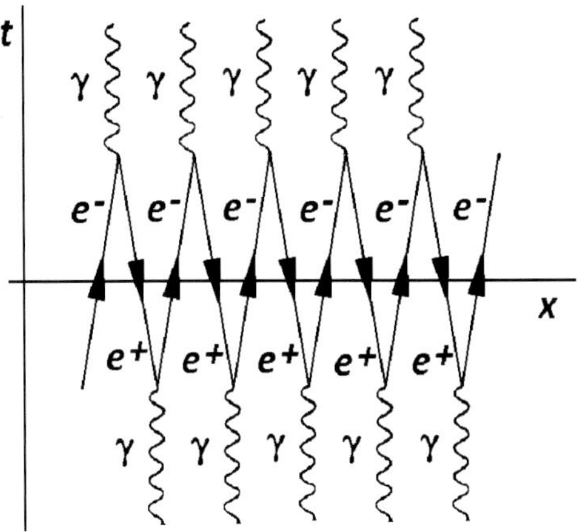

In an assumed reality where particles wander backward and forward in time, a big bang spacetime contraction might be pretty handy for turning the little guys around and keeping the swarms of particles balanced between forward time matter and backward time antimatter.

Physicists are pretty sure at this point that there is something like that in our past to turn antimatter particles around—namely, the big bang. Feynman-Stueckelberg and symmetry imply that there might also be something similar in our future to turn matter particles around. The official term is "big bang II"; "big crunch" is an unofficial term that gives a better picture of what will happen.

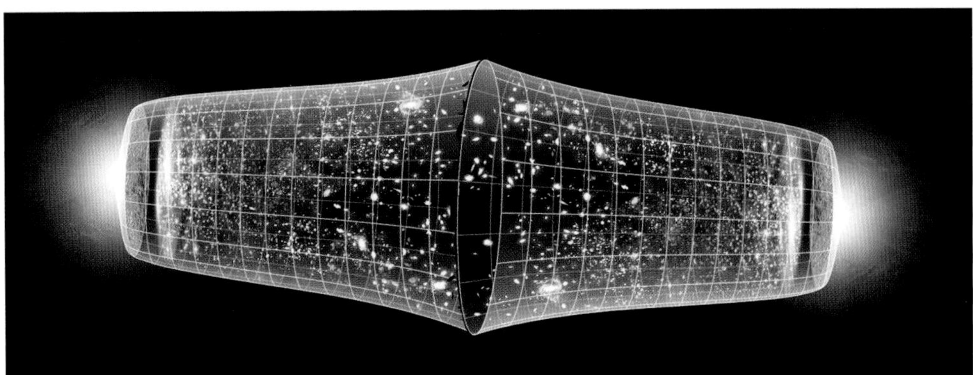

Fig. 128.3. Spacetime

Your humble author likes this idea of a symmetrical spacetime bounded by a big bang on one end and a big crunch on the other not for scientific reasons, but mostly just because it provides a really cool image: both the image shown above and the mental image of God holding the creation in his hands and then stretching out both time and space to make our universe.

The idea of a big bang II in the future fits pretty well with Scripture. There are several references in both the Old and New Testaments to stars falling from the sky:

"And all the host of heaven shall be dissolved, and the heavens shall be rolled together as a scroll: and all their host shall fall down, as the leaf falleth off from the vine, and as a falling fig from the fig tree."—Isaiah 34:4

"Immediately after the tribulation of those days shall the sun be darkened, and the moon shall not give her light, and the stars shall fall from heaven, and the powers of the heavens shall be shaken: and then shall appear the sign of the Son of man in heaven: and then shall all the tribes of the earth mourn, and they shall see the Son of man coming in the clouds of heaven with power and great glory."—Matthew 24:29–30

"But in those days, after that tribulation, the sun shall be darkened, and the moon shall not give her light, And the stars of heaven shall fall, and the powers that are in heaven shall be shaken. And then shall they see the Son of man coming in the clouds with great power and glory. And then shall he send his angels, and shall gather together his elect from the four winds, from the uttermost part of the earth to the uttermost part of heaven."—Mark 13:24–27

"And I beheld when he had opened the sixth seal, and, lo, there was a great earthquake; and the sun became black as sackcloth of hair, and the moon became as blood; And the stars of heaven fell unto the earth, even as a fig tree casteth her untimely figs, when she is shaken of a mighty wind. And the heaven departed as a scroll when it is rolled together; and every mountain and island were moved out of their places."—Revelation 6:13

If the stars were actually to move, we would not see them for millions and billions of years; but the stars might look like they were falling from the sky if their photon trails were shifting during a spacetime contraction.

Isaiah also mentions that the sun and moon become brighter at the end of this creation:

"Moreover the light of the moon shall be as the light of the sun, and the light of the sun shall be sevenfold, as the light of seven days, in the day that the LORD bindeth up the breach of his people, and healeth the stroke of their wound."—Isaiah 30:26

Once again, Scripture fits with the (maybe possible) cosmology. In a spacetime contraction, the sun would be getting closer, brighter, and much, much hotter. The other descriptions above, however, describe the sun as dark and the moon as blood red when the stars fall. These are places where Scripture does not fit this interpretation quite as well (unless God "turns off" the sun during the big crunch so that we don't get burned up).

There is one other point in the relationship between physics and Scripture that should be mentioned here. Genesis 1:4, if it does refer to the expansion of spacetime, implies that the expansion happened before there was any matter (as we think of matter) present in creation. There may have been swarms of virtual particles, but no gas and no rocks.

Big bang cosmology holds that spacetime inflation at the beginning was driven by the (very) rapid expansion of energy out from an initial, single point (they don't call it the big bang for nothing). The continuing expansion is still driven by an attachment between spacetime and a pervasive energy level associated with a vacuum called dark energy (very similar to the zero-point energy proposed as a mechanism for Dirac's negative energy particles). Dark energy was basically invented to provide a justification for the observed spacetime expansion. The dark energy model does provide a good fit to the observed distribution of redshift and luminosity that astronomers see in our universe, but the physical existence of dark energy has never been confirmed by experiment. It is just a guess based on the assumption of a natural world.

If we are correct that the "separation of light and darkness" describes the spacetime inflation, then Genesis 1:4 conforms to the description of gravitational effects in the rest of Scripture; they are always described as God setting boundaries. Here, also, the shape and size of spacetime—which general relativity tells us is the cause of gravity—is the result of actions by God, not the influence of matter.

There is some debate in physics and philosophy about the physical composition of spacetime. The two possibilities are that spacetime is some kind of substance, or that it has no physical existence at all; it is just a relationship between physical processes. Einstein apparently thought that spacetime is not a thing; it is just a relationship between processes. The assumed computational nature of creation in our interpretation provides a suggestion for how the expansion might have occurred if spacetime is not a substance. The expansion could be a change in the position attributes for the swarms of virtual probability amplitudes in spacetime and/or for the Fock quantum states available for particle probability amplitudes.

Genesis 1:5

"And God called the light Day, and the darkness he called Night. And the evening and the morning were the first day."

Hebrew:	Strong's Biblical Usage or Gesenius' Lexicon:
elohiym	rulers, judges, divine ones, angels, gods
qara	to cry out, to call, to recite, to proclaim
owr	(noun) light everywhere diffused, light cast, not a source, daylight, light of sun, moon, stars
yowm	day (not night), day (twenty-four hours), days (time), time period
choshek	darkness, obscurity, lightless
qara	to cry out, to call, to recite, to proclaim
layil	night (not day), midnight, gloom (low light)
ereb	evening, sunset, night (not day)
boqer	morning, sunrise, break of day
echad	one (number), each, first
yowm	day (not night), day (twenty-four hours), days (time), time period

God's act of naming the day and night has theological significance, but there does not appear to be a lot of physics happening in Genesis 1:6. However, an interesting implication of our interpretation does come up here. If the Feynman-Stueckelberg version of our time as all simultaneously existing is correct, then God is not in our time; our time is only a feature of creation and does not restrain God's perception the way it restrains our perception. This notion was used earlier to provide a physical justification for the Father's prophetic ability. We are also using it to explain the difference in timescales between the six "days" of creation (introduced here) and the millions and billions of years of science and natural philosophy: the six days are in God's time, while the millions and billions of years are in our stretched-out spacetime.

The interesting part of all of this is the implication that the *ereb* (sunset) and *boqer* (sunrise) mentioned in Genesis 1:6 (and five more times in Genesis 1) happen in God's time and God's reality, not in the creation. Some commentaries, both Christian and Hebrew, suggest that the evening and morning here are just imagery used to represent passing time; it was very common to reckon time in terms of sunsets or sunrises in ancient cultures. However, the commentaries apply that same, allegorical kind of logic to most of Genesis 1. The interpretation we are developing here, based on modern physics, assumes a very different point of view: the events described in Genesis 1 are very literal. They actually happened pretty much exactly as described. The terms used to describe events are often illustrative, chosen to convey an image, but the events themselves are assumed to be very concrete.

All of which implies that, according to our interpretation, there might be something very like sunrise and something very like sunset that happen at regular intervals to mark the boundaries of something very like days in God's reality.

Genesis 1:6

"And God said, Let there be a firmament in the midst of the waters, and let it divide the waters from the waters."

Hebrew:	Strong's Biblical Usage or Gesenius' Lexicon:
elohiym	rulers, judges, divine ones, angels, gods
amar	say, speak, utter
raqiya	extended solid surface, flat expanse, solid firmament
tavek	midst, middle, between two things, take from among
mayim	water
badal	to divide, to separate, to divide into parts, to make a distinction
mayim	water

Genesis 1:7

"And God made the firmament, and divided the waters which were under the firmament from the waters which were above the firmament: and it was so."

Hebrew:	Strong's Biblical Usage or Gesenius' Lexicon:
elohiym	rulers, judges, divine ones, angels, gods
asah	to do, to accomplish, to fashion, to make
raqiya	extended solid surface, flat expanse, solid firmament
badal	to divide, to separate, to divide into parts, to make a distinction
mayim	water
asher	who, which, that
tachath	the under part, beneath, instead of
raqiya	extended solid surface, flat expanse, solid firmament
mayim	water
asher	who, which, that
al	upon, above, over, in addition to, on the ground of, concerning
raqiyah	extended solid surface, flat expanse, solid firmament
ken	so, therefore, thus

Genesis 1:8

"And God called the firmament Heaven.
And the evening and the morning were the second day."

Hebrew:	Strong's Biblical Usage or Gesenius' Lexicon:
elohiym	rulers, judges, divine ones, angels, gods
qara	to cry out, to call, to recite, to proclaim
raqiya	extended solid surface, flat expanse, solid firmament
shamayim	sky, heaven
ereb	evening, sunset, night (not day)
boqer	morning, sunrise, break of day
sheniy	second (number), again, another
yowm	day (not night), day (twenty-four hours), days (time), time period

Up to this point, our interpretation has used the assumption of a computational reality to infer that the term *mayim* (water) is being applied to a computational environment that might look something like water to God but is not physical water as we know it. That assumption still works pretty well here on day two of creation. It will have to be dropped on day three when plants show up, but it still works here.

It still works because of the term *raqiya* (firmament), used in Genesis 1:6–8. The literal translation of *raqiya* is a solid, flat surface like a ceiling or a floor; it is used that way in other parts of Scripture (in Ezekiel's visions of cherubim for example; see Ezekiel 10:1). In Genesis 1:8 God names the *raqiya,* a solid surface, as *shamayim,* the sky. On day four the stars will be made in the *raqiya,* a solid surface.

The odd part is that, according to science and natural philosophy (which we fully accept here), the sky that we see in creation does not, except for the occasional bumps of the stars and planets, have anything solid about it. And here, on day two of creation, there aren't even any stars or (probably) planets yet—so there isn't anything solid about the sky at all.

Using the same logic as was applied for the term *mayim* earlier, then, we will assume the *raqiya* is a computational structure that will later be used to model the stars in the sky. It apparently looks more like a solid sheet than the *tehowm* (deeps of the sea) that describes the rest of the computational environment.

The creative terms used for the *raqiya* are both *amar* (to say) and *asah* (to make). If the tentative definitions for those terms suggested earlier are anywhere near correct, the *raqiya* was both prepared and planned before the creation started (as was suggested for *amar*) and developed as part of the creative process (as was suggested for *asah*).

In his 2003 paper on the possibility that our universe is a computational model ("Are You Living in a Computer Simulation?") philosopher Nick Bostrom pointed out that a computational environment made for the benefit of conscious minds would not really need to model every little detail. The model could vary in fidelity, with the parts that conscious minds are paying attention to modeled in much more detail than the parts they really can't see very well.

Earlier, in the description of the requirements of creation, I mentioned that the physical model of the universe is the easy part of creation; the really hard part is modeling life, especially conscious minds. Just a guess, but it may take more computational resources to model an anthill than it does to model the planet Jupiter.

The point here is that the model of the *shamayim* (sky) might not be a large part of the whole computational space devoted (*bara*) to creation. It seems pretty reasonable that, if it is a relatively small part of the whole network and if it has a different, denser interconnect structure, then the term *raqiya* would be an appropriate description.

Genesis 1:9

"And God said, Let the waters under the heaven be gathered together into one place, and let the dry land appear: and it was so."

Hebrew:	Strong's Biblical Usage or Gesenius' Lexicon:
elohiym	rulers, judges, divine ones, angels, gods
amar	say, speak, utter
mayim	water
shamayim	sky, heaven

qavah	bound (by a rope), wait (like a bound horse), look for, hope, expect
el	move toward, into, face toward, within, against (move or face away), between
echad	one (number), each, first
maqowm	place to stand, region, locality
yabbashah	dry land, dry ground
ra'ah	to see, to perceive, to have vision, to be seen

Genesis 1:10

"And God called the dry land Earth; and the gathering together of the waters called he seas: and God saw that it was good."

Hebrew:	Strong's Biblical Usage or Gesenius' Lexicon:
elohiym	rulers, judges, divine ones, angels, gods
qara	to cry out, to call, recite, proclaim
yabbashah	dry land, dry ground
erets	whole earth, earth with inhabitants, inhabited land, territory, ground
miqveh	yarn, gathering together, accumulation, hope, expectation
mayim	water
qara	to cry out, to call, recite, proclaim
yam	sea, lake, large river
elohiym	rulers, judges, divine ones, angels, gods
ra'ah	to see, to perceive, to have vision, to be seen
towb	good, pleasant, agreeable

Genesis 1:11

"And God said, Let the earth bring forth grass, the herb yielding seed, and the fruit tree yielding fruit after his kind, whose seed is in itself, upon the earth: and it was so."

Hebrew:	Strong's Biblical Usage or Gesenius' Lexicon:
elohiym	rulers, judges, divine ones, angels, gods
amar	say, speak, utter
erets	whole earth, earth with inhabitants, inhabited land, territory, ground
dasha	to sprout, to grow as a plant
deshe	young plant, grass
eseb	mature plant, edible plant
zara	to sow seed, to produce seed
zera	seed, sowing, children
periy	fruit, produce (of the ground), children, fruit of actions
ets	tree, wood, timber, stick
asah	to go, to accomplish, to fashion, to make
periy	fruit, produce (of the ground), children, fruit of actions
miyn	kind of animal, kind of plant
asher	who, which, that
zera	seed, sowing, children
erets	whole earth, earth with inhabitants, inhabited land, territory, ground

Genesis 1:12

"And the earth brought forth grass, and herb yielding seed after his kind, and the tree yielding fruit, whose seed was in itself, after his kind: and God saw that it was good."

Hebrew:	Strong's Biblical Usage or Gesenius' Lexicon:
erets	whole earth, earth with inhabitants, inhabited land, territory, ground
yatsa	to go out, to come out, to exit, to go forth
deshe	young plant, grass
eseb	mature plant, edible plant
zara	to sow seed, to produce seed
zera	seed, sowing, children
miyn	kind of animal, kind of plant
ets	tree, wood, timber, stick
asah	to do, to accomplish, to fashion, to make
periy	fruit, produce (of the ground), children, fruit of actions
zera	seed, sowing, children
miyn	kind of animal, kind of plant
elohiym	rulers, judges, divine ones, angels, gods
ra'ah	to see, to perceive, to have vision, to be seen
towb	good, pleasant, agreeable

Genesis 1:13

"And the evening and the morning were the third day."

Hebrew:	Strong's Biblical Usage or Gesenius' Lexicon:
ereb	evening, sunset, night (not day)
boqer	morning, sunrise, break of day
sheliyshiy	third, one third, third part, third time
yowm	day (not night), day (twenty-four hours), days (time), time period

Genesis 1:9–13, day three of creation, is the really hard part for an interpretation of Genesis 1 based on literal acceptance of the Scripture *and* acceptance of the science and natural philosophy of the world we see: on their respective faces, they do not agree at all here. Scripture tells us that real, physical water is gathered together into seas to produce real, physical dry land. They have to be real, physical water and real, physical earth because plants are going to grow in them. The earlier description of mayim (water) as an illustrative term referring to a computational environment just will not work anymore. On the other hand, science and natural philosophy tell us that our earth (and moon) and the water in our seas were all derived from stars, which will not be made until day four.

A possible resolution of the conflict will come from biology plus a little astrophysics, but first there are a few more verses, Genesis 2:4–6, that we can add to, possibly, fill in a few more details.

Genesis 2:4

"These are the generations of the heavens and of the earth when they were created in the day that the LORD God made the earth and the heavens."

Hebrew:	Strong's Biblical Usage or Gesenius' Lexicon:
el-leh	these
towledah	descendants, generations, families, races, history (of families)

shamayim	sky, heaven
erets	whole earth, earth with inhabitants, inhabited land, territory, ground
bara	to cut, to make by cutting, shape, fashion, create, make fat
yowm	day (not night), day (twenty-four hours), days (time), time period
Yehovah	the existing one, the proper name for the one true God
elohiym	rulers, judges, divine ones, angels, gods
asah	to do, to accomplish, to fashion, to make
erets	whole earth, earth with inhabitants, inhabited land, territory, ground
shamayim	sky, heaven

Genesis 2:5

"And every plant of the field before it was in the earth, and every herb of the field before it grew: for the L*ORD* *God had not caused it to rain upon the earth, and there was not a man to till the ground."*

Hebrew:	**Strong's Biblical Usage or Gesenius' Lexicon:**
siyach	bush, plant, shrub
sadeh	a plain, plowed and sown field, fields, agricultural area
terem	before, not yet, before that, previously, before the beginning
erets	whole earth, earth with inhabitants, inhabited land, territory, ground
eseb	mature plant, edible plant
sadeh	a plain, plowed and sown field, fields, agricultural area
tsamach	to sprout forth (as a plant), to spring up, to cause to grow

kiy	that, for, because, when, since, surely
Yehovah	the existing one, the proper name for the one true God
elohiym	rulers, judges, divine ones, angels, gods
lo	no, not, without, nothing
matar	to rain, to pour down rain
erets	whole earth, earth with inhabitants, inhabited land, territory, ground
ayin	nothing, emptiness, vacuum, not
adam	man, mankind, first man (Adam)
abad	to labor, to work, to do work, to work for another, to serve, to be worked, to compel labor
adamah	earth (soil), ground, field, land, a plot of land

Genesis 2:6

"But there went up a mist from the earth, and watered the whole face of the ground."

Hebrew:	**Strong's Biblical Usage or Gesenius' Lexicon:**
alah	to go up, to ascend, to climb
ed	mist
min	a prepositional construction meaning a part of, taken from
erets	whole earth, earth with inhabitants, inhabited land, territory, ground
shaqah	to drink, to furnish drink, to water (animals), to irrigate, to be watered
paniym	face, presence, person, surface, in front of
adamah	earth (soil), ground, field, land, a plot of land

Biology tells us that every other living organism on this earth depends on the primary producers, on the organisms that "eat" the raw minerals of the ground and the light from the sun and turn them into organic chemicals that will nourish the rest of us. Primary producers are almost entirely bacteria and Protista (single-celled eukaryotes). Even plants depend on soil bacteria to help reduce rocks to edible chemicals. In a sense, plants have an assisting role as primary producers: they are much easier for larger animals to eat than bacteria and probably taste a lot better too.

As well as providing food, primary producers condition our environment to make it fit for life. For example, even in the earth's relatively benign radiation environment, the unfiltered radiation intensity on the surface of the earth (especially UV radiation from the sun) is deadly to organic life. Most of the harmful radiation is currently filtered out by the high concentration of oxygen in our atmosphere, oxygen that was put there by bacteria and Protista plankton in the oceans.

Bacteria and Protista (and plants) made this planet suitable for our kind of life and sustain life every day; they are an absolutely crucial foundation for the existence of life in this creation. Therefore, when the time came to pick out a nice little planet to imbue with life (on day four), it might have been convenient to have a fully complete model of the primary producers first to make sure the planet would be suitable for all of the long years that it would take to fully model life (and us).

Looking again at the Hebrew, then, let's paraphrase Genesis 2:4: "These are the histories of the sky and ground divided [*bara*] in the day that the LORD God made [*asah*] the ground, the sky, and the plants." What is being described in Genesis 1:6–13 and, partly, in Genesis 2:4–6 is possibly the division of the model environment into three sections: a computation network that will later be used to model some other parts of creation, called "the waters above the firmament"; another, slightly different, kind of model environment called "the firmament," to model the earth and sky; and a third model environment, called "the waters under the firmament," which uses a simplified version of the earth model to develop the primary producers "before they were in the earth" (Genesis 2:5).

I call this early version of the earth described in Genesis 1:9–12 a simplified model because it had no star to make rain upon its surface, and according to the description, it only had one continent. Our earth has several continents, and it has had several continents through most of its geologic history.

Yet, while the "waters beneath the firmament" may have started as a simplified version of the model that we live in, there is still a lot that is happening in it. Matter appears here for the first time in creation, along with chemistry and the incredible, complex molecular biology of life: DNA, amino acids combined into proteins, metabolic pathways of proteins that build the cells of living organisms atom by atom "from the dust of the earth." Although they are not mentioned, bacteria are probably here in their thousands and millions of species, sharing a communal genome to provide the adaptability that they must have to survive and prosper in all the varied environments of the earth. Multicellular plants are here, with chemically based coordinate systems to map out the specialization of cells into tissues and large structures.

In so many ways, this "simplified" model is the heart of creation, the foundation layer that lets all the rest of life work.

The assumption that all of spacetime exists simultaneously from beginning to end tells us that the primary producer model also exists throughout all of time. It was not used briefly during the preparation for this creation and then discarded; it's still there, still modeling the primary producers, the bacteria and Protista that sustain life on earth, still daily providing us with the delicious fruits (literally) of God's generous providence.

The descriptions in Genesis 1:9–13 and Genesis 2:4–6 tell us that the mayim below the *raqiya* had plants sowing seed and trees bearing fruit. This implies that the primary producer model has the same millions and billions of years that science and natural philosophy see in our world. According to paleobotany, the study of plant fossils, and micropaleontology, the study of bacteria and Protista fossils, bacteria first showed up about 1800 MA (read more in *Microfossils*, 2005, by Armstrong and Brasier, and *Paleobotany*, 2009, by Taylor, Taylor, and Krings—an excellent and very thorough source for anyone interested in this fossil history). There are circumstantial indications of earlier bacterial life, but the Gunflint Chert in Canada, which has the oldest definite bacterial fossils, has a radiometric age of 1800 MA. Protista, single-celled eukaryote organisms, first definitely show up about 1200 MA in the form of *Bangiomorpha pubescens*, also in Canada. The oldest recognizable plant is *Baragwanathia longifora* at 421 MA. The Rhynie Chert in Scotland (407 MA) contains the first fungus in the known fossil record. The first plants with seeds show up about 391 MA. The first definite flowering plant fossil is *Archaefructus liaoningensis* at 125 MA.

(The dates quoted above are slightly different than dates for similar events quoted elsewhere in the book. The differences are due to the fog of paleontology. For many reasons there is often considerable time between the first *possible* appearance of a fossil category and the first *definite* appearance. The dates above are definite appearances. Some dates quoted elsewhere are for possible appearances.)

The image produced by our interpretational assumptions is that of a simplified version of a geologic model used for developing bacteria, Protista, and plants that persists for some part of the millions and billions of years in spacetime (still in its simple form) on day three of creation. The geologic model will get a lot more complex (still over the same millions and billions of years) when the big bang cosmology is added into the model on day four.

The Feynman-Stueckelberg view of time also provides us with a perspective for why the *raqiya* (the firmament) divides the *tehowm* (the deeps of the sea) into *mayim* (water) above and *mayim* below the *raqiya*. The *raqiya* apparently models the stars and galaxies, the astronomy of creation. As was mentioned earlier, science and natural philosophy tell us that the physical geology of the earth is probably part of the astronomical model in the *raqiya*. If the *mayim* "below" the *raqiya* models primary producers, bacteria, Protista, and plants, then the *mayim* "above" the *raqiya* might model the animals (coming later in creation).

In that case, huge amounts of information would need to continuously flow between the geologic model in the *raqiya* and the primary producer model in the *mayim* "below" the *raqiya*, as the geology sustains the plants and the plants alter the geology. There would also need to be a river of information flowing between the geologic *raqiya* and the *mayim* "above," as we and the animals all walk (and swim) the earth and change it.

If any of the above guesswork is even remotely true, it makes sense that the firmament would be placed to divide the waters from the waters; a creation model would work best if the geologic *raqiya* were in the middle, with an unobstructed flow of information to both of the biologic *mayim* models.

The geology of the primary producer model and the primary producers themselves all come into being via the creative term *amar* (to speak). My guess is, therefore, that the basics of geology and the basics of molecular biology were all planned before creation started and were programmed into the model on the third day. Looked at from a project perspective, that makes sense: the interactions between geology and the primary producers, the bottom layer of the food chain, is so essential, so fundamental for a creation filled with life, that they would have to be assured before the project could really start.

Genesis 1:14

"And God said, Let there be lights in the firmament of the heaven to divide the day from the night; let them be for signs, and for seasons, and for days, and years."

Hebrew:	**Strong's Biblical Usage or Gesenius' Lexicon:**
elohiym	rulers, judges, divine ones, angels, gods
amar	say, speak, utter
ma-owr	light source, luminary
raqiya	extended solid surface, flat expanse, solid firmament
shamayim	sky, heaven
badal	to divide, to separate, to divide into parts, to make a distinction
yowm	day (not night), day (twenty-four hours), days (time), time period
layil	night (not day), midnight, gloom (low light)
owth	sign, signal, distinguishing mark, flag, miracle, token
mow'ed	appointed place, appointed time, meeting
yowm	day (not night), day (twenty-four hours), days (time), time period
shaneh	year of time, year of age

Genesis 1:15

"And let them be for lights in the firmament of the heaven to give light upon the earth: and it was so."

Hebrew:	**Strong's Biblical Usage or Gesenius' Lexicon:**
ma'owr	light source, luminary
raqiya	extended solid surface, flat expanse, solid firmament
shamayim	sky, heaven

owr	(verb) to be light, to become light, to shine, to become bright
erets	whole earth, earth with inhabitants, inhabited land, territory, ground

Here, finally, is the big bang, the addition of matter into the spacetime model to form the stars and galaxies of the universe that we see around us. Matter that follows the distance and time previously stretched out for it in Genesis 1:4. Matter made of slight imbalances in the swarms of virtual particles that fill all of spacetime. Matter that is formed and changed by the probability amplitude interaction rules—the standard model of particle physics—set into spacetime in Genesis 1:3.

In keeping with the assumption that all of spacetime exists from beginning to end, what is added to creation here on day four is all of the millions and billions of years of the history of the matter universe, from the first, metal-poor galaxies that could not sustain life, to the world that we see around us today, to whatever fate lies in store for the universe when the sun and moon brighten and then go dark and the stars fall from the sky.

According to science and natural philosophy, one other thing added to creation on day four is the earth itself. It is formed from the solar system cloud; stratified into core, mantle, and crust; and covered with water by collisions with asteroids, comets, and meteorites from further out in the solar system. The churning of tectonic plates in the crust mixes water with rock to generate the geologic development of the continents with mountains, plains, and valleys.

Back in the *mayim* below the *raqiya*, the primary producer biologic model is now merged with the new geologic model to fill the seas of the newly added earth with bacteria and Protista plankton and to cover the terrain with grass, plants, and forests. The original, simplified model shifts to take on a form that is probably very similar to what we see around us today. At this point, the only thing missing is the larger animals.

Like the primary producer model, the basic astronomical/geologic model is brought into existence via the creative term *amar* (to say). The viewpoint here is the same as it was for the primary producers: the astronomy and geology are basic requirements for the sustenance of life in creation; they would have to have been worked out (at least as regards the basics) before the real action of creation could start.

Genesis 1:16

"And God made two great lights; the greater light to rule the day, and the lesser light to rule the night: he made the stars also."

Hebrew:	Strong's Biblical Usage or Gesenius' Lexicon:
elohiym	rulers, judges, divine ones, angels, gods
asah	to do, to accomplish, to fashion, to make
shenayim	two, second, double, both
qadowl	great, large, many, intense, loud, important, distinguished
ma-owr	light source, luminary
qadowl	great, large, many, intense, loud, important, distinguished
ma-owr	light source, luminary
memshalah	rule, realm, dominion, domain
yowm	day (not night), day (twenty-four hours), days (time), time period
qatan	young, small, insignificant, unimportant, less, least
ma-owr	light source, luminary
memshalah	rule, realm, dominion, domain
layil	night (not day), midnight, gloom (low light)
kowkab	star, stars

Genesis 1:17

"And God set them in the firmament of the heaven to give light upon the earth,"

Hebrew:	Strong's Biblical Usage or Gesenius' Lexicon:
elohiym	rulers, judges, divine ones, angels, gods
nathan	to give, to put, to set

raqiya	extended solid surface, flat expanse, solid firmament
shamayim	sky, heaven
owr	(verb) to be light, to become light, to shine, to become bright
erets	whole earth, earth with inhabitants, inhabited land, territory, ground

Genesis 1:18

"And to rule over the day and over the night, and to divide the light from the darkness: and God saw that it was good."

Hebrew:	**Strong's Biblical Usage or Gesenius' Lexicon:**
mashal	to make like, to assimilate, to lead, to rule, to have dominion, to reign
yowm	day (not night), day (twenty-four hours), days (time), time period
layil	night (not day), midnight, gloom (low light)
badal	to divide, to separate, to divide into parts, to make a distinction
owr	(noun) light everywhere diffused, light cast, not a source, daylight, light of sun, moon, stars
choshek	darkness, obscurity, lightless
elohiym	rulers, judges, divine ones, angels, gods
ra'ah	to see, to perceive, to have vision, to be seen
towb	good, pleasant, agreeable

Genesis 1:19

"And the evening and the morning were the fourth day."

Hebrew:	Strong's Biblical Usage or Gesenius' Lexicon:
ereb	evening, sunset, night (not day)
boqer	morning, sunrise, break of day
rebiy'iy	fourth, four square, fourth part
yowm	day (not night), day (twenty-four hours), days (time), time period

The same day of creation, more astronomy, more lights in the sky to give light upon the earth. This time though, the creative term is different. The concept of lights for the surface of the earth was expressed as *amar* (to say). The particular lights themselves are *asah* (to make). Guessing at the meaning of these terms within our interpretation, I would say the big bang cosmology was developed before the start of creation and only programmed into the model on day four. The particular results of the big bang, the sun and moon and actual stars that we see, are brought into detailed existence during the creation process.

As has already been noted, for reasons that we can only guess at, the astronomy of this universe appears to be the result of a Monte Carlo model—a model where what happens is based purely on random events. The apparently random nature of the astronomy of the universe, and by implication the geology of the earth, might provide a clue as to why the universe needs to be so very large.

Astrophysics tells us that planets with the right elemental composition, the right size, the right temperature, the right radiation environment, and the right orbital stability to continuously support life for the millions and billions of years that are apparently needed to build a vast, complex ecology like the one we see here on the earth, are very rare. In a Monte Carlo model, a model based on a purely random progression of events, there might not be even one in every galaxy that comes along.

One of the key prerequisites for life is the development and distribution of high atomic-number metals in the gases between the stars, gases that form solar systems and planets like ours. Galaxies taken as a whole tend to produce metals in proportion to their luminosity; the same nuclear processes that produce metals also produce abundant light. Our galaxy, the Milky Way, exhibits luminosity in the top 2 percent of the galaxies that we can see. It therefore probably also has metal concentrations that are in the top few percent of all galaxies, and it might have been one of the first galaxies in the universe to produce a suitable planetary environment.

If we assume that God seeded life on the first or one of the first suitable planets that became available within his model, simple math implies that the universe is about fifty times larger than it actually needs to be. In a Monte Carlo model, where results will depend on the statistical distribution of purely random events, a model that is fifty times larger than strictly necessary has at least two features: first, the probability that a suitable planet will appear at all is very nearly certain (it would be really irritating to have to do the whole thing over again because there weren't any suitable planets). Next, in a larger model, chance dictates an assortment of planets to choose from: this makes it much more likely that there will be something nice available, instead of having to make do with whatever comes along.

Genesis 1:20

"And God said, Let the waters bring forth abundantly the moving creature that hath life, and fowl that may fly above the earth in the firmament of the heaven."

Hebrew:	Strong's Biblical Usage or Gesenius' Lexicon:
elohiym	rulers, judges, divine ones, angels, gods
amar	say, speak, utter
mayim	water
sharats	to creep or crawl (like a reptile), to swarm like animals that creep, to multiply abundantly
sherets	reptiles, animals that creep, animals that swarm (insects, reptiles)
nephesh	breath, the soul, the mind, emotion, passion, living being
chay	living, alive
owph	wing, birds (winged animals), winged insects
uwph	cover (as with feathers), to fly, to fly away

al	upon, above, over, in addition to, on the ground of, concerning
erets	whole earth, earth with inhabitants, inhabited land, territory, ground
paniym	face, presence, person, surface, in front of
raqiya	extended solid surface, flat expanse, solid firmament
shamayim	sky, heaven

Genesis 1:21

"And God created great whales, and every living creature that moveth,
which the waters brought forth abundantly, after their kind,
and every winged fowl after his kind: and God saw that it was good."

Hebrew:	**Strong's Biblical Usage or Gesenius' Lexicon:**
elohiym	rulers, judges, divine ones, angels, gods
bara	to cut, to make by cutting, shape, fashion, create, make fat
gadowl	great, large, many, intense, loud, important, distinguished
tanniyn	great serpent, sea monster, great fish, dragon, crocodile
chay	living, alive
nephesh	breath, the soul, the mind, emotion, passion, living being
ramas	to creep (move on more than two legs), to crawl, to move lightly, to glide (like a snake or swimming animal)
mayim	water
sharats	to creep or crawl (like a reptile), to swarm like animals that creep, to multiply abundantly
miyn	kind of animal, kind of plant
kanaph	wing (as a bird wing), edge or extremity

owph	wing, birds (winged animals), winged insects
miyn	kind of animal, kind of plant
elohiym	rulers, judges, divine ones, angels, gods
ra'ah	to see, to perceive, to have vision, to be seen
towb	good, pleasant, agreeable

Genesis 1:22

"And God blessed them, saying, be fruitful and multiply, and fill the waters in the seas, and let fowl multiply in the earth."

Hebrew:	Strong's Biblical Usage or Gesenius' Lexicon:
elohiym	rulers, judges, divine ones, angels, gods
barak	to kneel down, to cause to kneel, to praise God, to ask God for blessing, to bless
amar	say, speak, utter
parah	to bear (carry), to bear fruit, to be fruitful, to bear young, to cause to be fruitful
rabah	to become numerous, to multiply, to become great, to make large, to increase
male	to fill, to make full, to satisfy
mayim	water
yam	sea, lake, large river
owph	wing, birds (winged animals), winged insects
rabah	to become numerous, to multiply, to become great, to make large, to increase
erets	whole earth, earth with inhabitants, inhabited land, territory, ground

Genesis 1:23

"And the evening and the morning were the fifth day."

Hebrew:	**Strong's Biblical Usage or Gesenius' Lexicon:**
ereb	evening, sunset, night (not day)
boqer	morning, sunrise, break of day
chamiyshiy	fifth
yowm	day (not night), day (twenty-four hours), days (time), time period

Genesis 1:20–23 describes the introduction of larger animals into the oceans and sky of the creation model. The introduction of marine animals in the sequence of events in Genesis 1 matches what the fossil record tells us both chronologically and developmentally. Chronological sequence is, of course, unimportant for an interpretation that considers each addition to the model as happening throughout all of the millions and billions of years in our time. But the fossil record also indicates that the first land animals were likely derived from very similar creatures living in the seas. The earliest land animal fossil currently known is *Pneumodesmus newmani,* a millipede radiometrically dated to 425 MA.[1] *Pneumodesmus newmani* is structurally similar to aquatic millipedes living at the time but has modifications (spiracle structures) that allow it to breathe air. Most land animal fossils show descent sequences that originate with aquatic creatures.

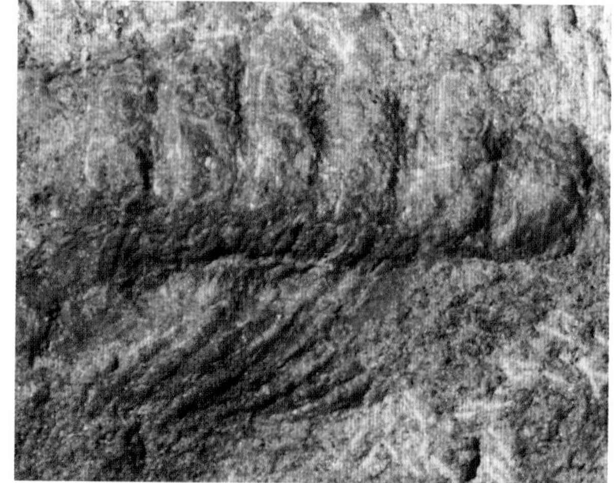

Fig. 129. Earliest Land Animal Fossil

Science and natural philosophy tell us that the development of the millions of species of living organisms that we see now in the world around us tends to follow the pattern set by *Pneumodesmus newmani*:

1 "Pneumodesmus." Retrieved c. 2014 from https://en.wikipedia.org/wiki/Pneumodesmus.

new species and new capabilities are often derived from minor changes to previously existing organisms. "Minor change" here is very much a relative term: aquatic and terrestrial millipedes may look very similar to an untrained eye, but the differences in genetic expression between water-breathing and air-breathing species—that is, the different embryonic development sequences of cell specialization based on chemical coordinate systems—are huge. Nevertheless, much of the genetic code for the various types of millipede is the same.

The overall picture for the development of life on earth that we get from science and natural philosophy is pretty much exactly what Genesis 1 tells us (from a certain perspective): the fundamental kinds of life (bacteria, Protista, multicellular animal phyla, and multicellular plant divisions) appear suddenly in the fossil record and then "multiply over the earth" with the incremental development of related species.

Genesis 1:20–23 does include events that were widely separated in our time: larger sea creatures first show up in the Cambrian Explosion around 542 MA. These were large compared to bacteria and Protista; they were still small by today's standards. Really large sea "monsters" appear later: plesiosaurs, for example, began leaving fossils around 205 MA. Definite avian fossils (birds) don't appear in the fossil record until 160 MA or so.[2]

In keeping with the assumption that time is as described by Feynman-Stueckelberg, what appears in the model on day five is not just a few, original sea creatures and birds but all of the sea creatures that swim the seas and all of the birds that fly over the earth throughout all of our time.

The creative terms used for aquatic animals and birds are both *amar* (to say) and *bara* (to cut). According to our definitions for those terms, the various kinds of animals were planned before creation started and required the allocation of dedicated computational capability. In this case, the *mayim* (water) above the *raqiya* (firmament) seems like it might be a candidate for the computational environment.

2 "Bird." Retrieved c. 2014 from https://en.wikipedia.org/wiki/Bird.

Genesis 1:24

"And God said, Let the earth bring forth the living creature after his kind, cattle after their kind, and everything that creepeth upon the earth after his kind: and it was so."

Hebrew:	Strong's Biblical Usage or Gesenius' Lexicon:
elohiym	rulers, judges, divine ones, angels, gods
amar	say, speak, utter
erets	whole earth, earth with inhabitants, inhabited land, territory, ground
yatsa	to go out, to come out, to exit, to go forth
chay	living, alive
nephesh	breath, the soul, the mind, emotion, passion, living being
miyn	kind of animal, kind of plant
behemah	large beasts (unable to talk), all large beasts, cattle (domestic beasts), wild beasts
remes	a reptile or reptiles, an animal that walks like a reptile, creeping things, moving things, gliding animal (snake or fish)
chay	living, alive
erets	whole earth, earth with inhabitants, inhabited land, territory, ground
miyn	kind of animal, kind of plant

Genesis 1:25

"And God made the beast of the earth after his kind, and cattle after their kind, and everything that creepeth upon the earth after his kind: and God saw that it was good."

Hebrew:	Strong's Biblical Usage or Gesenius' Lexicon:
elohiym	rulers, judges, divine ones, angels, gods

asah	to do, to accomplish, to fashion, to make
chay	living, alive
erets	whole earth, earth with inhabitants, inhabited land, territory, ground
miyn	kind of animal, kind of plant
behemah	large beasts (unable to talk), all large beasts, cattle (domestic beasts), wild beasts
miyn	kind of animal, kind of plant
remes	a reptile or reptiles, an animal that walks like a reptile, creeping things, moving things, gliding animal (snake or fish)
adamah	earth (soil), ground, field, land, a plot of land
miyn	kind of animal, kind of plant
elohiym	rulers, judges, divine ones, angels, gods
ra'ah	to see, to perceive, to have vision, to be seen
towb	good, pleasant, agreeable

Because science and natural philosophy tell us that land animals were incrementally derived from animals in the sea, it should not have been necessary to *bara* (partition) the *mayim* (water) when the land animals show up on day six; any required partitioning was already done. This is confirmed in Genesis 1:24–25: the creative terms used for land animals are *amar* (to say) and *asah* (to make). Land animals were conceptually planned before the start of creation with the specific creatures that we see derived by the creation model; both Genesis 1 and science and natural philosophy tell us exactly the same thing.

Once again, as with the sea animals and birds, what is added to the creation model here on day six is not just a few original species of land animal; what is added to the model is all of the land animals that live in creation throughout all of time: from *Pneumodesmus newmani*, to dinosaurs, to the animals now sharing this earth with us, to whatever animals will be creeping upon the earth at the end of time.

Genesis 1:26

"And God said, Let us make man in our image, after our likeness: and let them have dominion over the fish of the sea, and over the fowl of the air, and over the cattle, and over all the earth, and over every creeping thing that creepeth upon the earth."

Hebrew:	**Strong's Biblical Usage or Gesenius' Lexicon:**
elohiym	rulers, judges, divine ones, angels, gods
amar	say, speak, utter
asah	to do, to accomplish, to fashion, to make
adam	man, mankind, first man (Adam)
tselem	shadow, likeness, image
demuwth	appearance, model, pattern, likeness, image, similitude
radah	to tread with feet (like pressing wine), to subjugate, to rule, to dominate, to take possession of
dagah	fish
yam	sea, lake, large river
owph	wing, birds (winged animals), winged insects
shamayim	sky, heaven
behemah	large beasts (unable to talk), all large beasts, cattle (domestic beasts), wild beasts
erets	whole earth, earth with inhabitants, inhabited land, territory, ground
remes	a reptile or reptiles, an animal that walks like a reptile, creeping things, moving things, gliding animal (snake or fish)
ramas	to creep (move on more than two legs), to crawl, to move lightly, to glide (like a snake or swimming animal)
erets	whole earth, earth with inhabitants, inhabited land, territory, ground

Genesis 1:27

"So God created man in his own image, in the image of God created he him; male and female created he them."

Hebrew:	Strong's Biblical Usage or Gesenius' Lexicon:
elohiym	rulers, judges, divine ones, angels, gods
bara	to cut, to make by cutting, shape, fashion, create, make fat
adam	man, mankind, first man (Adam)
tselem	shadow, likeness, image
tselem	shadow, likeness, image
elohiym	rulers, judges, divine ones, angels, gods
bara	to cut, to make by cutting, shape, fashion, create, make fat
zakar	male (of humans or animals)
neqebah	female (of humans or animals)
bara	to cut, to make by cutting, shape, fashion, create, make fat

And here we are. According to the assumptions of this interpretation, Genesis 1:26–27 does not just describe the introduction of the first few human beings, it applies to all of us: all of the 100 billion or so of us who have ever, are now, or ever will be living, breathing people walking this creation. Just a tiny example demonstrating that the description in Genesis 1 applies to events over extended periods of our time: men and women are here described as being made at the same "time" on day six. Yet Genesis 2:21–22 describes woman as being made later, after Adam had been in Eden for a while.

Genesis 1 applies all three of the creative terms to us: *amar* (to say), *asah* (to make), and *bara* (to cut). According to our assumed definitions for those terms, *amar* implies that we were planned for and prepared before the creation model was started. This is amply confirmed in Scripture; it often speaks of God's plans for us, made before we were born.

Asah implies that we were developed as part of the creation model. Science and natural philosophy confirm that we were, like many other inhabitants of this creation, incrementally derived from creatures that probably already existed in the creation model. Scripture tells us that we are made in the image of God *(tselem,* like his shadow), and so we are. But the guts of the image, the internal working bits, are very definitely derived from our cousins among the other animals. Our DNA code, for example, is 72 to 97 percent identical to the genetic code of chimpanzees. We share a lot of our DNA sequence with other primates as well. Assuming that Genesis 1 is referring to our species, *Homo sapiens,* natural philosophy tells us that there were other, very similar species here in the creation before us: *Homo erectus, Homo ergaster,* and *Homo neanderthalensis,* for example. Genetic material has been recovered from *Homo neanderthalensis* that is 99.88 percent identical to ours.

Bara would mean that modeling space was allocated for us at the time we were added to the creation model. That makes sense from a scientific standpoint: it would take a lot of computer resources to model 100 billion or so conscious minds to the level of detail that we experience. The only hitch in our interpretation, though, is that we are fresh out of *mayim* (water). All of the modeling space described in Genesis 1, the *mayim* above and below the *raqiya* (firmament), have been accounted for with the primary producer model and the multicellular animal model. Providentially, Scripture provides an answer: we are described as living forever; the creation model of the *raqiya* and the two *mayims* is temporary. Computationally speaking, we might not really be a part of the creation model; we only interact with it.

The gospel of Mark recounts an event that may be compatible with the idea that our conscious minds have a somewhat flexible connection to this reality:

> *"And he cometh to Bethsaida; they bring a blind man unto him, and besought him to touch him.*
>
> *And he took the blind man by the hand, and led him out of the town; and when he had spit on his eyes, and put his hands upon him, he asked him if he saw aught.*
>
> *And he looked up and said, I see men as trees walking.*
>
> *After that, he put his hands again upon his eyes, and made him look up; and he was restored and saw every man clearly."*—Mark 8:22–25

This is a very interesting little bit of Scripture; it almost seems as if our Lord made a mistake. But our Lord is God and does not make mistakes. Though many commentators think the man's partially restored eyesight was simply blurry—that he could make out vertical figures but not features or shape—it seems to me that his response might indicate he saw people clearly, but he saw them as outlandishly tall. One way to look at this event is that the blind man temporarily saw through the eyes of a much smaller creature, a lizard or a mouse perhaps, making the men look very tall. After Jesus healed him the second time, he saw through his own eyes.

Some cases in medical history may add some background to this particular miracle. When people who have been blind from birth first acquire sight, it often takes them some time and practice to be able to compose an understandable image from what they see. For me, the most impressive feature of some of Jesus' healing miracles is the instantaneous adaptation of the healed individual to them. The healing of the blind, for example, includes suddenly imparting all of the visual memories and decoding procedures that we use to draw a sensible image from the light captured by our eyes; the healed are able to understand what they see from the instant of healing. Similarly, when the man who was crippled from birth had his legs healed, he also received all of the coordination and balance that we normally spend years learning as babies; he could walk from the instant of healing.

If the blind man in Bethsaida actually did see through the eyes of a small creature before seeing through his own eyes, it must, I think, have been deliberate, not any kind of a mistake. In order to see understandable images, he would first have needed the visual memories of the small creature to decode the sensory information from its eyes; he would then have needed his own visual memories to decode the images of his own eyes. There is a lot of work going on behind the scenes in this incident.

If all of this is correct, then Jesus may possibly have been showing us something about the connection between creation and our conscious minds. He may have been showing us that we are, in a sense, plugged in to this creation, not necessarily a part of it.

Genesis 1:28

"And God blessed them, and God said unto them, Be fruitful, and multiply, and replenish the earth, and subdue it: and have dominion over the fish of the sea, and over the fowl of the air, and over every living thing that moveth upon the earth."

Hebrew:	**Strong's Biblical Usage or Gesenius' Lexicon:**
elohiym	rulers, judges, divine ones, angels, gods
barak	to kneel down, to cause to kneel, to praise God, to ask God for blessing, to bless
elohiym	rulers, judges, divine ones, angels, gods
amar	say, speak, utter
parah	to bear (as in carry), to bear fruit, to be fruitful, to bear young, to cause to be fruitful
rabah	to become numerous, to multiply, to become great, to make large, to increase
male	to fill, to make full, to satisfy
erets	whole earth, earth with inhabitants, inhabited land, territory, ground
kabash	to trample with the feet, to subject or subdue to oneself, to force a woman
radah	to tread with feet (like pressing wine), to subjugate, to rule, to dominate, to take possession of
dagah	fish
yam	sea, lake, large river
owph	wing, birds (winged animals), winged insects
shamayim	sky, heaven
chay	living, alive

ramas	to creep (move on more than two legs), to crawl, to move lightly, to glide (like a snake or swimming animal)
erets	whole earth, earth with inhabitants, inhabited land, territory, ground

And here we are mentioned again. The sun and moon *mashal* (lead) the day and night. Our relationship to the creation is *radah* and *kabash,* oppress and rape. This is one of the places in Genesis 1 where the meaning of the original Hebrew does not really come across in most of the English translations. The King James Version of the Bible (and, apparently, most commentaries), for example, portrays the relationship of mankind to creation as a grant of authority: a decree by God that mankind is to rule over creation. The flavor in the Hebrew is, perhaps, more like a prophecy. Once we were added to the model, once all of the 100 billion or so of us who live in creation through all of time were added on day six, the whole of our impact on creation would have been laid out before God for him to see.

> *"And God saw that the wickedness of man was great in the earth, and that every imagination of the thoughts of his heart was only evil continually. And it repented the* Lord *that he had made man on the earth, and it grieved him at his heart."*—Genesis 6:5–6

Earlier I mentioned that we may have been added to creation right at the end, in the last few thousand years before the big crunch. This passage, I think, supports that notion. God knew what impact we would have on creation and tucked us in at the end to minimize the damage.

Genesis 1:29

"And God said, Behold, I have given you every herb bearing seed, which is upon the face of all the earth, and every tree, in the which is the fruit of a tree bearing seed; to you it shall be for meat."

Hebrew:	Strong's Biblical Usage or Gesenius' Lexicon:
elohiym	rulers, judges, divine ones, angels, gods
amar	say, speak, utter
hinneh	behold!, lo!, see!
nathan	to give, to put, to set
eseb	mature plant, edible plant
zara	to sow seed, to produce seed
zera	seed, sowing, children
paniym	face, presence, person, surface, in front of
erets	whole earth, earth with inhabitants, inhabited land, territory, ground
ets	tree, wood, timber, stick
periy	fruit, produce (of the ground), children, fruit of actions
ets	tree, wood, timber, stick
zara	to sow seed, to produce seed
zera	seed, sowing, children
hayah	to be, to become, to exist, to come into being
okiah	food

Genesis 1:30

"And to every beast of the earth, and to every fowl of the air, and to every thing that creepeth upon the earth, wherein there is life, I have given every green herb for meat: and it was so."

Hebrew:	Strong's Biblical Usage or Gesenius' Lexicon:
chay	living, alive
erets	whole earth, earth with inhabitants, inhabited land, territory, ground
owph	wing, birds (winged animals), winged insects
shamayim	sky, heaven
ramas	to creep (move on more than two legs), to crawl, to move lightly, to glide (like a snake or swimming animal)
erets	whole earth, earth with inhabitants, inhabited land, territory, ground
chay	living, alive
nephesh	breath, the soul, the mind, emotion, passion, living being
yereq	green (of vegetation), greenness, green plants, greenery
eseb	mature plant, edible plant
okiah	food

Genesis 1:31

"And God saw every thing that he had made, and behold, it was very good. And the evening and the morning were the sixth day."

Hebrew:	Strong's Biblical Usage or Gesenius' Lexicon:
elohiym	rulers, judges, divine ones, angels, gods
ra'ah	to see, to perceive, to have vision, to be seen

asher	who, which, that
asah	to do, to accomplish, to fashion, to make
mə'od	strength, force, strongly, very, exceedingly
towb	good, pleasant, agreeable
ereb	evening, sunset, night (not day)
boqer	morning, sunrise, break of day
shishshiy	sixth, sixth part
yowm	day (not night), day (twenty-four hours), days (time), time period

Philosophy from Genesis 1

What we have just seen is a possible interpretation of Genesis 1 based on four assumptions:

- The Scripture is literally true.
- Science and natural philosophy are mostly correct in what they tell us about the history and nature of the universe.
- We live in an eternalist reality: past, present, and future all physically, simultaneously exist.
- We live in a reality that is possibly based in mathematics; that may be a computational model or something like a computational model.

It is possible, using these four assumptions, to craft a story that fits the wording and description given in Genesis 1 pretty well. It is important, though, to remember that it is just a story; I cannot begin to make truth claims for this interpretation. If the whole thing seems implausible, something fetched from very far away indeed, then, dear reader, you fare well, because that is exactly what it is.

It is implausible, but it is not impossible.

The important point about this story is not that it is entirely or even mostly true—no one understands enough either about physics or about Scripture to know what the truth is. The important point is that it is possible to craft plausible hypotheses that are compatible with both Scripture and science (and natural philosophy). As long as it is possible for a single, plausible hypothesis to be compatible with both Scripture and science, there is not necessarily any conflict between them. They agree; they can both be true.

While Genesis 1 is (in my opinion) a good fit between physics and Scripture, as I've mentioned before, there are many places in Scripture where the fit is not as good. Our interpretational framework might fit quite well with the physics, but it is, I suspect, too simple to be a complete match for the Scripture.

Most importantly, it conflicts with the omniscience of God. One implication of the story told here is that God would only have become completely aware of the full repercussions of an action (such as the creation of mankind) after the action was complete in the creation model. A few bits of Scripture might imply the same (such as Genesis 6:5–6, quoted earlier), but there are many more that speak of predestination and of God knowing the details of our existence before we were made. On the whole, the idea that God was not completely aware of what was going to happen in his creation is almost certainly wrong.

Another problem is in the genealogies of Genesis 5 and 11. There are two places where a classical physics interpretation of Genesis conflicts with the timescales derived in science and natural philosophy: Genesis 1, with the six days of creation set against the millions and billions of years of astrophysics, geophysics, and geology, and the genealogies, where the times since the creation of Adam and the flood are in conflict with the timescales of archeology, paleontology, and especially physical anthropology.

The Feynman-Stueckelberg view of time as all simultaneously existing, and the consequent reinterpretation of Genesis 1 as describing events that occur throughout all of our time, does offer a fairly clear resolution to the conflict between the six days in God's time of Genesis 1 and the 14 billion or so years in our time deduced from the observations of science. Although the times are much shorter, the conflict regarding Adam and Noah is more difficult to resolve. The genealogies in Genesis 5 and 11 give times that add up to approximately six thousand years since Adam and Eve were in Eden and four thousand years since Noah and the flood. Roughly the same events have arguably occurred in the natural history of our world, but they were much longer ago than six and four thousand years. In natural philosophy, Adam and Eve lived between one hundred thousand and two hundred thousand years ago. The scriptural flood most likely happened about fifty thousand to seventy thousand years ago.

It is possible to apply the same story used in Genesis 1 to the genealogies in Genesis 5 and 11: the events in the Bible are told from God's perspective, so the times listed in Genesis 5 and 11 are in his time, not in our time. Just as the billions of years of geologic time could have happened during the six days of creation, the hundreds of thousands of years of our natural history on this earth may have taken only ~6,000 years in God's time.

Maybe. But although Genesis 5 can be made to fit, for reasons mostly scriptural, the Feynman-Stueckelberg story does not really fit in Genesis 11.

First, the times since Eden and the flood from the perspective of science and natural philosophy:

Scripture at least implies that Adam and Eve may have been the first *Homo sapiens*:

> *"Unto the woman he said, I will greatly multiply thy sorrow and thy conception; in sorrow thou shalt bring forth children; and thy desire shall be to thy husband, and he shall rule over thee."*—Genesis 3:16

The word translated as "sorrow" refers to the pain of childbirth; *Homo sapiens* have much larger skulls than preceding species of genus *Homo* and would be harder to bear.

Archeology and DNA molecular clock analysis place the first genetic *Homo sapiens* as living about one hundred thousand to two hundred thousand years ago depending on exactly how fossils are assigned to species. Molecular clock analysis, which supports the two hundred thousand year end of the range, basically counts up the number of DNA sequence changes that accumulate over time through DNA copying errors and divides the number of genetic differences by the average DNA replication error rate. Molecular clocks have debatable accuracy, partly because DNA error rates are not even remotely constant; they are known to change by orders of magnitude (factors of ten) for some organisms depending on environmental conditions. Archeology, which is probably a bit more reliable in this case, becomes conclusive at the lower estimate for the age of *Homo sapiens* of about one hundred thousand years or so (based on radiometric dating).

The case is similar for Noah and the flood. Genetic analysis and archeology both indicate that the number of human beings was probably reduced to a handful of individuals about fifty thousand to seventy thousand years ago (the usual term is "human population bottleneck"). The official scientific estimate for the population at the bottleneck is a few hundred to a few thousand persons; in Scripture, the number is eight. Mankind subsequently spreads out over the earth from a single location somewhere in southern Africa.

Human population genetics, the study of genetic relationships between groups of people, is most often based on the similarities and differences in selected parts of the human genetic DNA sequence. The two most commonly used gene sequences for human population relationships are Y chromosomes and mitochondrial DNA. Y chromosomes pass strictly from father to son; women do not have them at all. Mitochondrial DNA is present in both sexes but is always inherited from the mother. One reason that Y chromosomes and mitochondrial DNA are favored for molecular clock studies is that neither one participates in the genetic recombination (gene swapping) that is a normal part of sexual reproduction; their DNA sequences are more stable than other genes.

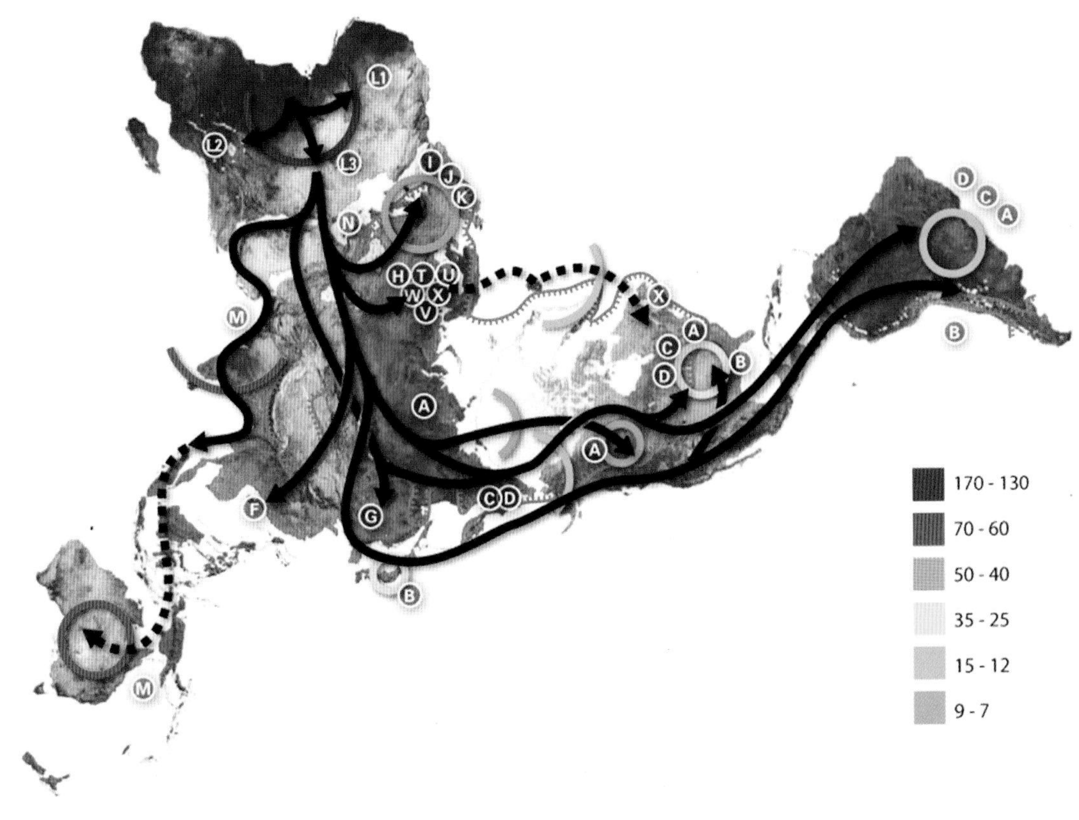

Fig. 130. Human Migration Routes Based on Mitochondrial DNA

The migration chart on the previous page is based on mitochondrial DNA. The colored circles represent estimated arrival dates (in thousands of years ago); the letters represent characteristic sequences in mitochondrial DNA. Y chromosome analysis gives a slightly different picture of gene distributions and arrival times. Other gene sequences (not mitochondrial DNA or Y chromosome) give a wide variety of dates and population relationships. That is another of the reasons that the validity of molecular clock analysis is questionable: the results are often inconsistent depending on which gene sequence is studied. Geneticists mostly agree to use one carefully selected gene sequence for descent tree and molecular clock analysis, because that particular sequence gives results that they like. Molecular clock analysis is more in the natural philosophy realm than it is technically science.

Incidentally, at the time of the human population bottleneck in Africa fifty thousand to seventy thousand years ago, there was one Y chromosome (male) DNA sequence and three mitochondrial (female) DNA sequences in the population. Scripture tells us that the human population of the ark was Noah and his three sons, who would have shared the same Y chromosome, and their four wives. Perhaps two of the wives were related to each other. Or perhaps Mrs. Noah did not have any female children after the flood.

Also incidentally, the human population bottleneck roughly coincides with the start of the Wurm ice age (our last glacial period) about seventy thousand years ago. I mention this because some of the classical physics analyses of Scripture suggest that the flood could have triggered an ice age if conditions were right, which they were at that time. (The important conditions in this case are solar radiation intensity and variations in the earth's orbit.) The scriptural description of the flood would make more physical sense if it, too, were associated with an icy sort of event: Genesis 7:19–20 describes the waters of the flood covering the highest hills by twenty feet or so. Mount Everest is 29,029 feet above sea level, so a literal interpretation of the scriptural description implies that the waters of the flood were five and a half miles deep. High mountains get covered with ice and snow all the time; there is nothing unusual about it. If the flood was accompanied by a sudden drop in temperature (as is physically likely), mankind could have been terminated with an efficient application of water in the form of ice and snow.

Scripture, however, does not support the ice age interpretation at all. The waters of the flood are described as *mayim,* liquid water. Hebrew for ice is *qerach;* snow is *sheleg*. If ice and snow were present in significant amounts, or if it got really cold, the extremely detailed description of the flood would probably have mentioned it. As one of my professors used to comment on test problems, "Nice try, zero."

Even taking the low ends of the ranges estimated by science and natural philosophy, the times are one hundred thousand years or so since Adam and Eve were in Eden and about fifty thousand years since the scriptural flood. Again, the scriptural timescale is much shorter. The genealogies listed in the King James Version plot out as shown in the figure below. Lifetimes are shown up to the birth of Abram, which is historically reckoned to have been about 1000 to 2000 BC, or roughly three to four thousand years ago.

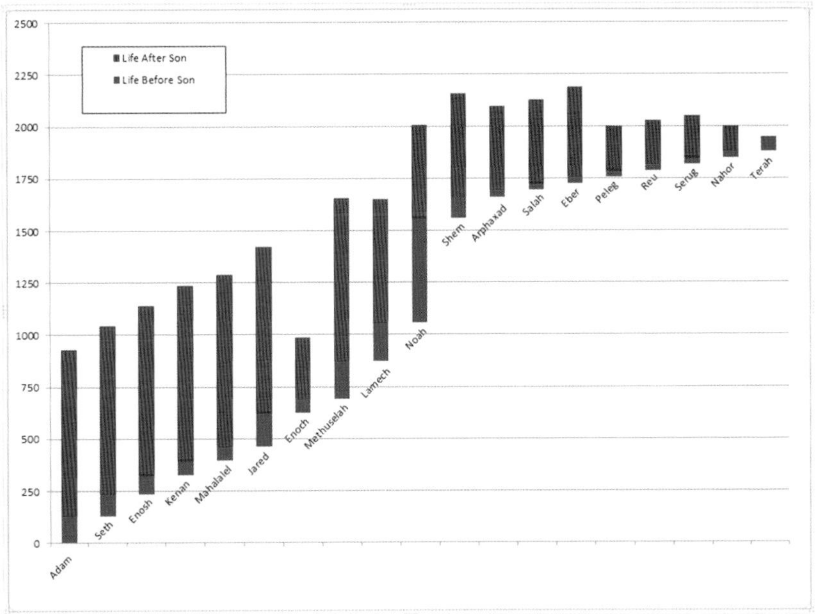

The flood happened two years before the birth of Arpahaxad, still about 3000 to 4000 years ago. Adam and Eve lived in Eden about 1800 years prior to that, or about 4800 to 5800 years ago.

Feynman-Stueckelberg can be applied to the genealogies by assuming that the times listed in Scripture are, like the six days of creation, in God's time, not in our time. In that case, the years of the lifetimes given in Scripture don't have any relationship to times that we might measure at all. The people listed in the genealogies would live approximately simultaneously (from God's perspective), and the times listed in Scripture would represent computational times needed to model their lives, not the lengths of the lives themselves. Under that assumption, the lifetimes would stack up

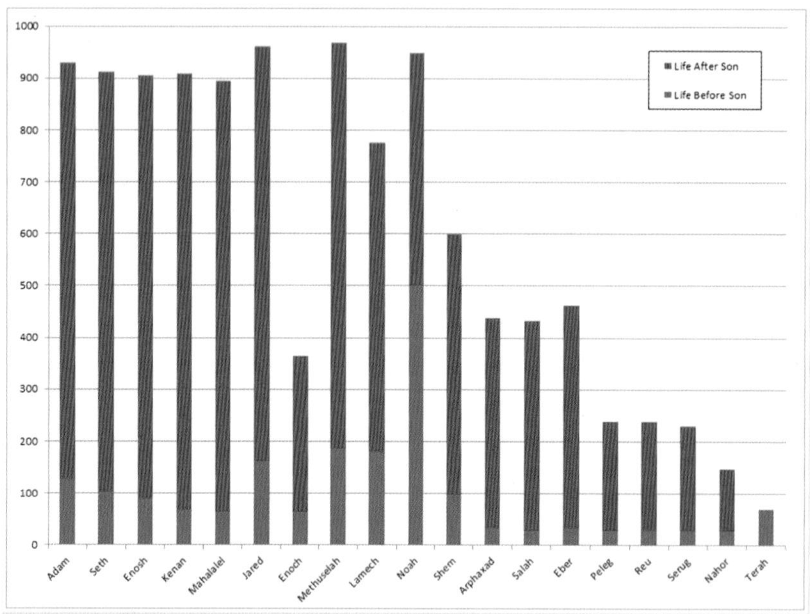

more like the figure above than like the chronological sequence shown on page 297.

But there are a couple of small problems with applying a computational time interpretation to the genealogies in Scripture. These problems don't definitely rule out the possibility that the years in the genealogies are in God's time, not in our time, but they make it hard to support. In particular, Scripture makes it hard to support.

In Genesis 1, every part of the Hebrew description of creation can be aligned with a consistent story derived from modern physics. In fact, there are elements of the description that only make physical sense in the context of a story pretty much like the one given here: mornings and evenings that occur before the sun and the stars exist; events described as happening in a single "day" that were spread out over millions of years in our world; etc.

The Hebrew in the genealogies, on the other hand, is just a plain recitation of births, deaths, and numbers of years; it is very much like the English translations have it. There is almost nothing in them that would indicate even circumstantially that the years described did not happen in our time. The only possible exception is the reference to the division of the earth in Genesis 10:25.

> *"And unto Eber were born two sons: the name of one was Peleg; for in his days was the earth divided; and his brother's name was Joktan."*—Genesis 10:25

This division might possibly refer to the covering of some or all of the land bridges that existed during the peak of the last ice age about twenty thousand years ago. The sea level dropped significantly (about four hundred feet) during the last ice age and exposed dry land to connect several areas that are currently separated by ocean: Siberia to Alaska, Great Britain to mainland Europe, Spain to Morocco, and several others. Those bridges were covered by ocean and the "earth was divided" when the glaciers of the ice age melted.

Next is the issue of the lengths of lifetimes for the people listed in the genealogies. The nine-hundred-year lifetimes listed already seem unreasonably long to us with our threescore and ten. In order for the ten generations from Adam to Noah to span fifty thousand years of chronological time in our world, those people would each have to have lived for several thousands of years. The same would need to be true for the generations between Noah and Abram.

Such long lives might be conceptually possible before the flood; a lifetime of even nine hundred years indicates that people in those days did not age the way we do. The fossil record for anatomically modern *Homo sapiens* does not conflict with this perspective; it doesn't necessarily support the idea, but it does not currently rule it out. Very few fossils have been found for humans in that particular time period (two hundred thousand to fifty thousand years ago; see Stanford, Allen, and Anton, 2013, *Biological Anthropology*). One possible reason for the lack of fossils is that not very many people died. Fossils are much more common for preceding species (*Homo erectus*, the archaic *Homo sapiens* group of species; and *Homo neanderthalensis*) and for *Homo sapiens* after the bottleneck.

Such long lives after the flood, however, are contrary to Scripture. God put a limit on the lives of humans before the flood in Genesis 6:3:

> *"And the Lord said, My spirit shall not always strive with man, for that he also is flesh, yet his days shall be a hundred and twenty years."*—Genesis 6:3

The genealogies of Genesis 11, the descendants of Noah's son Shem, confirm that lifetimes (if they are lifetimes) became much shorter after the flood.

If we assume despite all these issues that the times given in the genealogies are computational durations in God's time, we run into a similar sort of problem with the computational times themselves. Genesis 1 reports that all of creation was modeled in just six days. In the interpretation suggested here, that includes development and implementation of the physics model on day one, the organization of the computational space into structures to support the creation model on day two, modeling all of the primary producers (bacteria, protozoa, and plants) throughout all of time on day three, modeling all of the inanimate matter interactions in the universe throughout all of time on day four, modeling all of the multicellular animals in the seas and all of the birds throughout all of time on day five, and modeling all of the multicellular animals living on land throughout all of time plus organizing the computational environment to model 100 billion or so conscious minds (that would be us) on day six.

After God was able to do all of that in just six days, a computational interpretation of the times in the genealogies would imply that it took 130 years to model Adam's life before Seth was born and another 800 years to model the rest of Adam's life. If the times in the genealogies happen as they are described, one after another, and they are all added up, modeling all of the lives of mankind up to the birth of Abram would have taken 1948 years.

The whole idea of a computational reality is only an allegory; we don't know anything about the physical processes that underlie the operation of this creation. Even so, the (possible) modeling times for human lives seem a little long compared to the six days of creation.

To summarize, there is nominally a discrepancy of roughly 13,798,000,000 years between Scripture and physical science. The Feynman-Stueckelberg interpretation of time can be used to (possibly) eliminate 13,797,950,000 years of disagreement (99.9996 percent), covering the time since the big bang to the emergence and beginning stages of humanity, but it doesn't quite fit for the last fifty thousand years.

It would have been nice to be able to completely eliminate the disagreement between science and Scripture, but we really don't know enough to be able to do that yet. If our reality is fundamentally computational—if the evaluation of what is possible should be based on the limits of a computational model, not on the limits to behavior posed by physical law—then there is nothing "supernatural" about any of the events described anywhere in Scripture. They are all just physics; physics that we don't understand yet, but still just physics.

It might be reassuring, at this point, to remember what modern physics can tell us about time, which is not a whole lot. We have no idea what time physically is or how it really works. We know that time, like space, bends, stretches, shrinks, and twists. Feynman and Stueckelberg tell us that it even runs backward as well as forward.

With all of the uncertainty clouding our knowledge of time, a mismatch in the timescales should rightly be the least of our concerns. For example, general relativity tells us that time and space bend and stretch together. Astronomy tells us that our universe is expanding, that space is still stretching (at least it was 32 million years ago). Does that imply that time is also stretching? That the time that we measure as fifty thousand years might actually have been less than that? As far as I know, archeologists do not routinely apply corrections for general relativity to their dating estimates. Like most applications of general relativity in our normal world, any error in archeological time is probably really tiny, but the notion does introduce some uncertainty.

The major events in Scripture are, for the most part, also present in the history of our world, in geology, archeology, and paleontology. In some cases the timescales are a little off between the two. But what's a piddling little fifty thousand years or so between friends?

04

Speculation in Games

"You are so going to Hell."—My orthodox wife, Cynthia

And now for something completely different.

At this point, we have applied modern physics to the interpretation of Scripture and reached some fascinating possibilities (not conclusions, of course, but possibilities). The interpretation offered depended on the logical implications of two controversial proposals in physics: the Feynman-Stueckelberg view of time as all simultaneously existing and the notion that our reality might have a mathematical basis, that it might be some kind of computational model. Feynman-Stueckelberg provided a resolution for the difference in timescales between the account of creation in Genesis 1 and what we see and measure in the world around us. Looking at our world as if it might be a computational model provided us with a very flexible "reality," one that accommodates both some very odd physics and the many miracles and prophecies that are described in Scripture.

A question that pops up, though, is:

What if this universe *is* a computational model? What else might that imply?

This last section presents some of the broader logical implications of the proposal that our world might have a mathematical basis. It is strictly a scriptural apologetic, an argument for the truth of Scripture. It is also still just a story. The story provides, I think, two benefits to scriptural apologetics: logical support for the truth of Scripture and a possible rebuttal to one of the major points used by critics of the truth of Scripture.

One of the many battlegrounds in the debate between believers and nonbelievers over the truth of Scripture is called the first cause argument. First cause has been an issue in philosophy since Plato (425–348 BC) and an issue in theological apologetics since Saint Thomas Aquinas (1225–1274).

A version of the basic first cause argument, borrowed from Wikipedia, is:

1) Every finite and contingent being has a cause.
2) A causal loop cannot exist.
3) A causal chain cannot be of infinite length.
4) Therefore, a first cause (or something that is not an effect) must exist.[1]

There's a lot of philosophy jargon in this particular definition. Acceptance of the big bang cosmology by the physics community has given credibility to a much simpler version (also from Wikipedia), originally proposed by philosopher Al-Ghazali (1058–1111):

1) Whatever begins to exist has a cause.
2) The Universe began to exist.
3) Therefore, the Universe has a cause.[2]

When the big bang cosmology theory was originally proposed, the physics community resisted because it looked way too much like biblical creation ("Let there be light" = kaboom!). Physicists and cosmologists eventually accepted the big bang because the observational verification for it was quite good, and they were able to put a nice comfy 14 billion year barrier between the big bang and Scripture (a barrier I believe we can remove from the debate—which of course is one of the purposes for this book).

The debate is still being waged today between competing cosmological models and physical theories. Nonbelievers propose cosmologies that might be infinite (so they don't need a first cause), and believers point out that the math doesn't quite work out for that model; the supposedly infinite model really needs to be finite (and therefore, needs a first cause). Right now, in my opinion, it is early in the fourth quarter, the believers have a small lead in points, but the nonbelievers have the ball—so anything may happen. The nonbelievers will have scored if there is an announcement that the Large Hadron Collider at CERN has confirmed the physical existence of Kaluza-Klein

1 "First Cause Argument." Retrieved c. 2014 from https://en.wikipedia.org/).
2 "Cosmological Argument." Retrieved c. 2014 from https://en.wikipedia.org/wiki/Cosmological_argument.

supersymmetry particles. Watch for it on the evening news.

The first cause claimed by believers in the debate is, of course, God's act of creation. One of the standard rebuttals is that believers have not really supplied a first cause; they have only stretched the debate out a little, because they do not have a first cause for God. There is a sense in which that charge is a straw man argument; the subject under debate is the nature of our universe as revealed by science and natural philosophy, so the issue is properly whether our universe has a first cause, not whether our first cause has its own first cause. We can apply what we see in science and natural philosophy to understanding the nature of our universe, but we have precious little science regarding the origin or physical nature of God.

But there is also a sense in which the lack of a proposal for the origin of God is a valid criticism. It is not really relevant in the debate over the nature of our universe, but it is very relevant in the deeper inquiry into the fundamental nature of "reality." For nonbelievers, this universe *is* a fundamental reality; the particular bit that we see around us might be a tiny bubble in a much larger multiverse, but the universe or the multiverse are all that there is. For believers, this is a creation made by God. It will eventually be bulldozed under and replaced by something nicer and more permanent. Since it is made in something out of something, it cannot possibly be a fundamental reality. If we believers insist that this universe, this creation, is not a fundamental reality, there is nothing unjust in others asking, "Okay, so what is the fundamental reality?" The question is not relevant to the debate regarding the nature of our universe, but it does provide a nice entry into a different debate that is of interest.

One foundation of this speculation has been the notion that our reality might have a mathematical, computational basis. Nobody knows if that is true or not, but, according to the physics, it is definitely a possibility. If our reality is computational, three reasons come to mind for why it is that way:

1) Our reality is a computational model created by God.
2) Our reality is just naturally computational, with no intelligent actors involved.
3) Our reality is a computational model made by persons other than God.

Earlier, we assumed that this reality that we live in is a computational model made by God: a completely unnatural, created place. I mentioned briefly that it is possible to imagine a similar but different computational reality, one that is completely natural with no guiding intelligence, no creation involved. The first part of this chapter is a speculation about that kind of natural computational reality, how it might work and what might logically happen there.

In the previous section, we could ignore most of the details of how a computational reality might physically work; the presence of a directing intelligence implies that the details get handled somehow and we don't need to bother our pretty little heads with them. In the present speculation about a completely natural reality, there is no directing intelligence. Therefore, the details play a major role as we try to guess what can or can't, what might or probably won't, happen. So, oddly enough, this speculation will start with descriptions of a couple of computer games.

Conway's Game of Life

Mathematicians Stanislaw Ulam and John Von Neumann (the same John Von Neumann who invented modern computer architecture and who first implied that quantum localization might be related to conscious minds) proposed a new kind of puzzle for the entertainment of fellow mathematicians in the 1940s, while they were working together at Los Alamos National Laboratory (home of the Manhattan Project). The new puzzle type was called a cellular automaton. The rules were deceptively simple:

Divide some space into a regular grid of separate cells.

Each cell can have some number of states: on or off; red, green, or blue; whatever the heart may desire.

All of the cells change states at the same instant of time, called a tick.

The new state for a cell depends on the old state of the cell and the old states of the cells around it (its neighborhood), according to some rule.

For mathematicians, the entertaining part of the puzzle is figuring out grids, lists of cell states, and state change rules that produce interesting behavior. I call the rules deceptively simple because cellular automata are capable of extremely complex behavior. At the present time, the behavior of even the simplest cellular automaton (one dimensional line of cells and two cell states with very simple state change rules) is mathematically unpredictable; the only way to tell what a cellular automaton will do is to make one and try it.

The cellular automaton called the Game of Life was discovered in 1970 by mathematician John Conway. It uses a rectangular, two-dimensional grid (Cartesian coordinates again; very convenient here for computer screens and the pages of books like this one); two cell states, called "alive" and "dead"; and a really simple rule for cell state changes: Cells are born (turn on) if exactly three neighbors (out of eight) are alive. Cells stay alive (survive) if two or three neighbors are alive. Cells die (turn off) if fewer than two (zero or one) or more than three (four, five, six, seven, eight) neighbors are alive.

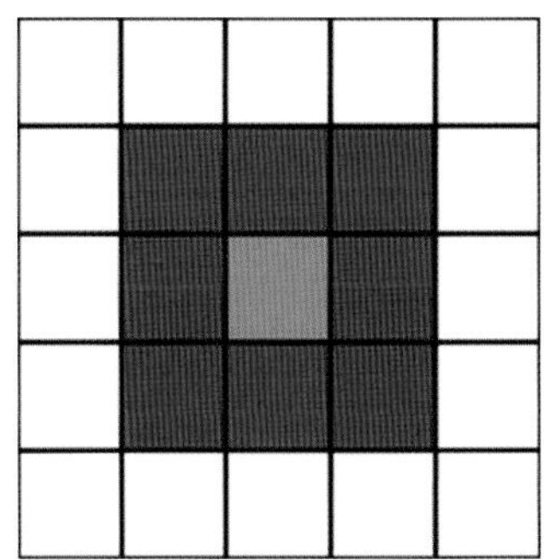

Fig. 130.3. 2-D Cellular Automata Neighborhood

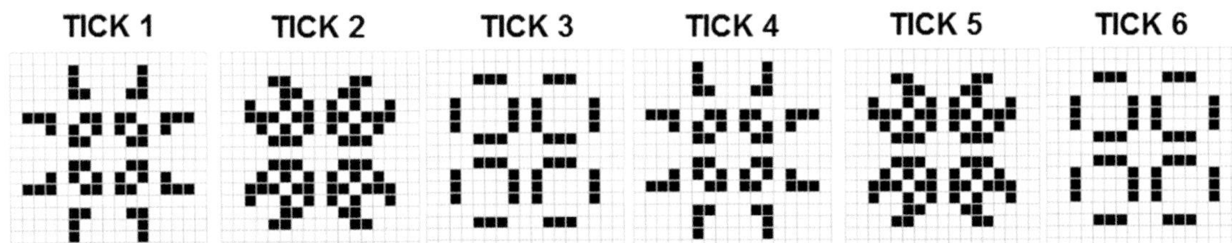

Fig. 130.4. Conway's Game of Life Pulsar Sequence

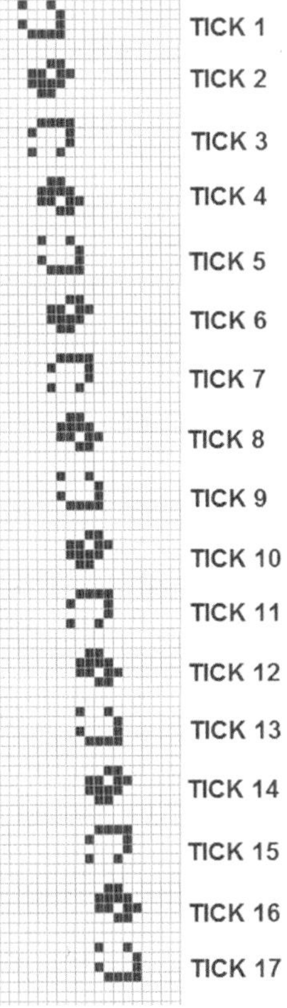

The particular rules for Conway's Game of Life produce an exceptionally lively cellular automaton. One simple example is the stationary oscillator called a pulsar, shown above in figure 130.4 (from Wikipedia). The figure on the right shows a moving pattern that is called a lightweight spaceship (also from Wikipedia[3]).

If you have a computer handy, I strongly recommend taking a look at the Wikipedia entry for Conway's Game of Life before reading on. The entry includes numerous video clips that show some of the dynamic capabilities of the game. There are stationary patterns of cells called still lifes, patterns that move across the screen (gliders and spaceships), patterns that produce gliders and spaceships (guns), and patterns that oscillate like the three-tick pulsar shown above. There are patterns called puffer trains and rakes, which move across the screen leaving trails of spaceships and guns.

3 "Conway's Game of Life." Retrieved c. 2018 from https://en.wikipedia.org/wiki/Conway%27s_Game_of_Life.

One of the best parts of the entry (at the time this is being written) is down at the bottom in the list of related articles, where you can find some of the best video clips on Wikipedia for Game of Life structures and actions. You can also find a very nice video on YouTube called "Epic Conway's Game of Life" that is entertaining.

Conway's Game of Life became popular in late 1970 when it was featured in a column by Martin Gardner in *Scientific American*. Several features of the game proved to be captivating to many audiences. First of all, of course, is that the game itself is cool; it was truly surprising that so much complex behavior could result from such a simple underlying structure.

Another intriguing aspect of the game is that some of the behaviors look very similar to particle physics. There are particles (cell structures) that propagate at constant speeds like photons; stable structures that emit and absorb "photons"; and structures composed of other, smaller structures. Particle physicist and computer scientist Stephen Wolfram has seriously proposed in *A New Kind of Science* (2002) that the physics of our world might be based on cellular automata—a proposal based on the many, many similarities between the physical behavior that we see in the world around us and the behavior of cellular automata.

For our purposes in this chapter, the best feature of the Game of Life is that it is possible to make structures in the game that can perform computations. Paul Rendell made the structure shown in figure 131 (from Wikipedia, of course; the same structure is shown in action in the YouTube video). It is capable of reading a series of stored instructions and performing actions based on those instructions. It has a memory based on the positions of still life structures and performs computations by setting switches to control the flows of gliders from glider guns.

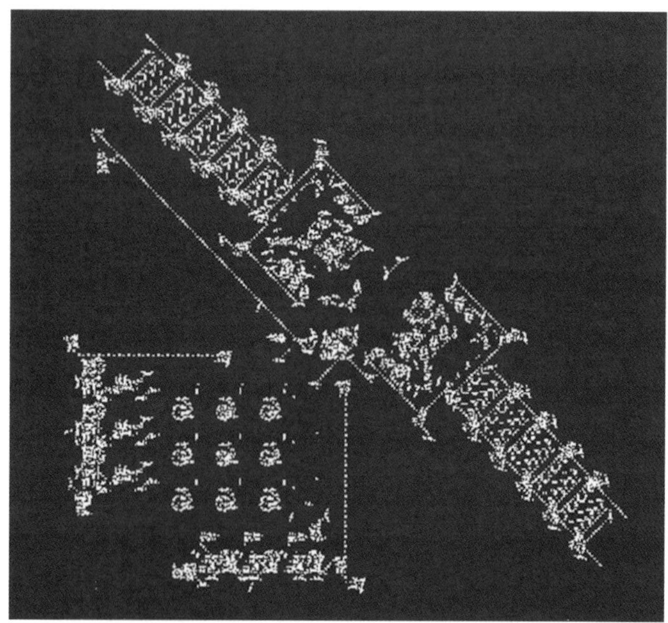

Fig. 131. Game of Life Computational Structure
Adapted from image by Andrew Trevorrow and Thomas Rokicki, structure by Paul Rendell

In the terminology of computer science, the Rendell structure is Turing complete: it is capable of performing any computation that can be performed by any digital computer.

Andrew Wade and Dave Greene have made versions of computational structures called replicators; these follow a list of instructions (a program) to build copies of themselves in other locations. Andrew Wade's replicator takes 34 million ticks to make a copy. Dave Greene's replicator copies both itself and the program it used to copy itself.

Incidentally, the computational structures with their flows of gliders look sort of like water when they are running; remember the *mayim* in the interpretation of Genesis 1?

Philosophy from Conway's Game of Life

Conway's Game of Life provides an illustration of one way that a reality with natural computation might work. All that is really needed is a kind of cellular automaton, a physics where points in space have a state that depends on the states of the points around them. If the states are right and the rules for changing states allow the same kind of flexibility that the Game of Life does, then perhaps we can imagine that the physics of the world we see around us might be the result.

One of the logical (not scientific) supports for the notion that our reality might be a kind of computer is that a computational reality is potentially much likelier to exist than a physical reality would be (remember Ockham's Razor, the *lex parsimoniae*). One battleground in the believer versus nonbeliever debate in science is called the anthropic fine-tuning principle. Anthropic fine-tuning was mentioned earlier in the section discussing the requirements of creation: it is the observation that the physical laws and the values of physical constants of this world are apparently exactly what they need to be to support the kind of life we enjoy. Very small changes in any of them would render our existence physically impossible. If one assumes that physical laws and constants can change and calculates probabilities for our existence based on physics, the odds are ridiculously small.

On the other hand, the requirements for a computational reality are much more likely to be satisfied in any random reality. All a computational reality would need to do is support an appropriate cellular automaton. Any of a zillion different variations of physics would likely work as well as any other.

Natural computation is only a little bit harder to imagine than a reality that supports a lively cellular automaton. Computational structures in the Game of Life are not random; they are very carefully constructed with a lot of work by very clever, talented people. They are not random, but they are also not all that large: the Rendell computing structure only uses a few thousand cells.

It is possible to "naturally" develop structures with interesting behaviors in the Game of Life; many of the oscillators and spaceships were originally found by starting with a random arrangement of cells and watching to see what happened. If one imagines a reasonably sized reality, about the same size as our universe for example, that supports a lively cellular automaton, it should not be difficult to imagine that computational structures or something like them might pop into existence here and there.

Some, perhaps most, nonbelievers have managed to convince themselves that living organisms came into existence on Earth from random conglomerations of naturally occurring chemicals. While many of the chemicals used by bacteria do occur naturally (amino acids, lipids, sugars, and RNA), the "computational program" required to produce a self-sustaining (chemolithoautotroph) bacteria (like Dave Greene's replicator in the Game of Life) requires about 500,000 DNA base pairs of information. The probability of producing one DNA genome of that size (let alone the rest of the critter; this is just the chance of producing the DNA sequence) is $1/4^{500,000}$ ($= 1/10^{301,030}$). There are probably lots of DNA genomes that would work nearly as well; several million or so of them have lived here on Earth at one time or another. But even if there are a billion viable bacterial genomes, the probability only improves to $1/10^{301,021}$. William Dembski has estimated that there have been about 10^{120} physical particle interactions in our universe in all of its history since the big bang. Statistically speaking, it is not possible that living organisms could be the result of a random process, almost no matter how many viable genomes there are. However, that doesn't mean they cannot result from a *natural process.* There are natural processes, like natural selection for example, that do have the capability for reducing the odds to numbers that are physically achievable.

The implication of the probability calculation above is only that, because of the vast amounts of "program" that living organisms must have, the process that produced them must have been entirely nonrandom (like natural selection). There cannot have been any purely random steps in it. Computational structures, on the other hand, can conceivably result from purely random events, as long as the reality in which they arise is sufficiently large and supports a lively cellular automaton. This is partly because they are so much smaller and simpler than living organisms (and therefore more likely to happen by pure chance), and partly because cellular automata are not as limited by physical laws as biological systems would be and can try more arrangements.

Cellular automata do have limits on what they can do, but those limits are much broader than the limits on particle behavior controlled by the standard model of particle physics. For anyone who can believe that living organisms might be the result of a random process, the possibility of natural computation should be a slam dunk.

All of the above implies that a rudimentary kind of computation might be possible in a natural environment that supports a lively cellular automaton, but that does not nearly get us to the kind of computational fundamental reality that could support the world we see around us. Remember that any kind of viable computational reality for our universe must be able to support the behavior we see in physics experiments. It must be able to support quantum computation, computational results that depend on superpositions of infinite possibilities. Quantum computation is extremely difficult, high-level mathematics. With all of our expertise in computer science, we can only do quantum computation by piggybacking on the quantum behavior of subatomic particles; we don't have clue as to how to do it from scratch.

It is relatively easy to imagine that rudimentary computation would naturally occur in a fundamental reality that supports a lively cellular automaton, but the much more advanced computational behavior that we see in our world needs more. It needs a nonrandom process like natural selection. In order to have natural selection, we need to introduce conflict into our computational environment. Conway's Game of Life provides an example of a lively cellular automaton. The next game will provide an example of conflict in a computational environment.

Core War

Conway's Game of Life is a single player, noncompetitive game; its entertainment value comes from watching the behavior of the patterns that evolve from the initial states of the cells that are assigned by the player.

Core War, by contrast, is a competitive computer game for two players, where the object of the game—like chess, checkers, or Go—is to destroy the opponent. But unlike those games, in which the opponents are people, in Core War the opponents are combative programs striving for dominance in a computer memory.

Core War was first proposed by D. G. Jones and A. K. Dewdney in 1984. The game uses a special programming language called Redcode, which runs in an "operating system" called the Memory Array Redcode Simulator (MARS, the Roman god of war).

Warrior programs are written in Redcode by players and then run against each other in the MARS program. The object of the game is to break up the opponent program so that it is no longer capable of providing legal instructions to MARS.

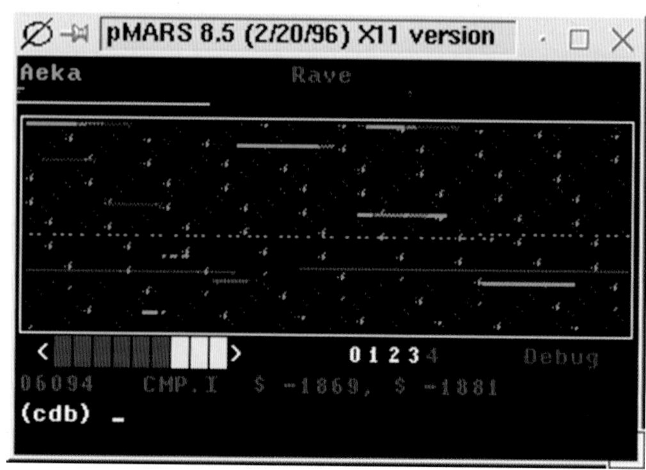

Fig. 131.1. Core War MARS Program

A few videos of Core War games have been posted on YouTube for interested readers; they show the action of the game but do not have the dramatic images that the Game of Life can generate. However, a few of the warrior program strategies are worth a closer look, as they provide examples of how conflict might work in a computational environment. These are taken from the Wikipedia entry for Core War. Most competitive warrior programs use combinations of these basic strategies.

Replicator

A replicator warrior makes multiple copies of itself and executes them in parallel. Left alone, a replicator will eventually fill the core with copies of itself. Replicators are hard to kill because all of the various copies have to be individually killed to win the game. Their weakness is that they are not very effective at killing the opponent warrior.

Scanner

A scanner warrior searches the core for the enemy and then launches targeted attacks. Scanners are most effective at killing replicators. Scanners are vulnerable to decoys that dissipate their attacks on useless targets. They also tend to be relatively large programs; they are easier to find and destroy than some of their opponents.

Bomber

A bomber warrior copies small bits of code, "bombs," to random locations in the core. Bombers are often effective against scanners because the bombs can distract the scanner, causing it to launch worthless, distracting attacks. Bomber programs can be small and fast. They are difficult for scanners to find.

Vampire

A vampire warrior constructs a "pit" trap and tries to entice enemy programs into the pit. Vampires are often modified scanners or bombers. The weakness of vampires is that, in order to entice an opponent into the trap, they leave their business cards all over the core. It is very easy to find a vampire.

Imp

Imps are very small programs that copy themselves around the core, similar to a replicator but smaller. Imps are particularly effective if they copy themselves in patterns called imp spirals.

Quickscanner

A quickscanner is a small scanner that searches only small volumes of the core so that it can launch attacks quickly. Quickscanners are effective against large opponent programs, which are easier to find. They are not effective against small opponents that are difficult to find.

Core Clear

A core clear warrior is a type of replicator that overwrites every memory location in the core.

Evolvers

Evolvers are computer programs that produce Redcode warrior programs using genetic techniques. Genetic algorithms make small changes to the warrior code and evaluate the effectiveness of the changes. Beneficial changes are incorporated and serve as a basis for further "evolution." Evolvers are, so far, capable of producing very effective small warriors, but they are not yet able to produce winning large warriors.

Philosophy from Core War

Conway's Game of Life is not usually a combative, competitive game. In the fundamental, cellular automaton reality of our speculation, however, there isn't just one pattern or one structure. In any sufficiently large reality, random chance will inevitably produce lots of replicating, expanding structures. The term "inevitable" applies for the same reasons that computational structures were considered a likely basis for our reality earlier: Game of Life expanding and replicating structures are often simple; they do not require large numbers of cells in order to expand and replicate, so the probabilities of random occurrence are quite reasonable. Also, a universe filled with a lively cellular automaton would likely be faster and more flexible at trying different options than our reality, bound by physical law, is.

Multiple expanding, replicating structures in the same space will, just as inevitably, collide. And when they do, they will attempt to expand and replicate right over each other. Both logic and the example of the Core War game imply that there are three possibilities when structures collide:

First, the structures ignore each other, and both keep right on expanding and replicating.

Second, both structures are disrupted and stop expanding and replicating.

Third, one structure "lives" and the other structure "dies."

And that third possibility, dear readers, is natural selection. Tough structures that can resist collisions will become larger and tougher; frail structures that are easier to disrupt will be terminated.

One additional point, though, is that disrupted structures are not necessarily obliterated; they might just be inactivated. The intricate bits and pieces could still be present but the precise timing and alignment required for expansion and replication would be missing, confused and disoriented by the random changes in cell states brought about by the collision. Even a tough, victorious structure might suffer damage: random changes that shift cell state composition, structural alignment, and timing.

Most random changes would, of course, degrade the expanding and replicating abilities of the overall structure. Some changes, though, might improve performance, making the overall structure tougher, faster, or more resilient.

And that, of course, is descent with modification by random mutation and natural selection.

This should all be starting to sound a little Darwinian.

Computational Evolution

At this point, we'll be using the mechanisms of Darwinian evolution to make some deductions about what would be likely to happen in the candidate fundamental reality that is being explored here: a physical environment that supports a lively cellular automaton and therefore offers the possibility of supporting natural computation.

Before we get into that part, however, it might be useful to explain why the same Darwinian evolutionary theories that believers have been opposing since they were first proposed 150 or so years ago have suddenly changed from being implausible to offering viable possibilities. The basic answer is that Darwinian evolution does not really work as an explanation for the diversity of life that we see around us in our physical world; natural selection works, and descent with modification is evident in the fossil record, but random mutation of DNA does not have the physical capability to provide enough candidate organisms for natural selection to have chosen the millions of living species that we see around us in the amount of time that has been available since the big bang. Biological organisms require far too much extremely specific information, coded in DNA sequences, in order to live and function at all. However, something like Darwinian evolution probably can work in an environment where the candidates are simpler and there are a lot more of them to choose from.

Here are a couple of very rough calculations to, I hope, show the difference in the two situations. The calculations are not meant to be really accurate (and they aren't), but they are simple and might help.

A little ways back I mentioned that the rough probability of finding a simple genome for the very first bacterial organism by a random search among all of the possibilities was roughly $1/10^{301,021}$. That number is only a wild guess—nobody really knows how many viable bacterial genomes there are—but the actual number of viable bacterial genomes is almost irrelevant. Even if there were $10^{300,000}$ viable genomes, and there almost certainly aren't anywhere near that many, the implication of the calculation is the same.

If we take William Dembski's estimate of the total number of particle interactions in our universe (10^{120}) throughout all of time since the big bang as a maximum number of possible tries, then we can do a rough estimate of the chance that our universe could randomly (not naturally, remember, just randomly) produce a single bacterium as, at most, $10^{120}/10^{301,021} = 1/10^{300,901}$. Forget about it.

Even if there were $10^{300,000}$ viable bacterial genomes, the chance of randomly producing a living bacteria would still be roughly $1/10^{901}$. The number of genomes does not matter; random (not natural) origination of life is a statistical impossibility.

We can do the same wild-guess sort of calculation for our hypothetical Game of

Life reality by assuming that the game operates in a space that is roughly the same size (92 billion light years in diameter), age (13.798 billion years), and resolution (cell spacing equal to the Planck length, 1.616×10^{-35}m; tick interval equal to the Planck time, 5.39×10^{-44} second) as our universe to estimate a total number of possible cell state changes at about 10^{226}; greater than but not enormously different than the 10^{120} number estimated for the much more limited physical reality that we live in.

The big difference comes when we calculate the chances of finding interesting structures. The Game of Life lightweight spaceship (from Wikipedia) shown to the right occupies a 7×7 (=49) block of cells.[4] The number of possible cell state configurations is $2^{49} = 5.6 \times 10^{14}$. The rough likelihood of producing lightweight spaceships is $10^{226}/10^{14}$; we would expect to produce about 10^{212} lightweight spaceships in the course of the game. If you went on a tour of the game space, you would probably need a flyswatter.

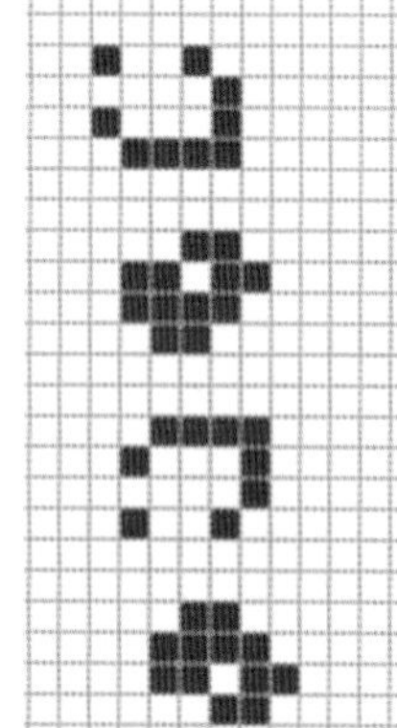

Without Darwinian evolution helping out, we would expect to routinely, at some times and some places, produce structures up to about 700 cells ($10^{226} \approx 2^{753}$). With Darwinian evolution lending a hand, as it almost certainly would, the sky is the limit.

So far in this speculation we have at least been paying lip service to the logical requirements of physics: conclusions should be mathematically logical and should not conflict with observations of the natural world. For the sake of brevity, this speculation in games will shift to the style of deduction and proof that is considered acceptable in evolutionary biology. I suspect it would be possible to continue the speculation with logical, mathematical justification for every step, but since there is a much easier path available, who has the time?

In evolutionary biology, all that is required to justify a developmental step is a plausible argument that the characteristic in question offers a competitive advantage to structures that have it. It is not necessary to present a scientifically logical mechanism that can physically accomplish the change; the magic of natural selection conquers all of those piddling little details. Agreement with observation is a convenience, but only a partial agreement is needed; observations that conflict with an evolutionary line of argument are obviously defective.

4 "Conway's Game of Life." Retrieved c. 2018 from https://en.wikipedia.org/wiki/Conway%27s_Game_of_Life.

Games and Evolutionary Biology

"There is abundant evidence that other cosmologies once existed in Israel. Scattered allusions to be found in the prophetic, poetic, and wisdom literature of the Bible testify to a popular belief that prior to the onset of the creative process the powers of watery chaos had to be subdued by God. These mythical beings are variously designated Yam (Sea), Nahar (River), Leviathan (Coiled One), Rahab (Arrogant One), and Tannin (Dragon). There is no consensus in these fragments regarding the ultimate fate of these creatures. One version has them utterly destroyed by God; in another, the chaotic forces, personalized as monsters, are put under restraint by His power.

"These myths about a cosmic battle at the beginning of time appear in the Bible in fragmentary form, and the several allusions have to be pieced together to produce some kind of coherent unity. Still, the fact that these myths appear in literary compositions in ancient Israel indicates clearly that they had achieved wide currency over a long period of time. They have survived in the Bible solely as obscure, picturesque metaphors and solely in the language of poetry."—Nahum Sarna, *The JPS Torah Commentary: Genesis*

It has been a long and winding road to this point in our speculation, so it might be useful to start with a short recap of where we are and what we are doing. This is a speculation about what might happen in a fundamental reality that supports natural computation. The "speculation" part means this is just a made-up story; we are making no claim that the reality described in this speculation is our reality (it probably isn't). It is a science fiction story that we are examining because it might be interesting, and because examining it may help us think about the nature of our reality in new ways.

The "fundamental reality" part implies that, just for the sake of this speculation, there is no God or any kind of intelligent actor involved in the physical operation of the reality we are exploring. Natural computation means computation that can happen on its own, naturally, without being made or programmed by an intelligent mind. (Not that computation happens automatically—part of this speculation is intended to provide an argument for why computation might begin—it's just that computation can happen naturally. It is possible.) Computation here means Turing computation, the capability to read a stored list of instructions and take actions based on those instructions.

To help define the possibilities so we can more easily craft the story, we have chosen a fundamental reality that supports a lively cellular automaton like Conway's Game of Life. There are many possible realities that would likely do just as well, but the Game of Life has really cool graphics available on Wikipedia and YouTube, so it's much easier to imagine how things might all work. Most importantly, as was mentioned earlier, Conway's Game of Life supports the essential requirements of this speculation: computation, natural selection, and descent with modification. (Technically, it's development by modification rather than descent with modification, more like bacteria than like multicellular animals, but descent with modification sounds more Darwinian. The results are the same.)

Finally, we will use a type of argument that is more like the justifications proposed in evolutionary biology, not the more demanding mathematical and logical approach that is generally required in physics. The scene of our story is a natural, evolutionary environment, very similar in many ways to the one assumed by evolutionary biology for our physical world. As was just shown in the last section, the Game of Life world of our story is more versatile than our physical world is; if something can logically happen here in our world, it can logically happen there.

The Story Begins

Once upon a time, there was a warm little pond. Oops, apologies. That's the wrong science fiction story. We'll try one more time.

Imagine, if you will, a vast Game of Life. The Game starts, as many of them do, with a random arrangement of cell states. Out of the clouds of random cells, out of the watery chaos, most cells turn off and vanish, but here and there, some structures persist. Some are stable still lifes that merely exist; they do nothing. Some are pulsars, which constantly shift their structure but do not move. Some structures move. Some grow. Some grow and move. Some produce smaller structures that move.

Growing and moving structures inevitably encounter still lifes and pulsars, the stationary structures that, because they are simple and small, fill the space of the Game. Some moving structures are broken up by stationary obstacles, but others persist, erasing the obstacles in their path or flowing around them and repairing the damage. They persist, but they are often changed by the encounters. Mostly they are degraded, but sometimes they are improved.

Moving structures may learn to sense the presence of obstacles and change direction to move around them. Many of the smaller moving structures can reflect, reversing their direction of movement when they encounter a still life (see Gosper's Glider Gun in Wikipedia for an example). Reflected scouts that return could trigger a shift in structure that causes them to change direction.

Wandering among the fields of pulsars and still lifes, moving and growing structures encounter each other. Some of the strategies used to persist among the stationary structures will work in encounters with other moving structures, but some won't. While moving structures are few and small (the military term is low force-to-space ratio), they will be able to shift directions and avoid each other. As they become larger, when there is less empty space (the military term is high force-to-space ratio), it will be harder for them to avoid other moving structures, and conflict will become much more common and much more direct. Structures that try to engulf and erase their mobile neighbors, as they did with the stationary structures, will discover opponents that engulf and erase right back.

Battle ensues.

Battle in the Game of Life

From here on, the development of our Game of Life structures is going to be dominated by the requirements of combat for the simple reason that winners live and losers die. The story is similar to the development of life here in our world. It will be driven by the competition for survival, but there are some important differences that will logically lead to a very different outcome. So, before we continue with the story of our Game of Life structures, what follows is a short discussion of battle in the Game of Life.

In our world, the competition between creatures that drives evolutionary development is limited by our physical existence and by our continuous need for food. Physically, individual animals have limited life spans; their speed is limited; the size and strength of their teeth and jaws is limited; tummies can only hold a limited number of their fellow creatures. It is not physically possible for any individual creature to dominate more than a tiny part of the earth, no matter how large and fierce it might be.

Physical limits to size do not apply in the same way in our hypothetical Game of Life. There is only one limitation on the size of a structure: the size of the game space. If there are survival advantages to size, it is likely that the competition will proceed until a lone survivor fills the entire Game of Life universe.

In our world, the ferocity of predators is limited because the food chain must be preserved. Any predator that is too good, that is too fast or too fierce or too voracious or too numerous, will destroy too much of the prey and then starve to death. One of the standard examples of a mathematical model in calculus is the predator-prey equations that show the oscillating relationship between the numbers of predators and prey.

As numbers of prey increase, it is easier for predators to find food. Well-fed predators breed more predators that eat more prey. As the numbers of prey decrease, the too-numerous predators struggle to find food, and many die of starvation. With fewer predators, the numbers of prey increase. And so on, and so on, and so on.

In the Game of Life described so far, there is no food, no metabolism, no compulsion to eat. There is no limit on the ferocity or appetite of the structures; there is only winning or losing, living or dying.

For Games of Life in our computers, the computers themselves supply the "energy" required for cell state changes. For a natural cellular automaton, no matter how lively it is, that would most likely not be true. Noether's theorem tells us that if physical behavior is consistent throughout the game space and from tick to tick, there must be conservation laws of some kind at play.

Our speculation would be fanciful indeed if it completely ignored the requirements of physics. So, to add a little (very little) scientific depth to it, we'll assume a simple conservation law just to see how it plays out. The simplest conservation law available, very similar to conservation of energy in our world, is conservation of cell "on" states. (A comment for accuracy: we are moving a little away from Conway's Game of Life here. Game of Life definitely does not conserve cell "on" states.)

If cell states are conserved, the still lifes and oscillators that fill the game space change from obstacles to "food"; casual avoidance by our hypothetical structures must change to aggressive consumption. In our physical world, the constant need for a steady supply of food puts a limit on the ferocity of competitors; they must not devour too many of the prey. In our Game of Life speculation, the availability of still lifes and oscillators is zero sum; there are only so many of them. Those not "eaten" by one structure will be consumed by its competitors. Any need for "food" in the Game of Life will intensify the competition. There is no limit on predator efficiency and ferocity, only limits on missed opportunities and timidity.

This Game of Life is far more competitive than our physical world could ever be. As stated before, if there are any advantages to size for our moving structures, the competition would likely proceed until there is only a single survivor that fills the game space.

In battle, there are many advantages to size.

In any battle of attrition, any conflict where both sides damage each other with roughly equal effectiveness, the larger structure will always win. But attritional conflict leaves even the victor weakened, easy prey for any intact structure that happens by before damage can be repaired.

Like the nations of our world, Game of Life structures would have two imperatives. One is to grow, to accumulate the size and resources that ensure victory in any decisive conflict. The other is to avoid, as much as possible, conflict that involves debilitating damage—to only engage in direct conflict when victory is assured at a reasonable cost. So, also like the nations of our world, the structures continuously spar, devouring the occasional small opponent while maneuvering for advantage against larger, more capable opponents.

Larger size also provides more opportunity for variety. Simply because they have more volume, larger Game of Life structures should be able to keep more kinds of defense and attack available for use against opponents. There is a rock-paper-scissors aspect to battle that makes variety an asset. In Core Wars, for example, the three main types of warriors—replicators, scanners, and bombers—trade dominance: scanners are effective against replicators, bombers against scanners, and replicators against bombers.

It is often much the same in human conflict. There is no attack that can't be repelled, no defense that can't be overcome. In classical warfare, before the deployment of cannon and rifles, a tactical balance had to be maintained between heavy and light infantry, heavy and light cavalry. Heavy cavalry (think mounted knights in armor) were effective against light infantry (archers) but could not beat heavy infantry (armored pikemen). Heavy infantry, however, were vulnerable to faster light infantry and light cavalry. Like Core War warriors that combine different types of attack and defense, ancient human armies typically combined infantry and cavalry and used them in combinations for both attack and defense.

Finally, larger size provides more opportunities to control the location and direction of a conflict. The military term is tactical maneuver. Attacks, and often defense, frequently have an orientation; they are stronger in a particular direction. The same is true in human conflict, where armies arrayed for battle typically have a front and a rear. There is a huge local (tactical) advantage if the opponent can be engaged by avoiding the prepared front and moving around a side to engage the unprepared rear; the military term is flanking attack. Flanking attacks are, practically speaking, much easier for a larger force to inflict on a smaller force. They are a major reason that the odds of a smaller force defeating a larger one tend to be low.

Returning to the moving, growing structures in our speculative Game of Life, the nature of battle in the game suggests some "physical" features that might be beneficial—some of which are quite complex. As the game proceeds, some features will evolve to become extremely complex. As mentioned before, evolution of complexity is far more likely in this Game of Life than it would be for the equivalent evolution of living organisms in our physical world. The basic structures that combine to build complexity (still lifes, glider guns) are much simpler than microbiological structures. The large, complex game structures, computers and replicators, are mostly assemblies of simple elements. That is not nearly as true for the molecular structures that compose living organisms; living organisms are more like three-dimensional jigsaw puzzles where every piece is different.

So what features might be evolved in this combative reality? In battle, senses would be crucial. Simple detection of obstacles has already been mentioned, but to be effective in attack and defense, senses should be more discriminating. They need to detect the approach of an opponent, the type and location of an attack (so that the proper defense and counterattack can be prepared), and the location and extent of damage so that repairs can be made.

Resistance to damage and repair of damage are also vital to any structure that survives its first few battles. Without repair, the results are the same as in a battle of attrition: the structure falls victim to any healthy structure that happens by. The simplest form of repair (because sensing and versatility are not required) is continuous waves of construction, expanding in all directions like water waves in a puddle (very much like a replicator in Core Wars). Incidentally, continuous construction would be a basic characteristic of any growing, moving structure, almost the definition of growing and moving in the Game of Life.

But in battle, the other side of the coin of simplicity is vulnerability. Any opponent structure that develops a counter to the waves of construction would eat a simple replicator for lunch. Effective repair in any long-lived structure would probably need to be versatile; it would be capable of building different structures appropriate to the conditions.

Coordination of attack and defense would also be handy. To resist an opponent's attack, an effective defensive structure would need to be placed in an appropriate location with a useful orientation. Attack type and location should be keyed to the arrangement of the opponents' defenses.

At more advanced levels of conflict, deception comes onto the stage: fooling sensors to show defense where there really is an attack; luring attacks into defensive ambushes; concealing the nature of attack and defense so that ineffective counters are deployed against them; decoys to draw attacks into useless targets.

It can all be quite complicated.

Intelligence

> *"Intelligence (from Latin* intelligere, *to comprehend): the ability to reason, plan, solve problems, think abstractly, comprehend complex ideas, learn from experience."*
> —Wikipedia[5]

Because of the potential for complexity in the management of conflict, intelligence would be a decisive advantage for battle in the Game of Life. When two opponents are physically matched, cunning and anticipation (accurate prediction of an opponent's future actions) will often bring victory and survival. In the history of human warfare, there are many examples of smaller armies defeating much larger opponents by the application of tactical cunning. One example is the three decisive battles between Alexander the Great of Macedon and the Persian Empire under Darius at Grannicus, Issus, and Gaugamela in 331 to 334 BCE. The Macedonians defeated larger forces in all three battles. At Gaugamela, the guys who were there on the Macedonian side claimed that the Persian army was over ten times larger than their own. Although they are not widely believed, that Alexander was extremely talented at warfare is not in question.

If intelligence can offer such a tremendous advantage in battle, it would certainly appear in our Game of Life speculation if there was any evolutionary path available for it at all. The same logic and arguments that support the natural, evolutionary

5 "Intelligence." Retrieved c. 2014 from https://en.wikipedia.org/wiki/Intelligence.

development of life and intelligence in our physical world must support a similar result in our speculative Game of Life. The incremental development that is evolution is much simpler and more likely in our speculative reality than it could ever be in our physical reality: the component parts are much simpler, the cellular automaton environment is more active than matter made of particles (meaning it has more opportunities to generate variations), and above all, our speculative reality does not have the same time limit that the big bang imposes on our physical world.

So how might such a path be laid out? Let's start with the simple response mentioned earlier: a change in direction when senses indicate a nearby obstacle. For a Game of Life structure, this would imply that the structure has the capability to change itself, to alter the arrangement of its cells in response to a sensory signal. Once the rudimentary capability to change structure in response to sensory signals is present, it is a short, incremental step to some of the other physical features that would benefit a Game of Life warrior: building defensive structures to meet an approaching attack, deploying attacking structures against an opponent's vulnerabilities, selecting attacks and defenses appropriate to the opposition's defenses and attacks.

All of these capabilities require, in a generic way, a structural ability to "read" events and perform sequences of actions in response to the events. In a very real sense, they require Turing computation: the ability to store instructions, read the stored instructions, and take actions based on the instructions. Just as computation in our technology has advanced from rudimentary calculations to Artificial Intelligence, it is not unreasonable to suggest that capability in our speculative, extremely competitive and evolving Game of Life might adapt and advance from rudimentary Turing computation to real intelligence.

> *"Consciousness (the meaning has changed over time, our current meaning is from the Latin phrase* conscius sibi, *knowing with oneself): awareness of external objects or something within oneself, the ability to experience or to feel."*—Wikipedia

The next step in development, the jump from intelligence to consciousness, is difficult to demonstrate in a logical derivation in the same way as the very basic argument just made for the development of intelligence. This is not because the necessary conditions are not available in our speculation, but because nobody knows what consciousness is. We all know that we have a "me" in there somewhere, but it turns out to be quite challenging to put a definitive, scientific finger on the details of what it is and how it works.

Since we have only a vague destination, our speculation is going to take a vague path to get there. Consciousness does have value for the survival of intelligent actors in the Game of Life, just as it does among us: it provides us with passion, with desire. We can write artificially intelligent programs that can engage in conversation that is indistinguishable from that of a human being. But computers don't start shouting and throwing things when the subject turns to religion or politics the way we do. They don't care; we do care. Passion, the fruit of consciousness, can provide an edge in battle. For opponents who are otherwise equal in every way, the one that fights harder will win more often than the one who just goes through the motions.

The purpose of all this speculation is to try to guess what might happen in a fundamental reality that supports natural computation. What we have so far is an evolutionary sequence that, to put a scale on the story, proceeds from small, unintelligent structures that shoot spit wads during recess to computing structures the size of solar systems that throw planets; from intelligent actors the size of galaxies shooting stars to universe-spanning, conscious geniuses that throw galaxies at each other.

What we have so far is an evolutionary sequence where the logical end is a single, extremely intelligent, very capable conscious being that literally and physically fills the universe.

One more little point and we'll be done here.

OODA Loops

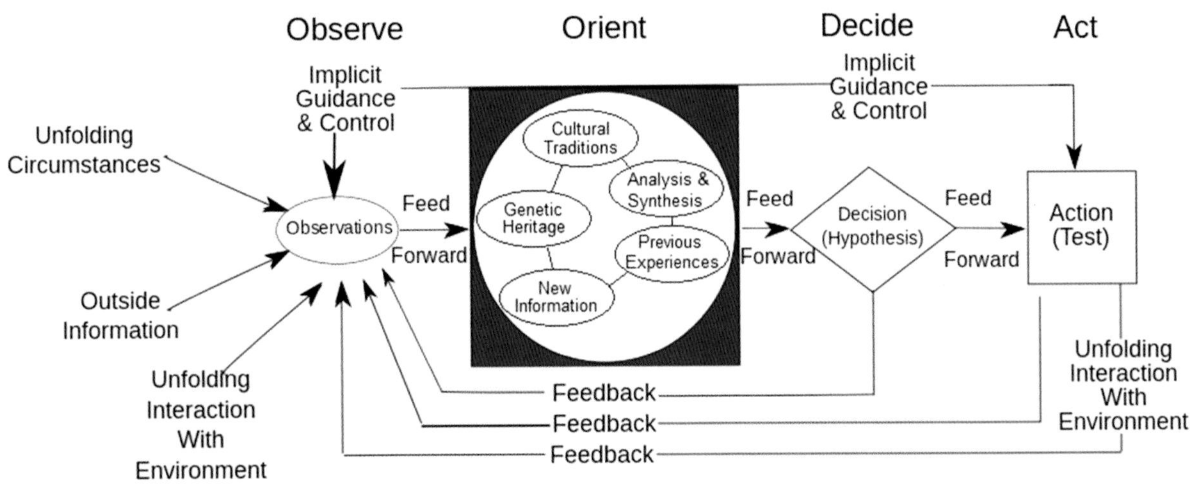

Fig. 132. John Boyd's OODA Loop

The OODA loop concept was developed by USAF colonel (and ex-fighter pilot) John Boyd as a part of his theoretical analysis of warfare called Patterns of Conflict. OODA stands for observe, orient, decide, act. The OODA loop is a model of the process that military organizations in particular use to direct their actions during battle.

In battle, scouts and frontline fighters in contact with the opponent report the positions and actions of the opponent (observe). The command organization analyzes this often fragmentary information and produces a model of the composition, distribution, and probable future actions of the opponent (orient). Based on the opposition model, command develops a plan for the distribution and actions of their own force (decide). The plan is communicated to the elements of the force, who then take actions as directed by command (act).

In a battle between organizations (or very large Game of Life structures), the speed of OODA loops is crucial to success. Many of the tactical actions in battle—the selection of the type of attack or defense and the positions of attacking and defending forces—depend for their success on the composition and positions of the opposing forces. A warrior with faster OODA loops will be able to shift composition and position before a slower opponent can place strong defenders in counter positions or direct attacks at locations where defense is weak or nonexistent. Most modern military organizations push the authority to make tactical decisions down as low as possible in the command hierarchy specifically to speed up their OODA loops.

The idea of OODA loops reveals a weakness of large warrior structures in our Game of Life speculation. As mentioned earlier, there are many advantages in battle to large size, but they do come with a price tag. Returning to a historical example mentioned earlier, one of the main reasons that Alexander's outnumbered Macedonians were able to defeat the much larger Persian army was that they could maneuver faster on the field of battle to exploit shifts in the Persian formations; the Macedonians had faster OODA loops. Many of the advantages that larger Game of Life warrior structures have would only be effective if they could still respond rapidly.

The simplest solution to the response time problem is the one mentioned earlier, which is used in many modern human warrior organizations: to distribute tactical decision-making to locations close to the scene of battle. One thing to remember, though, is that all of the competitive conditions that imply successful warriors need to be conscious and intelligent still apply for local decision makers.

The final result of our speculation, our science fiction story, is an evolutionary sequence where the logical end is a single, extremely intelligent, very capable, conscious being that literally and physically fills the universe—but this must also be a being that has an army of intelligent, conscious subordinates who direct the local, nitty-gritty details of battle.

Philosophy from Speculation in Games

Let's take a step back. What might be the logical consequences if our universe has a mathematical basis, as we've speculated?

As I mentioned before, three possible reasons come to mind for why our reality might be mathematical, why it might be something similar to the computational models that we make:

1) Our reality is just naturally computational, with no intelligent actors involved.
2) Our reality is a computational model created by God.
3) Our reality is a computational model made by persons other than God.

Which of those possibilities is the most likely? The speculation in computation focused on the idea that we live in a computational model made by God. The result of our speculation in games is that a naturally computational reality will logically—almost inevitably—produce a hierarchy of conscious, intelligent beings eerily similar to the full panoply of heaven described in Scripture—not just God himself, but the cherubim (the meaning of cherubim has been lost), seraphim (dragons), and legions of angels (messengers) as well. The specific argument made in the speculation in games was based on a lively cellular automaton and Conway's Game of Life, but those are really just examples. The Core Wars game implies that, although the specific details might be different in different realities, there would most likely be more than one computational "warrior" in any fundamental reality that supports natural computation. With multiple "warriors," competition for resources and natural selection would logically lead to much the same result as our speculation in games did. As long as there are no physical limits on the size of the "warriors" (as there are in our physical world), any reality that supports natural computation should, in the end, produce a single, extremely intelligent being that fills the available universe.

The analysis above implies that an environment that supports natural computation would probably not be anything like the world we see around us. Natural computation might produce someone who would have the capability to create our universe, but probably not our universe itself. But the analysis above is only speculation. What if some other chain of events could lead natural computation to produce something like our universe?

For that case we'll need some more physics to try to decide between natural computation and a creation made by God for our own reality. Particle physics tells us that, if our reality is computational, it is quantum computational. Our reality is based on the interference and superposition of infinite numbers of possibility distributions, each with infinite numbers of terms. As was mentioned before, quantum computation is not common or garden variety computation; it is extremely difficult. Also mentioned before, there is a good reason for quantum computation to be used in a creation made by God: in combination with eternalist, simultaneously existing time, it will produce results much more quickly for a long-term Monte Carlo simulation (which is what our reality appears to be). Quantum computation would be a logical choice for a creation if one happened to consider building computers the size of galaxies to be all in a week's work (as is implied by our speculation in games).

We know of no physical reason that a naturally computational environment would use quantum computation. Our lack of knowledge does not rule out the possibility, but it does reduce the likelihood. All of the comments by physicists regarding quantum mechanics: "nobody understands quantum mechanics"; "anyone not shocked by quantum mechanics has not understood it"; "the only thing that quantum mechanics has going for it is that it is unquestionably correct"; are expressions of the underlying, universal attitude of the physics community that quantum mechanics does not make any physical sense that we have been able to discern; it is just plain too weird to be real.

This being so, the quantum nature of our reality strongly implies that our reality is much more likely to be a creation made by God than any kind of natural computation. Even if it were a result of natural selection, there would need to be an identifiable benefit to quantum computation for it to result from natural computation. Because even small-scale quantum computation requires such heavy computational resources, it is hard to see how it would be competitive with more direct approaches.

The next alternative to consider is that we might be living in a computational model made by persons other than God, as suggested by philosopher Nick Bostrom ("Are You Living in a Computer Simulation?" *Philosophical Quarterly,* 2003). Mr.

Bostrom proposes that we might be living in a historical simulation made by our descendants. There are, of course, many other possibilities for persons that might engage in computational models like the one we (possibly) live in, but Mr. Bostrom's suggestion is among the most likely, and the logic applies in much the same way to most alternatives: it will all boil down to a matter of motivation. By the way, Mr. Bostrom uses the term "simulation"; as the alert reader may have noticed, I prefer to use the term "model," because this is our home that we are talking about. It is all very real to us.

Mr. Bostrom offers two philosophical choices that lead to three possible outcomes. There isn't any logical or scientific reason to decide one way or the other for either choice, so logically and philosophically, the three outcomes are equally likely.

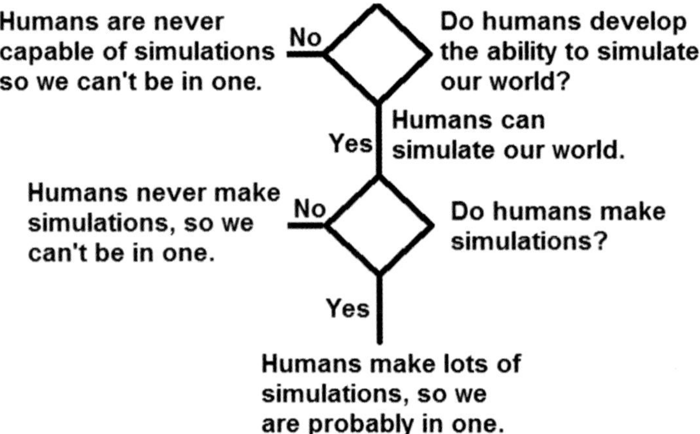

The choices and outcomes are shown in the diagram above. We will only consider the third outcome: that technologically advanced humans make lots of historical "ancestor simulations" with modeled conscious minds. There is nothing wrong with the first two logical outcomes: that humans never develop the advanced computer technology required to model conscious minds, or if they do, that they never use the technology to model conscious minds (it would be unkind to the modeled conscious minds). It's just that neither of those two outcomes is relevant to our speculation; neither of them provides a justification for a computational reality.

Mr. Bostrom suggests that, over time, lots of historical computer models would be created that include conscious minds. In his paper, he envisions that historical models would be of interest to historians (duh) and to individuals interested in their ancestors. I suspect that the major application would be games and vacations; your humble author is totally on board with touring the Cretaceous to see the dinosaurs as long as the tour vehicle is an M1A2 Abrams main battle tank.

If future humans make lots of historical computational models with lots of conscious minds in each one, then it would not be very long before modeled conscious minds would outnumber the original, biological minds. If modeled conscious minds greatly outnumber the original biological minds, then we are more likely to be modeled computational minds than biological minds.

It's all very philosophical.

To choose between a computational creation made by God and a historical simulation made by a person or persons unknown, we are going to apply the same physics as we used for natural computation. The detailed operation of our reality is described by quantum mechanics. Faster results for a Monte Carlo model are a good reason to use quantum mechanics in a creation made by God. This is not so true in the case of a creation made by someone else. It's not impossible that future modelers would choose to use quantum mechanics for a historical simulation, it's just that, as far as we can guess, a quantum-based reality takes a lot more computational resources than a reality based on classical mechanics. Why would anyone bother with probability amplitudes when there are much easier and cheaper approaches available?

Mr. Bostrom points out in his paper that it is not all that difficult to fake experimental results in a computer simulation; the quantum nature of our world could all be a sham. He also mentions that maintaining the sham would get more difficult as the modeled conscious minds (that would be us in this version of reality) build more and more semiconductor computers that depend on quantum mechanics for their operation; in order for those to work properly, the quantum behavior would have to be modeled.

One other tiny little point. Semiconductor electronics are not the only thing that depends on quantum behavior in order to operate. Photosynthesis, protein catalysis, and all of the chemistry that organic life depends on in turn depend on quantum physical behavior in order to work the way they do. As Dr. Feynman pointed out ("Simulating Physics with Computers," *International Journal of Theoretical Physics,* 1982), it is not feasible (as far as we know) to model the physical behavior of this world without quantum computation, which implies that any realistic model of our particular reality would have to use quantum mechanics.

This line of argument can dive in to epistemology ("How do we know what we know?") and solipsism ("I know that I exist, but how do I know that you exist?") and never stop going in circles. To avoid getting dizzy, we're going to stop at the first turn. Historical simulations by future humans with advanced technology would only need to model experiences, not the details of subatomic physics. The meticulously detailed world that physicists observe probably does not fit comfortably into that scenario. For that reason, it is, logically speaking, slightly more likely that this world that we live in is a creation made by God than it is likely to be a historical simulation.

05

Wrapping It All Up

"A reasonable doubt at a reasonable cost."—A lawyer's T-shirt

"We don't need to let go of the Bible. We just need to let go of Newton."
—My perceptive wife, Cynthia

So that's the story. At this point we get to ask one last question: How much truth is there in any of this story? The answer, unfortunately, is that nobody (except God) knows. Yet, while solid, proven truth is still beyond our reach, I think that believers can draw some reassurance from the story. Ironically, reassurance can come from our lack of knowledge.

This book has been a scriptural apologetic, an argument for the truth of Scripture. The argument was based on the picture of our reality provided by modern physics: relativity, quantum mechanics, and particle physics. It has also been based on two very unusual perspectives for our reality that are allowed by physics: the Feynman-Stueckelberg interpretation of antimatter and the proposal that our reality might be some kind of computational model.

For the last 150 years or so, aggressive nonbelievers have used the millions and billions of years of geologic time plus the evident antiquity of the fossil record and archeology to challenge the literal truth of Scripture, especially Genesis 1, 5, and 11. On their face, the timescales in Genesis are not compatible with the observations of natural philosophy.

I have suggested here that modern physics might offer a resolution to the apparent discrepancy between Scripture and natural philosophy. If we believers are willing to seriously consider the Feynman-Stueckelberg proposal that all of time might have a real physical existence, what Feynman called "the spacetime perspective," then the differences between natural philosophy time and scriptural time are reduced to a minor disagreement of interpretation.

With the spacetime perspective, Genesis 1 can be interpreted as a description of the creation of all of spacetime, from beginning to end, not just the creation of the earth and the universe at some instant in our past. In that interpretation, there is not necessarily any conflict between the times in Genesis and the times in natural philosophy; they might just be measuring two completely different realities: God's world and our world.

Please remember here that Feynman-Stueckelberg is not some whimsical speculation that somebody just made up (unlike much of this book). The negative time portrayal of antimatter in mathematics is a logical implication of the observed physical behavior in our world. It lies at the heart of the standard model of particle physics—at the heart of our fundamental understanding of how our world works. Feynman-Stueckelberg has been extensively verified by experimental observations. There is some disagreement among physicists about what it means philosophically, but the validity of the mathematics is currently beyond any reasonable doubt.

If we believers are willing to accept the possibility that a spacetime with millions and billions of years might be fully compatible with Scripture, some interesting doors open up in our evaluation of science and natural philosophy, including some theories that we can now interpret as being possibly correct:

- Big bang cosmology, with billions of years of stellar evolution
- Gas condensation models for the formation of the earth and the solar system
- Long, slow processes that have formed the geology of the earth's surface
- Life that has been present on the earth for many millions of years
- A fossil record that shows a long development of the millions of species that we see in the world around us
- Radiometric dating that, while particular dates may be debatable, shows a long chronological sequence for fossils and geology
- Archeology that shows our species present on the earth for many tens of thousands of years

In short, we can provisionally accept some theories in science and natural philosophy where the observational support is strong enough that in the past, aggressive nonbelievers have been able to use our opposition to portray our faith as ignorant and unscientific, our Lord's Scripture as untrue.

It is not really necessary to accept Feynman-Stueckelberg and an eternalist spacetime perspective as being physically true. The experimental support for the theory is probably not strong enough to justify a judgment of truth. It is, I think, enough to accept it as a real possibility, an idea that might be true. A Genesis that describes the creation of a spacetime containing millions and billions of years (of our time) in six literal days (of God's time) is a possible, perhaps even a reasonable, history.

If we believers can accept the possibility of an old universe and an old earth, the scientific debate regarding the nature of our world—whether it is a natural world or God's creation—shifts to different topics. If we can provisionally accept stellar evolution and geology, the disagreement with naturalists in physics shifts to cosmology and anthropic fine-tuning. If we accept the fossil record and archeology as potentially correct, the debate with naturalists in biology shifts to abiogenesis, original descent, and the molecular mechanisms of speciation. The scientific debate moves to the topics where scientists and natural philosophers who support the various Intelligent Design perspectives have been working for many years.

There are a couple of very good reasons to adopt Intelligent Design perspectives in the debate regarding the nature of our world, one personal and one very practical. On a personal level, the academic supporters of Intelligent Design have endured derision from their colleagues and professional persecution in the service of a consuming passion for scientific truth. I count it an honor and a privilege to be able to acknowledge justification of their efforts with a whole heart.

On a more practical level, it would be very convenient for believers to be able to accept the positions of Intelligent Design advocates because they are, in my opinion, winning the scientific debate. An enormous amount of scientific work has been done in the last ten to fifteen years that has filled in many of the gaps in our knowledge of theoretical physics, cosmological models, astronomical habitable zones, the fossil record, molecular biology, and the genetic operation and development of living organisms. Advocates of Intelligent Design in science and natural philosophy have been winning victory after victory after victory in the scientific debate. Their naturalist opponents have been largely reduced to ad hominem attacks (personal insults, for those of us who do not speak Latin), professional extortion, and the most degrading of all in a scientific debate: relying on judicial court decisions to justify their positions.

The other odd perspective offered in this presentation was the idea that our reality might be based on something like a computational model of subatomic processes. While the idea is arguably allowed by modern physics and supported by some physicists, it really is a whimsical speculation that I (and others) just made up; there isn't any experimental support for it at all. Even so, the computational model proposal is useful for scriptural apologetics as an allegory, as a picture of reality. A reality based on a computational model fits comfortably into our understanding and provides a flexibility that can easily accommodate the unusual events described in Scripture. Because of that flexibility, the perspective that our reality might have a computational basis offers possible responses to some of the more popular talking points of nonbelievers in the debate over the existence of God and the nature of our world:

- *"The miracles described in Scripture are physically impossible. They cannot have actually happened."*

  In a physical world, that would be true (that would be why they are called miracles). In a world with a computational basis, it would not be true. Events in a computational world would only be limited by the possibilities of computation, not by the limits of modeled physical interactions. As was mentioned earlier, the miracles described in Scripture would not be particularly difficult for anyone capable of creating and operating a computational model like the world that we see around us.

- *"The prophecies recorded in Scripture must have been faked. No one knows what the future holds."*

  In a presentist, physical world, that would be true. In an eternalist, computational world, it is not true. Like the miracles of Scripture, prophecies of future events are not a challenge when past, present, and future all simultaneously, physically exist—when all that someone outside the model needs to do to "see the future" is to look at what is right there in front of them.

- *"If this is a creation, it is not a very good creation. Pain and suffering are everywhere. We are prey to diseases. Our bodies are frequently defective. Evil triumphs. Many living organisms are just plain goofy. No good, loving God would make something like this."*

  There are a number of common theological responses to this criticism: God made this world, so he made it however he likes to accomplish whatever purpose he has for it; God originally made it to be better than this, and we chose to mess it up; focusing on the discomforts of this creation ignores God's generous providence, which is also a part of this creation (the food is great, for example); this creation is temporary, we are eternal: in a few thousand years whatever happens here isn't going to matter to us all that much; God is a lot smarter than we are, he knows what is coming next for us and we don't. Part of faith in God is trusting that whatever happens here is for our benefit. For example, if part of the purpose for this creation is training, to make us tougher and stronger or to help us see the value of his leadership by showing us an example of a world without God, then this is a truly excellent creation because it accomplishes those things very well indeed.

The notion that this might be a computational model adds another possible perspective: this temporary creation before the final creation might have some developmental purposes. God may have included us in the preparation for the final creation so that it would be more suitable for us (and we would be more suitable for it).

- *'There are natural, scientific explanations for how this universe came to exist and why it is the way that we see it. It is not necessary to invoke an all-powerful Creator to justify our existence."*

Even using classical physics, this assertion has always been debatable. If we add modern physics into the analysis, it becomes a real challenge to justify. Two primary arguments have been used to support the viewpoint that science naturally has all the answers: one is the conflict between geologic time and the evolutionary development of life versus the description of creation in Genesis; the other is that events described in Scripture don't seem to be compatible with the physical world that we see and measure.

If we accept the possibility that geologic time and the times in Genesis might be measuring different realities, there is not necessarily any conflict between them. If we accept the possibility that this reality might have a mathematical, computational basis, then physics might only see and measure a part of the things that can happen here. The events described in Scripture would not be unreasonable.

Without conflicting timescales and without a reality that is limited to the type of physical behavior we are accustomed to, the logical, scientific justification for a natural world needs to focus on different topics. On the classical physics side of the discussion about the nature of our universe, the questions shift to the areas described above:

Why did the big bang happen when it did and the way that it apparently did?

How did living organisms develop from naturally formed chemicals?

How did the original, relatively simple life forms that appeared here first develop into the millions of vastly more complicated life forms common in our world today?

What are the biological mechanisms responsible for the huge increases in genetic prescriptive information that would have been required for all of those new species?

In my opinion, science and natural philosophy do not currently have strong answers for any of those questions.

With modern physics, we can toss in a few more questions:

Why is the fundamental operation of our physical world based on the superposition and interference of possibility distributions?

Why does spacetime bend and stretch?

How does entanglement information pass between particle probability amplitudes at speeds faster than light?

Why is there a (possible) link between the choices of our conscious minds and the observed physical event called localization?

In my opinion, the science is a little fuzzy for those questions too.

Dear readers, naturalist science does not currently have answers for how this universe came to exist and why it is the way that we see it. Science and natural philosophy can tell us a lot about what it does, but not very much about what it is or why it is the way it apparently is.

I have examined the science and natural philosophy from both sides, both as a nonbeliever and as a believer. After considerable effort, I am unable to point to any observation or theory of science proven by experiment that supports the position that this is a natural, material universe that we live in. There may be some—my knowledge is limited in these areas—but they are not obvious.

- *"It may be difficult to explain our existence, but it is even more difficult to explain the existence of an all-powerful Creator. There are no proposals for the origin and physical existence of God."*

We do not have any science or natural philosophy regarding the origin and physical nature of God. We can only see and measure this world that we live in; there are limits to how well we understand even that. This book has offered a logical derivation that, on its face, might look like a proposal for the origin and physical nature of God, but it really is not. The derivation offered here was just a development of the logical consequences for a reality where computation could occur naturally, without any computers built by intelligent persons. An environment that supports natural computation is just one option for a reality with a computational basis. It's just one part of the argument. The problem with trying to step from that logical argument to any kind of real proposal for the origin and physical nature of God is that a reality that supports natural computation is not very likely. It may be more likely than our physical reality, but that's not saying much. Our physical reality has an absurdly low probability of existence.

It's just a story, that's all.

But there is, I think, one conclusion we can draw from the logic, even though it is just a story: a real, physical origin and a real, physical existence for God are not impossible; they are not incompatible with what science and natural philosophy tell us about this world.

Dear readers, we have finally arrived at the end of all speculation. At our current level of knowledge, science and natural philosophy do not conflict with Scripture in any definite way. It is possible to interpret what we know about our world to either support the events described in Scripture or not, depending on personal preference. In my opinion, science and natural philosophy lean more toward supporting Scripture than not.

The mathematics of Feynman-Stueckelberg has been experimentally verified; it is an accurate description of how our world works. Any supporter of a presentist reality has to reject the mathematics as physically inaccurate. There is no experimental or theoretical justification for rejecting what the mathematics tells us. The burden of proof for rejecting the physical implications of experimentally verified mathematics should properly lie with the rejection, not with accepting what the mathematics tells us.

A mathematical, computational basis for our reality is one possibility allowed by physics. As far as we know, it is conceptually possible to build a computational environment that could replicate the physical behavior we see in scientific experiments. It looks as if it would be extremely difficult, but it is not impossible. There are not a lot of other proposals for physical environments that would generate the quantum behavior that we see that are also fully compatible with experimental observations. For that reason, a computational reality is logically one of the more likely alternatives.

If this is a computational reality, then, as was discussed in the speculation in games, it is most likely that this is a creation made by God. There are possible reasons why a creation made by God would have quantum behavior. Because the computations are so much more difficult, it seems unlikely that a quantum reality would be used by a person or persons other than God or that a quantum reality would be a result of natural computation.

Our conclusion, therefore, should not be a surprise to any believer: as it says in Scripture, this creation attests to the existence of God.

PS: One last tidbit of advice. On Judgment Day, when we all meet God face-to-face, remember to be very courteous to the four *seraphim* (dragons) that Scripture tells us constantly attend the presence of the Father. If there is any truth at all to this speculation (which is doubtful, but why take the chance?), those four guys are probably his very best warriors.

Glossary

Antiparticles and antimatter

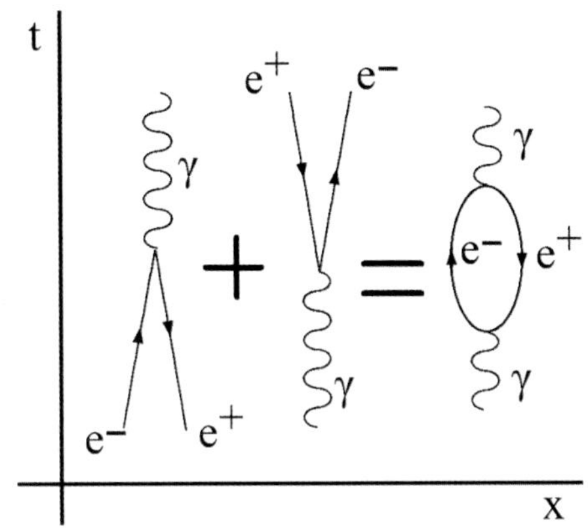

Antiparticles are versions of the fundamental particles (quarks or leptons; fundamental bosons do not have antiparticles) that have the same mass-energy charge as "normal" particles but have opposite electric charge (and possibly other charges). Antiparticles are frequently observed in cosmic rays and particle decay processes.

Antimatter is theoretically composed of atoms made of antiparticles: antielectrons (positrons) and anti-quarks. Antimatter hydrogen and helium have been made and/or observed, but no larger atoms have ever been seen.

Antiparticles and antimatter participate in pair annihilation and pair creation. In pair annihilation, particle and antiparticle meet and fluctuate into a photon with energy equal to the sum of the rest masses for the two annihilating particles. In pair creation, a photon with energy greater than or equal to the rest masses for two particles fluctuates into a particle and its antiparticle.

Pair creation and pair annihilation can combine to form vacuum fluctuations, where photons fluctuate to particles and antiparticles that exist for short times before fluctuating back into photons.

Ernst Stueckelberg and Richard Feynman have proposed that antiparticles may be the same as particles except that they travel backward in time.

Attributes (particles)

Attributes are properties of a particle that can change and define where the particle is and what the particle is doing: position (a vector, requires three values), orientation (a vector, requires three values), momentum (a vector, requires three values), kinetic energy (a scalar, one value), potential energy (a scalar, one value), and time (a scalar, one value).

The term *attribute* is used in this and a few other introductory books but is not in common usage in physics; a more common term would be kinematic or dynamic properties. I used *attribute* here to help distinguish between properties that describe behavior and properties that describe the nature of the particle (charges for example, called *properties* here). Real physics books tend to call all of them properties, so they can be a little more challenging to sort out.

Baryon

Baryons are quark group (hadron) subatomic (smaller than atoms) particles composed of three quarks. Protons and neutrons are baryons; each is composed of three quarks.

Big bang cosmology

The proposal that our universe originated with all of the energy concentrated in a single point about 13.798 billion years ago is based on astronomical observations.

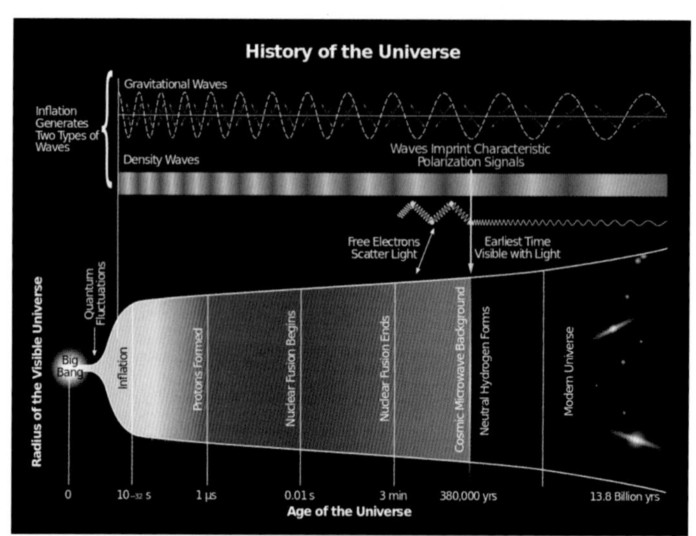

Fig. 132.3. Big Bang Cosmology

In 1929, Edwin Hubble used spectral measurements to observe that galaxies further than 32 million light years away tended to have light spectrums with lower (redder) frequencies. Redshift increased with distance. Redshift indicates that the galaxies are rapidly moving away from us; increasing redshift implies that more distant galaxies move away faster. The measured motions of distant galaxies implied that visible matter in our universe was expanding. Later, more precise measurements of redshifts indicated that the expansion rate has not been constant; it slowed down.

In 1968 and 1970, Hawking, Ellis, and Penrose used general relativity to calculate that the observed expansion was not just due to the movement of matter; space and time had to be expanding as well. They also calculated that space and time must have originated as a dimensionless point as well as the energy that became matter.

Quantum mechanics calculations for the big bang predict a distribution of matter, mostly hydrogen and helium, that matches the observed distribution. Quantum mechanics also predicts a residual "glow" of microwave radiation that was observed and measured in 1964. The uniformity of the cosmic microwave background (the residual glow) supports mathematical models that imply that spacetime grew very rapidly just after the big bang (called spacetime inflation).

Boson

Fundamental particles or particle ensembles that have integer values (0, 1, 2 . . .) of intrinsic angular momentum (spin). Particles with integer spin do not obey Pauli exclusion; there can be any number of bosons in a single quantum state. Fermions, particles with half-integer spin values (1/2, 3/2, 5/2 . . .) do obey Pauli exclusion; there can be only one fermion in any quantum state. Exchanges of fundamental particle bosons (photons, gluons, Z, W+, and W-) are associated with quantum interactions that change momentum, what we call forces.

c

"c" is the standard symbol in physics for the speed of light in a vacuum: 186,282.4 miles/second. The speed of light can be less in other media; the speed of light in glass, for example, is only about 124,188 miles/second.

The speed of light is always measured to have the same value regardless of the speed of travel and the direction of travel for the light source or the measuring equipment. Two instruments will measure light speed for the same event to be the same value (c) regardless of how fast they are traveling relative to each other.

The observation (and calculation) that c is always the same regardless of the movement of the light source or the measuring instrument is one basis for special relativity.

Cartesian coordinates

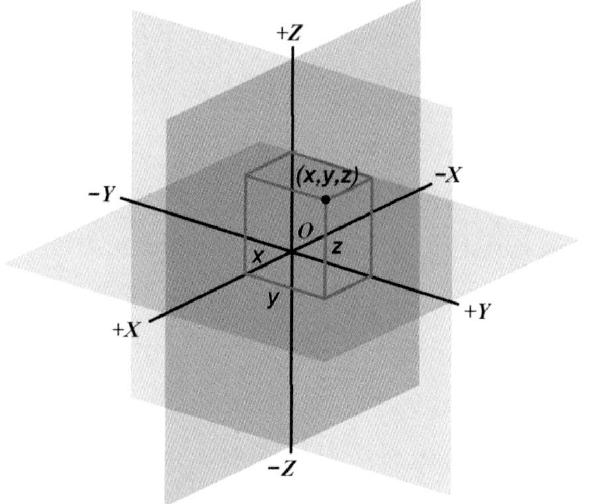

The fundamental tool of mathematical physics, Cartesian coordinates are used to assign numerical values to all physical variables that have locations or directions.

A Cartesian coordinate system consists of a point called an origin (O in the figure) and three perpendicular lines called axes (X, Y, and Z in the figure).

Any position or any other vector quantity in physics can be mathematically described with three measurements along the axes (x, y, and z in the figure).

Each axis has a positive direction, where measurements have positive number values. Measurements on the other side of the origin, in the negative direction, have negative number values.

Origin position and axis orientations are chosen for each calculation to make the calculation as simple as possible. The theories of physics must always work the same regardless of where the origin is or what directions the axes are.

Charge (particle)

Charges are particle properties that represent the susceptibility of the particle to the quantum interactions that we call fundamental forces.

Particles with color charge are susceptible to the strong nuclear force interaction.

Particles with weak isospin charge are susceptible to the weak nuclear force interaction.

Particles with electric charge are susceptible to the electromagnetic force interaction.

Particles with mass-energy charge are susceptible to the gravity force interaction.

The numerical value of a charge property relates strength of the force interaction for the particle to the rate that fundamental bosons are exchanged to mediate the force interaction.

Color charge

Color charge is a property of a fundamental particle that describes its susceptibility to the strong nuclear interaction (force); a particle must have color charge to participate in strong nuclear interactions (forces). The numerical value of color charge relates the strength of the strong nuclear force interaction for the particle to the rate that fundamental bosons (gluons for the strong nuclear force) are exchanged.

There are three types of color charge for matter particles, called red, green, and blue; and three types of color charge for antimatter particles, called anti-red, anti-green, and anti-blue. All three matter charges must be present to neutralize the strong force, or all three antimatter charges must be present to neutralize the strong force, or one matter charge and its antimatter charge (red and anti-red, for example) must be present to neutralize the strong force.

Fundamental particles with color charge (called quarks) are pulled into particle groups (called hadrons) by the strong nuclear interaction. Hadrons are always formed from quarks in ways that reflect the charges required to neutralize the strong interaction: three quarks form a baryon, three anti-quarks form an anti-baryon, a quark and an antiquark form a meson.

Complex number

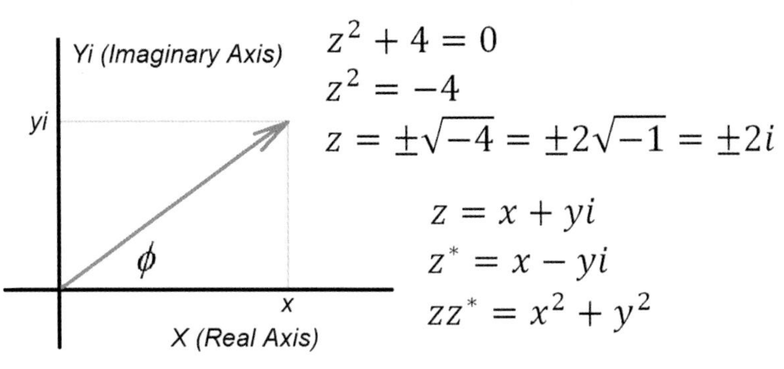

Complex numbers are required in mathematics to provide numerical values for the square roots of negative numbers. A complex number is written as x + yi where x is called the real part and y is the imaginary part. Complex numbers can be shown graphically in a Cartesian coordinate system with a real axis and an imaginary axis. i, the square root of −1, is the unit (the 1) of the imaginary axis.

Computation

As it is used here, computation is the type of computation done by a Turing machine: reading a stored list of symbols and performing actions based on the values of the symbols. More generally, computation is any type of calculation that follows a well-defined model, such as a defined sequence of operations (called an algorithm) or a body of rules that specify the passage of information between two systems (called a protocol).[1]

Computational core

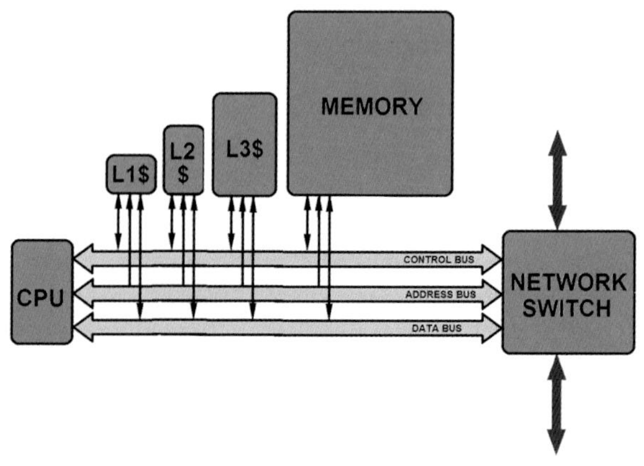

Parallel computers divide computational tasks up to be performed on many computational cores at the same time. Each computational core has all of the essential elements of a computer: a central processing unit (CPU), a system bus (control bus, address bus, and data bus), and associated memory. Each computational core is connected to a network switch that controls the flow of information between the computational core and the rest of the computer.

Conservation laws

In physics, a conservation law describes a particular measurable or calculable physical property of an isolated physical system that is conserved (does not change) as the system evolves over time.[2] Conservation of energy is the conservation law most frequently used here.

According to Noether's theorem, any physical behavior that does not change in time and space, that works the same way no matter where or when it happens, must have an associated conservation law. For example, for physical behaviors to remain consistent across time, energy must be conserved.

Cosmology

Cosmology is the study of the origin, evolution, and eventual fate of the universe.[3] Cosmological theories (like the big bang theory and spacetime inflation theory) are mathematical models of the origin, evolution, and eventual fate of the universe,

1 "Computation." Retrieved c. 2014 from https://en.wikipedia.org/wiki/Computation.
2 "Conservation Law." Retrieved c. 2014 from https://en.wikipedia.org/wiki/Conservation_law.
3 "Cosmology." Retrieved c. 2014 from https://en.wikipedia.org/wiki/Cosmology.

usually based on general relativity, quantum mechanics, and/or particle physics. Verification of cosmological theories is usually based on astronomical observations.

Coulomb force

Coulomb force (also known as electrostatic force) is the part of the electromagnetic interaction (force) that is due to the attraction (unlike, + and – , charges) or repulsion (like, + and + or – and –, charges) of stationary electric charges. Moving electric charges generate magnetic forces that contribute the rest of the electromagnetic interaction.

Dirac Sea

First proposed by Paul Dirac in 1930, the Dirac Sea is a theoretical model that describes a vacuum as an infinite sea of particles with negative energy. "Negative energy" here means less than the average value of the energy for the vacuum (called zero-point energy).

The term Dirac Sea as it is used here is also applied to the infinite cloud of virtual particles produced by vacuum fluctuations that theoretically fill the vacuum and form the "particles" that we see and measure. That application of the term is not common usage in physics; Dirac Sea is normally only used to describe the model proposed by Dirac.

e

"e" is an important number in mathematics. It has a value of approximately 2.71828. e was originally derived from calculations of compound interest. It can be calculated from the infinite series:

$$e = \sum_{n=0}^{\infty} \frac{1}{n!} = \frac{1}{1} + \frac{1}{1} + \frac{1}{1 \times 2} + \frac{1}{1 \times 2 \times 3} + \frac{1}{1 \times 2 \times 3 \times 4} + \ldots$$

(By convention, 0!=1)

e is an important number in physics because the e^x function is a kind of identity function for the derivative and integral operators in calculus: the derivative of e^x is e^x and the integral of e^x is e^x.

$$\frac{d}{dx} e^x = e^x \quad \int e^x dx = e^x + C$$

Electric charge

Electric charge is a property of a fundamental particle that describes its susceptibility to the electromagnetic interaction (force); a particle must have electric charge to participate in electromagnetic interactions (forces). The numerical value of electric charge relates the strength of the electromagnetic force interaction for the particle to the rate that fundamental bosons (photons for the electromagnetic force) are exchanged.

There are two types of electric charge, called positive (+) and negative (−). The electromagnetic force can either repel or attract particles that participate in the interaction, depending on the relationship between the electric charges of the particles: like charges (+ and + or − and −) repel; unlike charges (+ and −) attract.

Electromagnetic interaction (force)

The electromagnetic interaction (force) changes the momentum of (applies force to) particles that have electric charge. Only particles that have electric charge participate in the electromagnetic interaction. The electromagnetic interaction is a composite of two types of interaction that both require electric charge: an electrostatic, or Coulomb, interaction and a magnetic interaction. Electrostatic force or interaction (also known as a Coulomb force or interaction) is the part of the electromagnetic interaction (force) that is due to the attraction (unlike, + and − , charges) or repulsion (like, + and + or − and −, charges) of stationary electric charges. Moving electric charges generate magnetic force interactions that contribute the rest of the electromagnetic interaction.

Electrostatic forces

Electrostatic force (also known as Coulomb force) is the part of the electromagnetic interaction (force) that is due to the attraction (unlike, + and − , charges) or repulsion (like, + and + or − and −, charges) of stationary electric charges. Moving electric charges generate magnetic forces that contribute the rest of the electromagnetic interaction.

Energy

In classical physics, energy is the aggregate amount of work (force × distance) done to a physical system that is always equal to the amount of work the same system is able to do. Energy is conserved, meaning that it cannot be created or destroyed. Energy can change forms (from mechanical motion to heat, for example), but the total value of energy does not change.

In modern physics, energy (still the aggregate amount of work, by the way) is a dynamic property of particles (called an attribute in this book) called mass-energy charge. Mass-energy charge for a particle is the sum of rest energy, kinetic energy, and potential energy. Rest energy is effectively the lowest value of mass-energy charge that a kind of particle can have and still be that kind of particle. Kinetic energy is mass-energy charge that depends on the momentum of the particle. Potential energy is mass-energy charge that depends on the local arrangement of force interactions.

Mass-energy charge is the property of a fundamental particle that describes its susceptibility to the gravity interaction (force). Almost all particles have mass-energy charge, so almost all particles are susceptible to the gravity force interaction.

Particles can (and do) fluctuate into other kinds of particles. When particles fluctuate into different kinds of particles with different rest energy property values, the total value of mass-energy charge remains constant. If the new particles have lower rest energy, the kinetic and/or potential energy will increase to make up the difference; if the new particles have higher rest energy, the kinetic and/or potential energy will decrease. Particles can only fluctuate into other particles with higher rest energy if they have enough kinetic and/or potential energy to supply the additional rest energy.

Entanglement (quantum entanglement)

When quantum state particles interact in ways that link their probability amplitudes, they are described as being entangled. For example, when two particles "collide," their subsequent speeds and directions are restricted by energy and momentum conservation laws. If one of the particles is localized by a measurement, the probability amplitude for the other particle changes: it is restricted to a range of speeds and directions compatible with the value of the measurement. Localization of either particle changes the probability amplitude for the other particle.

Entanglement information, the change in the probability amplitude of the second particle, has been measured to pass between entangled particles at speeds that are much faster than the speed of light.

Eternalism

Eternalism is the philosophical viewpoint that all of time has a real, simultaneous physical existence. It is called eternalism because all of eternity exists. The contrary viewpoint is called presentism, the idea that only the present has a real, physical existence.

In physics, eternalism is supported by relativity because the shifting timescales predicted (and measured) by relativity theory make it impossible to define a present moment for the entire universe. Eternalism is also supported in particle physics by the Feynman-Stueckelberg interpretation of antimatter as particles traveling backward in time.

Some theories have been proposed that support presentism, but none of them so far have been verified by experiment or observation.

Fermion

A fermion is a fundamental particle or particle ensemble that has a net 1/2 integer value (1/2, 3/2, 5/2, 7/2 . . .) of intrinsic angular momentum (spin). Fermions are subject to Pauli exclusion, meaning that only one fermion can occupy a single quantum state. Particles or particle ensembles with integer values of spin (0, 1, 2, 3 ...) are called bosons and are not subject to Pauli exclusion; any number of bosons can occupy a single quantum state.

The particles that form the structure of matter (quarks and leptons) are all fermions and are all subject to Pauli exclusion. Pauli exclusion keeps atoms (and subatomic particles) physically separated into the extended structures that we call atoms, molecules, and substances.

Feynman diagram

A Feynman diagram is a graphical technique for summarizing the elements of the mathematical equations that describe interactions between quantum object probability amplitudes. It is drawn as a spacetime diagram (one spatial axis called x and one time axis called t) with lines representing quantum object probability amplitudes, and line intersections, called interaction

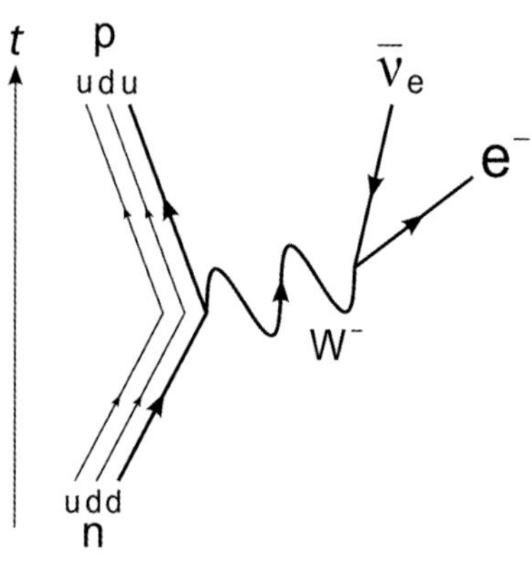

Fig. 132.9. Feynman Free Neutron Decay

vertices, representing interactions between probability amplitudes.

Feynman-Stueckelberg

The Feynman-Stueckelberg interpretation of antimatter is derived from the positive and negative exponent solutions to the Dirac equation describing the relativistic time evolution of quantum probability amplitudes for fermions:

$$\Psi(t) = e^{-i\alpha Et} \text{ and } \Psi(t) = e^{i\alpha Et}$$

In order to be mathematically valid, the exponent ($i\alpha Et$) must be negative. Dirac originally added two negative signs that would cancel out to form $-i\alpha(-E)t$. He referred to the rearranged term as a negative energy solution and proposed that it referred to a then-unknown new kind of matter called antimatter.

Feynman and Stueckelberg proposed an alternate rearrangement:

$$\Psi(t) = e^{-i\alpha E(-t)}$$

The physical implication of the Feynman-Stueckelberg rearrangement is that antimatter particles do not have negative energy; they travel backward in time. The Feynman-Stueckelberg negative time rearrangement resolves several problems with the application of relativity to quantum mechanics and is frequently used in quantum theory of particles. The implied physical interpretation is not widely supported by physicists.

Force

A force in physics (usually represented by an F in equations) is any interaction that changes the momentum of an object (F = dp/dt is one of Newton's laws of motion; p is momentum).

Force field

A force field in physics is a region of space where the value of force (the change of momentum for an object) can be calculated for every point in the space.

Fluctuations

In quantum physics, a fluctuation is a temporary change in the amount of energy at a point in space allowed by the Heisenberg uncertainty principle of energy and time.[4] Here, the term *fluctuation* is applied to changes in kind of particle, which require a change in rest energy.

Fock states

Fock states are a mathematical technique in quantum mechanics used for describing multi-particle systems as a sum of quantum states inhabited by populations of particles. In the simplified description of Fock states used here, the quantum states of a system are described as available probability amplitudes that can be inhabited by one (for a fermion) or more (for bosons) particles.

GA

An abbreviation of giga-annum, meaning one billion years ago.

GEV

An abbreviation of giga-electron volts/c^2, 1 billion EV/c^2. Electron volts/c^2 is a unit of mass frequently used to describe the mass-energy charge, particularly rest mass, of individual particles.

h

Planck's constant. Originally derived by Max Planck to describe the energy of photons as $E = h\nu$ (ν represents the frequency). Planck's constant occurs frequently in the mathematical models of quantum theory. For example:

De Broglie's equation for the wavelength of a particle: $\lambda = h/p$

Heisenberg's uncertainty relationships: $\Delta x \Delta p \geq h/4\pi$ or $\Delta E \Delta t \geq h/4\pi$

Hadron

A hadron is a composite particle made of quark fundamental particles bound together by the strong nuclear force interaction. Because the strong nuclear force can

4 "Quantum Fluctuation." Retrieved c. 2014 from https://en.wikipedia.org/wiki/Quantum_fluctuation.

be "balanced" in three different ways, there are three different types of hadron: baryons made of three quarks with red, green, and blue color charges; anti-baryons made of three anti-quarks with anti-red, anti-green, and anti-blue color charges; and mesons made of quark and anti-quark pairs with red and anti-red, green and anti-green, or blue and anti-blue color charges.

Heisenberg uncertainty

Heisenberg uncertainty is a mathematically derived relationship between complementary attributes of quantum state particles. Complementary attributes (position/momentum, orientation/angular momentum, energy/time) are limited in how small the possible ranges of values for both attributes can be: for example, if the range of values for position is very small, the range of values for momentum must be larger; if the possible range of momentum values is very small, the range of position values must be larger.

i

"i" is the symbol used in complex number notation to represent the square root of −1.

Interaction (quantum)

The term *interaction* is applied in physics to what are more commonly called forces because of quantum field theory. Physically, the strong nuclear force, weak nuclear force, electromagnetic force, gravitational force (possibly), and the phenomenon that we call inertial mass are interactions between quantum object probability amplitudes that involve the "exchange" of fundamental bosons (gluons for the strong nuclear interaction, W and Z bosons for the weak nuclear interaction, photons for electromagnetic interactions, gravitons for the gravitational interaction, and Higgs bosons for inertial mass).

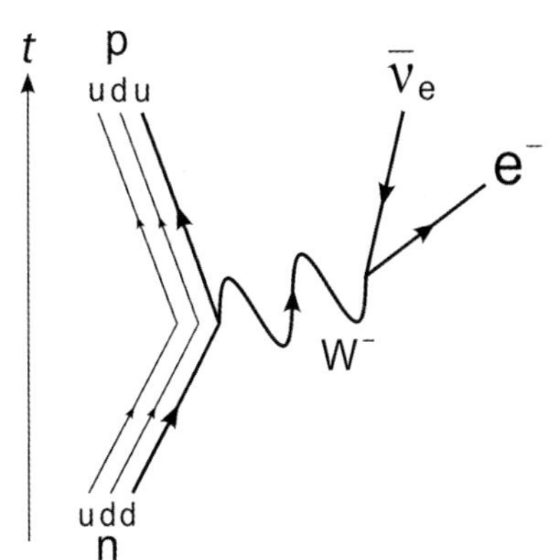

Fig. 132.12. Feynman Free Neutron Decay

Interaction vertices

On a Feynman diagram, a spacetime diagram that represents the mathematical elements of a quantum system, quantum object probability amplitudes are represented by lines, and quantum interactions are represented by line intersections called interaction vertices.

Interference (waves)

Wave interference is the superposing of two waves to result in a different wave pattern. Superposing (derived from *superposition*) means adding the numerical values of the wave amplitudes at every point to produce an interference wave that is the sum of the superposing waves.

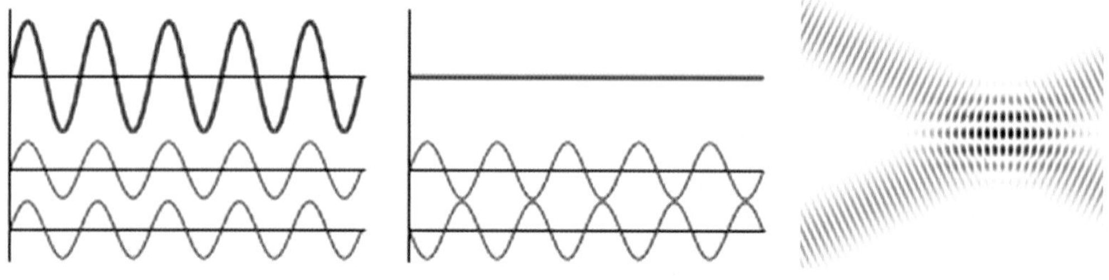

Fig. 132.13. Wave Superposition and Interference

Kinetic energy

Kinetic energy is the energy of an object with mass-energy charge (m) that is due to the motion of the object: $E_K = mv^2/2$ (or $E_K = pv/2$, since momentum, p, is mv)

In relativity, the value of kinetic energy for an object will change depending on the motion of the reference frame of the calculation; for the reference frame that moves with the object, kinetic energy is zero. There is a sum called the relativistic four-momentum that keeps a constant value regardless of the reference frame of the calculation: $p_x^2 + p_y^2 + p_z^2 - E^2/c$.

Lepton

A lepton is a fundamental particle that does not have color charge and does not participate in the strong nuclear force interaction. First-generation leptons are the electron and the electron neutrino. The leptons for the second generation of matter are the muon and the muon neutrino. Third-generation leptons are the tau and the tau neutrino.

Because they are not confined by the strong nuclear interaction, leptons can move about as individual particles. Electrons are found bound as parts of atoms (outside the strong-force-confined nucleus) and sometimes as individual particles. Electrical currents in metals, for example, are moving electrons.

Leptons have half-integer spin, so they are among the fermions and are subject to Pauli exclusion.

Localization

Localization is the transition of a quantum state object into a classical particle. Quantum state objects appear to exist as distributed waves of possibilities for attribute values mathematically described by the probability amplitude. All of the material in our universe spends almost all of its time in quantum state.

When quantum state objects morph into localized classical particles, the attributes of the particles will have specific values. The range and distribution of specific attribute values will conform to probability distributions calculated from the quantum state probability amplitude.

As far as we know, quantum state objects only localize into classical particles when we see them or when we do experiments on them. Localized classical particles are all that we ever see; quantum state objects always localize whenever we see them.

Lorentz contraction factor

In special relativity, the lengths of objects, time, and mass-energy charge all change when they are observed from a different reference frame (that is, by an observer traveling at a different velocity). The numerical value of the change is described by the Lorentz factor (usually represented by γ in equations):

$$\gamma = \frac{1}{\sqrt{1 - \frac{v^2}{c^2}}}$$

MA

MA is an abbreviation for mega-annum, meaning one million years ago.

Mass-energy charge

Mass-energy charge (usually represented by "m" in equations) is a property of particles that describes how the particles participate in the gravitational force interaction and in the behavior called inertial mass. Inertial mass means that particles accelerate in response to forces proportional to their current value of mass-energy charge ($a = F/m$ according to Newton's laws of motion).

Mass-energy charge has a minimum value that is associated with the rest energy of the particle ($m_{RE} = E_R/c^2$), but it increases with the kinetic energy ($\Delta m_K = E_K/c^2$) and the potential energy ($\Delta m_P = E_P/c^2$).

Matter

Matter is a concept of classical physics that is associated with substance, with the volume and weight (on Earth) of an object. The technical definition was: matter takes up space and has mass.

The matter concept of classical physics has not survived the transformation to modern physics. In modern physics there is no substance: everything is made only of energy in various forms. Nothing "takes up space": all of the fundamental particles are dimensionless points that are imbued with an illusion of bulk by Pauli exclusion. Unchanging mass has become mass-energy charge that changes at the drop of a hat (and the particles will spontaneously drop the hat).

Meson

Mesons are hadron (quark group) particles formed from a single quark and a single anti-quark.

MEV

An abbreviation of mega-electron volts/c^2, one million EV/c^2. Electron volt/c^2 is a unit of mass frequently used to describe the mass-energy charge, particularly rest mass, of individual particles.

Momentum

Momentum in physics (usually represented by "p" in equations) is the product of mass and velocity: $p = mv$. Momentum is often used in the mathematics of physics instead of velocity to describe the motions of objects, because forces acting on objects change momentum, not velocity by itself ($F = dp/dt$ is one of Newton's laws of motion).

In relativity, the calculated value of momentum changes depending on the reference frame of the calculation, that is, on how fast an observer is moving relative to the object. There is, however, a version of momentum called a four-momentum that has the same value regardless of how fast an observer is travelling: $p_x^2 + p_y^2 + p_z^2 - E^2/c^2$.

Network structure (network topology)

Network structure describes the arrangement of communications pathways between computers when they are connected to share information. Here, the term is applied to the arrangement of bus pathways and computational nodes in a parallel computer. Our parallel computers use linear networks with buses and nodes in a single line, ring networks with buses and nodes forming a circle, two-dimensional grids, or three-dimensional grids.

Neural networks have many bus pathways connecting computational nodes so that information can move very quickly.

Noether's theorem

Noether's theorem is a mathematical proof in physics that any behavior that remains consistent must have an associated conservation law to enforce its consistency. The application of Noether's theorem to particle physics uses the same complementary particle attributes as Heisenberg uncertainty: in order to have the same behavior in different positions in space, linear momentum must be conserved; in order to have the same behavior for any orientation, angular momentum must be conserved; in order to have the same behavior at different times, energy must be conserved.

OODA loop

OODA stands for "observe, orient, decide, act." The OODA loop is a model of the decision-making process that was originally developed to analyze military organizations, but it is applicable to any decision-making process.

Parallel computation

Parallel computation is an approach to the physical organization of the parts of a computer that works well for some types of problems. Problems that involve relatively simple calculations on large amounts of data can be done quickly using many small, simple computers connected together by a communications network. Parallel computers can have different arrangements of the communications network (network structure or topology); what network arrangement is most efficient can depend on the type of problem that needs to be done.

Particle

The term *particle* is used extensively in this book when, technically, it is not the correct term for the fundamental constituents of material. Oddly enough, the correct term in "particle" physics is quanta (plural) or quantum (singular). *Particle* is a concept from classical physics describing the idea that material is ultimately made of little, indivisible bits of substance. The classical particle concept did not survive the transition to modern physics.

In modern physics, it turned out that the fundamental constituents of material are not substance at all; there is nothing "solid" about them. Even the localized particles that we "see" in experiments are made only of energy. The quantum state objects (quanta) that seem to actually compose the material of our world may not even have energy; we have no idea what they are "made" of, but they are almost certainly not anything that we would call solid.

Mathematically, even quanta are probably not the fundamental constituents of material; the fundamental parts of material seem more likely to be quantum states that can be occupied by anonymous populations of quanta. Quanta seem, mathematically, to be collections of property and attribute values with aggregate sums preserved by conservation laws. That is, really, all that we currently know about them.

Potential energy

Potential energy is one of the forms of energy that is due to the position of an object in a force field (a region of space where the value of force, the change of momentum, can be calculated). Moving the object against the force increases potential energy; moving the object in the direction of the force decreases potential energy.

Presentism

Presentism is a philosophical conception of time as a physically existing present moment with a past and future that have no current physical existence. The concept of presentism is based on our perception of time as a sequence of experiences. There is no strong support for presentism in experimentally proven science. Relativity and quantum mechanics both at least imply eternalism, the concept that past, present, and future all have a simultaneous physical existence.

Primary producers

In biology, primary producers are organisms that "eat" naturally occurring material and/or energy (mostly rocks and sunlight) and produce organic compounds that other organisms must have to survive. In our ecology here on Earth, primary producers are mostly bacteria (both eubacteria and archea) and Protista (single-celled eukaryotes). Plants also participate in primary production, but they often require the assistance of bacteria or Protista to digest rocks.

Probability amplitude (Ψ)

A probability amplitude is a complex ($x + yi$) function used in quantum mechanics to describe the quantum state of an object. The probability amplitude is, basically, a sum of terms where each term is the product of a function that describes a possible state of the object and a complex ($x + yi$) factor that is associated with the possibility that the object will be in that state if it is localized.

"Possibility" here means that the complex factors are complex square roots of the probabilities for each of the terms of the probability amplitude: multiplying a complex factor times its complex conjugate yields the probability for the term.

Quantum state objects behave as though the probability amplitude has some kind of real, physical existence. Many of the odd experimental results that led to quantum mechanics were the result of the physical interactions of quantum object probability amplitudes with their physical surroundings. Atoms bond into molecules, for example, in physical configurations that are determined by the superposition and interference of the probability amplitudes of the electrons that surround each atom.

The mathematics of quantum mechanics describe the changes in probability amplitudes for quantum objects in response to their surroundings. When quantum state objects morph into localized classical particles, the values of particle attributes will be consistent with probability distributions calculated from the sums (superposition and interference) of all of the terms in the probability amplitude.

Properties (particles)

The properties of a particle are a collection of mathematical values that describe the behavior of the particle. Particle properties are a combination of values that are associated with the kind of particle (charges and internal symmetries; called "properties" in this book) and values that describe where the particle is and what it is doing (position, time, orientation, momentum, and energy; called "attributes" in this book).

Quantum computation

Quantum computation is similar to the binary digital computation that we mostly use in our computers, but it intentionally uses the properties of quantum state objects. Information is stored as quantum bits (qubits) rather than digital bits. Logical operations are done using quantum logic gate arrays instead of binary logic gate arrays.

In our binary digital computers, information is stored and manipulated as localized bits. In quantum computation, information is stored and manipulated in the form of quantum state probability amplitudes.

Quantum computation is projected to be much more efficient at solving some types of calculations that are very difficult or practically impossible for binary digital computers.

Quantum field theory

The version of quantum mechanics primarily described here is called classical quantum mechanics. Like classical physics, it has been superseded by more accurate mathematical models called quantum field theory. Classical quantum mechanics was used in this book because it is much easier to understand. The central argument of this book, that our world probably has a mathematical basis, is in my opinion supported even more strongly by quantum field theory than it is by classical quantum mechanics.

Quantum field theory models "particles" as oscillations of particle fields that permeate the entire universe, with a different field for each type of particle. There is one single electron field, for example, that extends throughout the universe; all real and virtual electrons are local oscillations of that field. Similarly, there is one electron neutrino field, one up quark field, one down quark field, one photon field, eight gluon fields, and so on.

A field is a region of space that can have some kind of number assigned to every point in it. Fermion (electron, up quark, down quark, etc.) fields have spinor values assigned to every point in the universe. A spinor is a special 4×1 spacetime vector with complex elements (four complex numbers) that obey Lie algebra for coordinate rotations. Boson (photon, gluon, W boson, Z boson, or Higgs boson) fields have vector values assigned to every point in the universe. A vector is a 3×1 spatial matrix with real number elements (three real numbers).

Particles are identical and indistinguishable because they are all oscillations of the same field. Each particle field has properties (what we describe as charges and conservation laws) that govern the interactions between them.

Most of the quantum mathematics described here, including the Klein-Gordon, Dirac, and Proca equations, renormalization, and Yang-Mills gauge theories, is actually done in quantum field theory, not in classical quantum mechanics.

Quantum logic gate

Quantum logic gates and quantum logic gate arrays perform logical operations in quantum computers. Quantum logic gates and arrays alter the probability amplitudes of quantum bits (qubits).

Quark

Quarks are fundamental particles that have color charge and participate in the strong nuclear force interaction. There are six "flavors" of quark: up, down, charm, strange, top, and bottom. Only the up and down quarks are stable; charm, strange, top, and bottom quarks are only observed in cosmic rays or particle accelerators. Quarks have never been observed as individual particles, they are always confined by the strong nuclear interaction into groups (called hadrons): baryons with three quarks; anti-baryons with three anti-quarks; and mesons with one quark and one anti-quark.

The protons and neutrons that compose atomic nuclei are quark group (hadron) particle ensembles with three quarks (baryons).

Qubit

A qubit, or quantum bit, is the unit of information storage for quantum computation. A qubit is stored in a quantum computer as a probability amplitude, a superposition of the possible values (0 or 1). Qubits localize to one of the possible values in accordance with probabilities calculated from the probability amplitude when they are read. The values of the complex (x + yi) factors that are used to calculate the probabilities for qubit localized values can be changed by quantum logic gates.

Radiometric dating

Radiometric dating in geology, paleontology, and archeology is based on the decay rates of radioactive isotopes of elements. Radiometric dating assumes that radioactive isotope decay rates have been constant throughout all of time.

Real particles

Real, as opposed to virtual, particles are quantum state probability amplitudes that persist after quantum interactions. Virtual particles (if they exist at all) only exist during a quantum state interaction or for short periods of time in vacuum fluctuations.

Renormalization

Renormalization is a mathematical technique for calculating particle behavior based on the presumption that what we call particles are actually infinite clouds of virtual particles and anti-particles with one extra real particle or anti-particle that creates a local imbalance of property values.

Rest energy

Rest energy is one of the three forms of energy (the other two are kinetic energy and potential energy). Rest energy is related to the minimum mass-energy charge value (m) that a kind of particle can have: $E_R = m_{MIN} \times c^2$.

Scalar

A scalar is a physical quantity in physics that can be described by a single number, that has no associated direction. In contrast, the other most common physical quantity is a vector, a physical quantity with a direction that requires three (for a spatial vector) or four (for a spacetime vector) Cartesian coordinate values to describe the quantity and its direction.

Spacetime

Spacetime is the term in physics that describes the idea that space and time are physically linked, that they cannot be treated separately in physical theories (mathematical models). The term was originally applied to describe mathematical transformations between reference frames in special relativity, where it is mathematically convenient to use a spacetime four-vector (x, y, z, ict) instead of treating space and time separately. In general relativity, the spacetime four-vector must be used to derive correct results. Space and time bend together to produce gravitational effects.

When Feynman proposed the negative time interpretation for antimatter and the associated implication that all of time must have a simultaneous, physical existence, he referred to it as "the spacetime perspective." To him, it was just a logical extension of the idea of spacetime in general relativity.

Spacetime diagram

A spacetime diagram is a picture of a (usually) two-dimensional Cartesian coordinate system with time along one axis and distance along the other axis. Spacetime diagrams are very commonly used in physics (and in this book) to illustrate concepts relating to spacetime. Feynman diagrams, like the one shown at right, are spacetime diagrams that represent the mathematics of quantum particle interactions.

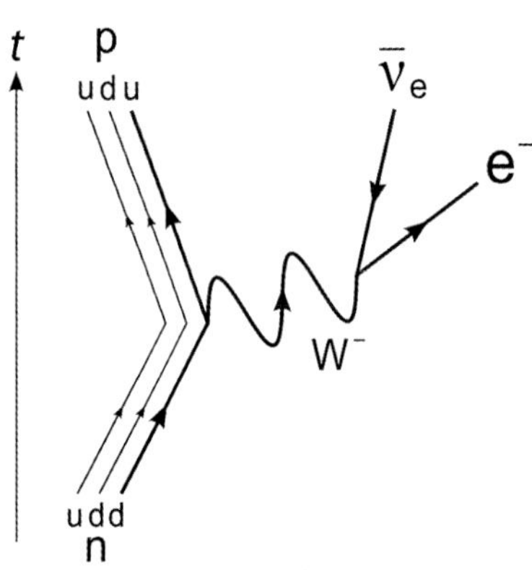

Fig. 132.15. Feynman Free Neutron Decay

Standard model of particle physics

The standard model of particle physics is a group of mathematical models that classifies subatomic particles and describes their interactions (forces) and fluctuations (changes in kind of particle).

Substance (stuff)

Substance is an idea from classical physics that material is made of solid, unchanging, atoms of matter. The idea of substance did not survive the transition to modern physics. In modern physics nothing is solid, everything changes constantly, and it is questionable whether the particles of matter have any real existence at all.

Superposition (waves)

Superposing (derived from *superposition*) means adding the numerical values of wave amplitudes at every point to produce an interference wave that is the sum of the superposing waves.

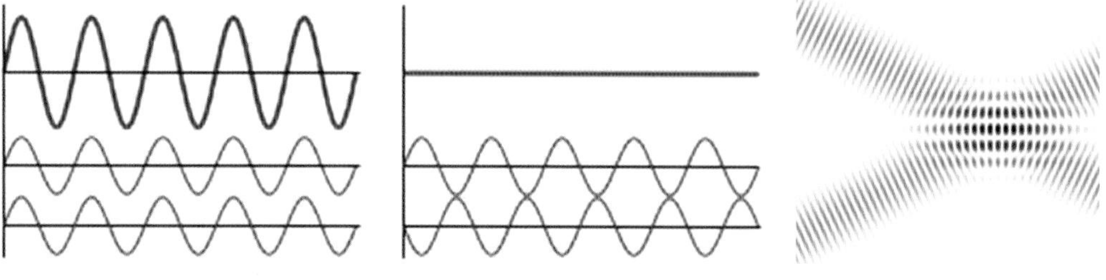

Fig. 132.16. Wave Superposition and Interference

Trophic web

The common usage name for a trophic web is "food chain." A trophic web is the pattern of predator-prey relationships (who eats who) in ecologies.

Vacuum fluctuations

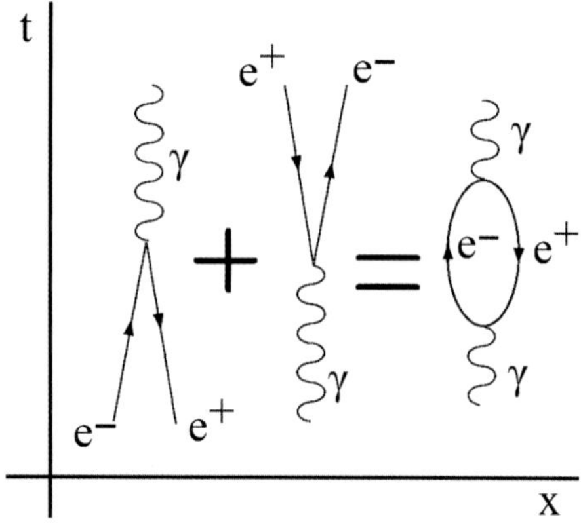

Vacuum fluctuations are spontaneous changes of fundamental bosons into matter/antimatter pairs of fundamental fermions (called pair creation) and recombination of matter/antimatter pairs of fundamental fermions back into fundamental bosons (called pair annihilation).

Vacuum fluctuations theoretically happen constantly and fill all of spacetime with infinite clouds of matter/antimatter fermion pairs.

Vector

A vector is a physical quantity with a direction that requires three (for a spatial vector) or four (for a spacetime vector) Cartesian coordinate values to describe the quantity and direction. In contrast, the other most common physical quantity is a scalar, a physical quantity that can be described by a single number (no direction).

Virtual particles

Virtual particles are theoretical (none have ever been observed) particles that exist only for short times during quantum interactions. Their existence is suggested by the mathematics of quantum field theory. In the Feynman diagram, the W boson is a virtual particle that participates in the decay of a neutron into a proton, an electron, and an electron antineutrino.

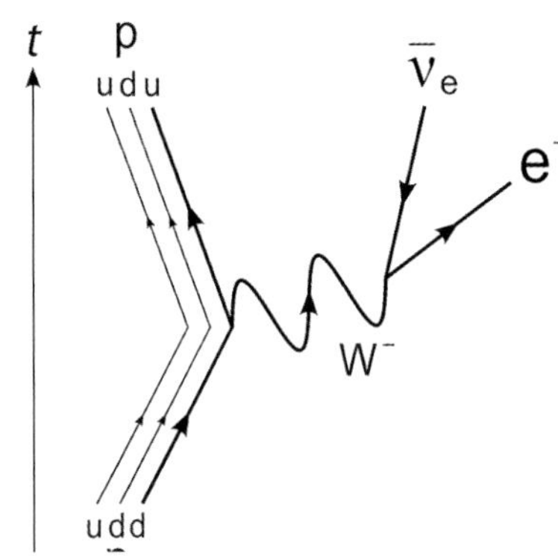

Fig. 132.18. Feynman Free Neutron Decay

Weak isospin charge

Weak isospin charge is a particle property associated with the weak nuclear force interaction. In quantum field theory, it relates to the rate of W and Z boson exchanges that mediate the force interaction.

Work

In physics, work is calculated as the product of the magnitude of a force times the movement of an object in response to the force (work = force × distance). Energy is the aggregate amount of work that has been done to an object: work done on an object increases energy; work done by an object decreases energy.

Yang-Mills gauge theories

As they are described here, Yang-Mills gauge theories are correction terms added to the energy balance equations of quantum mechanics (Schrodinger equation, Klein-Gordon equation, Dirac equation, and Proca equation) to conform to the light-speed limitations of special relativity. Yang-Mills gauge theories mathematically show the conformity of quantum mechanics particle theories to U(1), SU(2), and SU(3) Lie groups.

Annotated Bibliography

For garnering background information, I have found introductory college textbooks to be the most useful. Popular books on science, especially biological issues, tend (in my opinion) to be focused on naturalist apologetics and are often not trustworthy. Introductory textbooks for students entering a field are the best; they are normally written by experts in the field and tend to be very thorough. Even college textbooks written for survey courses (not for students entering the field) tend to focus on propaganda instead of science.

Quantum Mechanics

QED: The Strange Theory of Light and Matter by Richard Feynman (1985). This book is a great introduction to quantum mechanics. Dr. Feynman was one of the acknowledged stars in quantum physics and had a passion for explaining the subject to anyone who was willing to sit through a lecture. The example calculations focus on Feynman's path integral formulation.

Quantum Reality: Beyond the New Physics by Nick Herbert (1985 and 1987). This is a good introduction to quantum mechanics using Schrodinger's wave mechanics for the calculation examples. Nick Herbert is a philosopher, so *Quantum Reality* emphasizes the implications of the physics on the nature of our existence. It does a pretty good job of presenting some of the major interpretations of quantum mechanics. Just for reference, the view of quantum mechanics presented here is a slight twist on "Von Neumann's" extension of the Copenhagen interpretation (it wasn't actually Von Neumann who proposed the idea of observer-created reality, but that's what Dr. Herbert calls it).

Quantum Reality: Theory and Philosophy by Jonathan Allday (2009). This is a very thorough (and long) introduction to quantum mechanics with some introduction to quantum field theory. This book is a more challenging read; it uses Dirac's formulation and includes frequent presentations of how the mathematics for quantum mechanics is done. It also includes sections that discuss some of the major interpretations of quantum mechanics and their historical development.

Quantum Theory by David Bohm (1951 and 1979). This is a college-level introduction to quantum theory for physics students. Despite its age, it is still regarded as one of the best introductions to the mathematics of quantum mechanics. One of the parts I found interesting was the chapter on philosophical implications of quantum mechanics; some of the physical behaviors that Dr. Bohm dismissed as absurd have since been experimentally verified.

The Quantum Challenge: Modern Research on the Foundations of Quantum Mechanics by George Greenstein and Arthur Zajonc (2006). In my opinion, this is the best book out there about quantum physics. The book includes a very thorough discussion of the interpretational issues in quantum mechanics and the experiments that have been done to try to resolve them. This book is not an introduction. It is possible to get through it with no preparation, but it will make more sense after reading one or more of the introductory works mentioned above.

String Theories & M Theory

Warped Passages by Lisa Randall (2005). This book offers a presentation of the multi-dimensional physics implied by string theories and M theory. *Warped Passages* also includes a good description of general relativity and is exceptionally good at sharing the experience, the feel, of the mathematics of physics.

The Elegant Universe by Brian Greene (1999 and 2003). *The Elegant Universe* gives thorough description of string theories and is a bit easier to read than *Warped Passages*.

Particle Physics

Deep Down Things: The Breathtaking Beauty of Particle Physics by Bruce Schumm (2004). This book is a very nice introduction to the standard model of particle physics;

it's one of my favorites. Dr. Schumm does a particularly nice job of discussing some of the limitations of the physical theories; it's surprising how many of the experts forget to mention those little tidbits. It may be challenging for readers who have not been trained in introductory physics.

The Infinity Puzzle: Quantum Field Theory and the Hunt for an Orderly Universe by Frank Close (2011). This is a story of the development of the standard model of particle physics. It does give some description of the physics, but the focus is more on the story and the people involved in the effort.

Particle Metaphysics: A Critical Account of Subatomic Reality by Professor Dr. Brigitte Falkenberg (2007). Dr. Falkenberg has doctorates in both philosophy and particle physics. This book is basically a detailed presentation of particle physics intended for philosophers. It is not an introduction; it is an extremely thorough presentation of the material. There is not a lot of mathematics used in the presentation, so it is, in one sense, very readable. There is, however, a lot of physics jargon (unavoidable at this level of discussion) that is not defined in the text. Have an encyclopedia of quantum physics nearby while reading this.

Compendium of Quantum Physics, Concepts, Experiments, History and Philosophy edited by Daniel Greenberger, Klaus Hentschel, and Friedel Weinert (2009). This is an encyclopedia of quantum physics. It is not really intended as an introduction to the field, but it does help.

Modern Particle Physics by Mark Thomson (2013). This is an introduction to particle physics for physics students. It has lots of useful information even if you can't follow the mathematics.

"The Theory of Positrons" by Richard Feynman, *Physical Review*, 1949.

"Space-Time Approach to Quantum Electrodynamics" by Richard Feynman, *Physical Review*, 1949.

These are the original papers where Feynman proposed the Feynman-Stueckelberg interpretation of antimatter. They can be downloaded for free from the Internet; just do a search for the titles. There is nothing introductory about these papers. They are interesting to see, but I would recommend finishing all of the other books on quantum mechanics and particle physics first to have any chance at all of following what he is saying here.

Cosmology

A Universe from Nothing: Why There Is Something Rather Than Nothing by Lawrence Krauss (2012). This is a pretty good presentation of the naturalist side of the cosmology first-cause argument. It includes a good presentation of the observational justification for the big bang cosmology.

New Proofs for the Existence of God: Contributions of Contemporary Physics and Philosophy by Robert Spitzer (2010). This book presents the creationist side of the cosmology first-cause argument. It mentions a few things that Krauss left out (must have slipped his mind). It also has an interesting presentation of metaphysics for those unenlightened persons (like me) who think philosophers are mostly pretty goofy.

The Accidental Universe by Paul Davies (1982). A relatively short introduction to the physics of creation.

The Anthropic Cosmological Principle by John Barrow and Frank Tipler (1986). This is a serious tome, probably more than most would actually want to know about fine-tuning.

"Habitable Zones and Fine Tuning," Guillermo Gonzalez, in *The Nature of Nature,* 2011, edited by Bruce Gordon and William Dembski. This is a very nice, short but comprehensive presentation of fine-tuning. *The Nature of Nature* is a large compendium of scientific papers on the subject of creation, mostly from an Intelligent Design perspective, including history, philosophy, physics, biology, and more.

Physics of the Earth, fourth edition, by Frank Stacey and Paul Davis (2008). This is not strictly a book on cosmology, but it does have a very good presentation of solar system condensation models and solar system orbital dynamics. It also presents material on the condensation of the earth and the physics of geology. It is very thorough and very readable.

A Computational Universe?

A New Kind of Science by Stephen Wolfram (2002). Dr. Wolfram has seriously proposed that the physics of our world might be based on cellular automata because of the many, many similarities between the physical behavior that we see in the world around us and the behavior of cellular automata. Very long and very detailed.

Programming the Universe by Seth Loyd (2006). A quicker, simpler introduction to the idea that our universe might have a computational basis.

The Mind of God by Paul Davies (1992). This is a presentation of the physics of our universe that includes some material on the computational perspective.

"Are You Living in a Computer Simulation?" by Nick Bostrom, *Philosophical Quarterly* (2003). This is a relatively short paper that presents some of the technical issues associated with actually building a computational simulation of our universe.

"Simulating Physics with Computers" by Richard Feynman, *International Journal of Theoretical Physics* (1982). In this paper, Dr. Feynman demonstrates that it is not easy to accurately model the physical behavior of our world without using quantum computation. This paper has some historical significance because it is said to have inspired the development of quantum computation.

Biology and Genetics

Proteins, Structure and Function by David Whitford (2005). This is an introductory college textbook on proteins. I found it to be well written and very understandable. As usual with introductory college texts, it starts with the basics and is very thorough.

Molecular Biology of the Cell by Bruce Alberts, et al (2002). This is a (very large) introductory book on molecular biology. It has a thorough presentation and great graphics. It is, unfortunately, one of the standard texts for the field and is quite expensive; I found earlier editions to be much more reasonably priced.

Evolution: A View from the 21st Century by James Shapiro (2013). This book has a good presentation of the mechanisms of biological adaptability. The debate over whether this world occurred naturally or was created hinges on a few key issues. Adaptive mechanisms (the ways that organisms adapt to environmental changes) are, in my opinion, one of these, along with DNA modification processes and the configuration of protein sequence space. This book is advanced; it would be best to read an introduction to molecular biology first or have an encyclopedia of biology handy.

On the Origin of Phyla by James Valentine (2004). This is an excellent presentation of the fossil record relating to the original appearance of multicellular animals. It is very thorough; the only drawback to the book is that it may present more information than a casual reader ever wanted to know about early fossils. Based on comments in the book, I would guess that Dr. Valentine is philosophically a naturalist, but he presents material that is probably in conflict with the naturalist perspective anyway. A lot of naturalists leave out material that does not support the naturalist worldview. My compliments to Dr. Valentine; it is rare to find an academic who is a scientist first and only secondly a naturalist.

Paleobotany by Taylor, Taylor, and Krings (2009). This is an excellent source for anyone interested in this fossil history, very thorough. Even though the focus is on the fossil history of plants, *Paleobotany* has an excellent presentation of micropaleontology, the fossil history of microorganisms.

Microfossils by Armstrong and Brasier (2005). This is a reasonably priced, reasonably detailed presentation of the fossil record for bacteria and Protista. The illustrations are good.

Figure Credits

Fig. 8. Adapted from *The Blue Marble*. "File: The Earth as Seen From Apollo 17," https://commons.wikimedia.org/wiki/File:The_Earth_seen_from_Apollo_17.jpg, 1972, courtesy of NASA and Apollo 17 Crew, public domain.

Fig 11. Normal Distribution. Adapted from *Normal Distribution PDF* from Wikipedia Commons, https://commons.wikimedia.org/wiki/File:Normal_Distribution_PDF.svg. 2008. Inductiveload. Public domain.

Fig. 13. Compiled from: *Quartz* from "File: Quartz_oison," https://commons.wikimedia.org/wiki/File:Quartz_oisan.jpg, © 2014 by Didier Descouens, CC BY-SA 4.0 International; *Drop Closeup* from "File: Drop closeup," https://commons.wikimedia.org/wiki/File:Drop_closeup.jpg, © 2009 by Jos van Zetten, reprinted under CC BY-SA 2.0 Generic; *Purple Smoke* from "File: Purplesmoke," https://commons.wikimedia.org/wiki/File:Purplesmoke.jpg, 2007 by user Macluskie, public pomain; *Plasma Lamp* from "File: Plasma-lamp 2," https://commons.wikimedia.org/wiki/File:Plasma-lamp_2.jpg, © 2004 by Luc Viatour/https://Lucnix.be, reprinted under CC BY-SA 2.5.

Fig. 14. Illustration by Stuart Allen, using concepts from *Introduction to Special Relativity*, Helliwell, 1972.

Fig. 15. Illustration by Stuart Allen, using concepts from *Introduction to Special Relativity*, Helliwell, 1972.

Fig. 17. Based on figures in *Introduction to Special Relativity*, Helliwell, 1972.

Fig. 18. From "File: Daily satellite time dilation," https://commons.wikimedia.org/wiki/File:Daily_satellite_time_dilation.png. © 2012 by Wikimedia Commons user DVdm. Reprinted under CC BY-SA 3.0.

Fig. 21. *Dr. Niels Bohr* from Wikipedia article "Niels Bohr," 2018, https://commons.wikimedia.org/. 1922. By AB Lagrelius and Westphal. Public domain.

Fig. 22. *Richard Phillips Feynman (1918–1988)* from Wikipedia article "Richard Feynman," 2018, https://en.wikipedia.org/wiki/Richard_Feynman. 1965. By Nobel Foundation and Materialscientist. Public domain.

Fig. 24. From "File:Buckminsterfullerene-perspective-3D-balls," https://commons.wikimedia.org/wiki/File:Buckminsterfullerene-perspective-3D-balls.png. 2007. Illustration by Wikimedia Commons user Ben (Benjah-bmm27). Public domain.

Fig. 26. *Harmoniki* from "File:Harmoniki," https://commons.wikimedia.org/wiki/File:Harmoniki.png. © 2007 by Bartosz Firyn (Sarxos). Reprinted under CC BY-SA 3.0 Unported.

Fig. 27. Graphs by Stuart Allen, based on figures in Greenstein and Zajonc, *The Quantum Challenge*, 2006, p. 114–116, which were in turn based on Durr, Nonn, and Rempe, 1998, "Origin of quantum-mechanical complementarity probed by a 'which-way' experiment in an atom interferometer," *Nature*, 395, 33–37, figures 1, 2, and 4.

Fig. 28. Based on Based on *Standard Model of Elementary Particles* from"File:Standard Model of Elementary Particles," https://commons.wikimedia.org/wiki/File:Standard_Model_of_Elementary_Particles.svg, 2008 by MissMJ. Shared under CC BY 3.0 Unported.

Fig. 36. *Hadron Colors* from "File:Hadron colors," Wikimedia Commons, https://commons.wikimedia.org/wiki/File:Hadron_colors.svg. © 2009 by users Army1987 and TimothyRias, reprinted under CC BY-SA 3.0 Unported.

Fig. 39. Illustrations taken from Wikipedia article "Nucleon" circa 2014. *Quark structure neutron.svg*, https://commons.wikimedia.org/wiki/File:Quark_structure_neutron.svg. © 2006 by Arpad Horvath, reprinted under CC BY-SA 2.5 Generic. *Quark structure proton.svg* https://commons.wikimedia.org/wiki/File:Quark_structure_proton.svg. © 2006 by Arpad Horvath, reprinted under CC BY-SA 2.5 Generic.

Fig. 40. Diagram inspired by Bruce Schumm, *Deep Down Things*, 2004, p. 63.

Fig. 41. Author's work, based on Figure 5.7 and Equation 5.19 from Mark Thomson, *Modern Particle Physics* (p. 124–125). Cambridge, UK: Cambridge University Press, 2013.

Fig. 42. see *Fig. 26.*

Fig. 43. Based on *Standard Model of Elementary Particles* from"File:Standard Model of Elementary Particles," https://commons.wikimedia.org/wiki/File:Standard_Model_of_Elementary_Particles.svg, 2008 by MissMJ. Shared under CC BY 3.0 Unported.

Fig. 44. Author's work, based on Figure 7.1 from Mark Thomson, 2013, *Modern Particle Physics* (p. 161). Cambridge, UK: Cambridge University Press, 2013.

Fig. 45. Mark Thomson, 2013, *Modern Particle Physics*, p. 202, reprinted with permission of Cambridge University Press..

Fig. 46. **Left:** Illustration from "File: *Beta Negative Decay.svg*," https://commons.wikimedia.org/wiki/File:Beta_Negative_Decay.svg, 2007, by Joel Holdsworth, public domain. **Right:** Adapted from "*Kaon-decay.svg*," https://commons.wikimedia.org/wiki/File:Kaon-Decay.svg, © 2007 JabberWok, , reprinted under CC BY-SA3.0 Unported.

Fig. 47. Illustration inspired by Bruce Schumm, *Deep Down Things*, 2004, p. 90.

Fig. 48. see *Fig. 39.*

Fig. 51. Inspired by Schumm, *Deep Down Things*, 2004, p. 83.

Fig. 52. Inspired by Schumm, Figure 4.11, p. 85.

Fig. 53. Casimir Effect from "File:Casimir plates," https://commons.wikimedia.org/wiki/File:Casimir_plates.svg, © 2008 by user Emok, reprinted under CC BY-SA3.0 Unported.

Fig. 54. Plasma image from "File: Plasma-lamp 2," https://commons.wikimedia.org/wiki/File:Plasma-lamp_2.jpg. Copyright © 2004 by Luc Viatour / https://Lucnix.be. Reprinted under CC BY-SA 2.5.

Fig. 55. see *Fig. 45.*

Fig. 56. *The Planet, the Galaxy and the Laser* © 2007 by Y. Beletsky, ESO. Retrieved from https://commons.wikimedia.org/wiki/File:ESO-VLT-Laser-phot-33a-07.jpg in 2018. Reprinted under CC BY 4.0 International.

Fig. 57. Inspired by Bruce Schumm, *Deep Down Things*, Figure 7.8, page 199

Fig. 58. Information based on Schumm, *Deep Down Things*, 2004, Ch. 8.

Fig. 59. Illustrations by Wikimedia Commons users Joel Holdsworth (right, public domain) and JapperWok (left, © 2007). [See *Fig. 46.*]

Fig. 60. Inspired by Lancaster & Blundell, 2014, *Quantum Field Theory for the Gifted Amateur*, fig. 47.4, p. 441.

Fig. 61. Turing Machine illustration from "File:Maquina.png," https://commons.wikimedia.org/wiki/File:Maquina.png, 2005, by user Schadel. Public domain.

Fig 63. From "Z80 arch.svg," https://commons.wikimedia.org/wiki/File:Z80_arch.svg. © 2007 by user Apaloosa, reprinted under CC BY 3.0 Unported.

Fig. 64. From "Computer System bus.svg," https://commons.wikimedia.org/wiki/File:Computer_system_bus.svg, © 2011 by W. Nowicki, reprinted under CC BY-SA 3.0 Unported.

Fig. 66. See *fig. 64.*

Fig. 68.1. *Logic Gates* by Stuart Allen, licensed under CC BY-SA 3.0. Adapted from "Transistor pegelumsetzer.svg," https://commons.wikimedia.org/wiki/File:Transistor_pegelumsetzer.svg, 2010, by user Rolwand, Public domain; "TransistorANDgate.png" from https://commons.wikimedia.org/wiki/File:TransistorANDgate.png, © 2014 by user EBattleP, adapted under CC BY-SA 3.0 Unported; "Transistor OR gate.png," https://commons.wikimedia.org/wiki/File:Transistor_OR_Gate.png, © 2014 by user EBattleP, adapted under CC BY-SA 3.0 Unported; "SMOS XOR gate.svg," https://commons.wikimedia.org/wiki/File:CMOS_XOR_Gate.svg, © 2013 by user Software11, adapted under CC BY-SA 3.0 Unported; "TTL npn nand.svg," https://commons.wikimedia.org/wiki/File:TTL_npn_nand.svg, © 2006 by user sakurambo, adapted under CC BY-SA 3.0 Unported; *Cmosunbuff.png* from "NOR Gate," 2018, https://en.wikipedia.org/, 2009, by user Nkendrick, public domain.

Fig. 68.2. Gate Array for 8-Bit Adder
Adapted from *Adder Gate Array*, circa 2014, www.cpuville.com, © 2004 by Donn Stewart. Reprinted with the permission of Donn Stewart.

Fig. 69. Illustration from "Spacetime dimensionality.svg," https://commons.wikimedia.org/wiki/File:Spacetime_dimensionality.svg, 2010, by Max Tegmark, reprinted under CC BY-SA 3.0 Unported.

Fig. 70. Table of Nuclides—Elements with Stable and Unstable Isotopes
Adapted from *Table Isotopes*, https://commons.wikimedia.org/wiki/File:Table_isotopes_en.svg, 2009, by users Napy1kenobi and Silegg, reprinted under CC BY-SA 3.0 Unported.

Fig. 71. Nuclear Binding Energies. Adapted from *Binding energy curve – common isotopes.svg*, https://commons.wikimedia.org/wiki/File:Binding_energy_curve_-_common_isotopes.svg, 2007, by user Fastfission, public domain.

Fig. 72. Illustration from"Nucleosynthesis in a star.gif," https://commons.wikimedia.org/wiki/File:Nucleosynthesis_in_a_star.gif, 2008, uploaded by user Uber nemo. Originally from NASA website. Public domain.

Fig. 73. Based on Figure 22 from *Nuclides and Isotopes*, 2010, Knolls Atomic Power Laboratory, p. 30.

Fig. 74. *Tycho's Supernova Remnant* from "File:Tycho-supernova-xray.jpg, https://commons.wikimedia.org/wiki/File:Tycho-supernova-xray.jpg, 2003, by NASA/CXC/Rutgers/J. Warren & J. Hughes et al., public domain.

Fig. 75. From "Helix electron density myoglobin 2nrl 17-32.jpg," https://commons.wikimedia.org/wiki/File:Helix_electron_density_myoglobin_2nrl_17-32.jpg, 2010, by user Dcrjsr, reprinted under CC BY 3.0 Unported.

Fig. 76. *Extinction intensity.svg*, from https://commons.wikimedia.org/wiki/File:Extinction_intensity.svg, 2008, by user Smith609, GDFL/CC BY-SA 3.0. May be copied and distributed with attribution and share alike.

Fig. 77. *Wide field Imager view of a Milky Way look-alike NGC 6744* accessed from Wikimedia Commons, https://commons.wikimedia.org/wiki/File:Wide_Field_Imager_view_of_a_Milky_Way_look-alike_NGC_6744.jpg?uselang=en. © 2011 by

ESO, reprinted under CC BY 3.0 Unported. Originally from http://www.eso.org/public/images/eso1118a/.

Fig. 78. "Kuiper belt - Oort cloud-en.svg," accessed from https://commons.wikimedia.org/wiki/File:Kuiper_belt_-_Oort_cloud-en.svg. 2014. Courtesy of NASA, public domain.

Fig. 79. Illustration from "InnerSolarSystem-en.png," https://commons.wikimedia.org/wiki/File:InnerSolarSystem-en.png, 2006 by user Mdf, public domain.

Fig. 80. *Estrella tipos* from "Estrellatipos.png," https://commons.wikimedia.org/wiki/File:Estrellatipos.png, © 2013 by user Xenoforme, reprinted under CC BY-SA3.0 Unported.

Fig. 81. *Magnetosphere rendition.jpg,* from https://commons.wikimedia.org/wiki/File:Magnetosphere_rendition.jpg, 2005, by NASA, public domain.

Fig. 82. *Amino Acids and Peptides* adapted from: **Upper right**—*Chirality with hands.svg,* https://commons.wikimedia.org/wiki/File:Chirality_with_hands.svg, 2011, by NASA, public domain; **bottom**—*AminoAcidball.svg,* https://commons.wikimedia.org/wiki/File:AminoAcidball.svg, 2007, by user YassineMrabet, public domain.

Fig. 83. *Biological Amino Acids, Ball and Stick Models,* Compiled and adapted from images accessed through Wikimedia Commons and Wikipedia: **Glycine (Flexible)** from "Glycine-3D-balls.png, from https://commons.wikimedia.org/wiki/File:Glycine-3D-balls.png, 2007, by user Benjah-bmm27, public domain; **Alanine** from "L-alanine-3D-balls.png," https://commons.wikimedia.org/wiki/File:L-alanine-3D-balls.png, 2007, by Benjah-bmm27, public domain; **Leucine** from "L-leucine-3D-balls.png," https://commons.wikimedia.org/wiki/File:L-leucine-3D-balls.png, 2007, by Benjah-bmm27, public domain; **Isoleucine** from "L-isoleucine-3D-balls.png," https://commons.wikimedia.org/wiki/File:L-isoleucine-3D-balls.png, 2007, by Benjah-bmm27, public domain; **Valine** from https://commons.wikimedia.org/wiki/File:L-valine-3D-balls.png, 2007, by Benjah-bmm27, public domain; **Threonine** from https://commons.wikimedia.org/wiki/File:L-Threonine-3D-balls.png, 2010, by users Jynto and Ben Mills, public domain; **Aspartate** image from JSmol, https://chemapps.stolaf.edu/jmol, linked from "Aspartic Acid," 2018, https://en.wikipedia.org/, reprinted under GNU Lesser General Public License; **Serine** from https://commons.wikimedia.org/wiki/File:L-serine-3D-balls.png, 2010, by users Jynto and Ben Mills, public domain; **Glutamate** from https://commons.wikimedia.org/wiki/File:L-Glutamic-acid-3D-balls.png, 2011, by user Jynto, reprinted under CC0 1.0 Universal Public Domain Dedication; **Asparagine** from https://commons.wikimedia.org/wiki/File:L-asparagine-3D-balls.png, 2010, by users Jynto and Ben Mills, public domain; **Glutamine** from https://commons.wikimedia.org/wiki/File:L-Glutamine-zwitterion-3D-balls.png, 2011, by Jynto, reprinted under CC0 1.0 Universal Public Domain Dedication; **Cysteine** https://commons.wikimedia.org/wiki/File:L-cysteine-3D-balls.png, 2007, by user Benjah-bmm27, public domain; **Methionine** from https://commons.wikimedia.org/wiki/File:L-methionine-B-3D-balls.png, 2007, by user Benjah-bmm27, public domain; **Proline (kinks)** from https://commons.wikimedia.org/wiki/File:L-proline-3D-balls.png, 2007, by user Benjah-bmm27, public domain; **Lysine** from https://commons.wikimedia.org/wiki/File:L-lysine-monocation-from-hydrochloride-dihydrate-xtal-3D-balls.png, 2009, by user Benjah-bmm27, public domain; **Tryptophan** from https://commons.wikimedia.org/wiki/Image:L-tryptophan-3D-balls.png?uselang=it, 2007, by Benjah-bmm27, public domain; **Arginine** from JSmol, https://chemapps.stolaf.edu/jmol, linked from "Arginine," 2018, https://en.wikipedia.org/, reprinted under GNU Lesser General Public License; **Histidine** from "Histidine," 2018, https://en.wikipedia.org, 2009, by user Benjah-bmm27, public domain; **Phenylalanine** from "Phenylalanine," 2018, https://en.wikipedia.org/, 2007, by user Benjah-bmm27, public domain; **Phenylalanine** https://commons.wikimedia.org/wiki/File:L-phenylalanine-3D-balls.png, 2007, by user Benjah-bmm27, public domain. **Tyrosine** by Wikipedia user Jynto.

Fig. 84. *Space Fill Representation of a Protein (Chymotropsin, 2CGA) Showing Atom Positions.* Illustration by author, using the software RasMol and protein data from RCSB protein data bank, ID 2CGA by Wang, D., Bode, W., and Huber, R. NGL imager by AS Rose, AR Bradley, Y Valasatava, JM Duarte, A Prlić and PW Rose.

Fig. 86. *Comparison of Human and Whale Primary Structure for Myoglobin* by author, using information from Whitford, 2005, *Proteins, Structure and Function*, p. 40.

Fig. 87. Adapted from: *Alpha helix neg60 neg45 sideview*.png and *Alpha helix neg60 neg45 topview.png* from "Alpha Helix," 2018, https://en.wikipedia.org/wiki/Alpha_helix/, 2006, by user WillowW, reprinted under CC BY-SA3.0 Unported; *1gwe an-*

tipar betaSheet both.png from "Beta Sheet," 2018, https://en.wikipedia.org/wiki/Beta_sheet, 2006, by user Dcrjsr, reprinted under CC BY 3.0 Unported; *Beta turn.svg* from Wikipedia article "Turn (biochemistry)," 2018, https://en.wikipedia.org/wiki/Turn_(biochemistry), 2014, by user Muskid, reprinted under CC BY-SA 3.0 Unported.

Fig. 88. Adapted from: **Human thioredoxin** of PDB ID 4POL (Sridhar, chie-Leon, Badger, Nienaber, and Hausheer) (2014) BNP7787 *Forms Novel Covalent Adducts on Human Thioredoxin and Modulates Thioredoxin Activity* J Pharmacol Clin Toxicol **2: 1026**; **Fruit fly thioredoxin** of PDB ID 1THX (Saarinen, Gleason, and Eklund) (1995) *Crystal structure of thioredoxin-2 from Anabaena*. Structure 3: 1097-1108; NGL imager by A.S. Rose, A.R. Bradley, Y. Valasatava, J.M. Duarte, A. Prlić and P.W. Rose.

Fig. 89. *Typical Protein Peptide Chain Structures* is compiled and adapted from: *PDB 1PAR EBI.jpg*, https://commons-wikimedia.org/, 2009, by J. Swaminathan, public domain; *GFP 1ema ribbon fluor.png*, https://commons.wikimedia.org/wiki/File:GFP_1ema_ribbon_fluor.png, 2013, by user Dcrjsr, reprinted under CC BY 3.0 Unported; *Ribbon view of the Orange Carotenoid Structure 1M98.png*, https://commons.wikimedia.org/wiki/File:Ribbon_view_of_the_Orange_Carotenoid_Protein_Structure_1M98.png, 2015, by user Melnicki, reprinted under CC BY-SA 4.0 International; *Kindling fluorescent protein 1XMZ.jpg*, https://commons.wikimedia.org/wiki/File:Kindling_fluorescent_protein_1xmz.jpg, 2014, uploaded by user Esculapio, originally from RCSB PDB (www.rcsb.org) by Quillin, Anstrom, Shu, O'Leary, Kallio, Chudakov, and Remington, copyright holder allows any use of this image with attribution; *PDB 1tfi EBI.jpg*, https://commons.wikimedia.org/wiki/File:PDB_1tfi_EBI.jpg, 2009, by J. Swaminathan, public domain; *PBB Protein CDK5 image.jpg*, https://commons.wikimedia.org/wiki/File:PBB_Protein_CDK5_image.jpg, 2007, by user ProteinBoxBot, public domain.

Fig. 90. Compiled image under CC BY-SA 3.0. **Top left:** Illustration by Wikimedia Commons user Opabinia regalis, using RCSB protein data bank entry for 1AXC (Humphrey, W., Dalke, A. and Schulten, K., "VMD - Visual Molecular Dynamics", J. Molec. Graphics, 1996, vol. 14, pp. 33-38), created with software VMD (visualization software VMD was developed by the Theoretical and Computational Biophysics Group in the Beckman Institute for Advanced Science and Technology at the University of Illinois at Urbana-Champaign), reprinted under CC BY-SA 3.0; **Top right:** From the RCSB PDB (www.rcsb.org) of PDB ID 7AHL (Song, Hubaugh, Shustak, Cheley, Bayley, and Gouaux) (1996) Structure of staphylococcal alpha-hemolysin, a heptameric transmembrane pore, *Science* ***274****: 1859-1866,* created with NGL imager; **Bottom, left and right:** From the RCSB PDB of PDB ID 5M2B (M. Groll), created with NGL imager.

Fig. 91. Inspired by Whitford, 2005, *Proteins, Structure and Function*, p. 210. Compilation licensed under CC BY-SA 4.0. Adapted and compiled from—**Top Left:** From "Peptidoglycan en.svg," https://commons.wikimedia.org/wiki/File:Peptidoglycan_en.svg, 2008 by user Yikrazul (public domain); **Top right:** Lysozyme from RCSB PDB of ID 1HEW (J. C. Cheetham, P. J. Artymiuk, and D. C. Phillips) (1992), created with NGL imager; **Bottom**: by author.

Fig. 92. Adapted from "Ribose Structure 2.svg," https://commons.wikimedia.org/wiki/File:Ribose_Structure_2.svg, 2014 by user Fred the Oyster, reprinted under CC BY-SA4.0 International.

Fig. 93. **Left:** From "DNA chemical structure.svg," https://commons.wikimedia.org/wiki/File:DNA_chemical_structure.svg, 2007 by user Madprime, reprinted under Creative Commons CC0 1.0 Universal Public Domain Dedication; **Right:** From "DNA Structure+Key+Labelled.pn NoBB.png," https://commons.wikimedia.org/wiki/File:DNA_Structure%2BKey%2BLabelled.pn_NoBB.png, © 2011 by user Zephyris, CC BY-SA 3.0.

Fig. 94. Adapted and compiled using images from "Metabolic Metro Map.svg," https://commons.wikimedia.org/wiki/File:Metabolic_Metro_Map.svg, © 2016 by user Chakazul, CC BY-SA 4.0; "Glycolosis metabolic pathway 3 annotated.svg," https://commons.wikimedia.org/wiki/File:Glycolysis_metabolic_pathway_3_annotated.svg, © 2015 by Thomas Shafee, CC BY 4.0; "Glucokinse-1GLK.png," https://commons.wikimedia.org/wiki/File:Glucokinase-1GLK.png, 2008 by user Jag123, public domain; "File:1hox.jpg," Wikimedia Commons, https://commons.wikimedia.org/wiki/File:1hox.jpg, 2016 by user Astrojan using PDB ID 1HOX (Jeffrey, Lee, Chang, and Patel), CC BY 3.0; image of Fructose-1.6-bisphosphatse from the RCSB PDB (www.rcsb.org) of PDB ID 3FBP (entry by Moncoq, Morth, Bublitz, Laursen, Nissen, and Young), created with NGL imager;

"PDB 1bq3 EBI.jpg," https://commons.wikimedia.org/wiki/File:PDB_1bq3_EBI.jpg, 2009 by Jawahar Swaminathan and MSD staff at the European Bioinformatics Institute (http://www.ebi.ac.uk), public domain; "GAPDH with labels.png," https://commons.wikimedia.org/wiki/File:GAPDH_with_labels.png, © 2011, by user Vossman, CC BY-SA 3.0; "Phosphoglycerate kinase 3PGK.png," https://commons.wikimedia.org/wiki/File:Phosphoglycerate_kinase_3PGK.png, © 2013 by Thomas Splettstoesser, CC BY-SA 3.0; *"PDB 1bq3 EBI.jpg,"* https://commons.wikimedia.org/wiki/File:PDB_1bq3_EBI.jpg, 2009 by Jawahar Swaminathan, public domain; *"Enolase 2ONE wpmp.png,"* https://commons.wikimedia.org/wiki/File:Enolase_2ONE_wpmp.png, © 2006 by By Richard Wheeler (Zephyris), CC BY-SA 3.0; "Pyruvate kinase protein domains.png," https://commons.wikimedia.org/wiki/File:Pyruvate_kinase_protein_domains.png, 2012 by Thomas Splettstoesser, based on PDB: 1PKN, CC BY-SA 3.0.

Fig. 94.1. See *Fig. 92.*

Fig. 95. Adapted illustrations originally from: *"Microrna secondary structure.png,"* https://commons.wikimedia.org/wiki/File:Microrna_secondary_structure.png, © 2007 by user Opabinia regalis, CC BY-SA 3.0; *"TRNA-Phe yeast 1ehz.png,"* https://commons.wikimedia.org/wiki/File:TRNA-Phe_yeast_1ehz.png, © 2010 by user Yikrazul (using data from PDB ID 1ehz, rendered with PyMOL), reprinted under CC BY-SA 3.0 Unported; "50S-subunit of the ribosome 3CC2.png," https://commons.wikimedia.org/wiki/File:50S-subunit_of_the_ribosome_3CC2.png, © 2010 by user Yikrazul (using data from PDB ID 2CC2, rendered with PyMOL). Reprinted under CC BY-SA 3.0.

Fig. 96. From "File:*Chromatin Structures.png,"* https://commons.wikimedia.org/wiki/File:Chromatin_Structures.png, © 2006 by Richard Wheeler, reprinted under CC BY-SA 3.0 Unported.

Fig. 97. Based on Alberts, et al., 2002, *Molecular Biology of the Cell,* Chapter 6. Adapted from *Rnapol.png,* https://commons.wikimedia.org/wiki/File:Rnapol.png, 2010, by user Fdardel, reprinted under CC BY-SA 3.0.

Fig. 98. From "File:Transcription label.en.jpg," Wikimedia Commons, https://commons.wikimedia.org/wiki/File:Transcription_label_en.jpg, © 2007 user InfoCan, CC BY-SA 3.0.

Fig. 99. Illustration by author. Based on Alberts, et al, 2002, *Molecular Biology of the Cell*, p. 307, and "RNA Polymerase," *Wikipedia*, https://en.wikipedia.org/wiki/RNA_polymerase, circa 2014.

Fig. 100. Illustrations from "File:Simple transcription initiation1.png," Wikimedia Commons, https://commons.wikimedia.org/wiki/File:Simple_transcription_initiation1.png, 2007 by user Forluvoft, public domain; "File: *Simple transcription elongation1.png*," https://commons.wikimedia.org/wiki/File:Simple_transcription_elongation1.svg, 2007 by user Forluvoft, public domain.

Fig. 101. From "File:Ribosome mRNA translationen.svg," Wikimedia Commons, https://commons.wikimedia.org/wiki/File:Ribosome_mRNA_translation_en.svg, 2008 by user LadyofHats (Mariana Ruiz Villareal), public domain.

Fig. 104. Based on Yuh, et. al. 1994, "Complexity and organization of DNA-protein interactions in the 5′ regulatory region of an endoderm-specific marker gene in the sea urchin embryo," *Mechanisms of Development* 47, no. 2, p. 165–186, fig. 4.

Fig. 106. From "File:Cell membrane detailed diagram en.svg," Wikimedia Commons, https://commons.wikimedia.org/wiki/File:Cell_membrane_detailed_diagram_en.svg, 2007, by user LadyofHats (Mariana Ruiz Villareal), public domain.

Fig. 107. Compiled from Wikimedia Commons and Wikipedia images: "File:Signal transduction pathways.svg," https://commons.wikimedia.org/wiki/File:Signal_transduction_pathways.svg, © 2010 by user Cybertory, CC BY-SA 3.0; "File:P13K-Akt Pathway Activated by RTK.png," https://en.wikipedia.org/wiki/File:P13K-Akt_Pathway_Activated_by_RTK.png, © 2015 by user Tbatan, CC BY-SA 3.0; "File:Akt Substrates Involved in Cell Cycle Regulation.png," https://en.wikipedia.org/wiki/File:Akt_Substrates_Involved_in_Cell_Cycle_Regulation.png, © 2015 by user Tbatan, CC BY-SA 3.0; "File: *Akt Phosphorylation Substrates Affecting Apoptosis.png*," https://en.wikipedia.org/wiki/File:Akt_Phosphorylation_Substrates_Affecting_Apoptosis.png, © 2015 by user Tbatan, CC BY-SA 3.0; "File:Regulation of P13K-Akt Pathway in Feedback Loops.png," https://en.wikipedia.org/wiki/File:Regulation_of_P13K-Akt_Pathway_in_Feedback_Loops.png, © 2015 by user Tbatan, CC BY-SA 3.0.

Fig. 109. Illustration adapted from: *Copedpod*, from "File:Copepodkils.jpg," 2018, https://commons.wikimedia.org/wiki/File:Copepodkils.jpg, © 2005 by Uwe Kils, CC BY-SA 3.0; *Nordisk familjebok* [Book], vol.1, *Alger*, 1904, public domain, accessed from "File:Alger, Botydium granulatum, Nordisk familjebok.png," 2011 https://commons.wikimedia.org/wiki/File:Alger,_Botydium_granulatum,_Nordisk_familjebok.png; "File:Mikrofoto.de-Brachionus quadridentatus 6.jpg," 2011, https://commons.wikimedia.org/wiki/File:Mikrofoto.de-Brachionus_quadridentatus_6.jpg, by Frank Fox (www.mikro-foto.de), CC BY-SA 3.0 Germany; *Diatoms through the microscope.jpg* from Wikipedia article "Phytoplankton", 2018, https://en.wikipedia.org/wiki/File:Diatoms_through_the_microscope.jpg, 1983 by Gordon T. Taylor, public domain; *Phytoplankton - the foundation of the oceanic food chain.jpg*, from Wikipedia article "Phytoplankton", 2018, https://commons.wikimedia.org/wiki/File:Phytoplankton_-_the_foundation_of_the_oceanic_food_chain.jpg, 2009, by NOAA Mesa Project, public domain.

Fig. 110. From "File:Prokaryote cell.svg," https://en.wikipedia.org/wiki/File:Prokaryote_cell.svg, 2015, by Ali Zifan, reprinted under CC BY-SA 4.0 International.

Fig. 111. Adapted from "File:Tevenphage.svg," https://commons.wikimedia.org/wiki/File:Tevenphage.svg, © 2008 by users Adenosine and Pbroks 13, reprinted under CC BY-SA 2.5 Generic.

Fig. 112. From "Animal cell structure en.svg," https://commons.wikimedia.org/wiki/File:Animal_cell_structure_en.svg, 2006, by user LadyofHats (Mariana Ruiz Villareal), public domain.

Fig. 113. Images from "File:Xenophyophore.jpg," https://commons.wikimedia.org/wiki/File:Xenophyophore.jpg, 2002, courtesy of NOAA, public domain; "File:Discoaster pentaradiatus 05.jpg," https://commons.wikimedia.org/wiki/File:Discoaster_pentaradiatus_05.jpg, © 2008 by Hannes Grobe, CC BY 3.0; "File:DW-Radiolaria.jpg," https://commons.wikimedia.org/wiki/File:DW-Radiolaria.jpg, © 2001 by Patrick De Wever, reprinted under CC BY-SA 4.0 International; "Nitzschia-kerguelensis hg.jpg," https://commons.wikimedia.org/wiki/File:Nitzschia-kerguelensis_hg.jpg, © 2013 by Hannes Grobe, CC BY 3.0; "Calcidiscus-leptoporus hg.jpg,"
https://commons.wikimedia.org/wiki/File:Calcidiscus-leptoporus_hg.jpg,

1980 by Hannes Grobe/AWI, reprinted under CC BY 3.0 Unported; "Emiliania huxleyi coccolithophore (PLoS).png," https://commons.wikimedia.org/wiki/File:Emiliania_huxleyi_coccolithophore_(PLoS).png, 2011, by Alison R. Taylor (University of North Carolina Wilmington Microscopy Facility), CC BY 2.5 Generic; "Globigerinoides spp Pliocene.JPG," https://commons.wikimedia.org/wiki/File:Globigerinoides_spp_Pliocene.JPG, 2009, by user Antonov, public domain; "Discoaster surculus 01.jpg," https://commons.wikimedia.org/wiki/File:Discoaster_surculus_01.jpg, 2008, by Hannes Grobe, CC BY 3.0 Unported; "Discoaster variabilis 01.jpg," https://commons.wikimedia.org/wiki/File:Discoaster_variabilis_01.jpg, 2008, by Hannes Grobe, CC BY 3.0 Unported; "Diatom hg.jpg," https://commons.wikimedia.org/wiki/File:Diatom-half_hg.jpg, 2013 by Hannes Grob, CC BY 3.0 Unported; *Calocycloma sp. - Radiolarian,* https://commons.wikimedia.org/wiki/File:Calocycloma_sp._-_Radiolarian_(32163186535).jpg, © 2017 by Flickr user Picturepest, CC BY 2.0 Generic.

Fig. 114. Image from "Collapsed tree labels simplified.png," https://commons.wikimedia.org/, 2007, by Tim vickers, public domain. Additional labels added by Stuart Allen.

Fig. 115. Illustration is *spiral cleavage in gastropod Trochus,* from "Spiral cleavage in Trochus.png," https://commons.wikimedia.org/wiki/File:Spiral_cleavage_in_Trochus.png, © 2009 by Morgan Q. Goulding, CC BY 2.5 Generic.

Fig. 118. Illustration from "Hoxgenesoffruitfly.svg," https://commons.wikimedia.org/wiki/File:Hoxgenesoffruitfly.svg, 2007 by user PhiLiP, public domain.

Fig. 118.1. Adapted from *Smiley.svg,* 2018, https://commons.wikimedia.org/, 2006, by user Pumbaa80, public domain.

Fig. 119. Inspired by Valentine, 2004, *On the Origin of Phyla,* p. 186.

Fig. 120. Based on Valentine, 2004, *On the Origin of Phyla,* ch. 12, especially fig. 12.11 on p. 444.

Fig. 121. Illustration from "Rhynia stem.jpg," https://commons.wikimedia.org/wiki/File:Rhynia_stem.jpg, 2007, Plantsurfer, reprinted under CC BY-SA 2.0 UK: England & Wales.

Fig. 122. Based on information from Taylor, *Paleobotany*, and Wikipedia plant division articles

Fig. 123. From "Asaphus kowalewskii 3.jpg," https://commons.wikimedia.org/wiki/File:Asaphus_kowalewskii_3.jpg, 2006, by user DanielCD, public domain.

Fig. 124. From "Horizontal-gene-transfer.jpg," https://commons.wikimedia.org/wiki/File:Horizontal-gene-transfer.jpg, 2005, by Barth F. Smets, PhD, reprinted with permission per his email to Wikimedia Commons volunteer.

Fig. 125. From "Spindle diagram.jpg," https://commons.wikimedia.org/wiki/File:Spindle_diagram.jpg, 2011, by Peter Bøckman, public domain.

Fig. 125.1. *See Fig. 123*

Fig. 127. Adapted from "Calabi-Yau-alternate.png," https://commons.wikimedia.org/wiki/File:Calabi-Yau-alternate.png, 2007, by user Lunch, CC BY-SA 2.5 Generic; "CalabiYau5.jpg," https://commons.wikimedia.org/wiki/File:CalabiYau5.jpg, 2014, by Andrew J. Hanson, Indiana University, reprinted under CC BY-SA 3.0 Unported.

Fig. 128. *Timeline of the Universe* from "CMB Timeline300 no WMAP.jpg," https://commons.wikimedia.org/wiki/File:CMB_Timeline300_no_WMAP.jpg, 2006, NASA WMAP Science Team and Ryan Kaldari, public domain.

Fig. 128.3 Adapted from *Fig. 128.*

Fig. 129. *Pneumodesmus newmani.jpg* from Wikipedia article "Pneumodesmus," 2018, https://en.wikipedia.org/wiki/Pneumodesmus, 2007, by user Xenarachne, reprinted under CC BY-SA 2.5 Generic.

Fig. 130. From "Map-of-human-migrations.jpg," from Wikipedia article "Human genetic variation," 2018, https://commons.wikimedia.org/wiki/File:Map-of-human-migrations.jpg, 2005, by user Avsa, reprinted under CC BY-SA 2.5 Generic.

Fig. 130.3. Illustration from "CA-Moor.png," https://en.wikipedia.org/wiki/File:CA-Moore.png, 2012, by user Torchiest, reprinted under Creative Commons CC0 1.0 Universal Public Domain Dedication.

Fig. 130.4. *Pulsar oscillator from Game of Life* from "Game of life pulsar.gif," https://

commons.wikimedia.org/wiki/File:Game_of_life_pulsar.gif, 2009, by user Jokey-Smurf, public domain.

Fig. 131. Adapted from *Turing Machine in Golly.png*, https://commons.wikimedia.org/wiki/File:Turing_Machine_in_Golly.png, 2012, image by Andrew Trevorrow and Thomas Rokicki, structure by Paul Rendell, reprinted under the GNU General Public License.

Fig. 131.1. Image is a screenshot of Core War game in progress, *Core War PMars Screenshot.png*, https://commons.wikimedia.org/wiki/File:Core_War_PMars_Screenshot.png, 2005, by Ilmari Karonen, reprinted under the GNU General Public License.

Fig. 132. Adapted from *OODA.Boyd.svg*, https://commons.wikimedia.org/wiki/File:OODA.Boyd.svg, 2008, by Patrick Edwin Moran, reprinted under CC BY 3.0 Unported.

Fig. 132.3. *History of the Universe.svg* from https://commons.wikimedia.org/wiki/File:History_of_the_Universe.svg, 2010, by users Drbogdan and Yinweichen, reprinted under CC BY-SA 3.0 Unported.

Fig. 132.9. *Beta Negative Decay.svg*, https://commons.wikimedia.org/wiki/File:Beta_Negative_Decay.svg, 2007, by Joel Holdsworth, public domain.

Fig. 132.12. See Fig. *132.9*

Fig. 132.13. Adapted from: *Interference of two waves.svg*, https://commons.wikimedia.org/wiki/File:Interference_of_two_waves.svg, 2010, by user Haade, reprinted under CC BY-SA 3.0 Unported; *Interferences plane waves.jpg*, https://commons.wikimedia.org/wiki/File:Interferences_plane_waves.jpg, 2006, by user Effred, public domain.

Fig. 132.15. See *Fig. 132.9, 132.12*

Fig. 132.16. See *Fig. 132.13*

Fig. 132.18. See 132.9, 132.12

Index

C

H

I

K

L

M

N

O

P